THE PFI HANDBOOK

THE PFI HANDBOOK

Jason Fox
Partner
Herbert Smith

Nicholas Tott
Partner
Herbert Smith

JORDANS
1999

Published by
Jordan Publishing Limited
21 St Thomas Street
Bristol BS1 6JS

Copyright © Jordan Publishing Limited 1999

All rights reserved. No part of this publication may be reproduced, stored in a retrieval system, or transmitted in any way or by any means, including photocopying or recording, without the written permission of the copyright holder, application for which should be addressed to the publisher.

British Library Cataloguing-in-Publication Data
A catalogue record for this book is available from the British Library.

ISBN 0 85308 480 7

Typeset by Mendip Communications Limited, Frome, Somerset
Printed by MPG Books Ltd, Bodmin, Cornwall

DEDICATION

This book is dedicated by Jason Fox to Debbie, Olivia and James and by Nicholas Tott to Rowena, David and Rebecca.

ACKNOWLEDGEMENTS

Rather like the delivery of a PFI project itself, the production of this book has been very much a team effort. Numerous colleagues at Herbert Smith have contributed chapters across a range of specialisms. Without their input, it would have been impossible to achieve our objective of producing a comprehensive work that examines the many areas of law that PFI projects involve. We would like to thank the following for their contributions in the areas shown:

EU and Procurement Law (Chapter 3)	Adrian Brown
Public Law (Chapters 4 and 6)	Andrew Lidbetter
Construction Law and Dispute Resolution (Chapters 7 and 16)	Michael Davis
Finance and Projects (Chapters 8, 9 and 10)	Kelli Read, James Slessenger, David Wyles
Property (Chapter 11)	Chris de Pury
Overage and Tax (Chapters 12 and 14)	Neil Warriner
Planning and Environmental Law (Chapter 13)	David Brock
Employment Law (Chapter 15)	Andrew Brown

Thanks also go to other colleagues: Andrew Preece, Dorothy Livingston, Peter Frost and Peter Long for commenting on several of the chapters and to Jonathan Williams for preparing the Bibliography.

We would also like to thank Nigel Middleton, Head of PFI at Pricewaterhouse-Coopers, a former colleague from the early days of The Private Finance Panel Executive, who wrote Chapter 17 on Accounting for PFI Transactions, which brings logic and clarity to this immensely important and difficult area.

Finally, we would like to thank our former colleague, Stephen Barton, one of the outstanding projects lawyers of his generation and now a fellow of Jesus College Cambridge, for commenting on many of the early drafts of chapters and bringing to the benefit of this book his great experience, both as a practitioner and as an academic.

JASON FOX
NICHOLAS TOTT
February 1999

FOREWORD

The concept of using private finance instead of public funding has been around for at least 17 years, but it was only in 1992 that government took the matter seriously.

Even then, with the establishment of the Private Finance Panel in that year, progress was appallingly slow, although some sectors of government were quicker than others to spot the opportunities.

Following the election of the Labour Government in May 1997, a short review was commissioned with the objective of reinvigorating the PFI process and, since then, more rapid progress has been made with some £4 billion of deals closing in the first 18 months of the new Government.

Forward projections by the Government suggest that another £11 billion of deals will be done over the next three years, with transport, health, education, local authority and defence deals dominating.

PFI deals embody a fundamental change in the role of government as the public sector ceases to be an owner and operator of assets, and becomes instead a purchaser and procurer of services. Value-for-money must be the watchword: the added complexity of PFI deals is acceptable only if taxpayers' money goes further as a result.

I welcome this outstandingly clear and detailed *PFI Handbook*, which provides everything practitioners in both the public and private sectors need to know in order to conclude effective transactions for their mutual benefit.

SIR MALCOLM BATES
February 1999

PREFACE

The advent of the Private Finance Initiative has produced a sea change in government procurement and has in the process generated a major new industry. When we were both seconded to the Private Finance Panel in 1994 and 1995, during the early formulation of PFI policy, we could not have predicted the extraordinary development of the PFI which has since occurred and the explosion of work which it has generated for the legal and financial community. Nor could we have foreseen the prolonged gestation of some projects. The permanence of the PFI was confirmed by its survival following the change of government in May 1997 and its subsequent renaissance (due in no small part to Sir Malcolm Bates' Review and the Government's determination to implement his recommendations).

As the subject matter of this book confirms, a PFI transaction involves almost every aspect of legal practice, giving rise to a complex legal jigsaw of rights and obligations. Much of what you will read in this book is a distillation of many hours of discussion and negotiation on PFI projects, often late in the evening or early in the morning! The aim of the book is to draw together the disparate threads of PFI law and practice and to provide a guide to the processes (and pitfalls) of the PFI and the issues that face each of the parties.

We have endeavoured to state law and practice as at 1 December 1998.

JASON FOX
NICHOLAS TOTT
February 1999

CONTENTS

	Page
DEDICATION	v
ACKNOWLEDGEMENTS	vii
FOREWORD	x
PREFACE	xi
TABLE OF CASES	xxv
TABLE OF STATUTES	xxix
TABLE OF STATUTORY INSTRUMENTS	xxxii
TABLE OF CODES OF GUIDANCE ETC	xxxv
TABLE OF EC LEGISLATION	xxxix
GLOSSARY AND ABBREVIATIONS	xli

CHAPTER 1	THE BACKGROUND, EVOLUTION AND DEVELOPMENT OF THE PRIVATE FINANCE INITIATIVE	1
1.1	Introduction	1
1.2	What are the key aims and features of the Private Finance Initiative?	1
	The aims of the Private Finance Initiative	1
	Risk allocation and value for money	2
	Accounting treatment	4
	Affordability	5
	Types of PFI projects	5
1.3	The origins and development of the PFI	6
	Ryrie Rules	6
	Early private finance projects	6
	Private Finance Panel	7
	Universal testing	7
	PFI publications	8
	Departmental responsibility for the PFI	8
	Deals not rules	9
	Reinvigorating the PFI	10
	Institutional structure	10
	Improving the process	11
	Learning lessons	13
	Bid costs	14
1.4	Conclusion	14
1.5	Checklist 1: Key requirements for a PFI transaction	15
1.6	Checklist 2: The PFI – Key events	15

CHAPTER 2	THE CONTRACTING PARTIES, THEIR OBLIGATIONS AND THE CONTRACTUAL MATRIX		17
	2.1	Introduction	17
	2.2	The awarding authority's objectives	17
		Risk transfer	18
		Design risk	18
		Planning risk	19
		Completion risk	21
		Completion to time	21
		Completion to cost	21
		Completion to quality	22
		Operational risk	22
		Residual value risk	24
		Insolvency risk	25
		Value for money	28
		Other awarding authority objectives	28
	2.3	The consortium's objectives	29
		Minimising bid costs	29
		Delivering profit	29
		Risk transfer	29
		Limitation of recourse	30
		Liquidity of investment	30
	2.4	The debt funders' objectives	30
		Pass down of risk	31
		Limiting risk in the project company	31
		Take control early when things go wrong	31
	2.5	The contractual matrix	31
		The project agreement	31
		The property documents	34
		The funding agreements	34
		The debt funders' direct agreement	34
		Awarding authority collateral agreements	35
		Sub-contracts	35
		Performance bonds	35
		Collateral warranties	36
	2.6	Conclusion	36
CHAPTER 3	THE APPLICATION OF EUROPEAN UNION RULES ON PUBLIC PROCUREMENT TO PFI PROJECTS		37
	3.1	Introduction	37
	3.2	Scope: When do the procurement rules apply?	37
		The Public Sector Regulations	37
		The Utilities Regulations	38

		Works, supplies or services?	38
		Public works concessions	40
		The value thresholds	41
		Part A and Part B services	42
		National security exclusion	42
	3.3	The procedural requirements	42
		Choice of procedure: open, restricted or negotiated?	42
		Non-competitive negotiated procedure without OJ notice	44
		Competitive negotiated procedure with OJ notice	45
		Duty to advertise in the Official Journal	46
		Time constraints	49
		Pre-qualification	50
		Short-listing	51
		Contract award criteria	51
		The tenders/negotiations phase	52
		Is a two-stage negotiated procedure permissible?	53
		Negotiations with the preferred tenderer	54
		Post-award formalities and debriefing	55
CHAPTER 4		THE *VIRES* OF PUBLIC SECTOR BODIES TO UNDERTAKE PFI PROJECTS	57
	4.1	Introduction	57
	4.2	General principles	57
		Illegality	59
		Incidental powers	59
		Sufficient nexus	60
		Complete code	61
		Irrationality	61
		Wednesbury unreasonableness/perversity	61
		Relevant considerations	61
		Bad faith	62
		Improper purpose	62
		Unfairness amounting to abuse of power	62
		Unlawful delegation	62
		Fettering of discretion	64
		Fiduciary duty	64
		Procedural impropriety	65
	4.3	Local authorities	65

		Capital Finance Regulations	65
		Safe harbour provisions for lending to local authorities	66
		The Local Government (Contracts) Act 1997	66
	4.4	NHS trusts as statutory bodies and their statutory instruments	68
		The National Health Service (Private Finance) Act 1997	69
CHAPTER 5		THE TENDERING PROCESS AND TENDERING DOCUMENTATION	71
	5.1	Introduction	71
	5.2	Initial considerations	71
		Application of the Regulations on public procurement	71
		Choice of procedure	71
		Competition and value for money	72
	5.3	Tender process	72
		Summary	72
		Maintaining a level playing field	72
	5.4	Prior publicity	73
	5.5	Pre-qualification	74
		Dealing with expressions of interest	74
		Pre-qualification document	75
		Evaluating pre-qualification responses	76
		Debriefing unsuccessful candidates	77
		Re-evaluation	77
	5.6	The negotiations phase	78
		Structuring the negotiations phase	78
		Bid costs	78
		Number of tenderers	78
		Number of stages	79
		Interim submissions and changing requirements	82
		Setting realistic targets	82
		ITN	82
		Output specification	82
		Key constraints	83
		Commercial terms	83
		Evaluation criteria	83
		Terms and conditions	83
		Other ITN information	84
		Confidentiality	84
		Public sector comparator	85
		Accuracy of the ITN	85
		Revised ITN	85
		The interactive process	86

		Providing additional information	86
		Negotiations	87
	5.7	Bid submission and evaluation	88
		Bid evaluation	88
		Methodology	88
		Reference and variant bids	89
		Debriefing unsuccessful tenderers	90
		Continuing negotiations with preferred tenderer	90
		Negotiating price reductions: bridging affordability gaps	92
	5.8	Conclusion	92
CHAPTER 6		REMEDIES FOR BREACH OF THE TENDERING PROCESS	93
	6.1	Introduction	93
	6.2	Specific remedy for breach of the EU public procurement regime	93
	6.3	Action by the European Commission	95
	6.4	Judicial review	95
	6.5	Private common law remedies	98
CHAPTER 7		DESIGN AND CONSTRUCTION ISSUES	101
	7.1	Introduction	101
	7.2	The traditional construction project	101
	7.3	The structure of a PFI project	104
	7.4	Output specification	105
	7.5	Project company's proposals	106
	7.6	Construction-related provisions in the project agreement	107
		Project company's design and construction obligations	107
		Design development	108
		Project company's sub-contractors	110
		Guarantees and bonds	112
		Access and monitoring rights	112
		Decanting provisions	113
		Awarding authority's contractors	113
		Commissioning	114
		Completion	115
		Responsibility for latent defects	115
		Completion to time and to price	116
		Liquidated and ascertained damages	116
		Other issues	117
		Construction (Design and Management) Regulations 1994	117
		Housing Grants, Construction and Regeneration Act 1996	118

	7.7	Construction contract issues	119
		Typical types of PFI construction contracts	119
		Guarantees, bonds and retentions	121
CHAPTER 8		FINANCING PFI PROJECTS	123
	8.1	Introduction	123
	8.2	Overview of sources of finance	123
		Equity	124
		Bank debt	124
		Bond issues	125
		Lease financing	126
		Other sources	127
	8.3	Typical funding structure	127
	8.4	Funders' common concerns and objectives	128
		Risk allocation	128
		Completion risk	129
		Operating risk	129
		Pricing risk	129
		Revenue risk	130
		Awarding authority risk	130
		Change of law risk	130
		Land-related risk	130
		Sponsor/contractor risk	131
		Insurance	131
		Default and termination	132
		Debt funders' step-in rights	132
		Compensation for early termination	132
		Transferability	133
		Value for money reviews	133
		Security issues	133
	8.5	Key finance documents	134
		Credit agreement	134
		Purpose	135
		Drawdown requirements	135
		Conditions to each drawing	136
		Repayment formulae	137
		Representations and warranties	138
		Covenants	138
		Events of default	140
		Intercreditor agreements	140
	8.6	Refinancing of projects	141
		Annex 1	143
CHAPTER 9		DIRECT AGREEMENTS	145
	9.1	Rationale for direct agreements	145
		Introduction	145
		Scope of conventional security	145

	Nature of conventional security	146
	Floating charges	146
	Mortgages over shares in the project company	146
	The valuable assets	147
	Security over contractual rights	147
	Preservation of the income stream and risk allocation	147
	Additional protection and remedy	148
	Direct agreements with other contractual counterparties	148
9.2	Basic structure and effect of direct agreements	148
	Parties	148
	Purpose	149
	What is in it for the counterparties?	150
9.3	Principal terms of a typical PFI debt funders' direct agreement	150
	Introduction	150
	Notice of intention to terminate	151
	Step-in notice	151
	Means of taking over the project	151
	Step-in date	152
	Length of step-in period	152
	Pre-completion step in	152
	Step in following credit agreement events of default	153
	Credit agreement consequences of a termination notice	153
	Risks of going into possession	153
	Appointment of a receiver	154
	Appointment of a substitute entity	154
	Stepping out	155
	Step-in undertaking	155
	Pre-step in liabilities	155
	Step-in period liabilities	156
	Capping liabilities	156
	Nature of debt funders' liabilities	156
	Awarding authority's intervention rights	157
	Can the project agreement be assigned?	157
	Transferring the project to a third-party purchaser	158
	Identity of novatee	158
	Sensitive projects	158
	Revising the novation proposal	158
	The step-in period and novation	159

		How often can step-in occur?	159
	9.4	Other common provisions	159
		Consent to security	160
		Notification of credit agreement defaults	160
		Extension of remedy periods etc	160
		Payment instructions	160
	9.5	Recent developments	161
		Step-in undertakings	161
		Bond financing and direct agreements	161
	9.6	Conclusion	161
CHAPTER 10	NEGOTIATING THE PROJECT AGREEMENT		163
	10.1	Introduction	163
		Centralised guidance on project agreements	164
	10.2	Core issues	165
	10.3	Force Majeure, compensation events and relief events	166
		Force Majeure	166
		Compensation events	168
		Relief events	168
	10.4	Payment and performance	170
		Payment mechanisms	170
		Timing	170
		Payment elements	170
		Amount of payment	171
		Price adjustment and market testing	172
		Deductions	174
		Unavailability	174
		Performance points	175
		Over-performance	177
	10.5	Change of law	178
	10.6	Variations	180
		Restrictions	180
		Implementation	181
		Payment adjustments	182
	10.7	Termination	183
		Termination at will	183
		Project company default	184
		Awarding authority default	184
		Force Majeure	185
		Corrupt gifts	185
	10.8	Effect of termination	185
	10.9	Compensation	186
		Termination at will	186
		Project company default	186

		Awarding authority default	189
		Force Majeure	189
		Corrupt gifts	190
		Set-off	190
		Grossing up of termination payments	190
	10.10	Step-in	191
	10.11	Conclusion	192
CHAPTER 11	PROPERTY ASPECTS OF PFI PROJECTS		193
	11.1	Introduction	193
	11.2	The role of property in the PFI context	193
	11.3	Nature of the project	194
		Site identification	194
		Site risks	194
		Specific issues	195
	11.4	Nature of the property interest to be granted: Property structures	197
		Choice of structure	197
		Awarding authority as end-user/occupier	198
		Project company as end-user/occupier	198
		Awarding authority as ultimate end-user/occupier: structures	199
		Project company as end-user/occupier: structures	204
	11.5	Other matters	206
		Government Circular 6/93	206
		The Crichel Down Rules 1992	207
		Mixed-use properties	209
		Other restrictions	210
	11.6	When is the property structure to be imposed?	210
	11.7	Surplus property	210
	11.8	Conclusion	211
CHAPTER 12	OVERAGE/CLAWBACK		213
	12.1	What is overage/clawback?	213
	12.2	How did overage/clawback evolve?	213
	12.3	Why have overage for PFI projects?	214
		Timing	214
		Property sold without planning permission	214
		Windfall gains	215
	12.4	The form	215
		General	215
		What land interests will overage attach to?	216
		What disposals will trigger overage?	216

		When is overage payable?	216
		How is overage calculated?	217
		Anti-avoidance	218
		Administrative provisions	218
	12.5	Tax implications	219
		Back-to-back land contracts	219
		Direct contract	220
		Reduction in unitary payment	220
CHAPTER 13	PLANNING, ENVIRONMENTAL AND COMPULSORY PURCHASE ISSUES		221
	13.1	Planning	221
		Introduction	221
		The planning process	221
		The acceptable planning permission	222
		Conditions	222
		Planning agreements	223
		Preparing the planning application	224
		Risk transfer	225
		Surplus sites	226
		The special position of government departments in relation to planning	227
		Planning agreements with the Crown	228
	13.2	Environmental law	229
		Introduction	229
		Contaminated land: the problem	229
		Transferring risk to the private sector	230
	13.3	Compulsory purchase in PFI	231
		Introduction	231
		Issues	232
CHAPTER 14	TAX ISSUES		233
	14.1	Introduction	233
	14.2	PFI project structure	233
	14.3	Direct tax	234
		Public sector perspective	234
		Private sector perspective	234
		Start-up costs	235
		Construction costs	235
		Financing costs	238
		Other costs	238
		Timing of reliefs	238
	14.4	Indirect tax: VAT	241
		Private sector perspective	241
		Public sector perspective	242
	14.5	Stamp duty	244
		Public sector perspective	244
		Private sector perspective	244

	14.6	Surplus land	246
	14.7	Termination payments	247
	Annex 1		249
	Annex 2		250
	Annex 3		253

CHAPTER 15 — EMPLOYMENT LAW ISSUES — 255

15.1	Introduction	255
15.2	The Transfer Regulations	255
	The effect of the Transfer Regulations	255
15.3	The application of the Transfer Regulations	258
15.4	The *Suzen* decision	259
15.5	Developments post-*Suzen*	262
15.6	Documenting the impact of the Transfer Regulations	263
15.7	Transfer Regulations costs	266
15.8	Collective obligations	270
15.9	Changing terms and conditions of employment after a transfer	273
15.10	The 'Regulation 7' pension exclusion	276
15.11	Comparable pension arrangements	278
15.12	Enhanced pension benefits on redundancy and accrued pension rights	279
15.13	Proposals for pension law reform	281
15.14	Provision of information	281
15.15	Information concerning measures to be taken by the project company	283
15.16	Training and competence	283
15.17	Staff and convictions	284
15.18	Disciplinary action	285

CHAPTER 16 — DISPUTE RESOLUTION PROCEDURES — 287

16.1	Introduction	287
16.2	The panel or dispute review board	289
16.3	Alternative dispute resolution	289
16.4	Arbitration	290
16.5	Expert determination	291
16.6	Adjudication	292
16.7	Joinder of parties	293
16.8	Conclusion	294

CHAPTER 17 — ACCOUNTING FOR PFI TRANSACTIONS — 295

17.1	Introduction	295
17.2	Why accounting treatment is important	295
17.3	The accounting context	296
17.4	Treasury Guidance	297

	17.5	The Application Note approach	297
	17.6	The Treasury Guidance approach	300
	17.7	Differences and similarities	303
		Achieving consistency	304
		Exclusion of construction risk	305
		Presumptions about 'service performance' failures	305
	17.8	The future	306
CHAPTER 18		THE FUTURE PROSPECTS FOR THE PRIVATE FINANCE INITIATIVE	309
	18.1	Introduction	309
	18.2	Public/private partnerships	309
	18.3	Refinancing of projects	311
	18.4	The PFI process	311
	18.5	International PFI developments	313

BIBLIOGRAPHY AND USEFUL ADDRESSES	317
INDEX	331

TABLE OF CASES

References are to paragraph numbers.

AG v Great Eastern Railway Co (1880) 5 App Cas 473, 49 LJ Ch 545, 42 LT 810, HL	4.2.3
Adams (Barbara) and Others v Lancashire County Council and BET Catering Services Ltd [1997] ICR 834, [1997] IRLR 436, (1997) *The Times*, May 19, CA	15.10.2
Allied Maples Group v Simmons & Simmons [1995] 1 WLR 1602, [1995] 4 All ER 907, [1995] NPC 83, CA	6.2.6
American Express International Banking Corporation v Hurley [1985] 3 All ER 564, 1985 FLR 350, (1985) 135 NLJ 1034, DC	9.5.14
Anisminic v Foreign Compensation Commission [1969] 2 AC 147, [1969] 2 WLR 163, [1969] 1 All ER 208, HL	4.5.13
Associated Provincial Picture Houses Ltd v Wednesbury Corporation [1948] 1 KB 223, [1948] LJR 190, [1947] 2 All ER 680, CA	13.1.13
Becker v Home Office [1972] 2 QB 407, [1972] 2 WLR 1193, [1972] 2 All ER 676, CA	4.2.3
Betts and Others v Brintel Helicopters Ltd and KLM ERA Helicopters (UK) Ltd [1997] 2 All ER 840, [1997] ICR 792, [1997] IRLR 361, (1997) 147 NLJ 561, CA	15.4.9, 15.4.10, 15.4.11, 15.5.4, 15.6.4
Birkdale District Electric Supply Co Ltd v Southport Corporation [1926] AC 355, 95 LJ Ch 587, 134 LT 673, HL	4.2.23
Blackpool and Fylde Aero Club Ltd v Blackpool Borough Council [1990] 1 WLR 1195, [1990] 3 All ER 25, (1991) 3 Admin LR 322, CA	6.5.1, 6.5.4
British Sugar plc v NEI Power Projects Ltd and Another (1998) ITCLR 118, [1997] CLY 1751, CA	7.2.5
Bromley London Borough Council v Greater London Council [1983] 1 AC 768, [1982] 2 WLR 62, [1982] 1 All ER 129, HL	4.2.25
Burke v Royal Liverpool University Hospital NHS Trust [1997] ICR 730, EAT	15.9.9
Carltona v Commissioners of Works [1943] 2 All ER 560, CA	4.2.17
Case of the Master and Fellows of Magdalen College in Cambridge (1/615) 11 Co Rep 66B	14.3.1
Chaplin v Hicks [1911] 2 KB 786, 80 LJKB 1292, [1911–13] All ER Rep 224, CA	6.2.6
City of Dublin Steam Packet Co v O'Brien (1912) 6 TC 101	14.3.6
Commission v Denmark C-243/89, [1993] ECR I-3353, (1993) *Financial Times*, June 29, ECJ	3.3.37
Commission v Belgium C-87/95, [1996] ECR I-2043, ECJ	3.3.34, 3.3.37
Commissioners of Crown Lands v Page [1960] 2 QB 274, [1960] 3 WLR 446, [1960] 2 All ER 726, CA	4.2.22
Cornwall County Care Ltd v Brightman and Others [1998] ICR 529, [1998] IRLR 656, [1998] TLR 155, EAT	15.9.4
Council of Civil Service Unions v Minister for the Civil Service [1985] AC 374, [1984] 3 WLR 1174, [1984] 3 All ER 935, HL	4.2.1, 13.1.13

Cowell v Rosehill Racecourse Co (1937) 56 CLR 605   14.3.19
Credit Suisse v Allerdale Borough Council [1997] QB 306, [1996] 3 WLR 894,
 [1996] 4 All ER 129, CA   4.1.2, 4.2.14, 4.2.21
Credit Suisse v Waltham Forest London Borough Council [1997] QB 362,
 [1996] 3 WLR 943, [1996] 4 All ER 176, CA   4.2.7

ECM (Vehicle Delivery Services) Ltd v B Cox and Others [1998] ICR 631,
 [1998] TLR 369, (1998) *The Times*, 10 June, EAT   15.5.2–15.5.8

Fairclough Building Ltd v Borough Council of Port Talbot (1992) 62 BLR 82,
 33 Con LR 24, CA   6.5.2
Foreningen af Arbejdsledere i Danmark v Daddy's Dance Hall A/S (C-324/86)
 [1988] IRLR 315, [1989] 2 CMLR 517, ECJ   15.9.2
Frankling v BPS Public Sector Ltd EAT 442/98 (unreported), EAT   15.12.1, 15.12.3
Fry v Three C's (Lewisham) Ltd (1998) Employment Tribunal 2300189/98
 (unreported)   15.7.4

Gebroeders Beentjes BV v Netherlands (C-31/87) [1988] ECR 4635, [1990] 1
 CMLR 287, ECJ   3.3.34
Glendale Grounds Management v Bradley (1998) (unreported), EAT   15.9.10
Good v Epping Forest District Council [1994] 1 WLR 376, [1994] 2 All ER 156,
 [1993] JPL 127   13.1.8

Hazell v Hammersmith and Fulham London Borough Council [1992] 2 AC 1,
 [1991] 2 WLR 372, [1991] 1 All ER 545, HL   4.1.2, 4.2.5, 4.2.9, 4.3.4
Hotelera Internacional (C-311/92) (1994), April 19, ECJ   3.2.8

Jones v Swansea City Council [1990] 1 WLR 54, [1989] 3 All ER 162, (1990) 134
 SJ 1437, CA   6.4.2

Keymed (Medical & Industrial Equipment) Ltd v Forest Healthcare NHS Trust
 (1997) November 11, (unreported), HC   6.2.3

LM Tenancies 1 plc v IRC [1996] STC 880, [1996] 46 EG 155, [1996] 2 EGLR
 119, ChD   14.5.6

McCarthy & Stone (Developments) Ltd v Richmond upon Thames London
 Borough Council [1992] 2 AC 48, [1991] 3 WLR 941, [1991] 4 All ER 897,
 HL   4.2.6
Madras Electricity Supply Corporation Ltd v Boarland [1955] AC 667, [1955] 2
 WLR 632, [1955] 1 All ER 753, HL   14.3.1
Marren v Ingles [1980] 1 WLR 983, [1980] 3 All ER 95, [1980] STC 500, HL   12.5.4,
   12.5.12
Mass Energy Ltd v Birmingham City Council [1993] Env LR 298, CA   6.4.4, 6.5.2

Melluish (Inspector of Taxes) v BMI (No 3) Ltd; Melluish (Inspector of Taxes) v
BMI (No 6) Ltd; Melluish (Inspector of Taxes) v BMI (No 9) Ltd; Melluish
(Inspector of Taxes) v Barclays Mercantile Business Finance Ltd; Melluish
(Inspector of Taxes) v Fitzroy Finance Ltd; [1996] 1 AC 454, [1995] 3 WLR
630, [1995] 4 All ER 453, [1995] STC 964, HL 14.3.14

Oladehinde v Secretary of State for the Home Department. *See* R v Secretary of
State for the Home Department, ex parte Oladehinde; R v Same, ex parte
Alexander

R v Derbyshire County Council, ex parte Times Supplements Ltd (1991) 3
Admin LR 241, [1991] COD 129, (1991) 155 LG Rev 123, DC 6.4.2
R v Enfield London Borough Council, ex parte Unwin (Roydon) Ltd (1989) 1
Admin LR 1, [1989] COD 466, 46 BLR 1 6.4.2
R v Inland Revenue Commissioners, ex parte Unilever plc; R v Inland Revenue
Commissioners, ex parte Matteson's Walls Ltd [1996] STC 841, 68 TC 205,
[1996] COD 421, CA 4.2.15
R v Legal Aid Board, ex parte Donn and Co (a Firm) [1996] 3 All ER 1, (1996)
The Times, March 18, QBD 6.4.5, 6.4.7
R v Lewisham London Borough Council, ex parte Shell UK [1988] 1 All ER
938, (1988) 152 LG Rev 929, DC 6.4.2
R v Lord Chancellor's Department, ex parte Hibbit and Saunders (a Firm)
[1993] COD 326, (1993) *The Times*, March 12, (1993) *The Independent*,
March 16, DC 6.4.3, 6.4.4, 6.4.5, 6.4.7
R v Portsmouth City Council, ex parte Bonaco Builders and Others (1995) June
6, (unreported) 6.4.6, 6.4.7
R v Portsmouth City Council, ex parte Peter Coles; R v Portsmouth City
Council, ex parte George Austin (Builders) Ltd (1997) 9 Admin LR 535, 81
BLR 1, [1997] CLC 407, CA 3.3.34, 6.2.3, 6.4.6, 6.4.7, 6.4.8, 6.4.9
R v Secretary of State for Defence, ex parte Camden London Borough Council
[1994] EGCS 33, [1994] NPC 28 13.1.20
R v Secretary of State for the Home Department, ex parte Oladehinde; R v
Same, ex parte Alexander [1991] 1 AC 254, [1990] 3 WLR 797, [1990] 33 All
ER 393, HL 4.2.18
R v Somerset County Council, ex parte Dixon [1997] JPL 1030, [1997] COD
323, [1997] NPC 61, QBD 13.1.7
Rainbow Estates Ltd v Tokenhold Ltd [1998] 3 WLR 980, [1998] 2 All ER 860,
[1998] TLR 164, (1998) *The Times*, 12 March, ChD 11.4.22
Rask and Christiensen v ISS Kantineservice A/S (C-209/91) [1993] IRLR 133,
[1992] I ECR 5755, ECJ 15.3.2
Rederiaktiebolaget Amphitrite v The King [1921] 3 KB 500, [1921] All ER Rep
542, 91 LJKB 75 4.2.22
Roberts v Hopwood [1925] AC 578, [1925] All ER Rep 24, 94 LJKB 542,
HL 4.2.25
Rottenberg v Monjack [1993] BCLC 374, [1992] BCC 688, [1992] NPC 89 9.2.3
Rygaard Ledernes Hovedorganisation (acting on behalf of Ole Rygaard) v
Dansk Arbejdsgiverforening (acting on behalf of Stro Molle Akustik A/S)
(C-48/94) [1996] ICR 333, [1996] IRLR 51, (1995) *The Times*, October 20,
ECJ 15.5.9

Schmidt (Christel) v Spar – und Leihkasse de Früheren Ämter Bordesholm, Kiel
und Cronshagen (C-392/92) [1995] ICR 237, [1994] IRLR 302, [1994] I ECR
1311, [1995] 2 CMLR 331, ECJ 15.3.3

Sita (GB) Ltd v Burton [1997] IRLR 501, (1996) *The Times*, 5 December,
    EAT   15.10.5
Southampton City Council v Academy Cleaning Services (1993) *The Times*, 11
    June   6.5.2
Spijkers v Gebroeders Benedik Abbatoir CV (C-24/85) [1986] 2 CMLR 296,
    [1986] 3 ECR 1119, ECJ   15.4.3, 15.4.12
Standard Chartered Bank Ltd v Walker [1982] 1 WLR 1410, [1982] 3 All ER
    938, (1982) 126 SJ 479, CA   9.3.14
Stokes (Inspector of Taxes) v Costain Property Investments Ltd [1984] 1 WLR
    763, [1984] 1 All ER 849, [1984] STC 204, CA   14.3.14
Street v Mountford [1985] AC 809, [1985] 2 WLR 877, [1985] 2 All ER 289,
    HL   14.3.19
Süzen (Ayse) v Zehnacker Gebaudereinigung GmbH Krankenhausservice
    (C-13/95) [1997] All ER(EC) 239, [1997] ICR 662, [1997] IRLR 255, (1997)
    16 Tr LR 365, ECJ   15.3.6, 15.4–15.4.11, 15.5.1, 15.5.3, 15.5.4, 15.5.6

Tesco Stores Ltd v Secretary of State for the Environment and West Oxfordshire
    District Council [1995] 1 WLR 759, [1995] 2 All ER 636, [1995] JPL 581,
    HL   13.1.8

Wake v Hall (1883) 8 App Cas 195   14.3.15
Whent v T Cartledge Ltd [1997] IRLR 153, EAT   15.9.10
Wilson and Others v St Helen's Borough Council; Meade and Baxendale v
    British Fuels Ltd [1998] ICR 1141, [1998] IRLR 706, [1998] 3 WLR 1070,
    [1998] 4 All ER 609, HL   15.9.2, 15.9.5, 15.9.6, 15.9.9, 15.9.10, 15.9.11, 15.18.2

TABLE OF STATUTES

References are to paragraph numbers.

Arbitration Act 1996	16.4.2
s 1	16.4.3
Broadcasting Act 1990	
s 31(3)	14 *Annex* 1
Capital Allowances Act 1990	
Ch VI, Pt II	14.3.16
ss 1, 2	14.3.8
s 3	14.3.8, 14.3.9, 14.3.25
(5)	14.3.11
s 9	14.3.24
s 18(1)(b)	14.3.10
(c)	14.3.10
(d)	14.3.10
(da)	14.3.10
s 20	14.3.11
(6)	14.3.11
ss 22–24	14.3.8
s 24	14.3.12
(2)	14.3.12
(3)	14.3.25
s 38F	14.3.12
(1)	14.3.12
s 51(3)	14.3.17
s 52	14.3.17
s 73	14.3.24
s 83(2)	14.3.25
Channel Tunnel Rail Link Act 1996	13.3.2
Companies Act 1985	
s 35	4.1.1
s 263	8.2.2
Data Protection Act 1998	15.14.4
Deregulation and Contracting Out Act 1994	
s 69	4.2.19, 4.2.20
(1)	4.2.19
(2)	4.2.19
s 70	4.2.19
s 71	4.2.19

Employment Rights Act 1996	15.2.8
s 203	15.9.8
Environment Act 1995	
s 57	13.2.2, 13.2.3
Environmental Protection Act 1990	
Pt II	6.4.4
Pt IIA	13.2.2, 13.2.3, 13.2.4
s 61	13.2.2
Equal Pay Act 1970	15.7.6
Finance Act 1982	
s 129	14.5.2
Finance Act 1987	
s 55	14.5.2
Finance Act 1994	
s 241	14.5.4, 14.5.6, 14.5.7
(2)	14.5.4
s 242	14.5.4, 14.5.6, 14.5.7
(1)	12.5.5, 12.5.6
(3)	12.5.6, 14.5.4
Finance Act 1995	
s 37(2)	14.4.3
Finance Act 1996	8.2.9, 14.3.22
s 82	14.3.21
(2)–(4)	14.3.24
s 87	14.3.25
Sch 9, para 2(2)	14.3.25
Finance Act 1997	
s 37(3)	14.4.3
Finance (No 2) Act 1997	
s 39(9)	14.3.26
s 47	14.5.1
Finance Act 1998	
s 149	14.5.1
Health and Safety at Work Act 1974	7.6.37
Highways Act 1980	4.2.20
s 278	14 *Annex* 2, Pt 2
Housing Act 1988	11.3.11

xxix

Housing Grants, Construction and Regeneration Act 1996	16.1.4, 16.1.8, 16.6.3, 16.6.4, 16.6.5
Pt II	7.6.33, 7.6.38, 16.6.2
ss 104–107	16.6.1
s 104(1)	16.6.1
s 105	7.6.38, 16.6.2
ss 109–113	7.6.38
Income and Corporation Taxes Act 1988	14.6.6
Ch IV, Pt X	14.3.27
s 74	14.3.24
s 75	14.3.24
(1)	14.3.25
s 393	14.3.26
s 393A(1)(b)	14.3.26
(2)	14.3.26
s 401	14.3.7, 14.3.25
(1AB)	14.3.25
s 505	14.3.1
s 519	14.3.1
s 519A	14.3.1
Sch A	14.3.1, 14.3.24, 14.3.26
Sch D	14.3.1
Case I	14.3.7, 14.3.21, 14.3.24, 14.3.26, 14.6.3, 14.7.3
Case III	14.3.21, 14.3.24
Case VI	14.3.26
Sch F	14.3.1
Insolvency Act 1986	
ss 10, 11	9.1.2, 9.1.4
s 44(1)	9.3.14
Interpretation Act 1978	4.2.16
Landlord and Tenant Act 1927	11.4.22
s 18	11.4.22
Landlord and Tenant Act 1954	11.4.7, 11.4.32
Pt II	11.3.11, 11.4.26
Law of Property Act 1925	
s 109(2)	9.3.14
Law of Property (Miscellaneous Provisions) Act 1989	
s 2	11.4.8
Leasehold Property (Repairs) Act 1938	11.4.22
Local Government Act 1972	4.3.4
s 101	4.2.21
s 111	4.2.5, 4.2.7, 4.2.9
(1)	4.2.4, 4.2.5, 4.2.9
s 123	11.5.1
s 172	4.2.9
Sch 13	4.2.9
Pt I	4.2.9
Local Government Act 1980	6.4.6
Local Government Act 1988	6.4.6
Local Government and Housing Act 1989	
s 44(6)	4.3.4
s 50(3)	4.3.1
Local Government (Contracts) Act 1997	1.3.29, 4.1.2, 4.3.5, 4.3.6, 4.3.8, 4.4.7, 8.4.10
s 1	4.3.7
(1), (2)	4.3.7
s 2(1)	4.3.9
(6)	4.3.9
s 3	4.3.11
s 4(3), (4)	4.3.10
s 5	4.3.9, 4.3.12
s 6	4.3.12
s 7	4.3.13
Local Government (Scotland) Act 1973	
s 135	14 *Annex* 1
Merchant Shipping Act 1894	
Pt XI	14 *Annex* 1
National Health Service Act 1977	
s 97A(3)	4.2.27
(9)	4.2.27
National Health Service and Community Care Act 1990	4.2.4, 4.4.1
s 5(1)	4.4.1
(a)	4.4.1, 4.4.2
(b)	4.4.1, 4.4.3
(5)(b)	4.4.1
(7)	4.2.27
s 61(3)	14.5.2
Sch 2	4.4.1
para 16	4.2.4
Sch 3	4.2.4
National Health Service (Private Finance) Act 1997	1.3.29, 4.1.2, 4.4.4, 4.4.6, 4.4.7, 10.7.8
s 1(1)–(3)	4.4.5
National Health Service (Residual Liabilities) Act 1996	4.4.4, 8.4.10, 10.7.8

New Roads and Street Works Act 1991	4.2.20	s 55	13.1.20
New Towns Act 1981	14 *Annex* 1	s 75	13.1.20
New Towns Act (Northern Ireland) 1965	14 *Annex* 1	s 106	13.1.19, 13.1.22
		(6)	13.1.22
New Towns (Scotland) Act 1968	14 *Annex* 1	s 293(1)	13.1.20
		s 299	13.1.19, 13.1.20, 13.1.21
		s 299A	13.1.19, 13.1.22
		(5)	13.1.19, 13.1.22
		s 301	13.1.19
Perpetuities and Accumulations Act 1964		Trade Union and Labour Relations (Consolidation) Act 1992	
s 9	11.4.13	s 188	15.2.10
Planning and Compensation Act 1991		Transport Act 1968	
s 12	13.1.22	Pt II	14 *Annex* 1
Public Health (Control of Disease) Act 1984	14 *Annex* 1	s 56	8.2.10, 18.2.6
		Transport and Works Act 1992	13.3.2
Public Health (Scotland) Act 1897 Pt X	14 *Annex* 1		
		Value Added Tax Act 1994	
		s 33	14.4.3, 14.4.5, 14.4.6, 14.4.7, 14.4.9, 14.6.3, 14.6.4, 14.6.5, 14.7.2, 14.7.3, 14.7.4, 14 *Annex* 1
Race Relations Act 1976	14 *Annex* 2, Pt 2		
Rehabilitation of Offenders Act 1974	15.17.1	s 33(1), (2)	14.4.6
Rent Act 1977	11.3.11	s 41	14.4.3, 14.4.5, 14.4.6, 14.4.7, 14.4.8, 14.4.9, 14.6.4, 14.6.5, 14.7.3, 14.7.4, 14 *Annex* 2, Pt 1
Stamp Act 1891			
s 58	14.6.5	(3)	14.4.8
		Sch 9, Group 1, Item 1	14.4.2, 14.4.3
		Sch 10, para 2	12.5.7, 14.4.2
Taxation of Chargeable Gains Act 1992		para 2(3AA)	14.4.3
		para 3A(10)	14.4.3
s 17	14.6.5		
s 42	14.6.7		
s 256	14.3.1	Water (Scotland) Act 1980	
s 271(3)	14.3.1	s 109	14 *Annex* 1
Town and Country Planning Act 1990	13.1.19	Wireless and Telegraphy Act	14 *Annex* 2, Pt 2

TABLE OF STATUTORY INSTRUMENTS

References are to paragraph numbers.

Construction (Design and Management) Regulations 1994, SI 1994/3140   7.6.33, 7.6.34, 7.6.37
    reg 1   7.6.35
    reg 4   7.6.35, 7.6.37
    reg 21   7.6.37
Construction Contracts (England and Wales) Exclusion Order 1998, SI 1998/648   16.6.2, 16.6.3
Contracting Out (Highway Functions) Order 1995, SI 1995/1986   4.2.20

Local Authorities (Capital Finance) Regulations 1997, SI 1997/319   4.3.1
    reg 16   4.3.2
    regs 40–45   4.3.3
Local Authorities (Capital Finance) (Amendment) Regulations 1998, SI 1998/371   4.3.2
Local Authorities (Contracts) Regulations 1997, SI 1997/2862   4.3.11
    reg 3   4.3.11

National Health Service Trusts (Membership and Procedure) Regulations 1990, SI 1990/2024   4.2.27

Planning and Compensation Act 1991 (Commencement No 3) Order 1991, SI 1991/2272   13.1.22
Public Sector Regulations. *See* Public Services Contracts Regulations 1993; Public Supply Contracts Regulations 1995; Public Works Contracts Regulations 1991
Public Services Contracts Regulations 1993, SI 1993/3228   3.2.1, 3.2.2, 3.2.5, 3.2.6, 3.2.7, 3.2.8, 3.2.10, 3.2.11, 3.2.14, 3.2.16, 3.2.18, 3.2.19, 3.2.22, 3.3.1, 3.3.2, 3.3.12, 3.3.13, 3.3.16 (Table 4), 3.3.21, 3.3.23, 3.3.25, 3.3.30, 3.3.33, 3.3.37, 3.3.49, 5.2.1, 5.2.3, 5.3.1, 5.3.2, 5.4.1, 5.4.3, 5.5.2, 5.5.6, 5.5.9, 5.5.10, 5.6.4, 5.6.7, 5.6.25, 5.7.7
    reg 12   3.3.16 (Table 4)
    reg 14   3.3.25
    reg 32   6.2.1
    Sch 1, Pt A   3.2.20, 3.2.21, 3.3.1 (Table 1)
    Sch 1, Pt B   3.2.20, 3.2.21, 3.3.1 (Table 1)
    Sch 2, Pt D   3.3.13
Public Supply Contracts Regulations 1995, SI 1995/201   3.2.1, 3.2.2, 3.2.5, 3.2.6, 3.2.7, 3.2.8, 3.2.10, 3.2.11, 3.2.14, 3.2.16, 3.2.18, 3.2.19, 3.2.22, 3.3.1, 3.3.2, 3.3.12, 3.3.13, 3.3.21, 3.3.23, 3.3.25, 3.3.30, 3.3.33, 3.3.37, 3.3.49, 5.2.1, 5.2.3, 5.3.1, 5.3.2, 5.4.1, 5.4.3, 5.5.2, 5.5.6, 5.5.9, 5.5.10, 5.6.4, 5.6.7, 5.6.25, 5.7.7
    reg 29   6.2.1

Public Works Contracts Regulations 1991, SI 1991/2680   3.2.1, 3.2.2, 3.2.5, 3.2.6, 3.2.7, 3.2.8, 3.2.10, 3.2.11, 3.2.12, 3.2.14, 3.2.16, 3.2.18, 3.2.19, 3.2.22, 3.3.1, 3.3.2, 3.3.12, 3.3.13, 3.3.21, 3.3.23, 3.3.25, 3.3.30, 3.3.33, 3.3.37, 3.3.49, 5.2.1, 5.2.3, 5.3.1, 5.3.2, 5.4.1, 5.4.3, 5.5.2, 5.5.6, 5.5.9, 5.5.10, 5.6.4, 5.6.7, 5.6.25, 5.7.7, 6.4.6, 7.2.1
    reg 31   6.2.1

Town and Country Planning (Application) Regulations 1988, SI 1988/1812
    reg 2   13.1.4
Town and Country Planning (Assessment of Environmental Effects) Regulations 1988, SI 1988/1199   13.1.10
Town and Country Planning (General Development Procedure) Order 1995, SI 1995/419
    art 1   13.1.4
Transfer of Undertakings (Protection of Employment) Regulations 1981, SI 1981/1794   15.1.1, 15.1.2, 15.2.1, 15.2.2, 15.2.9, 15.3.1, 15.3.3, 15.3.4, 15.3.5, 15.3.6, 15.4.1, 15.4.8, 15.5.1, 15.5.2, 15.5.3, 15.5.4, 15.5.5, 15.5.9, 15.6.1, 15.6.3, 15.6.4, 15.6.5, 15.6.6, 15.6.8, 15.6.11, 15.6.12, 15.6.13, 15.7.1, 15.7.2, 15.7.3, 15.7.4, 15.8.9, 15.8.11, 15.9.1, 15.9.2, 15.9.6, 15.9.9, 15.10.1, 15.10.5, 15.12.1, 15.12.4, 15.13.2, 15.14.2, 15.14.5, 15.14.6, 15.15.1, 15.16.2, 15.17.1
    reg 7   15.2.4, 15.7.3, 15.10, 15.10.1, 15.10.2, 15.10.5, 15.12.1, 15.12.2, 15.12.4, 15.13.2
    reg 10   15.8.1
    reg 10(2)   15.8.3, 15.8.7
    reg 10(3)   15.8.7
    reg 10(5)   15.8.4
    reg 11(3), (4)   15.15.2

Utilities Contracts Regulations 1996, SI 1996/2911   3.2.3, 3.2.4
    reg 32   6.2.1

TABLE OF CODES OF GUIDANCE ETC

References are to paragraph numbers.

Accounting Standards
Application Note: *Amendment to FRS 5 Reporting the Substance of Transactions: The Privater Finance Initiative and Similar Contracts*,
   September 1998   17.3.5, 17.5.4, 17.5.6, 17.5.7, 17.5.10, 17.5.11, 17.6.1, 17.6.2, 17.6.3,
         17.6.5, 17.7.1, 17.7.2, 17.7.3, 17.7.4, 17.7.5, 17.7.6, 17.7.7, 17.7.10, 17.7.12,
               17.8.1, 17.8.2, 17.8.4

para F6	17.7.2
para F10	17.5.5, 17.7.2
paras F11, F12	17.5.6
para F17	17.5.7
para F19	17.5.6
para F20	17.5.7
para F21	17.5.7
para F22	17.5.7
paras F24–F80	17.5.9
para F50	17.5.8

FRS 5: *Reporting the Substance of Transactions*, 1994   17.3.3, 17.3.4, 17.3.5, 17.4.1,
        17.4.2, 17.5.1, 17.5.2, 17.5.6, 17.5.11, 17.7.1, 17.7.12, 17.8.1, 17.8.3

para 2	17.5.1
para 17	17.5.1
para 47	17.5.3
(b), (c)	17.5.3
para 51	17.5.3
para 52	17.5.4
SSAP 21, 1984	17.3.1, 17.3.2, 17.3.3, 17.3.4, 17.5.6, 17.6.2

Basic Contractual Terms – HM Treasury and Private Finance Panel, October
   1996   1.3.11, 1.3.25, 10.1.8

explanatory note	10.5.4
para 17.1	10.5.3
para 20	10.7.10

Bates Review (HM Treasury News Release 69/97)   1.3.17, 3.3.16, 3.3.30, 4.1.2, 5.5.8,
                           5.6.4, 5.6.15, 8.4.10, 10.1.7, 18.1, 18.2.1, 18.4.1, 18.4.6

Recommendation No 10	1.3.23
Recommendation No 14	18.4.4
Recommendation No 29	2.3.2

Breaking New Ground – towards a new partnership between the public and
   private sectors – HM Treasury   1.3.7, 1.6

Constructing the Team, July 1994   7.7.11
Crichel Down Rules. See Disposal of Surplus Government Land; Obligation to
   offer land back to former owners or their successors – The Crichel Down
   Rules

Department of the Environment Circular 18/84   13.1.19, 13.1.20, 13.1.21, 13.1.22
Disposal of Surplus Government Land; Obligation to offer land back to former owners or their successors – The Crichel Down Rules – Department of the Environment and the Welsh Office, October 1992   11.5.4, 11.5.5, 11.5.6, 11.5.7, 11.5.8, 11.5.9, 13.3.2

Further Contractual Issues – HM Treasury and Private Finance Panel,
- February 1997   1.3.11, 1.3.25, 10.1.8, 10.1.9
- para 2.2   10.4.1
- para 2.4   10.4.4, 10.4.20
- para 3.5   10.4.37
- para 4.3   10.4.29
- para 4.4   10.4.28
- para 7.4   10.10.3
- para 7.8   10.10.5
- para 9.3   10.7.2
- para 9.5   10.7.6, 10.9.6
- para 9.10   10.9.16, 10.9.19
- para 10.4   10.6.7
- para 10.5   10.6.3
- para 10.6   10.6.10

Government Accounting Rule DA011/96   12.3.2
Government Circular 6/93   11.5.1, 11.5.2
Government Procurement Agreement 1994   3.2.16, 3.3.41
- Art XIV   3.3.41
- Annex   3.2.16

Guidance on Project Agreements – Treasury Taskforce Draft, September 1998   8.6.3, 10.1.11, 10.2.1, 10.3.2, 10.3.4, 10.3.5, 10.3.7, 10.3.9, 10.3.12, 10.3.13, 10.3.15, 10.4.24, 10.5.5, 10.5.6, 10.7.2, 10.7.4, 10.7.6, 10.7.10, 10.9.13, 10.9.22, 10.9.24, 10.9.25, 18.4.1
- section 13.1.3   10.5.2
- section 13.9.4   10.5.4
- section 13.9.5   10.5.4
- section 14.2.4   8.6.3, 18.3.2
- section 20.1.2.2.2   10.9.17
- section 20.2.1   10.7.6
- section 20.2.2.3   10.9.6
- section 20.3.2.3.3   10.9.20
- section 24   8.4.15

HM Treasury Disposal Rules   12.3.3
- para 19   12.3.2
- para 20   12.3.2

JCT Standard Form of Building Contract with Contractor's Design (JCT 81)   7.2.2, 7.2.3, 7.2.4, 7.3.3, 7.7.2, 7.7.5, 7.7.6, 7.7.10

New Engineering Contract (2nd edition) (NEC)   7.7.10, 7.7.11, 7.7.12

Table of Codes and Guidance etc   xxxvii

Options A-F	7.7.11

Partnerships for Prosperity – Treasury Taskforce, November 1997   18.2.1
   para 1.04   1.2.7
   para 4.07   1.3.30
PFI in Government Accomodation – HM Treasury and Private Finance Panel, 2nd edition October 1996
   para 7.1   2.2.11
Policy Statement No 1 – *PFI and Public Expenditure Allocations* – Treasury Taskforce, October 1997   1.3.30
Policy Statement No 2 – *Public Sector Comparators and Value for Money* – Treasury Taskforce, March 1998   1.2.12, 1.3.34, 2.2.37
   section 5.1   5.6.22
Policy Statement No 3 – *PFI and Public Expenditure Allocations for Non-Departmental Public Bodies* – Treasury Taskforce, August 1998   1.3.29
Private Opportunity, Public Benefit – *Progressing the Private Finance Initiative* – HM Treasury and Private Finance Panel, November 1995   1.3.11, 1.6, 10.1.8
Protecting Parties to Local Authority Contracts: possible safe harbour provisions – Department of the Environment, Transport and the Regions, May 1997   4.3.5

Report by the Comptroller and Auditor General on the PFI Contracts for Bridgend and Fazakerley Prisons (HC 253, Session 1997–98, 31 October 1997)
   para 1.18   1.3.14
Risk and Reward in PFI Contract – HM Treasury and Private Finance Panel, May 1996   11.1.2

Selling Government Services into wider Markets, Policy and Guidance Note – HM Treasury (Enterprise and Growth Unit)   18.4.6
Step-by-Step Guide to the PFI Procurement Process – Treasury Taskforce, July 1997, Revised April 1998   1.3.11, 5.2.3, 5.5.14, 5.6.4, 5.6.29, 5.7.6, 5.7.14

Technical Note No 1: *How to Account for PFI Transactions* – Treasury Taskforce, September 1997   17.4.1, 17.4.2, 17.4.3, 17.5.11, 17.6.1, 17.6.2, 17.6.3, 17.6.4, 17.6.5, 17.6.6, 17.7.1, 17.7.2, 17.7.3, 17.7.4, 17.7.6, 17.7.12, 17.8.1, 17.8.2, 17.8.4
   paras 15, 16   17.6.3
   para 26   17.6.3
   para 28   17.6.4
Technical Note No 2: *How to Follow EC Procurement Procedure and Advertise in the OJEC* – Treasury Taskforce, June 1998   1.3.23, 3.2.9, 3.3.9, 3.3.16, 5.2.2

Transferability of Equity – HM Treasury and Private Finance Panel, October 1996   2.3.8, 10.1.8

Whitley Councils for the Health Service (Great Britain) General Council
   Conditions of Service   15.7.5
   section 46   15.12.1, 15.12.2
Writing an Output Specification – HM Treasury and Private Finance Panel, October 1996   1.2.3, 2.2.8, 5.6 13
   para 4.6.1   2.2.8

TABLE OF EC LEGISLATION

References are to paragraph numbers.

Council Directive 71/305/EEC concerning the co-ordination of procedures for the award of public works contracts, OJ [1971] L185/5 — 6.4.6

Council Directive 77/187/EEC on the approximation of the laws of the Member States relating to the safeguarding of employees' rights in the event of transfers of undertakings, businesses or parts of businesses (Acquired Rights Directive), OJ [1977] L61/26 — 15.1.2, 15.2.1, 15.2.4, 15.3.1, 15.3.2, 15.3.6, 15.4.3, 15.4.5, 15.4.7, 15.6.12, 15.9.2, 15.9 12

Art 3(3) — 15.10.1, 15.10.2

(3)(B) — 15.13.1

Council Directive 85/337/EEC on the assessment of the effects of certain public and private projects on the environment, OJ [1985] L175/40 — 13.1.10, 13.1.12

Council Directive 92/50/EEC relating to the co-ordination of procedures for the award of public services contracts, OJ [1992] L209/1 — 3.2.1, 3.2.20

Recital 16 — 3.2.8

Council Directive 93/36/EEC co-ordinating procedures for the award of public supply contracts, OJ [1993] L199/1 — 3.2.1

Council Directive 93/37/EEC concerning the co-ordination of procedures for the award of public works contracts OJ [1993] L199/54 — 3.2.1, 3.3.3

Council Directive 93/38/EEC co-ordinating the procurement procedures of entities operating in the water, energy, transport, and telecommunication sectors, OJ [1993] L199/84 — 3 2.3

Directive 97/11/EC — 13.1.10

EC Treaty (Treaty of Rome) 1957
Art 169 — 6.3.1

Statement Concerning Article 7(4) of Council Directive 93/37/EEC of 14 June 1993 OJ [1994] L 111/114 — 3.3.3

GLOSSARY AND ABBREVIATIONS

ASB	the Accounting Standards Board.
awarding authority	the public sector body (department, agency, NHS trust, local authority, etc) which is procuring a service through the PFI.
BAFO	best and final offer. Final priced bid submitted by tenderers following evaluation and/or negotiation of initial bids.
Bates Review	the review of PFI conducted by Sir Malcolm Bates (a founder member of the Private Finance Panel) which contained 29 recommendations which were announced and endorsed by the Government on 23 June 1997 (the results of the Bates Review are contained in Treasury Press Notice 67/97). A second Bates Review was announced in October 1998, reporting in February 1999.
benchmarking	a procedure for testing whether the standard and price of services is consistent with the market standard (if any), without any formal competitive tendering.
bidders	see tenderers.
change procedures	procedures in the project agreement for effecting variations (both mandatory and voluntary) to the physical facilities or the level or scope of services.
compliant bid	a bid which meets the awarding authority's stipulated requirements. An awarding authority may reserve the right to refuse to evaluate and reject a bid which is not compliant.
concession agreement	see project agreement.
consortium or the consortium members	the group of private sector participants who have come together for the purpose of tendering for a PFI contract.

contract term	the period over which the project company is engaged by the awarding authority, comprising the construction period and the operating period.
construction company	the company engaged by the project company to construct and/or refurbish the facilities which are the subject of the project.
construction period	the period of the design and construction/refurbishment of the facilities which are the subject of the project.
contract award notice	the notice published in the Official Journal following the conclusion of the project and the entering into of contracts between the awarding authority and the project company.
DBFO contract	a PFI contract providing for the design, building, financing and operation of facilities.
DCMF contract	a PFI contract providing for the design, construction, maintenance and financing of facilities. The term is synonymous with DBFO contract but is the expression used for PFI projects.
debt funders	the providers of debt finance to a project. In this context, the term is used to cover the provision of third-party debt finance including bank debt and bond finance (other than subordinated debt provided by the sponsors as a substitute for equity).
delay events	specified events excusing the project company from breach of its obligations and which entitle it to additional time to perform and often entitle it to compensation (where compensation is payable, these may be referred to as compensation events).
direct agreements	agreements between the initial parties to a contract entered into by the project company and one or more additional parties giving the additional party or parties the opportunity to step in to the contracts in place of the project company. See Chapters 2 and 9.

equity funders	the investors who subscribe for equity in the project company or provide quasi-equity in the form of subordinated debt.
FRS 5	the financial reporting standard entitled 'FRS 5: Reporting the Substance of Transactions' (issued by the ASB in 1994). See Chapter 17.
force majeure	a limited category of events outside the control of the awarding authority and the project company which may entitle the project company to compensation and ultimately give either party the right to terminate the project agreement. See Chapter 10.
full business case	the business case prepared by the awarding authority, following selection of the preferred tenderer, validating the affordability and value for money of the selected tender.
funders	collectively, the debt funders and the equity funders.
ITN	an invitation to negotiate and, ultimately, to submit priced bids, issued to tenderers by an awarding authority. This term is often used interchangeably with ITT.
ITT	an invitation to tender (by submitting priced bids) issued to tenderers by an awarding authority. This term is often used interchangeably with ITN.
market testing	a procedure for re-pricing the provision of services on a periodic basis by means of competitive tender.
negotiated procedure	one of the prescribed procedures under the EU procurement regime entitling the awarding authority to negotiate with tenderers at any stage during the tender process. See Chapter 3.
Official Journal, the Journal, OJ or OJEC	the Official Journal of the European Communities. The publication in which projects are advertised.
OJEC notice	a notice published in the Official Journal announcing details of the project and the procedure for bidding.

operating company	the company engaged by the project company to operate and maintain the facilities which are the subject of the project.
operating period	the period after expiry of the construction period, during which the project company operates and maintains the facilities. In some projects, interim services may be provided during the construction period.
outline business case	a business case prepared by the awarding authority to establish the need for the project and its outline parameters and scope, which, if approved, will lead to the commencement of the tender process.
output specification	the specification upon which tenders are invited to bid which sets out the awarding authority's requirements in non-prescriptive terms, leaving the tenderers with the responsibility for determining how to deliver those requirements.
overage or clawback	methods by which the awarding authority ensures that it can obtain a share of any increase in the value of land transferred to the project company over and above an agreed base value. See Chapter 12.
performance points	a system of scoring the standard of delivery of services by the project company. Accrued points may be translated into deductions from the unitary payment and ultimately count towards thresholds giving the awarding authority a right of termination.
4Ps	the Public Private Partnership Programme Limited, a company formed by the Local Authority Associations in England and Wales to promote PFI in local government.
PFI	the UK government's private finance initiative.
PFUs	Private Finance Units. Most central government departments now have a dedicated Private Finance Unit charged with the task of promoting PFI within that department.
PIN	prior information notice. A notice issued as part of the procurement process. See Chapter 3.

prequalification	the process by which the awarding authority selects a limited number of tenderers from those who have submitted an expression of interest in response to an OJEC notice.
PPP	public private partnership. A generic term for the development of projects involving both the public and private sectors (with varying levels of involvement and responsibility) of which PFI is one variant.
preferred tenderer	the tenderer selected by the awarding authority to be awarded the PFI contract. See Chapter 3.
Private Finance Panel or the Panel	the working group set up by the Conservative Government in 1993 to promote the PFI. See Chapter 10.
project agreement	the principal agreement between the awarding authority and the project company governing the project. Sometimes this agreement is referred to as the 'concession agreement'.
the project company	the company established by the preferred tenderer to be the contracting vehicle for a project.
PSC or public sector comparator	a benchmark used in the course of procurement against which the value for money of tenders is assessed by the awarding authority. It represents a notional cost estimate of the project based on the assumption that the facilities and services the subject of the project are acquired through conventional funding with the awarding authority retaining managerial responsibility and exposure to risk.
relief events	specified events excusing the project company from breach of its obligations but which do not entitle it to additional time or compensation.
reference bid	a bid which is submitted on the basis of (and complies with) certain prescribed requirements of the awarding authority.

service level specification	the specification (typically scheduled to the project agreement) setting out the standard to which the service must be delivered, often accompanied by an agreed performance monitoring regime.
shadow tolls	an expression developed in connection with the DBFO road projects connoting the payment of a notional toll by the awarding authority for each vehicle using the road.
sponsors or project sponsors	the private sector participants developing a project.
SPV	special purpose vehicle. The project company established by the sponsors which has as its sole purpose the delivery of a project.
tenderers	the consortia engaged in tendering for the award of a PFI contract. They may be referred to as 'bidders'.
TUPE	the Transfer of Undertakings (Protection of Employment) Regulations 1981. See Chapter 15.
the Treasury Taskforce or the Taskforce	the HM Treasury unit established following the Bates Review as the focal point for PFI across government. See Chapter 1.
unavailability	the test for determining deductions from the unitary payment by reference to standards for the provision of the facility (as opposed to the standard of associated services).
unitary payment	the payment by the awarding authority to the project company for the provision of the facility the subject of the project and associated services.
variant bid	a bid which does not comply with the prescribed requirements of the awarding authority for a reference bid but which a tenderer is proposing as offering better value for money.
vfm	value for money.

Chapter 1

THE BACKGROUND, EVOLUTION AND DEVELOPMENT OF THE PRIVATE FINANCE INITIATIVE

1.1 INTRODUCTION

1.1.1 This chapter sets out the basic principles of the Private Finance Initiative ('PFI') and traces the origins and development of the PFI, including its recent reappraisal by the Labour Government. It is intended as a basic route map for the PFI and the issues explored in detail in the following chapters.

1.2 WHAT ARE THE KEY AIMS AND FEATURES OF THE PRIVATE FINANCE INITIATIVE?

The aims of the Private Finance Initiative

1.2.1 The principal aim of the PFI is to involve the private sector in the provision of public services, shifting the role of the public sector from owner and provider to enabler and purchaser and guardian of the interests of the end-users, the general public. It is driven, in part, by the belief that the public sector should focus on its core functions, leaving the private sector to perform those functions which it can often do more cost-effectively and efficiently than the public sector. However, the key political driver behind the PFI is the desire to improve the nation's infrastructure and supporting public services without placing undue strain on scarce public funds and without having to increase taxation. Since the change of government in 1997 from Conservative to Labour, the focus has been on the investment opportunities of the PFI rather than on a reallocation of the roles and functions of the public and private sectors. To the extent that the Labour Government acknowledges any such reallocation, it does so in terms of the contributions which the public and private sectors bring to public/private partnerships.

1.2.2 The traditional procurement of public sector infrastructure and its related services, where the Government is owner and operator with responsibility for design and construction, has given way to the private sector assuming responsibility for design, construction, operation, management, maintenance and finance, with the public sector as the customer, or, sometimes, with the public itself as direct user, paying for the provision of a service.

1.2.3 The focus on the provision of a service by the public sector, rather than the purchase of a capital asset, underpins the PFI. By giving the private sector the responsibility for providing, maintaining and operating an asset, the public sector's motivation is to define a standard of service to be delivered to it (or to the general public, as end-user) leaving the private sector to determine the way to deliver that service. In other words, the public sector will prescribe a set of outputs (the 'what') leaving the private sector to determine the technical solution (the 'how'). By way of example, if the task is the delivery of constant hot and cold running water in a building, the output specification will be framed in terms of the provision of water to a certain number of people and a definition of what constitutes 'hot' (for example, water within a prescribed temperature band). The private sector's responsibility is to determine the quantity of water required, the capacity of tanks and the system necessary to ensure that there is always hot water.[1]

1.2.4 The focus on service provision was thought also to reinforce the fact that, from an accounting standpoint, the awarding authority was not purchasing an asset on deferred terms and so the transaction would not appear as a liability on the public sector balance sheet. However, as discussed in Chapter 17, this analysis has not been accepted by the Accounting Standards Board and, indeed, the service element of PFI transactions is not regarded by them as being a determining factor.

Risk allocation and value for money

1.2.5 By leaving the private sector to determine how to deliver the service, the awarding authority is able to transfer to the private sector certain risks which would otherwise have been borne by the awarding authority. Risk allocation is a fundamental element of the PFI. If the private sector is to be responsible for financing the provision of a capital asset and related services, how can the awarding authority justify reimbursing the cost of capital incurred by the private sector which will be in excess of the public sector's cost of capital? The answer is made up of a number of elements.

1.2.6 First, there is the ability of the private sector to access capital immediately to fund the provision of a capital asset at a time when corresponding public capital would not be available. However, that in itself would merely represent a disguised form of borrowing – a scheme to 'buy now and pay later' which has the benefit of facilities becoming available to the public sector earlier than they could otherwise have been afforded using public capital but, ultimately, at greater cost. The additional cost of capital may also be offset by the ability of the private sector to deliver the asset more cheaply and efficiently than under a traditional procurement. The manner of the design and construction of the asset under the PFI is a decision for the private sector, the test being that it meets the use requirements of the awarding authority (expressed on an output basis) rather than being bound by a design and construction solution prescribed by the awarding authority as would be the case in a traditional procurement. Experience of traditional procurements suggests that the public sector's prescribed solution has often suffered from over engineering and 'gold plating' to take account of every eventuality. It may well be that a natural reaction to obtaining scarce public capital to fund the construction of an asset is a desire to ensure that the asset procured will last. However, the cost of such over engineering can far outweigh

---

1   Guidance on how to frame the awarding authority's output requirements is contained in *Writing an Output Specification* (HM Treasury and Private Finance Panel) October 1996.

its benefits and, in particular, in a world where technological change and rapid obsolescence are inevitable, it rarely makes commercial or economic sense to build assets which will survive for generations.

1.2.7 The recent Treasury publication, *Partnerships for Prosperity*, contains examples[1] of the savings which can be achieved by using the PFI in place of a traditional procurement including:

- the first eight design, build, finance and operate ('DBFO') road projects delivered average cost savings of 15%;
- the Bridgend and Fazakerley prison projects achieved a 10% saving;
- NIRS 2 (the replacement national insurance recording system) is estimated to be 60% cheaper than the public sector equivalent would have been.

1.2.8 The cost of capital can also be mitigated if the private sector is able to generate additional third-party revenue from the asset, thus reducing the charge to the awarding authority. Provided the service can be delivered to the awarding authority in accordance with the output specification, the private sector should be free to provide services to third parties, subject always to the constraints of issues such as security (which may arise, for example, on defence-related projects).

1.2.9 Ultimately, in order to justify the extra cost of private sector capital, it is necessary for the private sector to bear certain risks inherent in the project.[2] The risk which is at the heart of the PFI is performance (ie continued delivery of the completed asset and related services). The awarding authority is purchasing a service and will pay only for the service delivered. In this way the private sector's capital at risk in the project will be repaid in full (together with a profit element) only if the asset and services are delivered to the requisite standard. There may also be an incentive on the private sector to complete construction of the asset and commence service operation as quickly as possible in order to trigger the obligation of the awarding authority to commence paying for the service. This is a radically different approach to that of a traditional public sector procurement involving a design and build contract. There, the awarding authority funds the provision of the asset by making stage payments without any ability to determine whether the asset will perform and few sanctions when it fails to do so. Under the PFI, the private sector is responsible for the performance of the asset throughout the contract period. Thus, long-term maintenance of capital assets and achieving the lowest overall 'life-cycle cost' for the assets and related services becomes the private sector's responsibility. That in itself is a major benefit to the public sector which has allowed periodic maintenance to become a front-line casualty in the battle for scarce public capital.

1.2.10 However, it must be remembered that every risk transferred has a price. The key to risk allocation is that the risk should be borne by the party who is best able to manage it. The awarding authority must be able to demonstrate that the price being paid for the private sector to bear a particular risk represents value for money. This is linked to the allocation of risks to the party best able to manage

---

1 *Partnerships for Prosperity* (HM Treasury) November 1997 paragraph 1.04.
2 The allocation of risk and its negotiation is discussed in detail in Chapters 2 and 10.

them. The price for transferring a particular risk may be prohibitively expensive (and thus poor value for money) if it is one with which the private sector is unfamiliar or one which is outside its control (for example, certain legislative risks). Equally important from the private sector's perspective is its ability to manage and control the risk. It will assess the probability of a risk occurring and its likely impact. In the final analysis, there may be certain risks which the private sector is unwilling to assume or price.

1.2.11 The allocation of risk, its pricing and the consequences of risk crystallising involve a delicate balance in order to achieve an acceptable outcome for the awarding authority and the private sector. The price charged by the private sector will reflect not only an assessment of the probability and impact of a risk occurring but also the consequences which may flow if the private sector is unable to perform its obligations. If the performance regime proposed by the awarding authority is too severe (by reference to the level of deductions for non-performance), this will affect the price which the private sector demands for bearing the risk. At the end of the day, the awarding authority must achieve a meaningful and realistic sanction for failure to perform and the private sector must have the incentive to bear the risk, in each case for a price which is value for money.

1.2.12 A value for money test must be applied whenever public money is involved in a PFI project. It is only in the case of truly financially free-standing projects (see **1.2.15**) that no value for money test is required.[1] A toll bridge project which relies on toll revenues but includes approach roads which are publicly funded would not be financially free-standing and a value for money test would be required.

Accounting treatment[2]

1.2.13 By achieving the correct allocation of risk, the finance required to develop and implement the project is not certain to be repaid, as full pay back will depend upon full performance by the private sector. This element is of fundamental importance: it distinguishes a PFI transaction from a 'take or pay' contract or a finance lease, where repayment is guaranteed. Were such a guarantee to exist in PFI transactions, it would result in the full value of the contract counting as a public sector liability at the outset of the transaction, which would score against public sector spending limits. This would either result in there being less public capital available for other purposes or would prohibit the transaction proceeding if it were in breach of the pre-set spending limits of the awarding authority in question. The off balance sheet treatment of public sector spending on PFI transactions was a fundamental issue for the previous Conservative Government and continues to be so for the Labour Government. This has brought into sharp focus the nature of the risks inherent in PFI transactions and their allocation between the public and private sectors. A delicate balance has to be struck between an allocation which produces the

---

1   For further information, see Policy Statement No 2 *Public Sector Comparators and Value for Money* (Treasury Taskforce) March 1998.
2   The accounting treatment of PFI transactions is discussed in detail in Chapter 17.

desired accounting treatment and one which also delivers a project which is value for money and affordable. It is at this point that the accounting treatment can be in danger of driving the risk allocation decision rather than allowing a decision based on the party who is best placed to manage the risk and whether it represents value for money.

Affordability

1.2.14 Ultimately the cost to the awarding authority of having transferred the risk must result in it making a stream of affordable payments. Affordability is an issue both at the outset of the transaction and over time. On the one hand, the payments must be capable of being met out of current spending allocations or forecast revenues. However, an equally important consideration is the long-term consequence of a committed stream of payments over a contract period of say 25 or 30 years. This commitment has to be taken into account when planning future spending. It remains to be seen how far the PFI spending being incurred today will squeeze and constrain future expenditure plans.

Types of PFI projects

1.2.15 There are three basic types of PFI project currently in development or operation.

Services sold to the public sector as purchaser and user

This represents the largest group of projects which has been promoted under the PFI since it was launched in 1992. The private sector is responsible for financing the provision of a capital asset and provides services in relation to that asset (including asset maintenance). Examples include the provision of prisons, hospitals and general government accommodation.

Financially free-standing projects

Here the private sector is responsible for the design, construction, operation, maintenance and financing of an asset, recouping its costs through charges direct to the ultimate end-user rather than a public sector entity. Examples of this type of project include the Second Severn Bridge and the Queen Elizabeth II Bridge at Dartford, both of which rely on tolls payable by the general public to generate the necessary income. Both these projects pre-dated the formal launch of the PFI and represent the principal type of private finance project which was developed before the advent of the PFI.

Joint ventures

These involve projects where there is a mix of end-user charges and public subsidy or contribution. This public subsidy or contribution can take several forms including direct subsidy (for example, through capital grants) or the contribution of assets (for example, surplus land or income generating assets) or a combination of both. Examples include urban regeneration projects, where land may be provided by the awarding authority in return for regeneration of a derelict site, and light rail schemes, where a capital grant is required to part fund the project, as the fare box revenue which can be recovered from passengers is insufficient to meet the full costs of the project.

1.3 THE ORIGINS AND DEVELOPMENT OF THE PFI

Ryrie Rules

1.2.16 The Labour Government is committed to exploring all forms of public/private partnership (of which the PFI is but one variety) and it may be that further variants emerge.[1]

1.3.1 The PFI was launched by the Conservative Government in the 1992 Autumn Statement of the then Chancellor of the Exchequer, Norman Lamont. However, the involvement of the private sector in the provision of projects which had traditionally been the preserve of government had its origins in the 1980s. By the beginning of the 1980s, the Treasury had established a committee led by Sir William Ryrie which reported in 1981 on the use of private finance to fund public sector projects. The product of that committee was the so-called 'Ryrie Rules' which set down the basis upon which private funding could be utilised. The principal rules were:

- privately funded projects had to be tested against a publicly funded alternative and shown to be more cost-effective;
- save in exceptional circumstances, a privately funded project would result in a pound for pound reduction in available public expenditure (although this was partially relaxed by the then Chief Secretary, John Major, in 1989).[2]

Early private finance projects

1.3.2 The combination of showing that private finance was more cost-effective than cheaper public funding and the displacement of public expenditure by private funding meant that private finance held little attraction for awarding authorities and few private finance projects were developed.

1.3.3 Of those that were developed, the earliest and highest profile private sector infrastructure project was the construction of the Channel Tunnel, the concession for which was awarded in 1985 and which has involved no public sector capital. Other projects included the Dartford Crossing, where a concession to design, build, finance and operate the Queen Elizabeth II Bridge was awarded in 1987 with the bridge opening in 1991, and the Second Severn Crossing, the concession for which was awarded in 1990 with the new bridge opening in 1997.

1.3.4 However, the projects in question were all transport-related. The difference which the PFI sought to make was to apply the concept of private sector involvement across all areas of government, including areas which had previously been the exclusive domain of the public sector.

---

1   For further discussion of the future development of the PFI, see Chapter 18.
2   This relaxation created the possibility for an element of private finance to be additional to public spending allocations. But see **1.3.8**.

Private Finance Panel

1.3.5 The original launch of the PFI in 1992 provided that:

- self-financing private projects were no longer required to be compared against a theoretical public sector solution;
- the private sector was encouraged to lead joint ventures with the public sector;
- there would be greater scope for the use of leasing by the public sector provided there was significant risk transfer and it offered value for money.[1]

1.3.6 The emphasis was very much on the funding of projects rather than the delivery of the asset and the service. It bore little fruit and the arrival of a new Chancellor, Kenneth Clarke, resulted in a relaunch in the autumn of 1993. This was coupled with the creation of a working group (the Private Finance Panel) under the chairmanship of Sir Alastair Morton. This group, consisting of representatives of the public and private sectors and supported by a full-time executive of secondees also from both the public and private sectors, was given the role of selling the PFI to the public and private sectors and kick-starting projects across government.

1.3.7 The establishment of the Private Finance Panel coincided with the publication by the Treasury of *Breaking New Ground – towards a new partnership between the public and private sectors*. The focus of this document was the creation of public/private partnerships, something which the current Labour Government also espouses. The difference between the Labour and Conservative approach to public/private partnerships is perhaps more apparent than real – the Conservative Government saw the PFI as *the* way to create public/private partnerships whereas the Labour Government, while supporting the PFI, views it as but *one* form of public/private partnership. It remains to be seen how the Labour Government proposes to develop other partnerships although it may be that greater emphasis is placed on the public accountability of the service provision element of the project, something which has been indicated in relation to the proposed upgrade of the London Underground system.[2]

Universal testing

1.3.8 In an attempt to encourage departments to identify suitable projects and embrace the PFI, it was announced in 1994 that the Treasury would no longer give approval to capital projects unless a PFI option had been tested. 'Testing' meant seeking expressions of interest and running a competition based on a PFI solution. Public capital provision was to be reserved for areas where private finance was inappropriate or would not produce value for money. Thus, any lingering notion there had been that PFI projects were additional to public spending allocations was firmly laid to rest.

---

1   This desire to increase the use of leasing never materialised, principally because the leasing industry was, in many cases, not the correct repository of the risks to be transferred.
2   See also Chapter 18.

1.3.9 The advent of universal testing saw an ambitious rolling out of projects across all sectors. This rush of projects coming forward caused consternation in the private sector: it was difficult to assess which schemes were likely to prove the most successful and attractive and this was coupled with limited resources within the private sector to devote to the expensive process of bidding for and developing projects. Within days of coming to power the Labour Government scrapped the universal testing requirement on the basis that it was clogging the process with schemes which were not viable and was wasteful of resources. In the NHS, a review and prioritisation exercise was undertaken immediately after the General Election in May 1997. As a result, in July 1997, the previous list of 37 acute general hospital PFI schemes was reduced to a priority list of 14. However, given the scarcity of public capital, it is still the case that the vast majority of major capital projects will come to fruition only through the PFI route. In the second wave of NHS capital projects announced in April 1998, there were 11 PFI projects, many of which had capital values (ie projected construction costs) in excess of £100m and only two publicly funded schemes (where the capital values were less than £30m).

1.3.10 The abolition of universal testing has been reinforced by the publication of priority lists of 'significant' PFI projects which have been 'road tested' for their suitability as PFI projects in order to enable them to come to the market and proceed to completion as smoothly and swiftly as possible.[1] A list of projects in the local authorities sector which will receive revenue support from central government has also been announced.

PFI publications

1.3.11 In November 1995, the Treasury and the Private Finance Panel published a consolidation of the theory, practice and achievements of the PFI entitled *Private Opportunity, Public Benefit – Progressing the Private Finance Initiative*. This was followed by a series of case studies and best practice guidance. This included guidance on the procurement process (*A Step by Step Guide to the PFI Procurement Process*, July 1997),[2] a set of basic boilerplate contract clauses (*Basic Contractual Terms*, October 1996) and a more discursive publication analysing the rationale behind some of the more contentious issues which arise in PFI transactions (*Further Contractual Issues*, January 1997).[3]

Departmental responsibility for the PFI

1.3.12 Private Finance Units ('PFUs') have been established in most government departments to monitor and promote the PFI and to act as a repository of best practice. They are staffed by a mix of civil servants and private sector individuals. In April 1996, the Public Private Partnerships Programme Limited

---

1 See **1.3.20** and **1.3.21** below.
2 Since superseded by the Treasury Taskforce publication of the same title dated April 1998.
3 Details of the guidance and case studies which continue to apply following the change of government in May 1997 are set out in the Bibliography.

('4Ps') was established by the Local Authority Associations in England and Wales to promote PFI in the local authority sector.[1]

Deals not rules

1.3.13 The mantra of the Private Finance Panel was that the PFI should be about 'deals not rules'. This was predicated on the basis that value for money and maximising the transfer of risk to the private sector would come from private sector innovation and keen competition. Applying prescriptive rules would act as an impediment and a constraint. In addition, because of the inexperience of both the public and private sectors in negotiating the early deals (coupled with a desire to demonstrate progress by signing transactions), there was a perception that the risk transfer achieved had been sub-optimal and could be improved upon in later transactions when both parties understood the nature and dynamics of the transactions in question.

1.3.14 However, the slow progress of early transactions resulted in failed political objectives, heavy deal costs and a concern that individual departments were 'reinventing the wheel'. This led to the formulation of more detailed principles for the PFI and a move towards establishing standard positions in relation to certain key commercial terms which eventually would evolve into model contracts which would streamline and expedite the process.[2] The experience of certain sectors, such as roads and prisons, has been that a standardised form of agreement has evolved over a series of transactions and the length of the bid process has reduced significantly. On the first prison project, the time from issuing the invitation to negotiate for the project to financial close was 17 months. The more recent projects have reduced this time period to 11 months.[3] A similar approach is being adopted in other sectors, notably health, where a consultation exercise has been conducted with a view to establishing benchmark commercial terms and, eventually, a model contract.

1.3.15 Although broad similarities will exist in PFI transactions across a range of sectors, certain issues will depend upon the precise nature of the project being undertaken and this may affect the speed with which transactions are closed. In part, this can be a reflection of the experience of the private sector with regard to the subject-matter of the project itself. The construction and maintenance of a road was well understood by the private sector before the PFI became the preferred method of procurement, as was the provision of IT services. As a consequence, transactions in each of these sectors have progressed more swiftly than in others, such as health, where the interface between the design and construction of a hospital, the operation of non-clinical services by the private sector and the provision of clinical services by the NHS has proved more problematic.

---

1   Both the PFUs and the 4Ps work closely with the Treasury Taskforce, whose role and functions are discussed at **1.3.20** and **1.3.21**. Details of the departmental PFUs, the 4Ps and relevant contact details are set out in the Bibliography.
2   See **1.3.23**, **1.3.24** and **1.3.25**.
3   See Report by the Comptroller and Auditor General on the PFI Contracts for Bridgend and Fazakerley Prisons (HC 253, Session 1997–98, 31 October 1997) paragraph 1.18.

1.3.16 Even in relation to generic issues such as compensation payable upon termination of the transaction, the approach to be adopted will depend on the precise circumstances of the transaction, the nature of the asset being provided and whether it is bespoke and required by the public sector after termination of the transaction (in which case the public sector would be expected to pay compensation reflecting the continued access to and use of the asset) or whether it is an asset which has alternative uses or income-generating capability and from which the public sector purchaser is prepared to walk away (in which event the public sector's liability to pay compensation would be reduced or may even not arise).[1]

Reinvigorating the PFI

1.3.17 With the election of a Labour Government in May 1997 came a reappraisal of the PFI and a focus on how it could realise its potential. As referred to earlier, the concept of universal testing for all capital projects, introduced by the Conservative Government in November 1994, was scrapped. In addition, Sir Malcolm Bates, a founder member of the Private Finance Panel, was asked to conduct a review of the PFI. The Bates Review made 29 recommendations which were announced and endorsed by the government on 23 June 1997.[2]

1.3.18 The Review recommended specific measures to reinvigorate and streamline the process, with a clearer definition and division of responsibilities on the public sector side. It also identified a need for central support for departments and proposed establishing a new Treasury Taskforce to provide necessary additional resources to ensure delivery of quality transactions.

1.3.19 The recommendations of the Bates Review fell into four categories:

- institutional structure;
- improving the process;
- learning lessons;
- bid costs.

The key outcomes of the Review were as follows.

Institutional structure

1.3.20 The Private Finance Panel was wound up and its executive disbanded. The new Treasury Taskforce is the focal point for the PFI across government, addressing policy issues and having a projects arm with a hands-on role in the execution of individual projects. This arm is intended to have a life span of approximately two years. Working with individual departments, the projects arm's role is to establish the commercial viability of significant projects *before* any procurement process commences. Qualification as a 'significant project' is determined by reference to one of four factors:

- size;

---

1   For further discussion of the determination of compensation on termination, see **10.9**.
2   The results of the Bates Review are contained in Treasury Press Notice 69/97.

- profile;
- replicability;
- ground breaking nature.

1.3.21 This pre-clearance and 'road testing' of projects before formal procurement is intended to allow projects to move more speedily towards signature. Key issues to be addressed in any pre-clearance include the prospects for achieving value for money, affordability, risk allocation, bankability and resourcing requirements (including the need for support from the Taskforce). The Taskforce is responsible for monitoring priority projects to ensure their delivery within agreed timetables. In February and October 1998, the Taskforce published lists of priority projects upon which it would be focusing its efforts.[1] Failure to make the priority list does not mean other projects will not proceed, and further projects will be road tested.

1.3.22 The focus for taking forward the PFI at government departmental level is the individual departmental PFU. The rationale behind the projects arm of the Taskforce having a limited two-year life is that expertise will become established within departments with the PFU as the monitor. As part of the attempt to standardise the PFI process, the Taskforce is publishing guidance on applying the PFI. All publications fall within one of four series:[2]

Series (i) Generic guidance;
Series (ii) Policy statements which detail policy issues arising from the implementation of the PFI (as opposed to implementation itself which is addressed in the Series (iii) publications);
Series (iii) Technical notes which provide guidance on how to implement certain aspects of the PFI;
Series (iv) Case studies of completed transactions. Individual departmental PFUs may also produce their own guidance.

Improving the process

1.3.23 The Review proposed certain standardisation measures. One area was the form and contents of the initial advertisement in the *Official Journal of the European Communities*.[3] Another recommendation was that individual departments establish standard or model contract terms in consultation with the Taskforce.[4] The Taskforce is to have the key role in this and has produced draft guidance on the contents of a standard PFI project agreement upon which consultation has been sought from the private sector and within the public sector. The stated objectives of the draft guidance are to achieve a common understanding of risks to be included in a PFI transaction, to achieve consistency

---

1   Details of the list of priority projects are contained in HM Treasury News Releases 17/93 and 171/98.
2   The list of publications current as at 30 November 1998 is set out in the Bibliography. Up-to-date lists are available by accessing the Treasury Taskforce Internet site: www.treasury-projects-taskforce.gov.uk
3   See Technical Note No 2 *How to Follow EC Procurement Procedure and Advertise in the OJEC* (Treasury Taskforce) June 1998 and Chapter 3.
4   See discussion at **1.3.14**, **1.3.15** and **1.3.16** and Chapter 10.

of approach and pricing across similar projects and to speed up the process of closing deals.[1] It has also produced a consultative draft model form Direct Agreement (building on a previous model produced by the Private Finance Panel Executive). The Treasury Taskforce has stated that the goal is to develop PFI contract structures which are commodity products and which are the accepted basis for each transaction.[2] They do not, however, advocate slavish standardisation across all sectors, recognising that there are aspects of PFI transactions which are unique to the particular sector. The scope for innovation is recognised as an important potential source of improved value for money and something which should not be constrained by the straitjacket of an inflexible standard contract. Although one of the tangible benefits of standardisation should be a reduction in the cost of negotiation, trying to force a bespoke transaction into a standard contract can prove a costly and frustrating exercise.

1.3.24 The pace at which standards and templates emerge will depend on the maturity of the sector in question. As mentioned at **1.3.14**, prisons and roads already have fairly well developed contract structures and accepted commercial terms. The NHS PFU is in the process of developing its own standards. Less well developed sectors, such as education and local authorities, will require several 'road tested' projects to have been 'run in' before consistent standards emerge.

1.3.25 The Taskforce has indicated that the publications *Basic Contractual Terms* (October 1996) and *Further Contractual Issues* (January 1997) produced by the Private Finance Panel and the Treasury represent a basis from which to develop a consistent approach on key issues across the public sector. Sharing experience from sector to sector is an obvious way of moving the process forward (subject always to preserving commercial confidentiality) not only in terms of identifying and promoting best practice but also warning against the mistakes and pitfalls of the past. However, little cross-fertilisation has occurred thus far.

1.3.26 All departments have been given the task of prioritising their PFI schemes (some of which may then become Taskforce priority projects).[3] Small-scale PFI projects should be grouped together, in particular, in the context of local authorities, health and education. This is a recognition that complex PFI transactions will give rise to certain costs which will apply irrespective of the transaction size. For a project to be attractive to the private sector and attract funding (particularly project finance) a certain critical mass is necessary. Bundling projects together is not a new concept. In the first water and sewerage PFI project in Scotland, awarded by the North of Scotland Water Authority, two separate projects in Inverness and Fort William were let as one project.

1.3.27 In the area of local authorities the Review raised the possibility of financing PFI schemes by issuing municipal bonds building upon the bond-financed PFI projects in roads and in health.[4]

---

1 For further discussion, see Chapter 10.
2 See Bates Review, Recommendation No 10 (HM Treasury Press Notice 69/97).
3 See **1.3.9** regarding the prioritisation of projects in the NHS.
4 For a discussion of bond and other financing techniques, see Chapter 8.

1.3.28 The thorny issue of the accounting treatment of PFI transactions was raised by the Review as an urgent issue with the need to produce Treasury guidance. Although this has been produced, the guidance is at odds with the Accounting Standards Board's treatment of PFI transactions.[1]

1.3.29 Departments were also requested to give assurance to funders of PFI transactions that funds would be made available to honour contractual commitments where the public sector counterparty is a non-departmental public body, in an attempt to avoid unnecessary attention on the covenant of such entities. The Taskforce has published a Policy Statement on this issue.[2] The issue of the *vires* of awarding authorities was identified as an area requiring action. Since the Review, legislation tackling this issue has come into force in relation to the NHS (National Health Service (Private Finance) Act 1997) and local government (Local Government (Contracts) Act 1997).[3] In the latter case in particular, the Department for the Environment, Transport and the Regions consulted widely within the private sector, producing legislation which was responsive to the concerns raised.

1.3.30 The Review also made it clear that the Treasury must maintain individual government departments' future expenditure allocations for contractual commitments arising under PFI transactions entered into. The Treasury Taskforce has published a Policy Statement on this issue[4] indicating that the expected payments due under PFI contracts entered into represent 'inescapable expenditure' which is 'effectively ringfenced'. The Policy Statement goes on to state that any future public expenditure savings which are to be achieved by across the board reductions on departmental expenditure baselines will not affect these hypothecated PFI commitments. As indicated at **1.2.4**, this may also have wider long-term implications for future departmental spending and investment plans.[5]

Learning lessons

1.3.31 The Review indicated that the training programme for civil servants needed to be refocused with a requirement for in-depth training. A new contract has been awarded to PricewaterhouseCoopers. This ought to enable departmental PFUs to achieve the necessary skill base to take forward projects in the medium term without the assistance of the Taskforce. In order to create a level playing field in negotiations, the public sector must have its own PFI specialists. The shortage of skills and expertise within the public sector is such that it cannot always be regarded as an equal partner with the private sector.

---

1 See **1.2.13** and Chapter 17.
2 Policy Statement No 3 *PFI and Public Expenditure Allocations for Non-Departmental Public Bodies* (Treasury Taskforce) August 1998, which adopts the same approach as set out in **1.3.30** in respect of individual departments.
3 See Chapter 4.
4 Policy Statement No 1 *PFI and Public Expenditure Allocations* (Treasury Taskforce) October 1997.
5 See also *Partnerships for Prosperity* (HM Treasury) November 1997, paragraph 4.07.

1.3.32 The Review emphasised the need for more case studies and specific guidance and the creation of a PFI library in the Treasury containing all documentation relevant to the PFI, including the documentation from completed transactions (omitting or restricting access to confidential information). As indicated at **1.3.25**, the sharing of knowledge and experience within the public sector has been patchy at best.

1.3.33 The Review made it clear that it was imperative for the new Taskforce to maintain frequent and active contact with the private sector to ensure that policy was responsive to the concerns of those who have hands-on experience of negotiating the transactions. This they are seeking to do through the issue of draft Policy Statements for consultation, their involvement in the current 50 priority projects and Taskforce conferences, the first of which took place in London in April 1998.

1.3.34 In the area of Public Sector Comparators, the Review identified that there had been confusion as to the way in which they were calculated and when they were required. The Taskforce has issued guidance on the calculation of Public Sector Comparators and also how to evaluate bids for value for money.[1]

Bid costs

1.3.35 The Review recommended that the Taskforce should have a remit to make projects more cost-effective by minimising bid costs. This is linked with their role of pre-clearing transactions before procurement. There should be a compulsory maximum of four short-listed bidders and, when a decision is taken not to proceed with the project which is unrelated to the viability of tenders received, bidding costs should be refunded.

1.3.36 The proposals put forward by the Bates Review have helped to clarify responsibilities and address the key structural and legal impediments to progressing the PFI. The focus on creating expertise within individual departments and the development of policy which is responsive to the concerns of the private sector will assist greatly in taking forward PFI under the banner of Public/Private Partnerships. By accepting the Bates Review in full, the Labour Government confirmed its belief in the benefits of the PFI, albeit as one method of securing public/private partnerships.

1.4 CONCLUSION

1.4.1 The PFI, as a policy, has developed out of a mixed bag of political objectives. On one level it can be viewed as the Conservative Government's creation to carry forward its ideological crusade to ensure the involvement of the private sector in areas where the privatisation solution was not a practical option. However, it exists also to meet the genuine political desire (and physical, social and economic need) to invest in the nation's capital stock, be it hospitals, public

---

1   Policy Statement No 2 *Public Sector Comparators and Value for Money* (Treasury Taskforce) March 1998. See also **1.2.5–1.2.12** and Chapter 2.

transport, roads or schools. That investment is required at a time when public capital is scarce (or rationed) and the UK, along with the other member states of the European Union, have their eye on economic and monetary union and the constraints imposed on public borrowing by the requirement to meet the Maastricht convergence criteria.

1.4.2 The progress of the PFI has, at times, seemed painfully slow but it is now generally accepted that its fundamental aims and objectives are the basis for public sector procurement across government for projects requiring significant capital investment. This has been reinforced by the renewed commitment to the PFI by the Labour Government and its desire to make it work more efficiently and effectively.

1.4.3 PFI projects are complex to negotiate and document. They involve the assessment and assumption of risk over lengthy contract periods. However, when made to work, they deliver badly needed investment.

1.5 CHECKLIST 1: KEY REQUIREMENTS FOR A PFI TRANSACTION

- There must be genuine risk transfer from the public sector to the private sector.
- The project must be value for money in relation to the public sector's expenditure.
- The year-on-year expenditure by the public sector must be affordable.
- The project should generally be off balance sheet for the public sector.

1.6 CHECKLIST 2: THE PFI – KEY EVENTS

Autumn 1992	PFI launched by Chancellor of the Exchequer
November 1993	Relaunch of the PFI
	Establishment of the Private Finance Panel
	Publication of *Breaking New Ground*
November 1994	Universal PFI testing for all capital projects introduced
November 1995	Publication of *Private Opportunity, Public Benefit*
May 1997	Labour wins General Election
	Universal testing abolished
	Review of the PFI by Sir Malcolm Bates announced
June 1997	Bates Review recommendations published
September 1997	Treasury Taskforce created
February 1998	List of 50 priority projects published
September 1998	Draft guidance on Project Agreements issued for consultation
October 1998	Second list of a further 30 priority projects published
November 1998	Second Bates Review of PFI announced

Chapter 2

THE CONTRACTING PARTIES, THEIR OBLIGATIONS AND THE CONTRACTUAL MATRIX

2.1 INTRODUCTION

2.1.1 This chapter examines the objectives of the three principal parties to a typical PFI transaction, the awarding authority, the consortium and the debt funders and considers in overview the matrix of legal agreements that are likely to be present. Many of these agreements are considered in greater detail in the subsequent chapters.

2.1.2 Paragraphs **2.2**, **2.3** and **2.4** examine, respectively, the objectives of the awarding authority, the consortium and the funders. Paragraph **2.5** reviews the key contracts that are likely to be present in a PFI project.

2.2 THE AWARDING AUTHORITY'S OBJECTIVES

2.2.1 Much has been said and written about the ideological basis of the PFI. What are the benefits from the public sector perspective of entering into an arrangement which will diminish its control and how can the private sector's greater cost of funding be offset by other savings that ultimately yield value for money for the public sector? The Treasury mantra is that under the PFI the awarding authority is purchasing a service and not (as was generally the case under previous procurement methods) buying assets. The reason for this (as outlined in Chapter 1) is that if an awarding authority is successfully to transfer to the private sector risks associated with a particular activity it should not be concerned with the 'means of production' for that activity, ie the assets used to provide it. It should be sufficient merely to prescribe clearly and unambiguously the outputs of that activity.

2.2.2 The extent to which the realities of the PFI actually meet this ideological precept is variable. Undoubtedly there are cases where it does. Take, for example, a PFI project for the disposal of a local authority's waste where the awarding authority indicates volumes of waste that it will require to be disposed of and agrees a price for doing this. To a large degree, the manner of disposal and the facilities or assets associated with it are not the awarding authority's concern. Contrast this with a project for the development of a new road where the contract will typically be entirely prescriptive as to the alignment of the road and many of its detailed characteristics. Even though there will be a long-term requirement placed on the project company to be responsible for the maintenance of the road, it is far more difficult to say, in any meaningful sense, that the awarding authority is 'purchasing a service'. The awarding authority is very much concerned with the physical assets being created, not least because, in the case of road project, at no point will the project company own the assets and, at the end of the concession period, the risks and responsibilities of ownership will necessarily revert to the awarding authority.

2.2.3 It is because of the diversity of subject-matter of PFI projects that it is inevitably difficult to generalise when considering the parties' objectives and common characteristics. However, at its highest level, the awarding authority's objectives will always be to transfer risks in a project to the private sector and to achieve value for money for any public sector contribution.[1]

2.2.4 Many of the elements of risk transfer that are so central to, and often contentious in, PFI projects are considered in further detail in Chapter 10. However, as risk transfer is at the heart of an awarding authority's objectives in any PFI project, it is worth considering here some of the key risks that the awarding authority is likely to wish to transfer. These are reviewed at **2.2.5** to **2.2.35**. The concept of value for money is considered at **2.2.36** to **2.2.39**.

Risk transfer

2.2.5 Risk transfer is the central ingredient of any PFI project. If the correct package of risks is transferred to the private sector, the efficient management of those risks by the private sector can more than offset the private sector's higher cost of borrowing.

2.2.6 Conversely, transferring the wrong package of risks will lead to poor value for money. The challenge, therefore, is to find the right package of risks. What is the correct package can be determined only on a case-by-case basis, although, as PFI matures, in each sector market practices are emerging that act as a guide. This has particularly been seen in the case of the roads and prisons sectors where there is a relatively well defined market and successive projects often have many characteristics in common. Even in those sectors, however, it is notable how the allocation of risk transfer is developing – in most cases, resulting in the public sector achieving greater risk transfer in later projects as the market becomes more mature and the risks become better understood by all parties involved. A number of the key areas of risk transfer are considered below.

Design risk

2.2.7 The transfer of design risk to the private sector is at the heart of the PFI. The awarding authority specifies the service it requires, in output terms, and the project company is responsible for delivering that service. Payment is against performance and levels of performance will be defined and graded to incentivise the project company to achieve high standards of performance and penalise it for poor performance. It is inherent in the principle of payment against performance that the private sector should be left free to specify and, where required, design the facilities required to provide the service. If the project in question involves a real risk in performance, naturally the private sector would not normally be

---

1   See **1.2.5** et seq.

prepared to accept a performance risk on facilities that have been specified or designed by the public sector.

2.2.8 There will, however, be particular cases where the awarding authority will insist on specifying that particular facilities are used or that particular specifications are met. The awarding authority must, however, recognise that, in so doing, it may well be negating the possibility of transferring design risk in that area and that there can be knock on implications for design risk in other aspects of the facilities. The Private Finance Panel publication, *Writing an Output Specification*, gives examples of cases where an awarding authority may need to prescribe technical requirements including where reasons of compatibility dictate that a particular system is used. Examples given are the communication systems to be provided by the private sector on a DBFO road project being compatible with the Highways Agency's own systems, and prison projects where a number of detailed requirements are typically imposed, with the following explanation being given:

> 'Because of political sensitivity as a result of the recent escape of Category A prisoners, the Prison Service considers that it is essential, even for PFI projects, for the purposes of assuring both Parliament and local communities where prisons are to be sited, that mandatory procedures specified in its own security manual will be followed by contractors.'[1]

2.2.9 One of the more troublesome aspects encountered in negotiating the transfer of design risk arises in connection with the concept of 'fitness for purpose'. It is not uncommon that draft documentation issued by awarding authorities contains a warranty to be given by the project company that the facilities will be 'fit for their intended purpose'. This requirement invariably proves contentious, with contractors being concerned both as to the uncertainty of the term, unless the purposes in question are agreed in detail in the specifications, and the possibility that the awarding authority's intended purpose may change over time. Frequently, the compromise reached is that the project company will warrant that the facilities (or services) will meet the requirements set out in the output specifications leaving the onus on the awarding authority to translate its intended purpose into more hard-edged terms and incorporate it into the detailed specifications.

2.2.10 The other rationale for seeking to transfer design risk to the private sector lies in the relationship between design risk and planning risk. The argument goes that if the public sector wishes to transfer planning risk, then it must leave the responsibility for design, which will have a direct bearing on the prospects of achieving the desired planning consents, with the private sector.

Planning risk

2.2.11 Planning risk will be relevant to almost all projects involving a significant element of new build. It is, however, an area where achieving risk

---

1   *Writing an Output Specification* (HM Treasury and Private Finance Panel) October 1996, paragraph 4.6.1.

transfer by the public sector has been notoriously difficult. The official line on this has been put as follows:

> 'Generally speaking the private sector will have wider experience in dealing with planning authorities than the public sector. Thus the government client should generally seek to transfer this risk. In a PFI accommodation procurement each bidder is likely, indeed encouraged, to offer different solutions, often based on different sites. In this instance it makes clear sense for the PSP [Private Sector Partner] to obtain their own outline and detailed planning permission.

> 'For accommodation solutions involving standard office buildings but on a specific site, the government client should at least speak to the local planning authorities and discuss their intentions in order to accelerate the process. Building a close relationship with the planning authorities can only help smooth the procurement process. Where there are clear planning constraints on an existing location or specific site that could lead to considerable delays, then the government client should obtain outline planning permission based on a flexible submission which provides maximum discretion to the private sector to put forward different and innovative design solutions.'[1]

2.2.12 The reality, however, is that achieving risk transfer other than in the limited context of the costs of pursuing planning consents, can be difficult. The reason for this is that where a planning consent is necessary for a project to go ahead, in practice the project documentation will almost always be made conditional on that consent being obtained. Not least, this is because experience has shown that, save in the most unusual circumstances, banks will not be prepared to advance funds until detailed planning permission has been obtained. In practice, the time and cost associated with obtaining detailed planning permission usually means that it is not obtained, indeed typically it will not even be applied for, until some time after a preferred bidder has been chosen. This means that the risk of planning being refused is shared because, if ultimately the planning application fails, there is no project and both parties are back at square one. The issue that therefore tends to get debated is the timing of application for the consent and the allocation of the cost of so doing if the consent is ultimately turned down or, indeed, if the project does not go ahead at all for some other reason.

2.2.13 Where a project involves the transfer of surplus sites to the project company as part of the consideration for the carrying out of a project, it may be possible to transfer planning risk to the project company in the sense that the project will go ahead on a predetermined basis as regards the payment arrangements whether or not the project company's desired planning permission on those surplus sites is achieved. However, there may be difficulties in getting the project company to underwrite robust values for surplus sites where a desired planning position has not yet been achieved by financial close. Even if the project company is willing to accept this risk, such a position may not give value for money and will almost always negatively impact certainty and affordability.[2]

---

1   *PFI in Government Accommodation* (HM Treasury and Private Finance Panel) 2nd edn, October 1996, paragraph 7.1.
2   See **13.1.18**.

Completion risk

2.2.14 Completion risk encompasses a number of separate aspects but, in essence, relates to the transfer to the private sector of the risk that facilities are completed and services become operational to time, to quality and to cost.[1]

Completion to time

2.2.15 Whether the facility in question is for some new public service such as a new hospital or road, or whether the facility is for use by government itself, perhaps securing cost savings or other benefits over existing facilities, it is almost always the case that the awarding authority will wish to see the facilities provided as early as possible. A completion date will be agreed upon and the project company will undertake to complete the project so that the services become operational by that date. Late completion may result in the loss of an amenity for the public or increased costs to the public sector or, sometimes, both. Accordingly, if completion is not achieved by the agreed completion date, the project company may be liable to damages. Often, liquidated damages will be agreed both to give certainty to the parties and also, from the project company's perspective, to limit the project company's exposure to a claim for damages. However, in every case the awarding authority will wish to test whether the imposition of liquidated damages delivers value for money given that the construction company will attach a price to this additional exposure.

2.2.16 Inevitably a range of factors both inside and outside the control of the parties may threaten the agreed timetable. Accordingly, the project company and the awarding authority will seek to agree the range of events which entitle the project company to an extension of time. These events are variously defined in project documentation as 'force majeure', 'compensation events', 'relief events' and 'delay events'. Distinctions are typically drawn between those events for which the project company will be granted time but not financial compensation (and, typically, no extension of the contract term) and those events which will entitle the project company both to time and financial compensation. Often the question of whether the risk is insurable by the project company will determine which category the event falls into. Distinctions are also sometimes drawn between events which entitle the project company to an extension of the completion date and a corresponding extension of the contract term and (typically where the event in question can be insured against) events where the project company is entitled to an extension of the completion date but gets no corresponding extension of the contract term.[2]

Completion to cost

2.2.17 It almost goes without saying that the onus is on the project company to complete the project to cost or, if it fails, to bear any cost overruns. In this respect, PFI contracts are no different from a well negotiated traditional

---

1 For further discussion of the issues arising in relation to determining completion, see **7.6.27**, **7.6.28** and **8.4.6**.
2 See **10.3**.

construction contract. Inevitably, however, there will be a limited category of events which will entitle the project company to an adjustment to the unitary payment or a lump-sum payment. Clearly such events will include matters entirely within the control of the awarding authority, such as requests for variations to the facilities or services, and breaches by the awarding authority of obligations it undertakes to the project company. There may, however, be a limited category of events outside the control of both parties, such as the discovery of fossils or antiquities or the occurrence of a change of law, where it is accepted that an adjustment to the unitary payment or a lump-sum payment will occur. These events are considered in more detail at **10.6**.

Completion to quality

2.2.18 Again, completion to quality is a risk which would normally be transferred entirely to the private sector. In the case of a project involving facilities that will be occupied, the definition of 'completion' or 'practical completion' will typically embody the achievement by the project company of the necessary standards set out in the specifications which will trigger the entitlement of the awarding authority to occupy or use the facilities and services and trigger the commencement of the payment of the unitary payment. Until these specifications are met, completion will not occur and not only will the project company not begin to receive payment but, as indicated earlier, it may also be liable in damages. Once the services are operational then the quality requirements continue to be regulated under a detailed performance monitoring and payment mechanism.

2.2.19 The pre-completion phase of a PFI project will usually be the most risky phase and the awarding authority will seek to protect itself during this period in a number of ways. First, it will wish to ensure that its payment obligations do not begin until completion has occurred. However, where a project involves a number of distinct phases or the taking over of some existing services prior to completion, the awarding authority may be prepared to accept some pre-completion payment obligations. Secondly, where the public sector is handing over assets to the project company as part consideration for the project, it will wish to see that it is not exposed to the insolvency risk of the project company in respect of the value of such assets. This risk is considered further below. Thirdly, it may require that the project company or one of the consortium post a bond or guarantee to cover claims that may arise against the project company prior to completion. Finally, the awarding authority may seek to enter into a direct agreement with the design and construction sub-contractors to the project company entitling it to step in and take over the key design and construction contracts in the event of a default by or insolvency of the project company.[1]

Operational risk

2.2.20 The transfer of operational risk in a project is an essential part of any PFI project. One of the central tenets of PFI is the principle of payment against

---

1 Performance bonds and direct agreements are considered at **2.5**.

performance and, with limited exceptions, the risk that facilities and services can be provided to the awarding authority throughout the contract term to the agreed output specification for the agreed unitary payment, will rest with the project company. Obviously, the scope and nature of what is contracted for will vary considerably. The prison projects are an example of a PFI project where the provision of the facilities, their maintenance and the core activity carried out within them, ie the custodial service, were contracted out. In many other PFI projects the scope of the services is more limited and confined, essentially, to the provision of physical facilities and their long-term maintenance but not the provision of the core activity carried out within them. Examples of this are projects for government accommodation and projects for new hospital facilities.

2.2.21 Naturally, in the context of the negotiation of project documents, it is the limited exceptions where the risk is not transferred to the private sector or where the risk is shared between the parties that are the subject of most attention. Clearly risks which are wholly within the control of the awarding authority will not generally be transferred to the project company and their occurrence will therefore entitle the project company to an adjustment of the unitary payment. An example of this is a variation to the services requested by the awarding authority. Where a risk is outside the control of both parties, such as a force majeure risk, then, as with the issue of completion risk referred to earlier, a distinction is often drawn between those events which excuse performance but do not entitle the project company to any financial compensation (often these are known as 'relief events') and those events which both excuse the project company from performance and entitle it to financial compensation. Again, the question of whether risks are insurable and, if they are, whether the awarding authority wishes the project company to take out insurance for these risks, often underlies the distinction. Leaving aside the question of 'price re-openers', it is worth re-emphasising the central importance of the payment mechanism in a PFI contract and the role which this plays in transferring operational risk.

2.2.22 The payment mechanism will naturally vary depending on the type of project concerned but, typically, will comprise one or more of the following components:

- an *availability element* which is paid in full if the facilities/service is fully available but which is withheld by reference to an agreed schedule if any part of the facilities or service is not available;
- a *performance element* which is paid in full if required performance standards are met, but which is subject to deductions where performance is sub-standard; and
- a *volume element* which varies with the amount or take up of the service.

2.2.23 In certain projects, primarily hospital projects, there may be discrete service fees within the unitary payment for particular services (a requisite if, as is the practice within the NHS, individual services are to be periodically market tested).

2.2.24 The development of a robust payment mechanism is essential to incentivising performance and can be an important factor in establishing the necessary degree of risk transfer for a project to achieve off balance sheet status from the point of view of the awarding authority.[1] It is, however, often one of the central battlegrounds in the negotiation between the parties involved. The project funders will be particularly concerned to limit the scope of performance deductions from the portion of the unitary payment that services the debt and to limit the impact of deductions on the project company either by requiring the project company to build up reserves or by ensuring the pass down of the operational risks to sub-contractors of acceptable financial standing.[2]

2.2.25 The presence of a volume element in the unitary payment is common, but its significance will vary considerably across the different types of projects. The DBFO road projects have been structured entirely around a volume-related payment mechanism with the project company receiving a notional toll or 'shadow toll' for each vehicle using the roads (with a banded structure so that the toll per vehicle varies with the total throughput on the road in a given period). The prison projects, however, contain no volume element as it became clear during the procurement process for the first two prison projects that the number of prisoners using a prison was not a risk which the private sector was prepared to take (the risk being heavily dependent on court sentencing policies and the allocation procedures for convicted criminals to particular prisons – both matters wholly within the control of the public sector). In hospital PFI projects, whilst the majority of the unitary payment will comprise the availability component there will typically be discrete service fees for certain services, a number of which will often contain volume-related elements – such as a payment per patient meal or a payment per tonne of waste disposed of.

Residual value risk

2.2.26 Residual value risk is the risk that facilities associated with a service will be required and will have a value at the end of the contract term. In terms of purist PFI philosophy this risk should generally pass to the private sector, as the public sector is merely buying a service for a given period and is not concerned with acquiring the assets associated with the service. In practice, however, the transfer of residual value risk is often more honoured in the breach than in the observance. Often this is because the facilities in question are so bespoke to the requirements of the awarding authority that there will never be any meaningful secondary market for them. Where this is so, the project company will price its service to the awarding authority on the basis that all the costs associated with acquiring, developing and maintaining the facilities are amortised during the contract term via the unitary payment.

2.2.27 Perhaps the most extreme example of this is in the case of the DBFO road projects where no ownership interest in the road will at any point be transferred to the project company and where, accordingly, the risks and rewards of ownership will necessarily return to the awarding authority at the end of the contract term (albeit that, at that point, the awarding authority can elect to

---

1 See Chapter 17.
2 This is difficult to achieve where the sub-contractor has a relatively weak balance sheet (eg many facilities management companies). For a further discussion of payment and performance, see **10.4**.

let another PFI contract). Another example is a prison where, although an ownership interest will be held by the project company during the contract term, arrangements are structured (usually via a lease granted by the awarding authority to the project company with a term coterminous with the contract term) so that ownership reverts to the awarding authority at the end of the contract term. The reason for this is partly the expectation that the facilities will be required by the Prison Service at the end of the contract term but also the reality that, because of the nature and location of most prison facilities, there would be little alternative use for the facilities at the end of the contract term and therefore the private sector will inevitably set its charges so that its entire capital costs are fully amortised through the unitary payment during the contract term. In such cases, however, it is usually necessary to identify and structure significant risk transfer in other areas (such as via the payment mechanism) in order to achieve off balance sheet status from the point of view of the awarding authority.[1]

2.2.28 Where, due to the location and/or nature of the facilities, there is a secondary market for them (such as the new rolling stock for the London Underground Northern Line or government accommodation in central city locations), it may well be possible for the awarding authority to transfer a residual value risk to the private sector and leave ownership of the facilities with the private sector at the end of the contract term. However, where it does so it is very common, in order to protect the awarding authority should it require continued use of the facilities at the end of the contract term, to structure within the contractual arrangements an option for the awarding authority to acquire the facilities for their open market value at the end of the contract term and/or to provide for a secondary term to commence (at the option of the awarding authority) at the end of the contract term. Naturally, if this route is adopted, the awarding authority will need to be satisfied that an adequate value for the facilities has been ascribed by the project company in its financial model and that the benefit of this has been translated into a reduced unitary payment.

Insolvency risk

2.2.29 The awarding authority's objective here will be to protect itself, both financially and in terms of ensuring the continuity of what are often vital public services, in the event of the insolvency of the project company. The project company will typically be a special purpose vehicle established with no, or limited, recourse to its consortium and will typically have no assets other than its interest in the project.

2.2.30 Perhaps the first point to note is that it is normal for PFI projects to be structured so that payment of the unitary payment does not commence until completion of the facilities and commencement of the service. The effect of this is that both the consortium and the funders will generally have committed the entire capital required for the project before the payment stream from the awarding authority commences. Therefore, the awarding authority may well have considerable financial security for the project company's obligations

---

1 See Chapter 17.

literally 'in the ground', ie in facilities or partly built facilities on land owned by the awarding authority (with the property arrangements being structured to ensure that any ownership interests of the project company can be terminated following a material and unremedied project company default).[1]

2.2.31 Where the awarding authority has agreed to incur a financial contribution prior to completion, the most common example being the transfer of surplus land to the project company in a project involving the rationalisation of an existing site or group of sites, the awarding authority will wish to ensure that it is not exposed to the insolvency risk of the project company in respect of the value of such a contribution. There are a variety of ways of mitigating this risk including:

- ensuring, through the timing of contributions/transfer of surplus land to the project company, that there is equivalent value or, indeed a multiple of that value, invested by the project company in the facilities (with insolvency-secure arrangements for the awarding authority to acquire and take these over on default);
- taking security over the project company's assets for the value of the contribution. The most common example of this is where surplus land is to be transferred by the awarding authority to the project company and immediately sold on to a developer. In this situation the cash proceeds of the on-sale might be placed in an account charged to the awarding authority with amounts being withdrawn from the account and used by the project company in the development in a way that meets the equivalent/multiple value mechanism described in the preceding paragraph;
- requiring the project company to post a performance bond by an acceptable surety for an agreed amount;[2] and
- delaying the contribution or transfer until completion of the facilities and commencement of the service.[3]

2.2.32 As to the more general issue of the risk of loss of bargain for the awarding authority on a default or insolvency of the project company, in most cases the risk can be mitigated by the arrangements for termination on the project company's default or insolvency. Leaving to one side for the moment the particular difficulties that will arise if the default or insolvency occurs during the very early phases of the project (for instance, the early part of the construction phase), in most cases adequate protection can be provided for the awarding authority through the contractual arrangements for compensation on termination. The usual method is to provide that ownership of the facilities passes to the awarding authority on the default/insolvency of the project company (in relation to land and fixed assets this being achieved via the property structures). Any compensation paid by the awarding authority to the project company (the awarding authority having, effectively, forfeited these assets) would be reduced

---

1   The consequences of this flow through to the provisions for compensation on termination which are dealt with at **10.9**.
2   See **2.5.7**. This will have value for money implications as the cost will be reflected in the unitary payment.
3   The awarding authority will need to assess whether this delay represents value for money.

to reflect the costs associated with the default such as increased costs of arranging for alternative contractors to take over the project.[1]

2.2.33 As to mitigation of the risk in the early phases of the project, one common method is to require the project company to post a performance bond.[2]

2.2.34 The position of the awarding authority in relation to securing the continuing use of non-fixed assets owned by the project company (such as equipment) that cannot be simply forfeited by the awarding authority under the property structures is more troublesome. In many projects completed to date this issue has not been addressed at all, the matter being left to be dealt with at the relevant time by negotiation between the awarding authority and the project company's liquidators/receivers. Inevitably, however, this exposes the awarding authority to particular risks where the nature of the project is such that the awarding authority may have an immediate and urgent requirement for continued use of certain non-fixed assets. Possible ways of improving the awarding authority's position are:

– for the awarding authority to take a charge over non-fixed assets to secure the project company's handback obligations (including an obligation to pass title to non-fixed assets to the awarding authority) in the event of its default or insolvency;
– to provide that the payment of compensation on termination is contingent on the project company complying with its handback obligations which should bring the project company's receivers or liquidators swiftly to the table; and
– for the awarding authority to retain legal title to key assets with the responsibility for their operation and maintenance resting with the project company.[3]

2.2.35 As regards ensuring continuity of service following a default or insolvency of the project company, the most common methods are:

– *prior to a termination of the project agreement* – to make provision in the project agreement for the awarding authority to have a range of self-help remedies such as step in rights;[4] and
– *following a termination of the project agreement* – to arrange, via direct agreements with the project company and key sub-contractors,[5] for the awarding authority to be able to step in and take over, in place of the project company, key sub-contracts such as the construction contract and the operating contract.

---

1 Further detail on the arrangements for compensation on termination are contained at 10.9.
2 See **7.6**. This will have value for money implications as the cost will be reflected in the unitary payment; see **2.5.10**.
3 This division of ownership and risk is encountered in a finance lease. It ought not to affect the off balance treatment of the project as economic rather than legal ownership is the key determinant.
4 See **10.10**.
5 See **2.5.6–2.5.8**.

Value for money

2.2.36 The second fundamental objective of the awarding authority in any PFI project is to secure best value for money. Usually this means minimising its financial contribution to the project. It will seek to secure this through the combination of its choice of contracting party, the rigours of a robust competitive process and the way in which it structures the commercial and contractual package between it and the project company (including, in particular, the optimal risk allocation).

2.2.37 Naturally the awarding authority will seek to select a party requiring the lowest financial contribution (in net present value terms over the contract term) but recognising that value for money is a function of, among other things, price, quality and the degree of risk transfer so lowest price will not always mean best value. In most cases, value for money will be determined by comparing the bids received. However, it is normal for a comparison also to be made by the awarding authority against a notional public sector comparator.[1]

2.2.38 In the simplest of projects the value for money calculation will be largely driven by the unitary payment bid by the tenderers. However, in more complex schemes, such as where there is to be a sharing of ancillary income generated by a project or the sharing of development gains above a predetermined threshold, the value for money calculation may need to take account of such potential benefits – although it is usual for awarding authorities heavily to discount benefits which are contingent or uncertain in the financial analysis of bids. In view of the growing political sensitivity to private sector parties enjoying 'windfall profits' in transactions with the public sector, mechanisms directed at enabling the public sector to share in unforeseen gains are becoming increasingly common. This area is considered in further detail in Chapter 10 and in Chapter 12 (in relation to disposal of surplus land or property).

2.2.39 The other general area an awarding authority will look closely at is the range of events that entitle the project company to re-open the agreed unitary payment. Although it is always more difficult to quantify the effects of contingent events, such as change of law, as opposed to headline figures for a unitary payment, it would be wrong to ignore such aspects altogether in the value for money equation.

Other awarding authority objectives

2.2.40 In addition to the overriding objectives of achieving risk transfer and value for money, the awarding authority will have a range of subsidiary objectives, depending on the type of project concerned. Typically these will include:

– ensuring early completion of the project;
– maximising its future flexibility through the contract (through variation mechanisms, break options etc);

---

1 See Policy Statement No 2 *Public Sector Comparators and Value for Money* (Treasury Taskforce) March 1998.

- limiting its commitments (in terms of undertakings required by the project company);
- ensuring ongoing service provision to the required standards; and
- ensuring that the project is off balance sheet for the awarding authority.

2.3 THE CONSORTIUM'S OBJECTIVES

2.3.1 Inevitably, in many respects the consortium's objectives will be the converse of the awarding authority's objectives, particularly in relation to the area of risk transfer. The key areas are as follows.

Minimising bid costs

2.3.2 The issue of abortive bid costs has been one of the most contentious issues for the private sector since the inception of the PFI. Potential sponsors will now look for well thought through schemes (with preference often now being given to schemes which have been 'road tested' by the Treasury Taskforce).[1] Bidders also now expect the Bates recommendation on bid costs to be observed.[2]

Delivering profit

2.3.3 Whilst the public sector may well have legitimate concerns about windfall profits in certain cases, particularly where uncertainties exist which have a significant financial impact, care must be taken not to lose sight of the fact that risk and reward go hand in hand, and if the public sector expect the private sector to accept genuine risk then they must accept the possibility of profits being made that may exceed those anticipated at the outset.

2.3.4 In terms of profit making, it is important to remember that a number of the consortium will often also have roles as key contractors in the project and for them the profit may derive both through dividends paid by the project company and through profits on these sub-contracts. Naturally, conflicts of interest will regularly present themselves and experience has shown that establishing contracts between the project company and its contractors on an arm's length basis at the outset can be an important factor in the long-term success of the project – particularly in terms of the ability of consortium members to sell on their investment in the project company in due course.

Risk transfer

2.3.5 As indicated above, at one level the consortium's objectives in relation to risk transfer will be the opposite to those of the awarding authority and a compromise must be found in the negotiation of the project agreement. Once risks have been accepted by the project company it will in turn seek to pass them down to sub-contractors or, in some cases, to third parties such as insurers. This

---

1   See **1.3.20** and **1.3.21**.
2   Bates Review, Recommendation No 29. See **1.3.35**.

risk transfer by the project company will be an important factor in ensuring bankability.[1]

Limitation of recourse

2.3.6 One of the objectives of the consortium members will be to limit their exposure to the project. One of the ways in which they will do this is by establishing the project company as a separate limited liability vehicle through which to run the project with their liability as consortium being limited to their agreed equity contributions. In the case of consortium members who are also contracting parties, it is common for limitations of liability to be included in the sub-contracts (although the debt and third-party equity funders will try to resist this).

Liquidity of investment

2.3.7 Inevitably, where significant risks are undertaken by a project company over a long contract term, the debt funders will insist on a significant equity contribution from the sponsors and/or third-party equity providers. Given the relatively weak balance sheets of many trade sponsors active in this market, particularly operating companies, there is an urgent need for participants to be able to recycle their equity investments to invest in new projects by selling on their investment, often early in the life of a project.

2.3.8 To stimulate the ongoing development of the PFI the government recognised early on that there was a need for authorities to be more liberal in the change of control restrictions imposed on project companies. Guidance[2] was issued by the Private Finance Panel which discourages restrictions on the private sector's freedom to transfer its interests in PFI projects save in exceptional cases.

2.4 THE DEBT FUNDERS' OBJECTIVES

2.4.1 This section considers in outline the key objectives of the debt funders in a PFI project. These objectives and the more detailed issues that go to 'bankability' are considered in more detail in Chapter 8.

2.4.2 Although the form and terms of documentation used to raise the debt finance will differ in significant respects depending on whether the project company raises its debt in the bank market or in the capital markets, in terms of the funders' position there are a number of general objectives common to both. At the end of the day, it must be borne in mind that the debt funders' profit for investing in a project will be an arrangement fee plus a margin and, with such limited upside, their appetite for risk is commensurately limited.

---

1   See Chapter 8.
2   *Transferability of Equity* (HM Treasury and Private Finance Panel) October 1996.

Pass down of risk

2.4.3 One of the general requirements that the debt funders will have is to ensure that as many as possible of the risks undertaken by the project company are passed down by the project company to sub-contractors of acceptable financial standing (such as design, construction and operating sub-contractors).

Limiting risk in the project company

2.4.4 Inevitably, certain risks such as traffic risk in a DBFO road project cannot be passed down to others, and the banks will rely on technical reports to quantify such risks and place requirements as to the reserves to be built up within the project company to cushion against them.

2.4.5 Where risks cannot be passed down to the sub-contractors, insured against or managed by the project company within reasonably quantifiable limits, the banks may insist that the project company limits its exposure to them. A common example of this is the risk of changes in law requiring capital expenditure where banks commonly insist that the project company cap its exposure to this under the project agreement.

Take control early when things go wrong

2.4.6 The debt funders will appoint technical experts to monitor the project through each of its phases and will wish to have the ability to take control early, usually through the appointment of a receiver, if things start to go wrong. They will require advance notice of any threatened termination of the project agreement by the awarding authority and will require the right to 'step in' and remedy matters or transfer agreements to a substitute vehicle under a direct agreement.[1]

2.5 THE CONTRACTUAL MATRIX

2.5.1 This section examines in outline the key contracts that are likely to be present in a PFI project. Figure 1 (below) illustrates the principal parties and contracts and Figure 2 (below) overlays on this some of the additional guarantees and collateral and direct agreements that may be present.

The project agreement

2.5.2 This is the principal agreement in any PFI contract and it will set out the relationship between and the rights and obligations of the awarding authority and the project company throughout the contract term. In a number of the earlier PFI projects, separate agreements were used to cover different aspects of the project (such as a 'development agreement' for the design and construction phase or an 'operating agreement' or 'facilities management agreement' for the operating phase). However, the current practice is for a single project agreement

---

1   See **2.5.5** and Chapter 9.

Principal Contract Structure

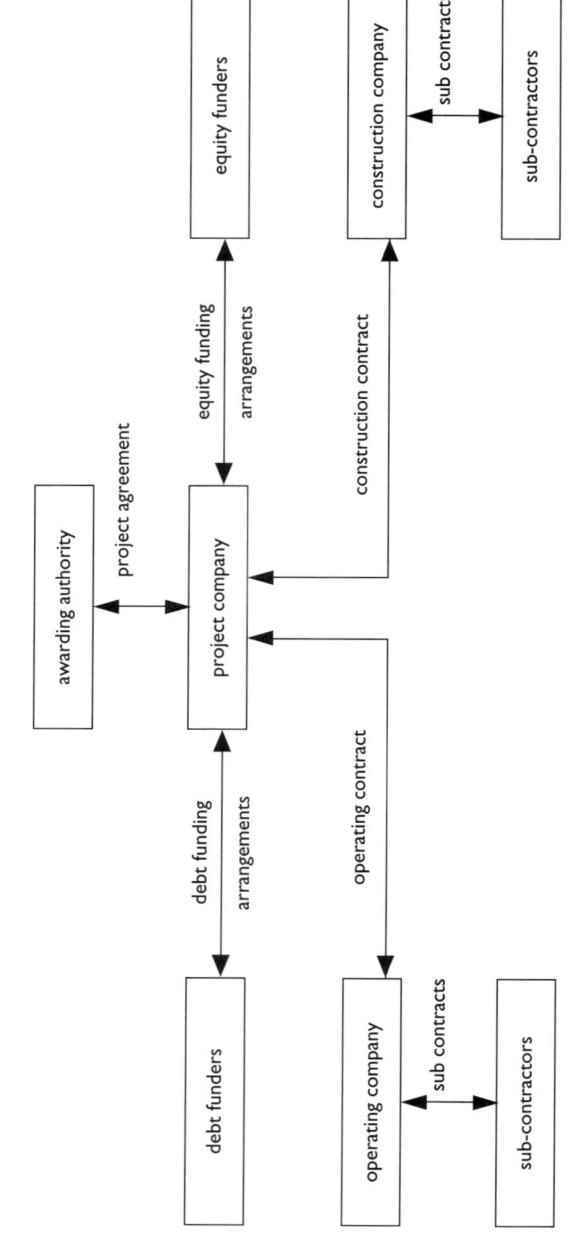

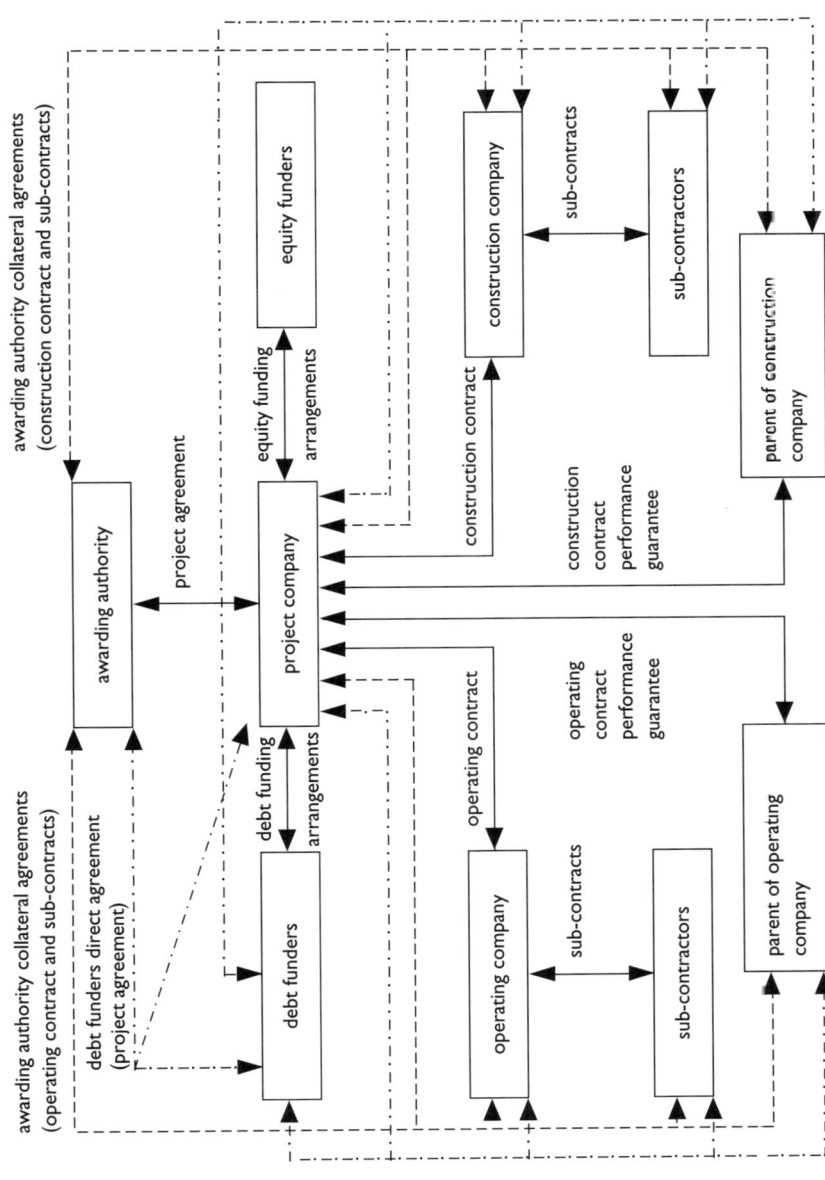

to cover all aspects. This removes some of the interface issues that may exist where the agreement is split into two or more separate documents, and is more consistent with the PFI philosophy of the 'purchase of a service' which is not severable into an asset and a service element.[1] The key provisions of the project agreement are reviewed in Chapter 10.

The property documents

2.5.3 Where a PFI project involves the development of land-based facilities, a property structure will need to be developed to reflect the respective interests of the awarding authority and the project company and the intended ownership position at the end of the contract term. A wide variety of structures have been used across the different sectors. The more commonly encountered structures include:

– the grant of a mere licence by the awarding authority to the project company (for instance, the DBFO road projects where no greater property interest could be granted to the project company or was needed by it);
– the grant of a headlease by the awarding authority to the project company with a sub-lease back to the awarding authority (for example, a number of the hospital projects where an interest in land was required by the project company in order to claim tax allowances[2] but the awarding authority was to be in occupation of the facilities throughout the contract term);
– the retention of the freehold by the awarding authority and the grant of a lease by the awarding authority to the project company for the contract term with no lease back (for example, the design, construct, maintain and finance ('DCFM') prison contracts); and
– the retention of the freehold by the project company and the grant of a lease by the project company to the awarding authority for the contract term (a number of the PFI projects for government accommodation where no ownership interest for the awarding authority is envisaged at the end of the contract term).

The property structures are reviewed further in Chapter 11.

The funding agreements

2.5.4 A comprehensive package of loan and security documents will be required by the debt funders usually supported by an agreed package of guarantees, collateral warranties and direct agreements. These agreements are reviewed further in Chapter 8.

The debt funders' direct agreement

2.5.5 The bank direct agreement is now an established part of the contractual matrix in all PFI projects. It is a tripartite agreement between the awarding

---

1   This is a particular issue in relation to the accounting treatment of PFI transactions. See Chapter 17.
2   See Chapter 14.

authority, the project company and the debt funders (or, in the case of a capital markets issue, the trustee for the bondholders) under which the awarding authority agrees to give the debt funders a period of advance notice of an impending termination of the project agreement and offer the debt funders the opportunity to step in (directly or, sometimes, via a nominee or other representative) to remedy the position and/or to find a substitute entity acceptable to the awarding authority to take over the rights and obligations of the project company under the project agreement. The form and content of the debt funder's direct agreement are reviewed in detail in Chapter 9.

Awarding authority collateral agreements

2.5.6 These have grown up as an extension of the concept underlying the debt funders' direct agreement, however their use, though increasing, is not yet widespread. The objective of the awarding authority direct agreement is to offer the awarding authority the opportunity of stepping into the shoes of the project company and taking over certain key contracts of the project company in the event of a termination of the project agreement (the bank direct agreement procedure having been gone through and not resolved matters).

2.5.7 In Figure 2, awarding authority collateral agreements are indicated in relation to both the construction contract and the operating contract. The intention behind these is that, if a default occurs during the construction phase, the awarding authority can ensure completion of the facilities by taking over the construction contract from the project company. Similarly, the awarding authority can take over the operating contract from the project company if the project agreement is terminated.

2.5.8 Where underlying contracts entered into by the project company enjoy the benefit of parent company guarantees, the authority would typically seek to enjoy a collateral agreement in relation to those as well.

Sub-contracts

2.5.9 A suite of sub-contracts will be put in place by the project company, passing down risks undertaken by the project company under the project agreement. It is very common for the project company to undertake none of the substantive activities itself but merely to be a vehicle for tying together the web of contracts associated with the project.

Performance bonds

2.5.10 These have been encountered principally in two scenarios. The first is where the awarding authority has required a performance bond to be posted in its favour by an acceptable surety to cover claims which may arise against the project company during the construction phase when, if a default were to occur, it is likely that the project company would not be good for any claim. In the case of a number of the DBFO road projects, performance bonds were required by the Highways Agency for an amount in the region of 10% of the capital value of the project. Clearly, however, such bonds will have a cost consequence which will feed back to the awarding authority and, as a result, their use is not widespread.

2.5.11 The second scenario is where debt funders have required performance bonds (on behalf of a key contractor) to be posted in their favour where they are not satisfied with the covenant of a contractor having regard to the magnitude of that contractor's obligations and the amount of its exposure to the project.

Collateral warranties

2.5.12 As is the practice in traditional development projects, debt funders will typically seek collateral warranties in their favour from key contractors and consultants appointed by the project company (and, indeed, sometimes sub-contractors beneath the prime contractors). In addition, awarding authorities have on occasion sought such collateral warranties in their favour. The value of such collateral warranties in favour of the awarding authority is principally in protecting the position of the awarding authority following a termination of the project agreement, in the event that losses suffered by the awarding authority exceed any value in the built or partly built facilities (ie the compensation calculation throws up a negative figure) or to cover the situation where a default or defect for which a contractor is responsible is discovered after the calculation of compensation on termination has been completed. However, where the compensation calculation throws up a negative figure it may well be that the debt funders seek to have a prior ranking claim in relation to a party who has given a collateral warranty both to the debt funders and the awarding authority.

2.6 CONCLUSION

2.6.1 As can be seen, reconciling the differing objectives of parties to a PFI project involves a complex set of contractual relationships. Clear trends are emerging as to how certain of these issues are to be resolved. However, as the following chapters demonstrate, many issues still fall into the melting pot of negotiation. Given the long-term nature of the contracts in question and the risk transfer which underpins them, this is perhaps not surprising.

Chapter 3

THE APPLICATION OF EUROPEAN UNION RULES ON PUBLIC PROCUREMENT TO PFI PROJECTS

3.1 INTRODUCTION

3.1.1 Most PFI projects are subject to rules laid down by the European Union ('EU') on public procurement. These rules are set out in a series of Council Directives which have been implemented into UK law by way of regulations. The procurement Directives form part of the wider programme of legislation, mostly introduced in the late 1980s and early 1990s, which was intended to create a single market for goods and services across the EU. The objective underlying the Directives is to ensure that public procurement is opened up to European-wide competition, with suppliers from any EU Member State being given an equal opportunity to bid for and win public contracts.

3.1.2 Whenever a PFI project is being contemplated, the procurement rules must be taken into consideration from the outset. The rules dictate the procedural framework that must be followed and lay down the broad principles governing the way in which the public sector ultimately chooses its private sector partner. As will be seen below, the procurement rules are unclear on a number of important issues which remain to be clarified by the British courts or the European Court of Justice. Despite these uncertainties, it is usually possible to undertake a PFI bidding process without being unduly hampered by the application of the procurement rules.

3.1.3 Awarding authorities are under a statutory duty to comply with the procurement rules. Any breach is actionable by an aggrieved supplier in the High Court and may also be the subject of a complaint to the European Commission. The potential sanctions for non-compliance are considered further in Chapter 6.

3.2 SCOPE: WHEN DO THE PROCUREMENT RULES APPLY?

The Public Sector Regulations

3.2.1 The Council Directives governing procurement by public sector authorities have been implemented in the UK by way of the following three statutory instruments:
– the Public Works Contracts Regulations 1991,[1] covering construction and civil engineering contracts;

---

1 SI 1991/2680, implementing an earlier version of Council Directive 93/37/EEC (OJ [1993] L 199/54).

- the Public Services Contracts Regulations 1993,[1] applicable to services contracts; and
- the Public Supply Contracts Regulations 1995,[2] covering contracts for the purchase or hire of equipment and goods.

3.2.2 These three sets of regulations (collectively 'the Public Sector Regulations' or 'the Regulations') apply to contracts awarded by the 'public sector' in its widest sense. Hence, they apply not only to central government departments and local authorities, but also to bodies 'governed by public law'. The last category is widely defined to encompass any organisation which is established to meet 'needs in the general interest' and which is predominantly financed, supervised or appointed by the State or other public authorities. The Regulations therefore apply to a wide range of public or quasi-public bodies, including:

- fire and police authorities;
- universities and maintained schools and colleges;
- National Health Service trusts and health authorities; and
- other non-departmental public bodies, such as the Audit Commission.[3]

The Utilities Regulations

3.2.3 A parallel but distinct set of procurement rules laid down in the Utilities Contracts Regulations 1996[4] applies to 'utility' companies operating in the sectors of water, energy, telecommunications and transport. Most utilities in the UK are already fully in the private sector. These include the privatised water and electricity companies, British Gas, airport authorities and regional railway franchisees. The main exceptions are London Underground, certain port authorities and Scottish water and sewerage authorities, which (at least for the time being) remain in the public sector.

3.2.4 Given the private sector status of most utilities in the UK, very few PFI projects are governed by the Utilities Regulations. These Regulations are not therefore considered further in the remainder of this chapter, which focuses instead on the Public Sector Regulations.

Works, supplies or services?

3.2.5 A preliminary issue in any PFI project is to determine which of the three sets of Public Sector Regulations applies. The answer depends upon the subject-matter of the contracts involved and is often far from straightforward.

3.2.6 Many PFI projects involve a combination of works, supplies and services. For example, a DBFO contract for a new hospital, prison or highway clearly has elements of all three. Any construction or renovation activities clearly constitute 'works' as covered by the Public Works Contracts Regulations 1991. The project might also include 'supplies' which would normally be caught by the Public

---

1   SI 1993/3228, implementing Council Directive 92/50/EEC (OJ [1992] L 207/1).
2   SI 1995/201, implementing Council Directive 93/36/EEC (OJ [1993] L 199/1).
3   A non-exhaustive list giving examples of such bodies is annexed to each set of Regulations. These lists are already significantly out of date.
4   SI 1996/2911, implementing Council Directive 93/38/EEC (OJ [1993] L 199/84).

Supply Contracts Regulations 1995, such as the provision of medical or gymnasium equipment. Most PFI projects also involve the provision of services, such as non-clinical support services (cleaning, catering, car park management, etc) for a hospital. These are, at least potentially, caught by the Public Services Contracts Regulations 1993.

3.2.7 The Regulations themselves give only limited guidance regarding the proper categorisation of such multi-faceted contracts. Where a contract involves a combination of supplies and services, it is the *relative value* of each element which determines which set of Regulations applies. For example, a PFI project involving the provision of fully serviced and maintained trains ought to be categorised as a supplies contract if the value of those trains exceeds the value (over the length of the contract) of the service of keeping those trains in good repair. This was an issue in the PFI project for the supply of new trains for the Northern Line of London Underground, where it was determined that the contract was one for supplies. Of course, apportioning precise values to the respective elements of such a contract may in itself be a complex matter.

3.2.8 An even more difficult issue can be distinguishing between works and services. The Regulations do not lay down any 'relative value' test as between works and services. Instead, it is necessary to look at the *main object* of the overall contract.[1] Applying this test to the example of a PFI contract for, say, a new hospital, the provision of new hospital buildings (works) could be said to be the main object of the project. It may also be noted that a works contract is defined very widely under the Regulations to include, *inter alia*, a contract 'under which a contracting authority engages a person to procure *by any means* the carrying out for the contracting authority of a work corresponding to specified requirements' (emphasis added).

3.2.9 On the other hand, PFI projects are usually described in terms of a service: for example, in the case of a new prison, the provision of a specified number of available prisoner places and facilities over a given period. Moreover, remuneration for carrying out the project takes the form of periodic payments relating to the provision of the service, rather than a lump-sum payment designed to cover the capital building costs. In this way, the building risk is effectively transferred to the private sector. These latter factors suggest that a typical PFI contract would be more suitably categorised as being one for services. However, each project must be analysed on its own facts. The latest Treasury Taskforce guidance comments:[2]

'The characterisation of a PFI proposal as a 'service provision' does not imply that the proposal will automatically be classified as a service contract under EC rules,

---

1   This is confirmed by the 16th recital to Services Directive 92/50. Support for this approach can also be derived from a case ruled upon by the European Court of Justice: C-311/92 *Hotelera Internacional* of 19 April 1994. The case involved the award of a concession to open and operate a hotel casino, including a requirement to invest at least 1 million pesetas in fitting out the hotel. The Court of Justice implied that the contract was not a works contract because the fitting out works were merely 'incidental' to the main (services) object of the award.
2   See Technical Note No 2 *How to Follow EC Procurement Procedure and Advertise in the OJEC* (Treasury Taskforce) June 1998.

however. It is feasible that a PFI project could be structured as a long-term service provision but still be a works or a supply contract.'

3.2.10 Ultimately, the categorisation of a PFI project as works, supplies or services is not usually critical, because the procedural requirements under the different Regulations for works, supplies and services are broadly similar. The most significant differences between the three sets of Regulations are in the threshold values above which the Regulations apply (see **3.2.16**) and in the grounds on which a competitive negotiated procedure may be used (see **3.3.7**). The threshold for works, above which the Public Works Contracts Regulations 1991 apply, is much greater than the threshold for application of the Regulations governing supplies and services contracts. Nevertheless, most significant PFI projects will exceed even the higher threshold laid down in the Public Works Contracts Regulations.

3.2.11 Otherwise, the rules under all three sets of Regulations are very similar. The choice of applicable Regulations determines the section of the Tenders Electronic Daily ('TED') database in which the contract notice will appear.[1] One possible course in cases of doubt is to advertise the PFI project as both a works contract and a services contract, so that a notice appears in both the works and services sections of the Official Journal. There is no downside in publishing two concurrent notices, but in practice this very rarely happens and compliance with one or other set of Regulations is generally considered to be sufficient.

Public works concessions

3.2.12 Under the Public Works Contracts Regulations 1991, public works concessions are treated as a distinct category of contract, being defined as:

> 'A public works contract under which the consideration given by the contracting authority consists of or includes the grant of a right to exploit the work or works to be carried out under the contract.'

3.2.13 Some PFI projects fall into this category. The private sector partner may be given the incentive of being able to charge users for the service or construction which they provide, in exchange for carrying out the works or services and bearing the risks of the transaction. Examples of concessions have included projects for the construction of major new bridges, such as the Skye, Second Severn and Queen Elizabeth II bridges, for which part of the consideration was a right given to the private sector partner to charge a toll on users of the completed bridge. The contract to construct the Channel Tunnel Rail Link was also awarded as a public works concession.

3.2.14 The procurement Regulations lay down special provisions for public works concessions. These rules are much less onerous than those for other works contracts. The only procedural obligation imposed upon the authority awarding the concession is a requirement to publish a notice in the Official Journal, advertising the authority's intention to award the concession and allowing at least 52 days for receipt of tenders or of requests to participate. The firm or consortium which wins the concession is itself obliged to publish a notice in the

---

1   See **3.3.13** and **3.3.19**.

Official Journal if and when it intends to award to third parties any works sub-contract worth more than £4,016,744. Having done so, the concessionaire must allow at least 37 days for interested parties to request to participate.

3.2.15 Apart from these advertising requirements, the procurement rules impose no further procedural obligations on either the awarding authority or the concessionaire. Thus, concessions are not subject to the various provisions, described in **3.3** et seq, regarding pre-qualification of candidates, negotiations and award criteria.

The value thresholds

3.2.16 The procurement Regulations only apply to contracts worth more than a specified threshold. The thresholds are expressed in euros, with the sterling equivalent being determined every two years. For the two-year period 1 January 1998 to 31 December 1999, the thresholds in pounds sterling are as follows:

- £4,016,744 for works contracts;
- £104,435 for supplies and services contracts awarded by organs of central government;[1] and
- £160,670 for supplies and services contracts awarded by other public bodies, such as local authorities.

3.2.17 For the purposes of the above thresholds, the value of a contract should usually correspond to the amount of consideration which the awarding body expects to give under the contract. Where a PFI project involves a combination of works, supplies and/or services, the relevant figure is the total value of the entire project, assuming that all elements are to be awarded to a single contractor or consortium.

3.2.18 The Regulations lay down a number of rules on contract valuation. For example:

- in the case of a public works concession, it is necessary to estimate the monetary value of the consideration which the authority would have given if the contractor had not been given the right to exploit the works;
- for long-term or indefinite contracts for services or the lease of products, the projected value over the first four years of the contract is taken (that is, the monthly value is multiplied by 48); and
- if a supplies or services contract specifies option clauses, the awarding authority must presume that all the options will be exercised and so take the maximum possible value.

3.2.19 The Regulations specify that a single purchasing requirement may not be split up into lots with the intention of avoiding the procurement rules. If an awarding authority sub-divides what is essentially a single contract into smaller units, the value of each part has to be added together to determine whether the

---

1   This lower threshold for central government reflects the obligations of the EU under an international accord known as the Government Procurement Agreement ('GPA'), which was entered into with a number of third countries, including the US and Japan, in 1994. The bodies to which this lower threshold applies are listed in an Annex to the GPA. They include central government departments as well as NHS trusts and health authorities.

relevant threshold is met. Various 'aggregation' rules are laid down in order to reinforce the principle. Hence, separate contracts to build or extend different parts of a single building or structure would usually have to be aggregated. This might not be the case, however, where different parts of a project are to be carried out in different locations or at different times, for example where there are phased contracts to build separate but adjoining sections of a motorway. Each case should be judged on its particular facts.

Part A and Part B services

3.2.20   Whereas contracts for (virtually) all works and supplies are covered by the procurement Regulations, the coverage of services is more piecemeal. When laying down the rules for services contracts in Council Directive 92/50/EEC, the EU decided that the rules should only apply in full to those categories of services where there is real potential for cross-border competition. Consequently, services under the procurement rules are divided into two separate bands.

- Services listed in Schedule 1, Part A of the Public Services Contracts Regulations 1993 ('Part A services'), which are subject to the Regulations in full.
- Services listed in Schedule 1, Part B ('Part B services'), which are subject only to the rules on technical specifications and post-award notices, but exempt from all other procedural requirements.

The most important examples of services in either category are listed in Table 1.

3.2.21   Both annexes cross-refer to the Community Product Classification ('CPC') which defines the various categories of service in more detail. A large PFI project will frequently involve services falling into different categories, some of which fall under Part A (for example, information technology services) and others under Part B (for instance, legal services and clinical medical services). In such a case, the full Regulations only apply if the Part A services are worth more than the Part B services.

National security exclusion

3.2.22   There is a general exclusion, under each set of Regulations, for contracts which are classified as secret, which must be accompanied by special security measures or where the basic interests of UK security so require. There is little case law clarifying the scope of this exclusion, but it can be expected to apply in relation to any genuinely security-sensitive PFI projects involving the UK's military or intelligence services. Thus, some PFI projects undertaken, for example, by the Ministry of Defence or GCHQ may benefit from this exemption.

3.3 THE PROCEDURAL REQUIREMENTS

Choice of procedure: open, restricted or negotiated?

3.3.1   Under the Public Sector Regulations, public authorities have to award contracts according to one of four types of procedure:

Table 1: Examples of Part A and Part B services

Part A services (covered)	Part B services (largely excluded)
Maintenance and repair	Hotel and restaurant services
Land transport	Rail transport
Telecom services (but not voice telephony)	Water transport
Financial services	Legal services
Computer (IT) services	Security services
Accounting/auditing	Education services
Management consultancy	Health and social services
Architectural and engineering services	Recreational, cultural and sporting services
Advertising services	Other services
Building-cleaning/property management	
Publishing/printing	
Sewage/refuse disposal	

- *open* procedure: all interested suppliers may submit a tender;
- *restricted* procedure: the awarding authority invites expressions of interest and only those suppliers short-listed by the awarding authority may submit a tender;
- *negotiated* procedure: the awarding authority consults suppliers of its choice and negotiates the terms of the contract with one or more of them;
- *design contest:* the awarding authority calls for architects or designers to put forward plans or designs for a particular project and the winning design is then selected by a jury.[1]

3.3.2 Awarding authorities can always choose to use the open or restricted procedures, whereas a negotiated procedure may only be used in certain circumstances prescribed in the Regulations. The open procedure will rarely, if ever, be suitable for PFI projects because (unlike the restricted procedure) it gives no opportunity for the awarding authority to limit the number of tenders it has to consider. The open procedure is not therefore considered further in this chapter.

3.3.3 The disadvantage of both the open and restricted procedures is that the authority is bound to make its choice of preferred bidder solely on the basis of

---

1 This procedure is rarely used in practice and is not covered further in this chapter.

the written tenders that are submitted. There appears to be no scope for meaningful negotiation with bidders, either before or after submission of the tender. This limitation is not spelled out in the procurement Directives or Regulations themselves, but is apparent from a joint statement issued by the Council and the Commission at the time when Directive 93/37/EEC (concerning public works contracts) was adopted. That statement declares that:

> 'In open and restricted procedures all negotiations with candidates or tenderers on fundamental aspects of contracts, variations in which are likely to distort competition, and in particular on prices, shall be ruled out; however, discussions with candidates or tenderers may be held but only for the purposes of clarifying or supplementing the content of their tenders or the requirements of the contracting authorities and provided this does not involve discrimination.'[1]

3.3.4 In relation to PFI projects, the awarding authority will want to enter into detailed discussions and negotiations with short-listed bidders, as part of the process for selecting a preferred bidder. Consequently, awarding authorities usually have a strong preference for using a negotiated procedure. It is therefore relevant to consider the grounds on which such a procedure is available. It should be noted that there are in fact two types of negotiated procedure: a competitive version which is pre-advertised in the Official Journal and a non-competitive version which does not have to be advertised. The grounds on which these procedures are available are considered in the following sections.

Non-competitive negotiated procedure without OJ notice

3.3.5 In a number of exceptional circumstances, an authority is entitled to use a negotiated procedure without publishing a prior notice in the Official Journal and without holding a competition. In other words, the authority can turn

Table 2: Summary: Which award procedure?

Open procedure   – Any interested party may tender   – Not suitable for PFIs
Restricted procedure   – Short-list invited to tender   – No post-tender negotiations   – Too inflexible for PFIs
Competitive negotiated procedure   – Available if prior pricing or precise specifications not possible   – Strongly recommended for PFIs
Non-competitive negotiated procedure   – Only allowed on exceptional grounds (eg extreme urgency)   – Rarely available for PFIs

---

1 Statement concerning Article 7(4) of Council Directive 93/37/EEC of 14 June 1993, OJ [1994] L 111/114.

directly to the firm or consortium of its choice. The most important grounds on which such a procedure is available are as follows:

- where no tenders or no appropriate tenders are received by the authority in response to an open or restricted procedure;
- when, for technical or artistic reasons or for reasons connected with the protection of exclusive rights, the contract may only be carried out by a particular supplier;
- when, for reasons of extreme urgency brought about by events which were unforeseeable by and not attributable to the awarding authority, the time limits prescribed under the open and restricted procedures cannot be respected; or
- for additional works or services not included in an existing contract which have, through unforeseen circumstances, become necessary for the carrying out of the contract, provided such additional works or services are strictly necessary to complete the original contract or cannot be separated from it without great inconvenience. As a further condition attached to this ground, the total value of the additional works or services may not exceed 50% of the value of the original contract.

3.3.6 The European Court of Justice has on a number of occasions emphasised the exceptional nature of these grounds and indicated that the onus lies upon the awarding authority to justify its recourse to them. It can be expected that these grounds will arise only very rarely in the context of PFI projects. Moreover, the absence of an advertised competition would run counter to the government's policy of fostering competition for such projects.

Competitive negotiated procedure with OJ notice

3.3.7 Under the competitive version of the negotiated procedure, a prior notice must be published in the Official Journal, calling for candidates to apply to participate. Such a procedure is permitted on several grounds. Two of these grounds are potentially applicable to PFI projects, being:

- exceptionally, when the nature of the works or services, or the risks involved, do not permit prior overall pricing; or
- when the nature of the service being procured, particularly in the case of intellectual or financial services, is such that contract specifications cannot be established with sufficient precision to permit a contract award using the open or restricted procedures.

3.3.8 The somewhat vague wording of these grounds is open to different interpretations and there is as yet no judicial guidance on precisely when the grounds apply. Nevertheless, reliance has regularly been placed upon one or other of the grounds in relation to PFI contracts, so as to justify use of a competitive negotiated procedure. For example, where a contract to design and build an acute general hospital is involved, the uncertain nature of the risks being transferred to the private sector could be argued to mean that it is not possible to price the transaction in advance. It remains to be seen whether a court would support such an interpretation, particularly as this ground is stated to be exceptional. Alternatively, if the contract as a whole is for services, it may be the case that the contract specifications for those services cannot be drawn with 'sufficient precision' to enable bidders to tender against them in an open or restricted procedure.

3.3.9 While the European Commission has not yet expressed a formal view on this practice,[1] the UK Treasury advocates the use of the negotiated procedure for most PFI projects. It has stated in published guidelines that 'a competitive negotiated procedure is already permitted by the directives in certain clearly defined circumstances which are very likely to apply to PFI projects'.[2] The Treasury has also publicised the fact that an attempt by the Prison Service in 1993 to use the restricted procedure in relation to two PFI prison projects (Bridgend and Fazakerley) had to be aborted when all of the tenders submitted were found to be non-compliant. Consequently, with the consent of all the short-listed bidders, the Prison Service switched to use of the negotiated procedure.

3.3.10 In practice, most firms bidding for PFI work would accept the need for negotiation. It is therefore unlikely that an interested party would bring an action against an authority solely on the ground that it should not have used the negotiated procedure.

3.3.11 The issue of whether or not recourse to the negotiated procedure is justified remains a question of fact and degree which has to be decided on a case-by-case basis. Nevertheless, the negotiated procedure is in practice used for the large majority of PFI contracts and the remainder of this chapter will therefore focus primarily on the requirements under that procedure.

Duty to advertise in the Official Journal

3.3.12 Where a project involves a relevant works contract, the awarding authority is required to publish a prior information notice (or 'PIN') in the Official Journal 'as soon as possible after the decision approving the planning of the works contract'.[3] The purpose of the PIN is to give interested parties advance notice of the forthcoming works contract, but it does not call on contractors to respond at this stage. The PIN must give brief details of the forthcoming contract, following the standard format annexed to the Regulations.

3.3.13 Once the authority is ready to begin the bidding process, it must submit a contract notice for publication in the Official Journal.[4] The notice again has to follow a standard layout, which is set out in an annex to the Regulations. For example, the appropriate form of notice for a negotiated procedure under the

---

1 The Commission does state in its Green Paper on Procurement, published in November 1996, that a competitive negotiated procedure may be justified for complex works and services contracts relating to Trans European Networks, where the Commission is very keen to encourage private sector involvement.
2 Technical Note No 2 *How to Follow EC Procurement Procedure and Advertise in the OJEC* (Treasury Taskforce) June 1998.
3 The requirement is a little different under the Public Services Contracts Regulations. These require the publication of a PIN on an annual basis, giving prior notice of forthcoming contracts for services in those categories where the authority expects to award contracts the total value of which exceed £584,901.
4 The notice now appears only on the Tenders Electronic Daily ('TED') database, the paper version having been discontinued. See **3.3.19**.

Table 3: A competitive negotiated procedure

> Approval of PFI project plan
>
> [Publish prior information notice (PIN) in OJ]
>
> Publish contract notice in OJ, allowing at least 37 days (or 15 if urgent) for reply
>
> Short-list candidates (at least three) per qualification criteria
>
> [Debrief rejected candidates]
>
> Issue Invitation to Negotiate
>
> Negotiate, with or without formal tenders
>
> Select preferred tenderer per award criteria
>
> [Debrief rejected bidders]
>
> Final negotiations to contract signature
>
> Publish award notice within 48 days

Public Services Contracts Regulations 1993 is set out at Sch 2, Part D to those Regulations. This model form sets out 15 points on which information must be given. These are set out in Table 4 below.

3.3.14 Great care needs to be taken in drafting the contract notice, as it sets the parameters for the entire project. If the contract notice is incomplete or poorly drafted, it may be open for interested parties subsequently to claim that all or part of the project has not been properly advertised. In extreme cases, this might even lead to the bidding process having to be recommenced with publication of a new notice in the Official Journal.

3.3.15 It is important to specify in clear terms all of the requirements that may be covered by the project. For example, if a hospital redevelopment project includes the provision of non-clinical services, such as catering, security and information technology, the notice should specify these. If redevelopment opportunities in relation to surplus land are present, that should be mentioned. Similarly, if the awarding authority wishes to retain the flexibility to divide the project into lots, the notice should make this clear. The total length of the notice should not exceed 650 words, so there is a limit to the degree of detail that can be included. The authority may cross-refer to other documents, available on request, for more complete information.

3.3.16 One of the recommendations of the Bates Review was that a degree of standardisation should be introduced for the wording of OJ notices relating to PFI projects. The Treasury has subsequently set out some recommendations on this in a Technical Note.[1] The Note states that 'key standard wording' should be inserted in the 'other information' section of OJ notices as follows:

---

1   Technical Note No 2 *How to Follow EC Procurement Procedure and Advertise in the OJEC* (Treasury Taskforce) June 1998.

Table 4: Negotiated procedure notice under Public Services Contracts Regulations 1993

1. Name, address and telephone, telegraphic, telex and facsimile numbers of the contracting authority.
2. Category of services and description. CPC reference number.
3. Place of delivery.
4. (a) Indication of whether the provision of the services is reserved by law, regulation or administrative provision to a particular profession;
   (b) Reference to the law, regulation or administrative provision;
   (c) Indication of whether legal persons should indicate the names and professional qualifications of the staff to be responsible for the provision of service.
5. Indication of whether service providers can offer some or all of the services required.
6. If known, the number of service providers which will be invited to tender or the range within which that number is expected to fall.
7. Where applicable, non-acceptance of variants.
8. Period of contract or time limit, if any, for completion of the services.
9. Where applicable, the legal form to be assumed by a grouping of service providers to whom the contract is awarded.
10. (a) Where applicable, justification for use of the shorter time limits [in accordance with reg 12];
    (b) Final date for the receipt of requests to participate;
    (c) Address to which they must be sent;
    (d) Language(s) in which they must be drawn up.
11. Any deposits and guarantees required.
12. The information and formalities necessary for an appraisal of the minimum standards of economic and financial standing, ability and technical capacity required of the services provider.
13. Where applicable, the names and addresses of services providers already selected by the contracting authority.
14. Other information.
15. Date of despatch of the notice.
16. Date(s) of previous publications in the Official Journal.

'This requirement is considered suitable for the application of the Private Finance Initiative (PFI) or an alternative Public Private Partnership (PPP). Service providers who respond to this requirement will ultimately be required to make firm proposals for funding the project in accordance with this application. The contracting authority reserves the right not to award a contract.'

3.3.17 The Treasury's Note also recommends that the standard wording to cover variant bids should be:

'Variant bids will be permissible, provided the contracting authority agrees that the core requirements will be met.'

3.3.18 The above wording put forward by the Treasury is entirely sensible. There is, however, little scope for further standardisation of the wording of these notices. The critical part of the notice is the description of the project and the awarding authority's broad requirements, and this description clearly has to vary from project to project.

3.3.19 The contract notice must be sent, preferably by fax, to the Office for Official Publications of the European Communities in Luxembourg,[1] who will arrange for its publication. The notice will appear in electronic form on the Tenders Electronic Daily ('TED') database, which is available in CD-ROM format or online through the Internet or X25 network. The TED database is located at http://www.echo.lu/ted. Notices also used to appear in paper form in the Daily Supplement (or 'S series') to the Official Journal, but for reasons of cost this printed publication was discontinued on 30 June 1998.

3.3.20 Advertisements regarding the PFI project may not be placed in any national publication until after the contract notice has been sent to the Official Journal. Any national notices may not contain information which adds to or contradicts the information set out in the Official Journal notice.

Time constraints

3.3.21 In both restricted and (competitive) negotiated procedures, the Regulations require the awarding authority to allow a minimum of 37 days for interested parties to respond to the contract notice in the Official Journal. That period begins to run from the date on which the notice is sent to the OJ publishers (and not from the subsequent day on which the notice actually appears). It is only after the expiry of that period that the authority can select its short-list of pre-qualified tenderers.

3.3.22 The 37-day time limit may be shortened to 15 days where the longer period (37 days) is 'rendered impracticable for reasons of urgency'. Where this happens, the process is usually described as an 'accelerated' procedure. The rules do not expand upon what may or may not constitute sufficient urgency. It is clear that the test is less stringent than the 'extreme urgency' ground (referred to at **3.3.5**) under which the need to hold an advertised competition may be dispensed with altogether. Indeed, in condemning recourse to that 'extreme urgency' ground, the European Court of Justice has on a number of occasions said that the awarding authority should instead have used the accelerated time limits.

3.3.23 The Regulations do not lay down any further time constraints as regards conduct of a negotiated procedure. As for the restricted procedure, the Regulations prescribe that, when the authority invites its short-list of bidders to submit tenders, it must allow at least 40 days, as from the date of that invitation,

---

1　Fax number: 00 352 29 294 2670.

for submission of tenders. This 40-day period may be shortened to 26 days where a PIN has been published, or to 10 days where urgency renders the longer period impracticable.

Pre-qualification

3.3.24 Once interested parties have come forward pursuant to the contract notice, the awarding authority will proceed to the pre-qualification (or 'pre-selection') stage. This involves the authority verifying that the interested parties satisfy its minimum requirements as regards financial standing and technical capability (including relevant experience). The authority will then select a short-list from amongst the candidates that do satisfy those minimum pre-qualification requirements. Those on the short-list are then invited to tender (in a restricted procedure) or to negotiate (in a negotiated procedure).

3.3.25 The Regulations set out a number of grounds on which candidates may be automatically excluded.[1] These grounds relate to the integrity and financial solvency of the candidate. For example, a candidate may be excluded if it is in the process of a bankruptcy or liquidation, if it has been found guilty of a criminal offence or grave professional misconduct, or if it makes serious misrepresentations in supplying information to the awarding authority.

3.3.26 The procurement rules go on to prescribe in some detail the factors that the awarding authority may take into account for the purpose of pre-qualifying candidates. These rules on pre-qualification criteria generally reflect the type of factors which an awarding authority would probably wish to take into account, in any event, when assessing the suitability of candidates for a PFI project. Relevant pre-qualification factors fall into three broad categories:

- *financial standing:* the type of evidence that the authority may take into account includes appropriate bank statements, financial accounts and details of turnover;
- *technical capacity:* this may be evidenced, *inter alia*, by the educational and professional qualifications of the candidate's managerial staff and details of works carried out in the last five years and/or services over the past three years; and
- *ability* of the service provider, taking into account in particular his skills, efficiency, experience and reliability.

3.3.27 The Treasury Taskforce has issued a draft Technical Note which provides for the standardisation of information required from prospective tenderers. The draft Note recommends that those responding to advertisements for PFI projects should be asked to supply information in the format of a standard questionnaire. This information will then be stored on a database of the type previously operated by the Department of the Environment, Transport and the Regions for construction contractors and consultants. For any future applications, the applicant is then simply able to provide its database reference number rather than having to forward details of its qualifications every time. The

---

1   Regulation 14 of the Public Services Contracts Regulations 1993.

Treasury indicates that the fee for enrolment on the database is small and that the system will be entirely voluntary. Those who prefer to send details of their qualifications on a contract-by-contract basis remain free to do so. It can be seen, however, that enrolment on the database will be in the contractor's interests since it will avoid the unnecessary duplication involved in resubmitting relevant information each time they apply to participate in a project.

3.3.28 The awarding authority is left considerable discretion to decide upon the precise details of how it conducts the pre-qualification process. The procedure may involve preliminary interviews with, or presentations by, the candidates. Moreover, the awarding authority may wish to use a detailed scoring system, possibly with different weightings being given to different factors. It is fairly clear from the rules that the awarding authority should not at this stage have regard to the proposals which the candidates intend to put forward. Such matters have to be assessed in the tenders/negotiations phase by reference to the authority's award criteria.[1]

Short-listing

3.3.29 At the end of the pre-qualification exercise, the authority has to select a short-list which it will invite either to tender or to negotiate. It must make this choice from among those candidates which meet its minimum pre-qualification criteria. If a relatively large number of candidates (say, eight) are adjudged to meet those criteria, the authority will usually wish to reduce that number to a smaller short-list of, say, three or four. The rules do not specify how an authority must arrive at this short-list. A sensible course would be to select those candidates which *best* meet the authority's pre-qualification criteria, but the rules do not expressly require this.[2]

3.3.30 There is scope for debate as to the ideal number of candidates to short-list. The Bates Review recommended a compulsory maximum of four. The Regulations specify that, in a competitive negotiated procedure, the number selected to negotiate must be *at least three* (assuming that there are at least three suitable candidates). For the restricted procedure, the Regulations do not specify a minimum but do state that the number invited to tender 'shall be sufficient to ensure genuine competition'. Again, it would appear that three is a reasonable minimum number.

3.3.31 The issue of whether an awarding authority can subsequently reduce the number of candidates still further (perhaps to just two), after a preliminary round of tenders or negotiations, is considered at **3.3.39**.

Contract award criteria

3.3.32 The awarding authority is required to specify clearly in advance, in either the Official Journal or the contract documents, the criteria upon which it will select its preferred bidder. In PFI projects, the most common practice is for

---

1 See **3.3.33**.
2 Further commentary on the evaluation of pre-qualification responses is set out at **5.5.7–5.5.12**.

the award criteria to be specified in either the invitation to tender or the invitation to negotiate which is sent to the short-listed bidders.[1]

3.3.33 The procurement rules require the authority to award the contract to the bidder which puts forward the 'most economically advantageous offer'.[2] The term equates broadly to the notion of 'best value for money' and, as such, is compatible with the underlying objectives of the PFI. It is up to the awarding authority to decide upon (and specify) the criteria by which it will identify the most economically advantageous offer. The Regulations merely give a non-exhaustive list of factors that the authority may use. These include period for completion, quality, aesthetic and functional characteristics, technical merit and price.

3.3.34 The duty to specify all relevant criteria in advance is a strict one. The ruling of the Court of Appeal in the *Portsmouth* case[3] indicates that an awarding authority is not entitled to take into account any award criteria which it fails to mention either in the contract documents or the Official Journal notice. Indeed, that case went so far as to find that, where the award criteria are not properly specified, the contract must be awarded on the basis of lowest price only. It is therefore vitally important that the awarding authority gives a clear written statement of its intended award criteria.

3.3.35 Case-law in the European Court of Justice[4] indicates that the award criteria should focus firmly on the proposals of the bidders for carrying out the contract. The authority should not, at this stage, have regard to 'pre-qualification' criteria such as the size and relevant experience of the bidder consortium or its members. Strictly speaking, those factors should only be taken into account at the pre-qualification phase. In practice, it may sometimes prove difficult to draw a clear-cut line between the pre-qualification and award criteria.

The tenders/negotiations phase

3.3.36 Where a restricted procedure is being used, the short-listed candidates are invited to submit written tenders setting out their proposals for carrying out the project. As explained above, the preferred bidder must be chosen on the basis of a comparison between the written tenders and it appears that there should not be any significant negotiation on terms. It is for this reason that public authorities generally prefer to use the negotiated procedure when awarding PFI projects.

3.3.37 The Regulations (like the Directives that they implement) do not prescribe in any detail the process to be followed in a negotiated procedure, particularly in the phase between pre-qualification and contract award. Clearly,

---

1   The criteria could also be set out in other 'contract documents', such as any pre-qualification briefing sent to all interested candidates.
2   The rules also allow for the alternative award basis of lowest price only, but it is difficult to envisage that it would ever be appropriate to award a PFI project solely on the basis of price.
3   *R v Portsmouth City Council, ex p Peter Coles and others* (1997) 9 Admin LR 535. Support can also be found in the European Court of Justice ruling in *Commission v Belgium* C-31/94 (re Walloon Buses) [1996] ECR I-2043.
4   Such as C-31/87 *Gebroeders Beentjes BV Netherlands* [1988] ECR 4635.

the procedure entails detailed discussions between the awarding authority and the bidders. In practice, the procedure usually also includes the presentation of formal written tenders.

3.3.38 Perhaps the overriding requirement to be borne in mind is the prohibition (also applicable in other stages of the award procedure) against unfair discrimination. The European Court of Justice has stated that the principle of equal treatment of bidders lies at the heart of the EU procurement rules.[1] This principle implies, for example, that any significant information regarding the awarding authority's requirements should be given to all the short-listed tenderers.

Is a two-stage negotiated procedure permissible?[2]

3.3.39 A recurring issue in PFI award procedures is whether, and to what extent, the awarding authority can 'whittle down' the number of short-listed bidders. For example, the authority may originally pre-qualify six bidding consortia and then wish to reduce that number to three short-listed bidders from whom it receives fully costed bids. The procurement rules neither expressly allow for, nor prohibit, the conduct of negotiations in two stages, with some of those short-listed tenderers being eliminated from the process before the final stage of receiving costed bids. Moreover, this issue has not yet been addressed in any procurement case before the European Court of Justice. It is therefore necessary to consider whether such conduct is compatible with the principles underlying the procurement rules.

3.3.40 One of the principal aims of the procurement legislation is to ensure that there is open competition for public contracts. The legislation provides that adequate competition is ensured if at least three candidates are invited to negotiate in a negotiated procedure. However many are invited, the number ultimately of course has to be narrowed down to one. If, at some intervening stage, only a smaller number of candidates (perhaps as few as two) are selected for a final procedure of elimination, that does not mean that there has been a lack of competition. Indeed, given the costs of submitting full tenders and negotiating upon them, it could be argued that the interests of competition are best served if the final selection stage is limited to only two or three candidates.

3.3.41 It is submitted that the procurement rules do not prohibit the kind of two-stage negotiation process described, provided the early elimination of candidates can be justified on objective, economic grounds.[3] The overall negotiation process must be conducted with a view to identifying the most

---

1   *Commission v Denmark* C-243/89 [1993] ECR I-3353 ('the *Storebaelt* case'), at para 33, and also *Commission v Belgium* C-87/95 [1996] ECR I-2043 at para 51.
2   See also **5.6.5–5.6.8**.
3   Some support for this view may be gleaned from the international accord known as the Government Procurement Agreement (GPA) which governs procurement as between the EU and certain third countries. Article XIV of the GPA states, *inter alia*, that 'Negotiations shall primarily be used to identify the strengths and weaknesses in tenders ... entities ... shall ensure that any elimination of participants is carried out in accordance with the criteria set forth in the notices and tender documentation'.

economically advantageous tender, in terms of the awarding authority's evaluation criteria. Any early elimination of candidates must be justifiable by reference to those criteria. It would probably not be sufficient to justify such elimination solely by reference to the costs or inconvenience of admitting a larger number of candidates to the final 'tender' stage.[1] Instead, the elimination decision ought to be made by reference to the relative quality of the proposal being put forward by each short-listed tenderer. The awarding authority must therefore have sufficient information on each tenderer's proposals in order to carry out such a comparative assessment. It may be difficult to claim that such an assessment has taken place if elimination takes place at a very early stage of the negotiations and in particular if there has not yet been any detailed discussion of pricing or financial arrangements.

3.3.42 There is an argument that the awarding authority must have received fully costed tenders from all short-listed tenderers before being able properly to assess which pre-qualified candidates are most likely to offer the most economically advantageous tender. However, it is submitted that something less than this will suffice, particularly as price is not the only bid evaluation criterion.

3.3.43 The awarding authority could hold an initial round of exploratory 'negotiations' with all six pre-qualified tenderers, basically consisting of presentations by each tenderer followed by a question and answer session about the tenderer's proposals, including price. If, at the end of that (relatively brief) process, the awarding authority has objective grounds for believing that three of the six short-listed candidates are more likely than the other three to satisfy its stated award criteria, then it ought to be able to proceed to invite full bids only from the three preferred candidates.

3.3.44 The rather vague provisions in the legislation, together with the lack of case law, mean that this issue remains something of a 'grey area'. Until it is clarified, the above analysis must remain somewhat speculative and there is clearly a need to proceed with caution. In particular, awarding authorities must be careful to avoid any suggestion of unfair discrimination.

Negotiations with the preferred tenderer

3.3.45 The awarding authority will ultimately select one 'preferred' tenderer which it considers to have put forward the most economically advantageous offer. Having selected that preferred tenderer, it is usual for there to be a further period of detailed negotiation between the awarding authority and that tenderer prior to a final agreement being entered into for the project. Experience shows that this final period of negotiation may run for many months, while details of the project and the financing arrangements are worked out.[2]

3.3.46 Final negotiations with the preferred tenderer, as well as being commercially imperative, are not of themselves incompatible with the procurement rules. An infringement might occur, however, if those negotiations result in

---

1   Conversely, this factor is clearly permissible when deciding how many tenderers to short-list (and invite to negotiate) at the pre-qualification stage.
2   See **5.7**.

a significant change either to the scope of the project itself or to the offer put forward by the preferred tenderer.

3.3.47 In particular, any major alteration could invalidate the fairness of the selection of the preferred tenderer's original offer as the most economically advantageous one. For example, if the preferred tenderer manages to negotiate a reduction in its obligations under the project or an increase in its remuneration, the unsuccessful tenderers may have good grounds to argue that there has been unfair discrimination. Whether such an infringement occurs is a question of fact and degree which can only be judged on a case-by-case basis.

Post-award formalities and debriefing

3.3.48 Within 48 days of the award of the contract, the awarding authority is obliged to send a short notice to the Official Journal setting out brief details of the award. The notice must follow the model format set out in an annex to the Regulations.

3.3.49 Under the Regulations, the awarding authority must keep a written record documenting each stage of the award procedure. HM Treasury and the European Commission are entitled to ask to see a copy of this record.

3.3.50 Whenever a candidate is eliminated, whether at the final award stage or earlier, it may request reasons for its rejection. If so, the awarding authority is required to give written reasons within 15 days. The rules do not specify the level of detail to be given in the awarding authority's reasons, but general principles suggest that they must be sufficient to enable the candidate to understand why it was unsuccessful.

Chapter 4

THE *VIRES* OF PUBLIC SECTOR BODIES TO UNDERTAKE PFI PROJECTS

4.1 INTRODUCTION

4.1.1 In the same way that issues of *vires* constrain the activities of private sector bodies, so public sector bodies will also be constrained by *vires* issues, but those companies or individuals dealing with public sector bodies do not have the benefit of provisions analogous to the Companies Act 1985, s 35. Briefly, public sector bodies will be constrained by the terms of any governing legislation and other general public law principles.

4.1.2 The importance of complying with *vires* requirements has been highlighted in a number of cases where transactions between the public sector and private sector have been held to be unenforceable on the basis that the public sector body was acting outside its powers. For example, in *Hazell v Hammersmith and Fulham LBC*[1] interest rate swaps transactions were held to be outside the terms of the relevant local government legislation, and in *Credit Suisse v Allerdale BC*[2] a scheme involving the construction of a swimming pool and the construction and sale of time-share units was *ultra vires* the Council. Cases such as these raised concerns about the legality of PFI transactions (which were echoed and reinforced by the Bates Review[3]) and have resulted in two new Acts, the National Health Service (Private Finance) Act 1997 which came into force on 15 July 1997 and the Local Government (Contracts) Act 1997 which came into force on 30 December 1997. The operation of both pieces of legislation is discussed in this chapter.

4.2 GENERAL PRINCIPLES

4.2.1 The possible invalidity of a public law decision by a public body can be classified under three main heads:[4]

- illegality;
- irrationality;
- procedural impropriety.

A flow-chart illustrating these main heads and the grounds under those heads is set out in Figure 1.

---

1 [1992] 2 AC 1.
2 [1997] QB 306.
3 See **1.3.29**.
4 Per Lord Diplock in *Council of Civil Service Unions v Minister for the Civil Service* [1985] AC 374.

Figure 1: Awarding authority powers

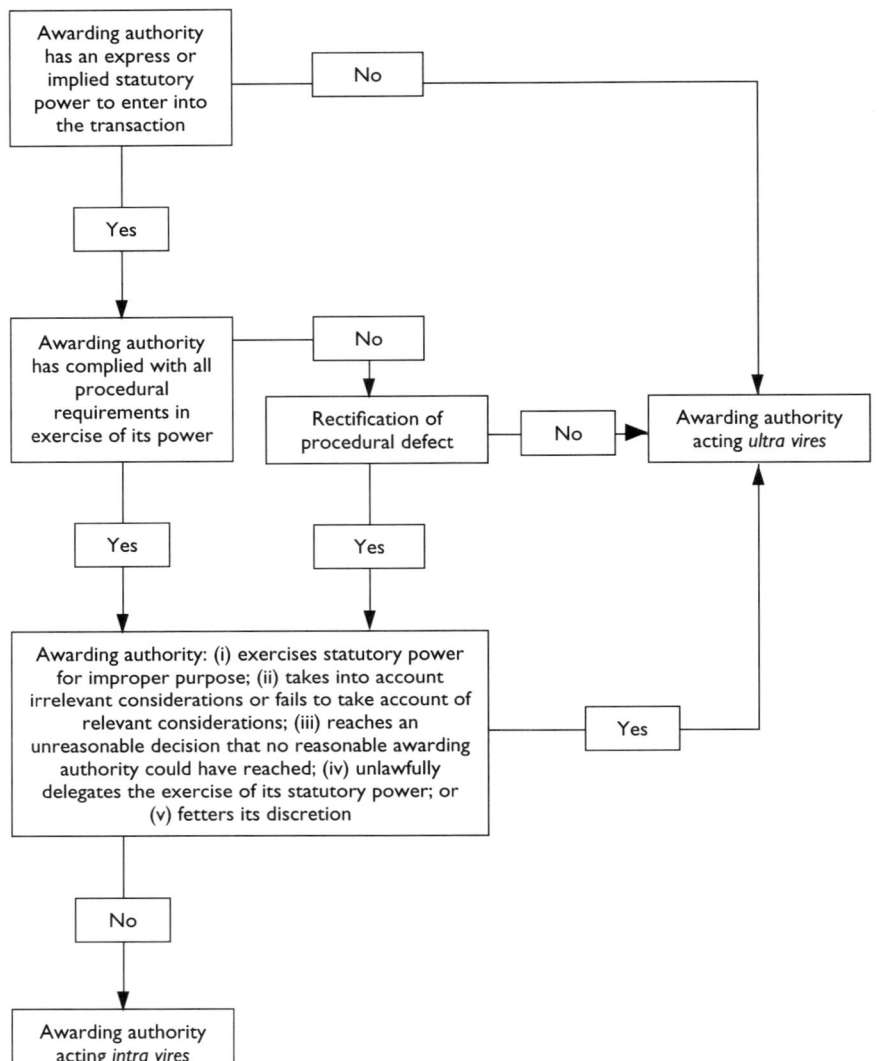

Illegality

4.2.2 Awarding authorities such as local authorities, health authorities and NHS trusts are creatures of statute. Their powers derive solely from the statute in question. Central government, ie the Crown and government ministers, may act under the Crown's prerogative, which confers unfettered legal power, but where legislation expressly or impliedly limits central government's powers in any sphere of activity, such legislation will constrain the activities of central government. Thus, if a public authority acts outside the scope of the wording of legislation, its act will be tainted by illegality.

Incidental powers

4.2.3 As a matter of statutory interpretation, a public body will have the power to do things which are reasonably incidental to its express statutory functions. This is apparent from *AG v Great Eastern Railway Company*.[1]

4.2.4 The relevance of implied incidental powers may be seen in the context of NHS trusts. NHS trusts encountered problems in the early development of the PFI in hospital projects, stemming mainly from the fact that the National Health Service and Community Care Act 1990 contains no express powers for NHS trusts to enter into PFI projects. In the absence of an express power, an NHS trust may seek to rely upon the incidental powers conferred by para 16 of Sch 2 to the 1990 Act,[2] which states:

> '(1) Subject to Schedule 3 to this Act, an NHS trust shall have power to do anything which appears to it to be necessary or expedient for the purpose of or in connection with the discharge of its functions, including in particular power:
>
> (a) to acquire and dispose of land and other property;
> (b) to enter into such contracts as seem to the trust to be appropriate;
> (c) to accept gifts of money, land or other property, including money, land or other property to be held on trust, either for the general or any specific purposes of the NHS trust or for all or any purposes relating to the health service; and
> (d) to employ staff on such terms as the trust thinks fit.
>
> (2) The reference in sub-paragraph (1)(c) above to specific purposes of the NHS trust includes a reference to the purposes of a specific hospital or other establishment or facility which is owned and managed by the trust.'

A similar provision arises in the context of local government PFI projects where the Local Government Act 1972, s 111(1) states:

> 'Without prejudice to any powers exerciseable apart from this section but subject to the provisions of this Act and any other enactment passed before or after this Act, a local authority shall have power to do any thing (whether or not involving the expenditure, borrowing or lending of money or the acquisition or disposal of any property or rights) which is calculated to facilitate, or is conducive or incidental to, the discharge of any of their functions.'

---

1 (1880) 5 App Cas 473. See also *Becker v Home Office* [1972] 2 All ER 676.
2 Although there is now specific legislation to deal with PFI (see **4.4.4–4.4.7**).

4.2.5 However, it is important to note the limitations on the ambit of incidental powers. This may be seen from the cases in the local government context. In *Hazell v Hammersmith and Fulham LBC*,[1] the banks accepted that local authorities had no express power to enter into a swap transaction but argued that swap transactions were within the scope of s 111(1). The House of Lords, however, found that the swaps transactions went beyond what was permitted by s 111. The usefulness of s 111(1) has been severely curtailed by *Hazell* and subsequent cases. Two of the key restrictions which emerge from the judgments are described below under the headings as 'sufficient nexus' and 'complete code'.

Sufficient nexus

4.2.6 There must be sufficient nexus between the function and the activity which is said to be incidental to it. For example, in *McCarthy & Stone (Developments) Ltd v Richmond upon Thames LBC*[2] the Council had passed a resolution that a charge of £25 be made for inquiries relating to speculative development proposals made by prospective purchasers of land or property. Under protest, *McCarthy & Stone* paid for two such consultations between themselves and the Council's planning officers prior to making formal applications for planning permission. They then sought judicial review of the Council's policy and a declaration that the Council had no power to charge the fees in question. The House of Lords held that a charge could not be made unless the power to charge for it is given by express words or by necessary implication. Those words impose a rigorous test going far beyond the proposition that it would be reasonable, conducive or incidental to charge for the provision of a service. Charging was incidental (ie unnecessary) to the power to give consultations, which was itself incidental to the Council's duty to deal with planning applications.

4.2.7 In *Credit Suisse v Waltham Forest LBC*,[3] the London Borough of Waltham Forest set up a joint venture with the National Leasing Finance Co Limited. The joint venture company purchased property with the benefit of a loan from Credit Suisse which was to be repaid through the proceeds of the rents and the eventual sale of the properties. Waltham Forest gave a guarantee to Credit Suisse to meet the amount of the loan. When property prices collapsed and the company could not meet the outstanding amount of the loan through disposals, Credit Suisse called on the guarantee. Hobhouse LJ held that the primary exercise of any power that existed under s 111 was setting up, and taking a shareholding in, the joint venture company. However, the grant of the guarantee and the indemnity were to facilitate the borrowing by the company at advantageous rates and these transactions were remote from the actual function of housing the homeless or the acquisition of housing for the purpose of providing accommodation. Hobhouse LJ concluded that they related to an exercise in property speculation on borrowed money and the needs of a trading company, not to the needs of the Council and the discharge of its functions.

---

1   [1992] 2 AC 1.
2   [1992] 2 AC 48.
3   [1996] 3 WLR 943.

4.2.8 These cases in the local government context demonstrate the difficulty of relying on the incidental powers in any PFI transaction, be they in the central government, local government or NHS sectors.

Complete code

4.2.9 A statutory regime may effectively preclude the transaction by providing a complete code which it is not possible to supplement by relying on s 111(1). The House of Lords in *Hazell* considered this issue. The Court found that the word 'functions' in s 111 embraced all the duties and powers of a local authority. Accordingly, a local authority could do anything calculated to facilitate or which is conducive or incidental to the local authority's function of borrowing. However, s 172 of the Local Government Act 1972 directed that Part 1 of Sch 13 'shall have effect with respect to the powers of local authorities to borrow and lend money and with respect to their funds'. The House of Lords found that Sch 13 established a comprehensive code which defined and limited the powers of a local authority with regard to its borrowing. Since there was a comprehensive code in Sch 13 there could not be additional incidental powers to enter into swap transactions.

Irrationality

4.2.10 There are various reasons why a decision by a public body may be invalid on the grounds of irrationality.

Wednesbury unreasonableness/perversity

4.2.11 *Wednesbury* unreasonableness arises where the power under which the decision-maker acts has been exercised perversely. The principle emerges from the judgment of Lord Greene MR in *Associated Provincial Picture Houses Ltd v Wednesbury Corporation*[1] who stated that a court would intervene if a decision was so unreasonable that no reasonable authority could ever come to it. Providing the terms of the proposed PFI contract are commercially sensible and represent the decision-maker's bona fide view of what is in the interests of the public sector party after taking appropriate advice, unreasonableness should not be an issue for PFI projects.

Relevant considerations

4.2.12 A second possible attack on the basis of irrationality is a failure to take account of a relevant consideration or taking into account an irrelevant consideration. It is more difficult to guard against this than against an attack based on *Wednesbury* unreasonableness and the parties to the transaction should take appropriate advice to minimise the risk of a finding that a relevant consideration has been ignored or an irrelevant consideration taken into account. The parties should look at the transaction from the awarding authority's viewpoint in the legal and commercial context and seek to ensure that all relevant legal and factual matters have been taken into account (and no irrelevant ones

---

1   [1948] 1 KB 223.

included) in, for example, those reports which formed the basis of the decision to enter into the PFI transaction.

Bad faith

4.2.13 A transaction with an awarding authority may be struck down where it was entered into in bad faith.

Improper purpose

4.2.14 An awarding authority should only act for proper purposes. This principle of administrative and local government law was reiterated by Neill LJ in *Allerdale* where it was held that the purpose of a scheme was to circumvent a local authority's borrowing limits and was therefore an improper purpose.

Unfairness amounting to abuse of power

4.2.15 This is an emerging head of public law invalidity coming, in particular, from tax cases. If the person or organisation dealing with an awarding authority 'puts his cards face upwards on the table' and is led to act to his detriment because of representations by the awarding authority, it may be an abuse of power for the awarding authority to resile from this position.[1] It would be surprising if this were to arise in the context of a PFI transaction.

Unlawful delegation

4.2.16 Where powers are entrusted to certain public bodies specifically, those powers may only be exercised by the body or officer on whom the power has been conferred, unless a delegation of the power is authorised (either by express words or by necessary implication). It is worth noting that powers are frequently conferred upon the 'Secretary of State' without naming his department. Under the provisions of the Interpretation Act 1978, the effect of not naming a department is that the powers are exercisable by any Secretary of State. In practice, the administration of each Secretary of State is confined to his own department, and the term 'Secretary of State' in any particular statutory context accordingly refers to the Secretary of State whose department normally deals with the subject-matter of the provision. The Treasury will also have to give its approval if the value of a PFI contract is in excess of departmental delegated limits. In the case of documents transferring an interest in land, it would be necessary to use the seal of each Secretary of State in whom land has been vested.

4.2.17 In the context of a PFI project involving central government, there are two possible means of delegation involved in a PFI contract: delegation of the Secretary of State's powers to a departmental official and delegation of the Secretary of State's or departmental official's powers to the project company. In relation to the former, strictly speaking there is no question of delegation but, rather, the official is acting as the alter ego of the Minister, under what is known as the Carltona principle.[2]

---

1   See for example *R v Inland Revenue Commissioners, ex p Unilever* [1996] STC 681.
2   See *Carltona v Commissioners of Works* [1943] 2 All ER 560.

4.2.18 The language of a statute can expressly limit the Minister's power to devolve or delegate and require him to exercise a power in person. However, in *Olahinde v Secretary of State for the Home Department*,[1] it was held that the Carltona principle was not merely an implication which would be read into a statute in the absence of any clear contrary indication, but was a common law constitutional principle, which could not be excluded by implication unless a challenge could be mounted on the basis that the decision to devolve authority was Wednesbury unreasonable. The exercise of powers conferred on the relevant Secretary of State by a departmental official is not likely to constitute unlawful delegation provided it does not conflict with or embarrass the departmental official in the discharge of his specific statutory duties under the relevant legislation.

4.2.19 The problem of the *vires* of delegation to a project company has been addressed in both local and central government by the enactment of the Deregulation and Contracting Out Act 1994 (the 'Contracting Out Act'). Section 69(1) of the Contracting Out Act states:

'This section applies to any function of a Minister or office holder:

(a) which is conferred by or under any enactment; and
(b) which, by virtue of any enactment or rule of law, may be exercised by an officer of his; and
(c) which is not excluded by section 71[2] below.'

Section 69(2) of the Contracting Out Act states:

'If a Minister by order so provides, a function to which this section applies may be exercised by, or by employees of, such person (if any) as may be authorised in that behalf by the office-holder or Minister whose function it is.'

4.2.20 Orders made under s 69 of the Contracting Out Act include the Contracting Out (Highway Functions) Order 1995, SI 1995/1986. This enables the Secretary of State for Transport to authorise another person, or that person's employees, to exercise functions conferred on him by or under the Highways Act 1980, the New Roads and Street Works Act 1991 and various other pieces of legislation. A typical PFI contract for a DBFO road therefore provides that the project company is authorised by the Secretary of State to exercise various functions conferred on the Secretary of State 'by or under' a series of provisions of the New Roads and Street Works Act 1991 and Regulations made under that Act.

4.2.21 In the context of local authorities, under s 101 of the 1972 Act, a local authority may arrange for the discharge of any of its functions by a committee, a sub-committee or an officer of the authority or by any other local authority (subject to certain express exceptions). However, it is not open to a local

---

1   [1991] 1 AC 254.
2   Section 71 excludes a function from s 69 (and s 70) if its exercise would constitute the exercise of jurisdiction of any court or tribunal, its exercise or failure to be exercised would interfere with an individual's liberty, it is a power or right of entry, search or seizure, or if it is a power or duty to make subordinate legislation. However, certain provisions, particularly those provisions relating to the enforcement of council tax, do not receive the benefit of s 71.

authority to delegate its functions to a company or any other third party unless expressly authorised to do so.[1]

Fettering of discretion

4.2.22 An awarding authority cannot act so as to fetter itself in the manner in which it discharges its functions in the future.[2] The concern in a PFI project is that an awarding authority cannot bind itself by long-term contracts in such a way as to fetter future executive action and the exercise of discretion. As a matter of construction, the freedom of awarding authorities to exercise their discretionary powers (derived either under statute or under common law) for the public good will never be impliedly excluded.[3] For an awarding authority to be deemed to be fettering its discretion, express wording must be included in the contract, having the effect that the contract can only be performed in such a way as to fetter the awarding authority's discretion, in which event the contract may be unenforceable.

4.2.23 As far as commercial contracts (including PFI project agreements) are concerned, it may in certain circumstances be held that an apparent 'fetter' is nothing more than consideration for the benefit the awarding authority is getting by virtue of that contract. Any contract is bound to be a fetter on future executive discretion in some way and all such provisions cannot be unenforceable. If they were, no party would be able to contract with any public authority with any degree of security and the capacity to contract would be inhibited to an intolerable degree. The nature of the fetter can, however, only be determined on a case-by-case basis.[4]

4.2.24 In PFI projects, care should be taken to ensure that aspects relating to land and building plans do not appear to fetter the discretion of the Secretary of State for the Environment, Transport and the Regions in relation to his planning functions (for example, to decide planning appeals). It will also be important to ensure that the PFI contract enables the public sector body to set outputs and vary them (thus retaining discretion and the ability to act in the public interest).

Fiduciary duty

4.2.25 There is authority for the proposition that a local authority owes fiduciary duties to the ratepayers (and presumably council tax payers).[5] Thus care should be taken when assessing the value for money of a PFI project from the local authority's viewpoint.

---

1 *Credit Suisse v Allerdale BC* [1997] QB 306.
2 See *Rederiaktiebolaget Amphitrite v The King* [1921] 3 KB 500 and *Commissioners of Crown Lands v Page* [1960] 2 QB 274.
3 *Commissioners of Crown Lands v Page*, above.
4 *The Birkdale District Electric Supply Co Ltd v Southport Corporation* [1926] AC 355.
5 See *Roberts v Hopwood* [1925] AC 578; *Bromley LBC v Greater London Council* [1983] 1 AC 768.

Procedural impropriety

4.2.26 Procedural impropriety relates to the express statutory procedures which must be complied with and also the rules of natural justice. In the context of local authorities, for example, it will be important to check that the awarding authority has complied with its own standing orders.[1]

4.2.27 In relation to NHS trusts, under s 5(7) of the 1990 Act, the Secretary of State may by regulation make general provision with respect to the chairman and directors of an NHS trust and their proceedings. Those regulations, the National Health Service Trusts (Membership and Procedure) Regulations 1990, SI 1990/2024, require trust boards to adopt standing orders, the content of which is determined by the board. Standing orders provide the framework for the conduct of the trust's business, such as provisions as to membership of the board, calling meetings, sealing of documents and declarations of interest. Standing Financial Instructions (or 'SFIs') are issued in accordance with financial directions issued by the Secretary of State under the provisions of ss 97A(3) and (9) of the National Health Service Act 1977 for the regulation of the conduct of the NHS trust in relation to financial matters. The project company (and its funders) will clearly be concerned to ensure compliance with all such procedural provisions.

4.3 LOCAL AUTHORITIES

Capital Finance Regulations[2]

4.3.1 A number of amendments have been made to the capital finance regime to encourage the use of PFI in the local authority sector. These amendments were reaffirmed by a consolidating statutory instrument which came into force on 1 April 1997: the Local Authorities (Capital Finance) Regulations 1997,[3] as subsequently amended. The aim of the particular regulation is that projects meeting PFI criteria require reduced or no credit cover,[4] depending on the precise circumstances, and in many cases may also attract revenue support from central government.

4.3.2 Regulation 16 (as amended by the Local Authorities (Capital Finance) (Amendment) Regulations 1998)[5] sets out a definition of a 'private finance transaction': namely a contract under which the private sector provides the local authority with an asset for use by the authority in connection with the discharge of its normal functions. The regulation places no restriction on the nature of any interest the authority may have in the property or when this may be acquired. The contract must provide for variable payments by the authority (which must

---

1 But see **4.3.9**.
2 This is an extensive topic in its own right, a detailed examination of which is beyond the scope of this chapter. The Department of the Environment, Transport and the Regions has produced various guides summarising their regulations – see the Bibliography.
3 SI 1997/319.
4 Credit cover is defined in the Local Government and Housing Act 1989, s 50(3) and comprises permitted borrowings under a credit approval, certain available capital receipts or available revenues.
5 SI 1998/371.

be determined in set ways) and the scale of these variable payments can only be changed in accordance with strict conditions.

4.3.3 Other regulations of particular relevance to PFI transactions include reg 40 which applies to full-scale DBFO schemes involving a considerable degree of 'risk transfer' to the private sector, and its effect, provided its conditions are met, is to reduce to nil the initial cost of the credit arrangement, thus eliminating altogether the need for credit cover. Similarly, regs 41 and 42 provide for an abatement of credit cover in the case of buildings which are either replacement buildings (reg 41) or buildings which are additional to existing stock (reg 42). A similar scheme is also provided for in the context of local authority heating and lighting systems (regs 43 to 45).

Safe harbour provisions for lending to local authorities

4.3.4 Protections exist for third parties transacting with local authorities in certain circumstances. Section 44(6) of the 1989 Act provides:

> 'A person lending money to a local authority shall not be bound to enquire whether the authority have power to borrow the money and shall not be prejudiced by the absence of any such power.'

This provision provides a lender with a 'safe harbour' from any want of power in relation to borrowing transactions. It was not sufficient to afford protection in *Hazell* where the House of Lords held that swaps entered into between the London Borough of Hammersmith and Fulham and the bank were not covered by corresponding provisions of the Local Government Act 1972 (which were replaced by s 44(6) of the 1989 Act) and were *ultra vires* and void.

4.3.5 In May 1997, the Department of the Environment, Transport and the Regions released a discussion note entitled *Protecting Parties to Local Authority Contracts: possible safe harbour provisions*. Although the Department reiterated that it had no reason to believe that partnership contracts associated with the delivery of core local services were outside authorities' powers, it recognised that the private sector parties would wish their interests to be protected in the unlikely event that a contract were found to be unlawful for the authority. Consequently, it offered for discussion a 'safe harbour' option. This initiative led to the Local Government (Contracts) Act 1997.

The Local Government (Contracts) Act 1997

4.3.6 The Local Government (Contracts) Act 1997 (the '1997 Act') came into force on 30 December 1997. It seeks to provide protection to parties entering into financing contracts with local authorities and it is particularly designed to encourage PFI transactions with local authorities.

4.3.7 The Act sets out the basic power of local authorities to enter into principal PFI contracts (ie 'provision contracts') and direct agreements with project financiers.[1] Under s 1, it is only statutory provisions 'conferring or imposing a function on a local authority' which confer power on the local authority to enter

---

1   1997 Act, s 1(1) and (2). See Chapter 9 for a discussion of direct agreements.

into a 'provision contract'. Accordingly, the 1997 Act is unlikely to have any application in relation to PFI transactions based on the fulfilment by the local authority of any implied functions. Further, the 1997 Act does not empower local authorities to enter into contracts or agreements (other than direct agreements) which are ancillary to the main provision contract. Section 1 refers to discharge of the relevant function 'by the local authority'. It does not therefore address the specific issue of whether or not a PFI transaction is *ultra vires* by reason of the improper delegation by the local authority of its functions to the private sector. It is still necessary to look carefully at the legislation under which those statutory functions are conferred, to ensure that delegation is possible.

4.3.8 The objective of the 1997 Act is not to remove the issue of *ultra vires* completely but rather to seek to ensure that the private sector is adequately compensated for the setting aside of *ultra vires* contracts. The private sector's main source of comfort is therefore contained in the remainder of the 1997 Act, which deals with the treatment of certified contracts.

4.3.9 The 1997 Act provides that certified contracts have effect, or are deemed always to have had effect, as if the local authority had power to enter into them and exercised such power properly in doing so, ie certified contracts are deemed to be *intra vires*.[1] This deeming provision does not operate so as to prevent questions being raised on judicial or audit review.[2]

4.3.10 Certified contracts are contracts relating to 'the provision or making available of services ... for the purposes of, or in connection with, the discharge by the local authority of any of its functions'[3] and which operate or are intended to operate for a period of at least five years. They also include contracts entered into (in connection with such a contract) with a person who makes a loan to or provides any form of finance for a party to that contract (other than the local authority) or any insurer of or trustee for such a person.[4] The consequence of this wide definition is that most contracts connected with PFI projects will be covered.

4.3.11 The certification requirements are laid out in s 3 of the 1997 Act and in associated regulations (the Local Authorities (Contracts) Regulations 1997)[5] A local authority must ensure that a copy of every certificate issued by it is given to each person with whom the authority has entered, or is to enter, into the contract in relation to which the certificate is issued.[6]

4.3.12 Although the 1997 Act allows public law rights of challenge, that is, the judicial and audit review of contracts entered into by local authorities,[7] it provides a fallback aimed at protecting the position of the private sector party where, on such a review, it is found that the local authority did not have the

---

1   1997 Act, s 2(1).
2   1997 Act, ss 2(6) and 5.
3   1997 Act, s 4(3).
4   1997 Act, s 4(4).
5   SI 1997/2862.
6   Ibid, reg 3.
7   1997 Act, s 5.

necessary powers to enter into a particular contract. It provides for what are called 'relevant discharge terms'.[1] These are contractual pre-agreements relating to what is to happen if a certified contract is subsequently struck down by public law challenge. The legislation seeks to preserve the enforceabiltity of these 'relevant discharge terms' even where, on judicial or audit review, a local authority is declared to be acting *ultra vires*.

4.3.13 Even the lack of such relevant discharge terms is not the end of the statutory protection. Where a court determines or orders that the certified contract does not have effect and no relevant discharge terms exist (or are themselves set aside), the innocent counterparty to the contract is entitled to be compensated as if the contract had been terminated by reason of repudiation by the local authority.[2] The 1997 Act attempts to provide protection to the private sector from the consequences of the *ultra vires* acts of local authorities in every scenario. Although it must be borne in mind that, as a matter of principle, it is impossible to oust judicial review[3] and that until the courts have considered the efficacy of the provisions seeking to protect the private sector there will remain residual doubts as to whether they provide complete protection, it would be surprising if this proves to be a problem in practice.

4.4 NHS TRUSTS AS STATUTORY BODIES AND THEIR STATUTORY INSTRUMENTS

4.4.1 NHS trusts are statutory bodies constituted under the National Health Service and Community Care Act 1990. Section 5(1) of the 1990 Act gives the Secretary of State power to establish NHS trusts by statutory instrument:

'(a) to assume responsibility, in accordance with this Act, for the ownership and management of hospitals or other establishments or facilities which were previously managed or provided by Health Authorities or Special Health Authorities; or
(b) to provide and manage hospitals or other establishments or facilities.'

Under s 5(5)(b) of the Act, every NHS trust has the functions conferred on it by its constituting statutory instrument and by Sch 2 to the 1990 Act. A typical statutory instrument creating an NHS trust provided that the trust was established for the purpose specified in s 5(1)(a) of the 1990 Act and, for example, the trust's functions in relation to acute services were to own and manage hospital accommodation and services provided at one or more specific named hospital sites.

4.4.2 There were two main areas of difficulty with the typical statutory instrument. First, the trust was stated to be established under s 5(1)(a) of the 1990 Act. The wording of that subsection seemed to be confined to the ownership and management of existing hospitals, establishments and facilities. It was thought that this would probably not authorise the trust to develop (or procure the

---

1   1997 Act, s 6.
2   1997 Act, s 7.
3   See *Anisminic v FCC* [1969] 2 AC 147.

development of) completely new facilities. Secondly, the typical establishment order stated that the functions of the NHS trust were to own and manage hospital accommodation and services at specific sites, impliedly excluding every other site from such provision.

4.4.3 Typical amendments to the establishment orders of NHS trusts were that the trust was established for the purpose specified in s 5(1)(b) of the Act and that the trust's functions were to provide and manage hospital accommodation and services at any of the existing hospitals, any new site identified for the PFI project and any other premises for the time being associated with any of those hospitals. Some PFI projects will involve the disposal of surplus land owned by the trust. It may be that this land only becomes surplus during the development phase. An establishment order which lists, as one of the NHS trust's functions, ownership or provision of hospital accommodation at a specified site (which is later to become surplus) gives rise to a problem. The NHS trust will require power at the outset of the project to sell the land as and when it becomes surplus. However, if its function at that point is to provide hospital accommodation at that site it cannot also contract to sell it. The solution is to seek an amendment to the establishment order removing a reference to the specific site and relying on the wording relating to premises for the time being associated with the main hospital.

The National Health Service (Private Finance) Act 1997

4.4.4 In the early days of the development of PFI projects in the NHS, certain fundamental issues of concern were identified and the opinion of leading counsel was sought on several occasions. One issue related to the covenant strength of an NHS trust and was addressed by the National Health Service (Residual Liabilities) Act 1996. The other related to the power of an NHS trust to enter into a PFI transaction. This issue was of acute concern to the funders of the project company. The consequences of an NHS trust lacking the requisite power were catastrophic and, based on their experience of the local authority cases discussed above, not merely a theoretical risk. Even though opinion was divided on whether there was a problem, the mere existence of doubt was enough to convince the government of the need for legislation.[1] The result was the National Health Service (Private Finance) Act 1997 (the '1997 NHS Act').

4.4.5 Section 1(1) of the 1997 NHS Act provides that the powers of an NHS trust include power to enter into 'externally financed development agreements'. Section 1(2) provides that an agreement is an externally financed development agreement if it is certified as such in writing by the Secretary of State. Section 1(3) provides that the Secretary of State may give such a certificate if:

'(a) in his opinion the purpose or main purpose of the agreement is the provision of facilities in connection with the discharge by the trust of any of its functions; and
(b) a person proposes to make a loan to, or provide any form of finance to, another party in connection with the agreement.'

---

1 It should be noted that counsel's opinion had been obtained in relation to the local authority cases that there was not an *ultra vires* problem.

4.4.6 Unfortunately, the wording of the 1997 NHS Act has given rise to a number of problems of interpretation. For example, many PFI projects are documented using a number of separate agreements. It may be that, on its construction, the main purpose of an individual project document is not the provision of facilities but, for example, the documentation of the applicable payment mechanism. On a strict interpretation of the 1997 NHS Act, such a project document might not be certifiable *per se*. For this reason, NHS PFI projects tend to be documented in one agreement. Another problem may arise where it proves necessary to make amendments to a project document in respect of which a certificate has been given. Since the 1997 NHS Act does not provide for the certificate to cover amendments made after the date of the certificate, it may be necessary to seek recertification of the whole document, however minor the amendments.

4.4.7 There are significant differences in the approach of the 1997 NHS Act and the Local Government (Contracts) Act 1997. The former merely addresses issues of illegality by certification of a transaction as an externally financed development agreement (which the trust has power to enter into). The 1997 NHS Act does not assist if the complaint is that a PFI project is tainted by irrationality. By contrast, the local government legislation addresses the issue of irrationality and, although it remains to be seen how effective the concept of upholding relevant discharge terms will prove to be, there is at least an attempt to protect those who contract with local authorities from an attack based on irrationality.

Chapter 5

THE TENDERING PROCESS AND TENDERING DOCUMENTATION

5.1 INTRODUCTION

5.1.1 Choosing the appropriate tender process is a key issue for the awarding authority to address early in the PFI process. This chapter aims to examine some key issues which the awarding authority will need to address when conducting a tender process for the procurement of a PFI project and the documentation required to give effect to and facilitate the tender process. It also looks at the potential concerns of private sector tenderers involved in bidding for PFI projects.

5.1.2 This chapter focuses on the formal tender process which should be implemented once the awarding authority has made the decision to pursue a PFI option. It does not address the preliminary steps[1] preceding a formal tender process which need to be undertaken in order for an awarding authority to make a decision as to whether to pursue a PFI option.

5.2 INITIAL CONSIDERATIONS

Application of the Regulations on public procurement

5.2.1 Once it has been decided that a PFI option should be pursued and an outline business case has been completed, the key question which needs to be addressed is whether the particular project falls within the Public Sector Regulations which govern public procurement. Chapter 3 deals in detail with this. In most instances, the Public Sector Regulations will apply and, therefore, govern the way in which a tender process is structured and conducted.

Choice of procedure[2]

5.2.2 As discussed in Chapter 3, existing PFI guidelines[3] recognise that the negotiated procedure is the most appropriate means of procuring the majority of PFI projects. This allows an awarding authority to seek the views and tap the ideas of the private sector at various stages of the tender process on an iterative basis. With each iteration, an awarding authority should be able to define its

---

1 For example, the carrying out of an option appraisal and preparation of an outline business case.
2 Chapter 3 describes each of these different types of procedure and the rules which dictate the particular procedure which an awarding authority may adopt.
3 Technical Note No 2 *How to Follow EC Procurement Procedure and Advertise in the OJEC* (Treasury Taskforce) June 1998.

requirements with greater clarity and with a better understanding of the private sector's concerns. This in turn should enable tenderers to ensure that they are using the correct building blocks to develop their proposals as they move through each stage of the tender process.

Competition and value for money

5.2.3 The competitive procurement process is not driven wholly by the requirements of the Public Sector Regulations. Competition in the procurement process forms an integral part of PFI philosophy. It is one of several means of ensuring that PFI solutions provide value for money. Existing PFI guidelines recommend the limited use of a non-competitive approach to procuring projects.[1] This, coupled with the narrow grounds justifying the non-competitive procurement of public contracts under the Public Sector Regulations, means that it is rare for PFI projects to be procured without resorting to some form of competition.

5.3 TENDER PROCESS

Summary

5.3.1 For the reasons outlined above, the vast majority of PFI projects will be procured under the competitive version of the negotiated procedure provided for under the Public Sector Regulations. The remainder of this chapter will, therefore, focus on the tender process and documents that will typically be used when implementing that procedure in the procurement of a PFI project. This process is summarised in the table below. Detailed explanations of each step in the process are provided in the remaining sections of this chapter.

Maintaining a level playing field

5.3.2 In conducting any tender process, an awarding authority must abide by the principle of equal treatment of bidders which lies at the heart of the EU regime on public procurement; an awarding authority will be subject to an over-arching duty to maintain an unbiased non-discriminatory and truly competitive environment. This principle is not confined to the procurement of projects falling within the Public Sector Regulations. The need to maintain an objective and non-discriminatory tender process is also important in minimising the risk of legal challenges to an awarding authority's decisions on traditional administrative law grounds.[2]

---

1   *A Step by Step Guide to the PFI Procurement Process* (Treasury Taskforce) April 1998.
2   See Chapter 6.

Table 5: Tender process

Stage	Phase	Summary	Paragraph
1	Prior Publicity	– interested parties invited to submit expressions of interest	5.4
2	Pre-qualification	– interested parties invited to provide pre-qualification responses – responses evaluated and pre-qualified parties selected to proceed to next phase	5.5
3	Clarification and Negotiations	– pre-qualified parties (ie tenderers) invited to participate in clarification exercise and/or commence negotiations – conduct of negotiations and clarification exercise – (possibly) interim bid submissions	5.6
4	Final Bid Evaluation	– point at which negotiations cease and bids are evaluated	5.7
5	Selection of Preferred Tenderer	– party submitting most economically advantageous proposal selected to implement project – continuing negotiations with preferred tenderer culminating in commercial and financial close	5.7

5.4 PRIOR PUBLICITY[1]

5.4.1 The formal tender process usually begins with the advertisement of the project. The Public Sector Regulations require projects being procured under the negotiated procedure to be advertised across the EU through the publication of notices in the Official Journal of the European Communities. Essentially, the Regulations require an awarding authority to publish three notices:

– a prior information notice which gives no more than an indication of an awarding authority's intention to seek expressions of interest;
– a contract notice which opens the project to competition by calling upon interested candidates to apply to participate in the tender process; and
– a contract award notice once the contract has been let.

---

1   See **3.3.12–3.3.20**.

5.4.2 In addition to publishing these notices in the Official Journal, an awarding authority may wish to publicise the project through other means such as advertising in the national press or relevant trade periodicals. An awarding authority should ensure that any additional advertisements placed are phrased in a manner consistent with the notices placed in the Official Journal.

5.4.3 Projects falling outside the Public Sector Regulations need not be advertised in the Official Journal. Nonetheless, if they are to be competitively procured, some form of publicity will be required in order to generate a sufficient level of competitive interest in the projects. There are no hard and fast rules as to how these projects should be publicised and public sector bodies usually have their own internal procurement rules and policies which govern how these projects should be advertised. However, as a general rule, any publicity material (for example, trade journal or newspaper advertisements) inviting expressions of interest should be drafted in a similar fashion to a contract notice placed in the Official Journal.

5.5 PRE-QUALIFICATION

Dealing with expressions of interest

5.5.1 After receiving expressions of interest, an awarding authority will move on to the pre-qualification stage of the tender process by issuing a pre-qualification document to interested parties inviting them to submit further information about themselves. There are two ways in which an awarding authority may approach the pre-qualification stage:

– it may begin the culling process at the first hurdle so that only a select number of interested parties are invited to provide pre-qualification responses; or
– it may invite *all* parties submitting expressions of interest to provide pre-qualification responses.

5.5.2 If an awarding authority is intending to adopt the first approach, it should make its intention clear when advertising for expressions of interest in the project. The problem with this approach, however, is that interested parties are unlikely to provide a consistent level of information as to their technical capabilities and economic standing[1] when submitting their initial expressions of interest. There will, therefore, be an element of pre-judgment involved in any selection process undertaken at such an early stage.

5.5.3 Ultimately, the first of the two options outlined above involves an awarding authority having to bear some risk (however small) of challenges to any decision to exclude parties from submitting pre-qualification responses. The second approach outlined above is, therefore, usually preferable. In any event, the field of interested parties is likely to go through a natural culling process once further information about the project is released. For instance, there may be

---

1   The Public Sector Regulations only permit an awarding authority to assess candidates' technical capability and economic standing. See **3.3.26**.

parties who are only interested in isolated aspects of a project (for example, the IT aspects or equipment provision). Those parties may have expressed their interests in the project in their individual capacities, but may subsequently seek to pre-qualify as part of a multi-disciplinary consortium of companies. Parties may also refrain from submitting pre-qualification responses if they decide that the project is too large or complex for their resources.

Pre-qualification document

5.5.4 Interested parties are usually invited to apply for pre-qualification by way of a pre-qualification document. This document serves two primary purposes:

- it should aid the process of natural selection described at **5.5.1** by providing sufficient information about the project to enable interested parties to decide whether they have the appropriate resources and expertise to pursue the project; and
- it will be the means by which an awarding authority will seek information from parties wishing to pre-qualify as to their economic standing and technical capability.

5.5.5 A pre-qualification document should, therefore, contain information such as:

- background information about the awarding authority, its functions, and its project management/advisory teams;
- background information about the project including the strategic and political context within which it is being promoted;
- an outline of the intended scope of the project;
- a projected timetable for the procurement programme including, in particular, a deadline for the submission of pre-qualification responses and an expected date by which parties will be informed of their success or failure to pre-qualify;
- a brief explanation of the tender process leading up to the selection of the preferred tenderer;
- the criteria against which parties will be pre-qualified to proceed to the next stage of the tender process;
- a clear statement of the information which parties seeking to pre-qualify will be required to provide in their pre-qualification responses;
- a simple procedure and the awarding authority's points of contact for dealing with any queries which parties may have about the project or any information with which they have been provided; and
- general terms and conditions of the pre-qualification exercise.

5.5.6 The level of detailed information which an awarding authority needs to impart at the pre-qualification stage will vary from project to project but a balance needs to be struck in all cases. On the one hand, sufficient information should be provided to enable interested parties to gauge the scale and complexity of the project and to respond with adequate information for the awarding authority to carry out its evaluation of the pre-qualification responses. On the other hand, an awarding authority will need to avoid overloading candidates with unnecessary information requests at this stage. For instance, it should not be necessary for a pre-qualification document to include output specifications or risk allocation matrices for the project (even in draft); the Public Sector Regulations do not permit candidates to be evaluated for proposals as to technical solutions or risk allocation at the pre-qualification phase. A general outline of the scope of the project should give interested parties a sufficient indication of the scale and complexity of the project. Indeed, the inclusion of unnecessary information within the pre-qualification document could detract from the usefulness of the document as a marketing tool.

Evaluating pre-qualification responses[1]

5.5.7 The primary function of the evaluation exercise to be conducted at the pre-qualification stage is for the awarding authority to verify that candidates satisfy its minimum requirements as regards financial standing and technical capability. The awarding authority will need to ensure that interested parties respond with a sufficient and consistent level of information to enable it to carry out its pre-qualification evaluation exercise. A common means of addressing this concern is for candidates to be supplied with pre-qualification questionnaires which set out a standard format for the provision of pre-qualification responses and supporting information. It is important for the awarding authority to ensure that the questions asked of candidates sit squarely with the criteria against which candidates' responses will be evaluated. It is equally important for the awarding authority to ensure that it asks the appropriate questions of the appropriate parties. The problem here is that parties often seek to pre-qualify as consortia of companies comprising, for instance, special purpose project companies, building contractors, service providers, equity financiers and advisers. The awarding authority will need to ensure that each member of each consortium provides the appropriate level and type of information to enable it to carry out its pre-qualification evaluation.

5.5.8 The burden on the awarding authority to develop its own pre-qualification questionnaires will be lifted once the Taskforce issues its standard form questionnaire in response to the recommendations of the Bates Review.[2] A standardisation of approach would also ease the private sector's burden of having to navigate round a multitude of variations on the same theme.

5.5.9 The procurement rules under the Public Sector Regulations prescribe in some detail the factors which may be taken into account for the purposes of the pre-qualification evaluation exercise. An awarding authority procuring a project which falls within the Public Sector Regulations must, therefore, be guided by those Regulations as to the bases upon which it evaluates candidates and the information it takes into consideration when carrying out such an evaluation.

5.5.10 Although the Public Sector Regulations prescribe the specific factors which an awarding authority is entitled to evaluate and the information which the authority is entitled to consider (technical capability and financial standing)

---

1 See also **3.3.24–3.3.28**.
2 See **3.3.27**.

they do not prescribe any methodology for the qualitative assessment of those criteria. Indeed, the Regulations do not give any guidance as to the relative importance which should be ascribed to each of the two evaluation criteria. The awarding authority therefore has some discretion to devise its own systems and methods (including scoring devices and weighting mechanisms) for evaluating candidates' technical capability and financial standing. An awarding authority is not required to draw comparisons between the pre-qualification responses. However, awarding authorities commonly adopt evaluation methodologies to compare the candidates' relative level of general competence by measuring the *extent* to which each candidate satisfies the pre-qualification criteria. The candidates are then ranked according to how best they satisfy those requirements.

5.5.11 By the end of the evaluation exercise an awarding authority must be in a position to:

- identify candidates which fail to meet its minimum pre-qualification requirements for further participation in the tender process; and
- select (from the remaining candidates that have satisfied its minimum pre-qualification requirements) an appropriate number of tenderers to proceed to the negotiations phase of the tender process.

5.5.12 Achieving the second of these objectives presents little difficulty where only a limited number of candidates (say, three or four) has managed to satisfy the awarding authority's minimum pre-qualification requirements. Where, however, a larger number of candidates meets the awarding authority's minimum criteria, the awarding authority may select those candidates that best meet the pre-qualification criteria. Alternatively, it could invite *all* the candidates that have met its pre-qualification criteria to participate in a two-stage negotiations process.[11]

Debriefing unsuccessful candidates

5.5.13 Unsuccessful candidates may request a debriefing from the awarding authority. An awarding authority is obliged to provide reasons for not pre-qualifying candidates, although awarding authorities are normally circumspect about the debriefing process so as to minimise the risk of providing information that could lead to their decision being challenged by unsuccessful candidates.

Re-evaluation

5.5.14 Existing PFI guidelines[2] recommend that once the pre-qualification exercise has been completed, an awarding authority should not have to re-evaluate a pre-qualified party's general technical competence or financial strength unless new information emerges which gives the awarding authority reason to doubt its original assessment. A re-evaluation may be required where,

---

1   *See* **5.6.5–5.6.8**.
2   *Step by Step Guide to the PFI Procurement Process* (Treasury Taskforce) April 1998.

for instance, a pre-qualified consortium decides to alter the make-up of the consortium. The general competence of that consortium could be adversely affected if the proposed change involved, say, the withdrawal of a key consortium member (for example, the main provider of equity finance or the building contractor). An awarding authority should, therefore, require all pre-qualified consortia to give it prior notice of any proposals to change their consortium structures.

5.6 THE NEGOTIATIONS PHASE

Structuring the negotiations phase

5.6.1 The awarding authority will have to make an early decision as to how the negotiations phase of the tender process should be structured. The matters which an awarding authority will need to consider include:

- the number of tenderers that should be pre-qualified to participate in the negotiations phase;
- the number of interim steps tenderers should be required to undertake prior to the submission of their final bids; and
- the work packages tenderers are required to deliver at each step in the process.

The factors which the awarding authority should take into account when addressing these issues are outlined in the remainder of this section.

Bid costs

5.6.2 The awarding authority must be mindful of private sector concerns over bid costs. The amount of work required of bidders must be proportionate to the value of the project and the number of bidders pre-qualified. As a rule, the larger the field of competition, the less individual tenderers will be prepared to put at risk.

Number of tenderers

5.6.3 To an extent, the number of parties selected to participate in the negotiations phase will depend on the number of candidates applying for pre-qualification. An awarding authority may not, therefore, be able to make a firm decision as to the number of tenderers it should include in the negotiations phase until the outcome of the pre-qualification exercise is known. It should, however, be able to form a view, based on early market soundings and the experiences of others on similar projects, as to the number of candidates likely to be interested in seeking pre-qualification. It should, therefore, be able to develop a strategy (albeit provisional) for the negotiations phase based on the number of tenderers it would expect to involve.

5.6.4 Ultimately, an awarding authority's flexibility with regard to selecting an appropriate number of tenderers may be fairly restricted. Under the Public

Sector Regulations, an awarding authority must pre-qualify a minimum of three tenderers to participate in the negotiations phase of the project (assuming, of course, that there are at least three candidates that satisfy the authority's minimum pre-qualification requirements). It should also be noted that the Bates Review recommends 'a reduction in the number of bidders – compulsorily to a maximum of four'. The Treasury Taskforce's *A Step by Step Guide to the PFI Procurement Process* recommends that 'the final tender list ... be limited to the least number of contenders needed to ensure genuine competition. In general, this would be three, or at most four'. A two-stage negotiations phase (discussed below) would not appear to be precluded provided that no more than four short-listed tenderers are selected to make full and final bids.

Number of stages

5.6.5 There are two basic approaches to structuring the negotiations phase of a project. These approaches (together with examples of each approach) are summarised in the table below.

Table 6: Structuring the negotiations phase

Approach	Summary	Examples
OPTION 1: 'Single Stage'	The preferred tenderer is selected from the original short-list of pre-qualified tenderers; there is no intermediate point in the process at which the original field of short-listed tenderers is culled.	EXAMPLE 1 – three tenderers are pre-qualified to negotiate – invitation to negotiate issued – after a period of negotiations, all three tenderers submit fully costed proposals – clarification of bids and further negotiations – awarding authority selects the most economically advantageous bid EXAMPLE 2 – four tenderers are pre-qualified to negotiate – invitation to negotiate issued – after an initial negotiation period, all four tenderers make interim submissions – awarding authority revises its requirements in response to interim submissions – revised invitation to negotiate (or, invitation to tender) issued

Approach	Summary	Examples
		– (possibly) further negotiations – all four tenderers submit fully costed proposals based on authority's revised requirements – awarding authority selects most economically advantageous bid
OPTION 2: 'Two Stage'	Following pre-qualification, a long-list of pre-qualified tenderers is drawn up. At an intermediate point in the process, a short-list of tenderers is chosen from the previous long-list of tenderers. The preferred tenderer is selected from the subsequent short-list.	EXAMPLE 1 – four tenderers are pre-qualified to negotiate – invitation to negotiate issued – after a period of initial (and limited) negotiations, all four tenderers submit initial bids – awarding authority selects two out of the four tenderers to proceed with further negotiations and excludes the other two from further participation in the process – after secondary negotiations, the two tenderers left in the competition submit 'best and final' bids – awarding authority selects the most economically advantageous bid
		EXAMPLE 2 – five tenderers are pre-qualified to negotiate – invitation to negotiate (or invitation to submit outline proposals) issued – after a period of limited negotiations, all five tenderers submit outline proposals or interim bids – awarding authority short-lists three out of the five tenderers to proceed with tender process and excludes the other two from further participation in the process

Approach	Summary	Examples
		– awarding authority revises its requirements in response to interim submissions and negotiates more extensively with the three short-listed tenderers
		– revised invitation to negotiate (or, invitation to tender) issued
		– all three short-listed tenderers submit fully costed proposals based on authority's revised requirements
		– awarding authority selects most economically advantageous bid

5.6.6 The legality of the two-stage tender process (Option 2) is explored at **3.3.39** to **3.3.44**. An advantage of this approach (and, indeed, a single-stage approach involving interim submissions) is that the awarding authority may be able to secure more detailed and tailored bids than in a single-stage tender and maximise the negotiating position it has during the competitive phase of the tender process.

5.6.7 The two-stage approach could also be useful in the procurement of a particularly complex or novel project. For instance, a project may be so technically complex that an awarding authority could only justifiably enter into detailed negotiations with tenderers that possess the specific technical competence to deal with the particular circumstances of the project. The Public Sector Regulations do not allow the awarding authority to evaluate candidates' proposals relating to the implementation of the particular project at the pre-qualification stage. An awarding authority could, therefore, require all pre-qualified tenderers to submit outline technical proposals at an interim stage in the negotiations process. Once those proposals are assessed, a limited number of tenderers that satisfy (or best satisfy) the authority's minimum technical requirements could then be short-listed to continue negotiating with the authority.

5.6.8 Another example of when a two-stage approach could be appropriate is where in terms of satisfying an awarding authority's pre-qualification criteria the difference between a relatively large number of pre-qualified parties (say, four) is marginal but the awarding authority only has sufficient resources to pursue full scale negotiations with a limited number of tenderers (say, two).

Interim submissions and changing requirements

5.6.9 An awarding authority may require formal interim submissions to be made whether or not those interim submissions are intended to be used by the authority to reduce the field of tenderers. In other words, an awarding authority could also require tenderers to make interim submissions as part of a single-stage approach to the negotiations phase (Option 1). These formal submissions could be used to establish a basis upon which to commence negotiations. An awarding authority could also use tenderers' interim submissions to test the viability of the original assumptions underlying its requirements. If necessary, the authority could then refine its requirements in response to the concerns and issues which emerge from the tenderers' interim submissions. However, an awarding authority must ensure that any refinements to its requirements made during the course of the tender process do not take the scheme beyond the boundaries of the project as originally advertised in the Official Journal and also that the commercial confidentiality of tenderers' submissions is observed.

5.6.10 Ultimately, an awarding authority will want to end up with a realistic set of requirements against which tenderers can submit affordable proposals that meet those requirements and represent value for money. The feedback which tenderers give during the course of the negotiations phase can be instrumental in achieving this objective. This feedback can be sought and given in a variety of ways (for example, formal presentations by tenderers; face to face discussions or negotiations) but the certainty attached to formal written submissions makes them a particularly useful way of gauging tenderers' ideas and concerns.

Setting realistic targets

5.6.11 The disadvantage of requiring tenderers to make formal submissions is that these will add to their bid costs. An awarding authority should, therefore, take a reasonable approach to:

- the number of formal submissions which tenderers will be required to make during the course of the tender process;
- the matters and issues which need to be addressed in each formal submission; and
- the way in which formal submissions are required to be made.

ITN

5.6.12 At the commencement of the negotiations phase, the awarding authority will need to issue a package of tender documentation to the tenderers that have pre-qualified. This chapter refers to this documentation as the Invitation to Negotiate ('ITN'). The typical key contents of an ITN are outlined below.

Output specification

5.6.13 The awarding authority will need to set out its requirements for a project in output terms. With projects that involve both a construction and a services element, the output specification(s) often comprise two separate elements: a design and works specification and a services specification. Guidelines[1] exist as to how these should be drafted but the key principle for the awarding authority to bear in mind when specifying its requirements is that it should avoid being overly prescriptive; tenderers must be given sufficient scope to be innovative.

Key constraints

5.6.14 Although the awarding authority should allow as much room for innovative solutions as possible, its particular circumstances may be such that there are immutable restrictions on the scope of the project. For instance, the awarding authority may have to be located at a particular site or it may not be permitted (say, for security reasons) to outsource certain services. These necessary restrictions on the solutions which tenderers may propose should, therefore, be clearly articulated.

Commercial terms

5.6.15 The awarding authority will need to provide tenderers with its intended approach to risk allocation. This may be done in a variety of ways ranging from the provision of a matrix outlining the risk profile, through to the provision of detailed draft contracts. Much will depend on the negotiating strategy which the awarding authority intends to adopt.[2] As has already been mentioned, the awarding authority should bear in mind that tenderers may not be prepared to incur a large amount of legal costs in undertaking a detailed review of full draft contracts in the early stages of the tender process, particularly if there is a wide field of competition. It may be more appropriate for 'heads of terms' to be issued as part of initial ITN documentation provided to tenderers and for full draft contracts to be introduced at a later stage before final bids are submitted. However, the move toward standardised or model contracts (led by the Bates Review)[3] should eventually reduce the burden of this part of the tender process.

Evaluation criteria

5.6.16 The criteria against which tenderers' submissions will be evaluated should be clearly stated.[4] If a two-stage approach to the negotiations phase is adopted, tenderers should be informed of the criteria against which their submissions for each stage will be evaluated.

Terms and conditions

5.6.17 An awarding authority will need to set out clear guidelines and instructions as to the conduct of the negotiations phase. The matters which need to be covered include:

– a timetable for the remainder of the tender process;

---

1   *Writing an Output Specification* (HM Treasury and Private Finance Panel) October 1996.
2   See **5.6.28–5.6.30**.
3   See **1.3.8**.
4   This is compulsory – see **3.3.32–3.3.35**.

- guidelines for the carrying out of clarification exercises and the conduct of negotiations;
- instructions for the submission of bids and any interim proposals (including instructions relating to the format in which bids must be submitted and the submission (if relevant) of reference bids and variant bids);[1]
- other terms of the tender process including any rules as to how tenderers should approach the process (for example, specific prohibition on collusive tendering; requirements as to confidentiality; disclaimers relating to information provided by the awarding authority;[2] rules governing access to and use of data room).[3]

Other ITN information

5.6.18 The matters referred to at **5.6.13** to **5.6.17** are by no means exhaustive as to the information which an awarding authority should provide to its tenderers. Ultimately, the information provided by an awarding authority should be sufficient to enable the tenderers to submit fully costed final bids. A balance does, however, need to be struck and an awarding authority should avoid overloading the tenderers with unnecessary information. The tenderers will only have a limited amount of time to assimilate the information before having to submit their proposals.

5.6.19 Where the volume of information that tenderers may require is extensive, the awarding authority may set up a data room to hold any secondary and supporting information. A data room could also be used to store confidential or particularly sensitive information which would otherwise have to be circulated among the tenderers. An awarding authority wishing to use a data room should ensure that, in the interests of maintaining a level playing field, all tenderers are permitted an equal opportunity to gain access to the data room.

Confidentiality

5.6.20 There may be confidential information which an awarding authority will want to include in an ITN. The awarding authority should, therefore, consider whether to require tenderers to provide confidentiality undertakings prior to the release of the ITN. An awarding authority wishing to procure confidentiality undertakings will need to identify the appropriate parties required to give those undertakings. These may include the members of the consortium, its advisers, financiers and any identified contractors who are not consortium members. Where the membership of a tendering consortium fluctuates during the course of the tender process changes should be notified to the awarding authority and further confidentiality undertakings obtained.

---

1   See **5.7.4** and **5.7.5**.
2   See **5.6.23**.
3   See **5.6.19**.

Public sector comparator

5.6.21 As part of its preparatory work leading up to the decision to put a project out to tender under the PFI, the awarding authority will have developed an outline business case making the case for pursing a PFI solution to its requirements. An outline business case will usually include a fully costed reference project or draft public sector comparator which tests whether an affordable investment option exists. The public sector comparator will usually be refined to take account of the issues which emerge as a result of the PFI process and, after such refinement, provide a benchmark for measuring the value for money of tenderers' proposals.

5.6.22 The awarding authority will need to give careful consideration to whether it releases the outline business case and/or the public sector comparator (in its original form) as part of the ITN. Given that the public sector comparator will be one of the factors which they will be bidding against, tenderers will be keen to see it even if only in its original form. The draft public sector comparator could assist the tenderers in ensuring that their proposals are affordable. The downside, however, of releasing the draft public sector comparator to the tenderers is that it may curb private sector innovation. Less adventurous tenderers could be tempted to play around at the margins of the public sector comparator instead of pursuing a truly innovative solution which may also be more affordable. Full details of the public sector comparator should only be released to tenderers where there is strong competition. In other cases, disclosure should be limited to the conceptual basis of the public sector comparator and the methodology used in its construction.[1]

Accuracy of the ITN

5.6.23 A typical ITN usually includes a general disclaimer relating to the accuracy of the information contained in the ITN. Indeed, such a general disclaimer is commonly extended to all documents issued by the awarding authority during the course of the tender process. That is not to say, however, that an awarding authority will never have to stand by the information it provides to the tenderers. Much of the information contained in an ITN will form the basis of the contract which an awarding authority will eventually enter into with the preferred tenderer. The awarding authority can, therefore, expect to have to warrant the accuracy of certain information under the terms of that contract.

Revised ITN

5.6.24 The overall approach taken by the awarding authority to the tender process may mean that it will issue a revised version of the ITN or a further set of tender documentation (for example, an Invitation to Tender ('ITT') or Final Bid Instructions) at a later stage in the tender process (eg following the short-listing of tenderers or prior to the submission of final bids). The contents of this

---

1 Policy Statement No 2, *Public Sector Comparators and Value for Money* (Treasury Taskforce) March 1998, section 5.1.

subsequent document (which, for the sake of convenience, is referred to in this section as the ITT) will usually mirror or contain specific aspects of the contents of the ITN discussed above. Generally, the considerations which apply to the drafting of the ITN will also apply to the drafting of the ITT. Indeed, the ITT is often no more than a revised version of the ITN with:

- updated output specifications, key constraints, commercial terms and other pricing information; and
- new instructions to tenderers as to the submissions to be made in response to the ITT.

The interactive process

5.6.25 The Public Sector Regulations do not prescribe the process of 'negotiations' which should take place in the period between pre-qualification and award of the contract. However, the awarding authority will need to ensure that it maintains a level playing field throughout the tender process. As part of this requirement the awarding authority will need to ensure that, so far as possible, all tenderers are given equal access to staff, premises etc and that the confidentiality of tenderers' proposals is respected. Maintaining a level playing field and safeguarding tenderers' confidential information are matters which need to be addressed throughout the tender process. This is best achieved by ensuring that the process of interaction between the awarding authority and the tenderers is structured, controlled and that all meetings are minuted.

Providing additional information

5.6.26 During the course of the tender process, tenderers are likely to ask questions calling for the clarification of information or documentation in their possession or for the provision of additional information. There is nothing to prevent the awarding authority from requiring all such requests to be reduced to writing and routed through its designated points of contact. In practice, however, tenderers may raise queries in meetings with the awarding authority and/or over the telephone.

5.6.27 In keeping with the principle of equality of treatment in general, any such clarifying or additional information should be communicated to all tenderers and not confined to the tenderer that raised the query. However, any such response should not compromise the position of the tenderer that raised the query in the first instance. Accordingly, clarification circulars should:

- not disclose the identity of the tenderer whose query has given rise to the need for the circular;
- not reveal the nature of the query which was raised or, indeed, the motivations or innovative ideas behind that query; and
- avoid revealing any aspect of the approach adopted by the tenderer raising the query.

Negotiations

5.6.28 The precise point in the negotiations phase at which 'negotiations' (in the sense of full scale debate and discussions geared to reaching a compromise or mutual agreement) should commence will depend very much on the way in which the negotiations phase is structured. Generally, early discussions between the awarding authority and the tenderers will be focused on clarifying and raising issues as opposed to trying to resolve or agree those issues. Usually, negotiations will only commence in earnest after the first formal submissions have been made and a basis on which to negotiate has been established.

5.6.29 In deciding on an appropriate strategy and timetable for the conduct of negotiations, the matters which an awarding authority should consider include the following.

How many sets of separate negotiations can it resource?
The number of tenderers selected to enter into full scale contract negotiations may be limited by the resources available to the authority.

How should the contract documents be developed?
It may not be practicable to seek to get individual tenderers to sign up to a detailed contract if (say) it is intended to conduct three sets of negotiations in parallel. The resources on either side of the negotiating table which will need to be devoted to trying to reach agreement on the minutiae of a contract will be considerably more than that which would be required to reach agreement on the broad principles of risk allocation. The awarding authority should consider, therefore, whether a more effective approach would be to use a 'heads of terms' as the basis for initial negotiations and to introduce a detailed draft contract at a later stage (for example, prior to final bid submissions or, perhaps, after a preferred tenderer has been selected).

Should there be a common document for negotiations or should each set of negotiations be allowed to take its own course?
On the one hand, the awarding authority could negotiate with each tenderer on the basis of a draft contract (or 'heads of terms') which is common to all tenderers and continue to do so after each iteration. In other words, it would only look at compromising its opening position on issues of general concern to all tenderers or to apply any specific concession made to a particular tenderer across the board. With this approach, the tenderers would submit final bids on the basis of identical commercial terms.

Alternatively, an awarding authority could treat each set of negotiations in isolation such that at the end of the exercise, it will end up with different sets of commercial terms particular to each individual tenderer. The disadvantage of this approach is that the comparison of bids will be complicated by the fact that they have been submitted on the basis of different commercial terms. A possible solution to this problem could be to require all tenderers to submit 'reference' bids on the basis of standard commercial terms but to submit variant bids based on the particular commercial terms agreed with the authority.[1]

---

1 See **5.7.4–5.7.6**.

To what extent can agreement be reached on matters of risk allocation?
Existing PFI guidelines[1] recommend that parallel 'negotiations should be aimed at pinning down the commercial terms of the contract, and ensuring that the contracted outputs will be delivered'.

5.6.30 As many contract terms as possible should be agreed between the awarding authority and individual tenderers before a preferred tenderer is selected. However, the awarding authority will need to take a realistic view about the extent to which these commercial terms can, in fact, be pinned down before a preferred tenderer is selected. In practice the limiting constraint is usually the willingness of tenderers to commit resources to legal negotiations prior to the selection of the preferred tenderer (including negotiations with the tenderer's proposed funders).

5.7 BID SUBMISSION AND EVALUATION

Bid evaluation

5.7.1 In selecting a preferred tenderer, the awarding authority will need to evaluate the proposals embodied in the tenderers' final bids to identify the tenderer that has proposed the most economically advantageous solution. This evaluation exercise will clearly need to take account of any post-submission discussions between the awarding authority and the individual tenderers and/or any supplementary submissions made as a result of these discussions.

5.7.2 Although the 'most economically advantageous offer' is the sole basis upon which the preferred bidder may be selected, an awarding authority may apply any number of criteria in trying to identify the 'most economically advantageous offer'. The awarding authority must, however, notify the tenderers of the criteria it intends to use to evaluate their bids (as highlighted at **5.6.16**, a vital component of the ITN will be a statement of the authority's intended bid evaluation criteria). The awarding authority must adhere strictly to the evaluation criteria that it specifies.

Methodology

5.7.3 The Regulations do not prescribe any particular methodology for the qualitative assessment of the tenderers' proposals and it will be up to the awarding authority to devise appropriate mechanisms for the evaluation of bids. Outlined below are some of the general issues which the awarding authority will need to address when developing its bid evaluation methodology.

- In effect, the bid evaluation process requires the awarding authority to use the specified bid evaluation criteria for the purposes of comparing the relative merits of each of the bids. Ultimately, the awarding authority's evaluation methodology should enable it to rank the tenderers according to

---

1   *A Step by Step Guide to the PFI Procurement Process* (Treasury Taskforce) April 1998.

the *extent* to which each of their bids can be described as 'economically advantageous'.
- The methodology will need to incorporate a weighting system which reflects the varying levels of importance of each of the evaluation criteria.
- The 'most economically advantageous offer' does not necessarily equate with the 'lowest priced offer'. The evaluation methodology should, therefore, reflect the trade-offs between cost and benefit which the awarding authority is prepared to make.
- The evaluation methodology must, however, reflect the fact that there may be certain immutable criteria or minimum bid requirements which must be met in order for a bid to be compliant. In a sense, the extent to which a tenderer has satisfied each of these requirements does not fall to be considered until it has first been determined that the tenderer has, in fact, achieved the relevant minimum requirements. The awarding authority should give careful consideration to the matters which it regards as minimum bid requirements. It should avoid setting these minimum thresholds at levels which are too idealistic, otherwise it may find itself in receipt of non-compliant bids from all the tenderers, thus having to invite the submission of revised bids or, even worse, receipt of an apparently compliant bid from only one tenderer which is otherwise an unattractive bid.
- The bid evaluation methodology to be adopted should also address the fact that the awarding authority will rarely be comparing 'like with like'. Tenderers are likely to propose different technical solutions at different prices. Those proposals will also be based on the assumption of different levels of risk transfer. The awarding authority's bid evaluation methodology should, therefore, include mechanisms which compensate for the fact that different bids will have different bases, so that sensible comparisons can be drawn between the competing bids. One way of introducing a degree of consistency to the process is considered in **5.7.4** to **5.7.6**.

At the time of writing the Taskforce has issued to Departments for consultation draft guidance on the selection of preferred bidders. However, this has not yet been publicly released.

Reference and variant bids

5.7.4 It is common for awarding authorities to invite each tenderer to submit more than one bid. Such an approach allows the tenderers more scope for innovation. It also enables the awarding authority to establish some ground which is common to all the tenderers by requiring each of them to submit a standard or reference bid based on certain fixed assumptions. Tenderers will be encouraged to innovate by submitting further bids (variant bids) which do not have to comply with those fixed assumptions.

5.7.5 Typically, tenderers will be required to submit reference bids based on a standard risk allocation profile. They may then submit variant bids premised on risk profiles which deviate from that standard risk profile. Having a set of reference bids based on common assumptions as to risk transfer may assist the awarding authority in assessing the pricing implications of each of the tenderers' approaches to the allocation of risk. However, the benefit of this approach may be lost if the awarding authority is unrealistic in the risk position it proposes for the reference bids (with the consequence that all of the tenderers depart from it significantly).

5.7.6 Existing PFI guidelines[1] recommend that 'the standard bid should be standard only as regards commercial issues ... there should not be any "standard" requirement as regards technical or operational issues (except where these form part of the constraints on the procurement as a whole)'.[2]

Debriefing unsuccessful tenderers

5.7.7 The Public Sector Regulations require an awarding authority to provide each unsuccessful tenderer with the reasons for its failure to be appointed the preferred tenderer. The awarding authority may choose to debrief each unsuccessful tenderer orally. Whatever mode of communication it uses, the awarding authority will need to take the same precautions it would take when giving its reasons for not pre-qualifying candidates.[3] In particular, an awarding authority should ensure that the reasons given to a tenderer are expressed as being by reference to that tenderer's inability to meet the awarding authority's specified evaluation criteria.[4]

Continuing negotiations with preferred tenderer

5.7.8 The appointment of the preferred tenderer will mark the end of the competitive phase of the tender process. From the awarding authority's point of view, it would be ideal if a competitive environment could be maintained through to contract signature and/or financial close. The commercial reality, however, is that a tenderer (and its debt funders) will only be prepared to commit the substantial resources required to bring a project to commercial and financial close after that tenderer has been selected as the preferred bidder. Debt funders, in particular, will not be prepared to incur the costs of carrying out a due diligence exercise while the tenderer they are backing is still in the process of competing for the project. In practice, therefore, an awarding authority can expect to engage in potentially lengthy tripartite negotiations with the preferred tenderer and the debt funders, before a project can be brought to financial close.

5.7.9 Once a preferred tenderer has been selected, any downward pressure on price exerted by the force of competition will ease. The awarding authority will need to limit the opportunities for the preferred tenderer and its funders to re-open negotiations over previously settled issues, particularly if that involves a price increase. In a sense, the awarding authority's entire strategic approach to the tender process will need to be geared to limiting the scope of negotiations undertaken outside the competitive environment. It should aim to maintain the competitive environment for as long as reasonably possible and seek to settle as

---

1   *A Step by Step Guide to the PFI Procurement Process* (Treasury Taskforce) April 1998.
2   See **5.6.14**.
3   See **5.5.13**.
4   See also **3.3.50**.

many issues as possible while it still possesses the lever of competition. In some cases, this could mean having to delay the selection of the preferred tender and going back to the tenderers to get them to improve their bids. The awarding authority should seek to get as close as possible to being in the ideal position of receiving a comprehensive set of full and final bids based on agreed commercial terms. Against that, however, an awarding authority will need to avoid setting unrealistic targets for the tenderers while they are still in open competition.

5.7.10 Outlined below are some of the specific steps the awarding authority may take to limit the diluting effects which subsequent negotiations with the preferred tenderer and the debt funders may have on the targets achieved during the competitive stages of the tender process.

5.7.11 The selection of the preferred tenderer could be backed up by the appointment of a reserve preferred tenderer (the tenderer that has proffered the second 'most economically advantageous' proposal). That second-placed tenderer should be invited to keep an offer on the table for as long as possible. This device may, however, be of limited utility; the more protracted the negotiations between the awarding authority and the preferred tenderer, the less likely that the awarding authority will resort to the reserve bid on offer or that the reserve tenderer will be in a position (or willing) to enter the fray.

5.7.12 The awarding authority will need to assess the 'deliverability' of each of the bids submitted by the tenderers in order to satisfy itself that the preferred tenderer's proposals are realistic. Even if the awarding authority takes the view that a proposal is in some respect unrealistic or undeliverable, it may still wish to pursue that proposal. For instance, an awarding authority may believe that a particular proposal cannot realistically be implemented within the requisite timeframe. It may, nonetheless, adjudge the proposal to be the 'most economically advantageous' on offer. In such a situation, it will, at the very least, enter into negotiations with the preferred tenderer in the knowledge that it will have to make certain concessions to bring the project within the requisite timeframe. It may even be prepared to have to meet an increase in price. An awarding authority's 'deliverability' assessment may lead it to conclude that a particular tenderer's proposed funding package may be under-costed. It may still decide to appoint that tenderer as the preferred tenderer with the knowledge that concessions may have to be made subsequently.

5.7.13 There is a fine line between, on the one hand, the assessment of 'deliverability' and, on the other hand, second-guessing the tenderers by unilaterally reworking their proposals. The latter proposition does not sit squarely with notions of risk transfer. The awarding authority will need to guard against unnecessarily interfering with the tenderers' ideas and proposed solutions under the guise of 'deliverability'. Concerns as to deliverability are usually better addressed in the clarification process.

5.7.14 The awarding authority should require all parties (including the debt funders) associated with each bid to provide sufficient evidence of their commitment to the terms of their bid. Indeed, existing PFI guidelines[1]

---

1   *A Step by Step Guide to the PFI Procurement Process* (Treasury Taskforce) April 1998.

recommend that funders should be asked to provide evidence of their approval of the risk profile embodied in the bids they are backing. The awarding authority should take a realistic approach to the levels of commitment which need to be demonstrated. It may otherwise run the risk of receiving non-compliant bids which fall foul of this particular condition. Debt funders, in particular, will frequently provide their commitment, subject to due diligence after the selection of the preferred tenderer. Ultimately, the provision of appropriate assurances will not of itself preclude any back-tracking on the part of a tenderer and/or its constituent members. It does mean, however, that a party will need to have compelling reasons to put its professional reputation at stake before reneging on its prior assurances.

Negotiating price reductions: bridging affordability gaps

5.7.15 Once the preferred tenderer has been selected, there may be an upward pressure on price depending on the level of detailed commercial agreement which has been reached prior to selection of the preferred tenderer. The awarding authority may require price reductions in order to ensure the project remains affordable. This can be achieved either by challenging the preferred tenderer's pricing assumptions or by accepting an adjustment to the risk allocation (which does not impact on the accounting treatment) in order to drive down the price. In addition, the commercial pressures on the preferred tenderer and the debt funders should not be underestimated. They will be keen to unlock the returns which come with the implementation of the project and will, therefore, have a genuine interest in finding the means to make their proposals affordable.

5.8 CONCLUSION

5.8.1 An effectively managed tender process is essential to delivering successful PFI projects. When used effectively, the tools of competition and negotiation will go some way to ensuring that tenderers' solutions are innovative, represent value for money, are affordable and are deliverable. However, the competitive environment cannot realistically be sustained right through to contract award and financial close. Final negotiations between the awarding authority and the preferred tenderer will be conducted outside that competitive environment. In practice, if these negotiations entail a significant number of price sensitive issues they will undermine the value of any prior competition and usually result in a deterioration in value for money (and potential affordability problems) for the awarding authority. If there is one major factor which should drive the strategic approach the awarding authority takes to a tender process, it is the need to limit the scope and duration of the negotiations which remain to be carried out after the preferred tenderer has been selected.

Chapter 6

REMEDIES FOR BREACH OF THE TENDERING PROCESS

6.1 INTRODUCTION

6.1.1 There are a number of avenues which may be open to a tenderer who is aggrieved by a decision made during the tendering process:

- a claim under the specific mechanisms for seeking redress for breach of those regulations which implement the EU public procurement regime into domestic law;
- a complaint to the European Commission alleging a breach of the requirements of the EU public procurement regime;
- judicial review; and
- a private law claim for breach of an implied contract or possibly tort.[1]

6.2 SPECIFIC REMEDY FOR BREACH OF THE EU PUBLIC PROCUREMENT REGIME

6.2.1 There are four statutory instruments setting out Regulations which implement the Directives on public procurement.[2] These each set out a specific mechanism for claiming in respect of a breach of the particular Regulations concerned.

The provisions for remedies are broadly similar in each case and are found as follows:

- Public Works Contracts Regulations 1991, reg 31;
- Public Services Contracts Regulations 1993, reg 32;
- Public Supply Contracts Regulations 1995, reg 29; and
- Utilities Contracts Regulations 1996, reg 32.

6.2.2 Actions under these Regulations must be brought in the High Court. The rights of action laid down in the Regulations are available to any person:

- who seeks or sought to be or would have wished to have been, the person to whom a relevant contract (ie one caught by the Regulations in question) is awarded; and

---

1 Generally see S Arrowsmith 'Protecting the interests of bidders for public contracts; the role of the common law' [1994] CLJ 104 and S Arrowsmith 'Law of Public and Utilities Procurement' (Sweet & Maxwell, 1996) at pp 28–40.
2 See **3.2**.

- who is a national of and established in an EU member state or in certain other 'relevant states', being the three non-EU countries covered by the European Economic Area ('EEA') Agreement (Norway, Iceland, and Liechtenstein) and certain Eastern European countries that have signed up to Association Agreements with the EU.

6.2.3 Actions must be brought promptly, and in any event within three months from the date when grounds for bringing the proceedings first arose, unless the Court considers there is a good reason for extending this period.[1] This time-limit is similar to that applicable to judicial review. In addition, before commencing the action, the plaintiff must first inform the awarding authority of the alleged breach and of his intention to bring proceedings in respect of that breach. The decision in *R v Portsmouth City Council, ex p Coles*[2] confirms that this pre-notification requirement is a strict one and a failure to comply with it may lead to the claim being rejected.

6.2.4 Although some aspects of this specific procedure bear a resemblance to judicial review (the time-limit, for example) there is nothing in the Regulations which specifies that any proceedings should take the form of an application for judicial review. It therefore appears that the correct approach is to proceed by way of a writ action alleging a breach of the Regulations.[3]

6.2.5 Where the contract has not yet been entered into, the High Court has the power to:
- make an interim order (injunction) suspending the contract award procedure, or suspending the implementation of any decision or action taken by the awarding authority in the course of such a procedure; and
- if satisfied that a decision or action taken by an awarding authority or utility was in breach of its duty of compliance:
  - order the setting aside of the decision or action or order the contracting authority to amend any documents; and/or
  - award damages to a supplier who has suffered loss or damage as a consequence of the breach.

If the contract in question has been entered into, the Court does not have the power to order any remedy other than an award of damages.

6.2.6 There is no guidance as to how damages should be quantified, but the compensation would be likely to cover all or part of the costs of participating in the bidding process and might also compensate the plaintiff for its loss of the potential profit which it stood to make if it had been selected to carry out the PFI project. Any award of damages may well depend, however, on the tenderer

---

1. In *Keymed (Medical & Industrial Equipment) Ltd v Forest Healthcare NHS Trust* (unreported, 11 November 1997, High Court) the period was extended because the delay by Keymed in bringing proceedings was not long and was to an extent the fault of the Trust. The date from which the three-month period runs is an objective one and is not limited to knowledge of the existence of a breach.
2. (1997) 9 Admin LR 535.
3. See **6.4** as to whether it would be possible to allege a breach of the UK regulations incorporating the EU procurement regime in judicial review proceedings.

demonstrating that but for a breach of the Regulations he would have been awarded the contract. The alternative is that the Court works on the principle that damages should be payable in any event but on the basis of multiplying the expected profits by the probability of the plaintiff being awarded the contract, ie the principle of loss of a chance.[1]

6.3 ACTION BY THE EUROPEAN COMMISSION

6.3.1 An aggrieved party may lodge a complaint with the European Commission. When the Commission becomes aware of alleged infringements of the procurement rules, it has the power to call upon the national authority to justify its procurement procedure and to rectify any infringement. If the Commission is not satisfied with the response, it may commence infringement proceedings against the UK government under Article 169 of the EC Treaty. It may not, however, proceed directly against the awarding authority itself. Such proceedings may ultimately lead to the UK government being condemned by the European Court of Justice for having breached its Community obligations. In serious cases, the Commission may also apply for an interim order suspending the contract award procedure.

6.3.2 The European Commission only proceeds to formal legal proceedings in a small number of procurement cases each year. To date, there has not been a ruling of the European Court against the UK in the field of procurement (although a couple of actions against the UK are pending). Nevertheless, the risk of a complaint to the Commission in respect of a PFI project cannot be ruled out, particularly as such complaints give complainants the possibility of causing considerable political embarrassment to the awarding authority without obliging the complainant to resort to potentially expensive litigation in the national courts.

6.4 JUDICIAL REVIEW

6.4.1 An aggrieved tenderer may seek to proceed by way of judicial review. This is the normal procedure by which third parties have been able to challenge the actions and decisions of public authorities in the UK. A fundamental point, however, is that judicial review is only available if the decision under challenge has a sufficient public law element. There is a debate as to whether procurement decisions by public bodies have a sufficient public law element such that they fall within the ambit of judicial review or whether instead such decisions are of a private commercial nature only.

6.4.2 Initially, a number of cases established that public procurement procedures by public authorities could be the subject of judicial review proceedings.

---

1 See for example *Chaplin v Hicks* [1911] 2 KB 786 and *Allied Maples Group v Simmons & Simmons* [1995] 1 WLR 1602.

In *R v Lewisham LBC, ex p Shell UK*,[1] it was held that the local authority's decision not to deal with firms having South African connections, which was motivated by a desire to put pressure on the apartheid system, was reviewable because it was made for a purpose not contemplated by the statute conferring the authority's procurement powers. This approach was followed in *R v Enfield LBC, ex p Unwin (Roydon) Ltd*[2] where the local authority had, in breach of the principles of natural justice, suspended a contractor from its approved list in the context of an investigation into alleged wrongdoing by the contractor. The decision of the Court of Appeal in *Jones v Swansea City Council*[3] also cast doubt on the view that contract powers are inevitably outside the scope of public law. Finally, in *R v Derbyshire County Council, ex p Times Supplements Ltd*,[4] the local education authority responded to articles in *The Sunday Times* criticising one of its councillors by deciding to cease advertising for teaching posts in the Times Educational Supplement. Times Supplements successfully applied for judicial review on the grounds of bad faith.

6.4.3 However, a more restrictive approach was adopted in *R v The Lord Chancellor's Department, ex p Hibbit and Saunders*.[5] The applicants were disappointed tenderers who had failed to obtain a contract for court reporting services. They sought judicial review claiming the Lord Chancellor's Department had negotiated with bidders after the receipt of tenders contrary to statements in the tender documents and that it had acted contrary to expectations in allowing some tenderers, but not the applicants, to submit bids according to altered specifications. Rose LJ referred to various cases concerning the link between public law and employment law and stated that judicial review only applied to decisions which are statutorily underpinned or involve some other public law element. The Court concluded that the applicants' legitimate expectations had been infringed but that there was no element of public law sufficient to render the decision amenable to judicial review.

6.4.4 The approach in *Hibbit and Saunders* was followed in *Mass Energy Ltd v Birmingham City Council*[6] concerning tenders leading to the award of a waste disposal contract by the Council under Part II of the Environmental Protection Act 1990. A rejected tenderer challenged the Council's decision to choose one tenderer with whom it negotiated improved terms. The Court of Appeal held that under the statutory provisions of the Act, the Council was only under a duty to act commercially. There was no specific statutory duty to act fairly and the Council had not therefore breached the Act. The Court consequently refused leave to move for judicial review, but indicated that the rejected tenderer's remedy may lie in private law.

---

1   [1988] 1 All ER 938.
2   (1989) 1 Admin LR 50.
3   [1990] 1 WLR 54.
4   (1991) 3 Admin LR 241.
5   [1993] COD 326.
6   [1993] Env LR 298.

6.4.5 However, the results of these cases contrast with *R v Legal Aid Board, ex p Donn and Co (A firm)*[1] where Ognall J found that the procedure of a Legal Aid Committee, in awarding a contract to solicitors for the conduct of a multi-party action, was justiciable in public law. The judge rejected the respondent's argument, based on the *Hibbit and Saunders* ruling, that the fact that the performance of the contract by the solicitor was of public importance could not of itself make the matter justiciable in public law. He held that, although there was no universal test, an overall impression must be formed, both of the selection process itself and its consequences, taking into account the public importance of the conduct of the litigation. Therefore, quite independently of any private remedy that may have been available, the public dimensions of the matter made it justiciable in public law.

6.4.6 In *R v Portsmouth City Council, ex p Bonaco Builders and Others*,[2] other bidders challenged the Council's decision to award certain contracts for housing works to its own direct labour department. At first instance there were challenges based on the EU Works Directive 71/305, the Public Works Contracts Regulations 1991 and the compulsory competitive tendering rules of the Local Government Act 1980 as amended by the Local Government Act 1988 and the challenges also included an allegation of breach of a legitimate expectation. In respect of the legitimate expectation challenge, Keene J doubted whether the decision had sufficient public law elements to make it susceptible to judicial review even though the process of awarding public works contracts was subject to considerable statutory underpinning. Keene J did, however, consider the challenges based on the specific procedures required by the EU Directive and the domestic legislation and granted relief in respect of part of the claim. On appeal in *R v Portsmouth City Council, ex p Coles*,[3] the Court of Appeal did not need to consider whether the more general claim based on legitimate expectation was subject to public law and had to consider only the claims based on the Directive and Regulations. The Court of Appeal's judgment proceeds on the basis that the case was appropriate for judicial review although it is unclear from the judgment whether or not the point was argued.

6.4.7 Therefore, the applicability or otherwise of judicial review in the procurement area is unclear because it is not certain what effect the decision in *Hibbit and Saunders* has had on the earlier cases. It is also unclear as to where the decision in *Donn* fits in and how the *Portsmouth City Council* case affects the position.

6.4.8 A further consideration is that there is a general principle of administrative law that relief may be withheld in judicial review proceedings where an applicant has failed to pursue an alternative remedy. However, this principle is by no means inflexible and it does not appear that the specific regime for remedies in the Regulations referred to at **6.2.1** will lead to the refusal of relief in judicial review proceedings. That judicial review may still be appropriate is indicated by the statement in the Regulations that their application is 'without

---

1   [1996] 3 All ER 1.
2   6 June 1995, unreported.
3   (1997) 9 Admin LR 535.

prejudice to other powers of the Court'. Moreover, in *R v Portsmouth City Council, ex p Coles* the Court of Appeal was willing to entertain a judicial review application despite the existence of the procurement regulations with their specific procedures although *ex p Coles* was concerned with various grounds of challenge including alleging a breach of the relevant Directive itself and was not confined to an alleged breach of the Regulations.

6.4.9 One possible approach is to say that the procurement decision only involves public law where there is some particular statutory underpinning or where the selection process and public importance of the task to be performed by the preferred tenderer are such that the procurement decision brings in public law. It appears from the *Portsmouth City Council* case that a claim that a decision is *ultra vires* the specific wording of the Regulations or the relevant EU Directive may be the subject of judicial review although some caution is needed because the point does not appear to have been fully argued in that case. An alternative approach is to look at the grounds of challenge. Thus, for example, where there are allegations of illegality or bad faith or improper purposes, the court might be more inclined to find a decision reviewable than where the argument is based on, for example, a breach of a procedural legitimate expectation. This would appear slightly unprincipled but would have the merit of reconciling some of the earlier cases.

6.4.10 The overall position at this stage in those PFI projects where there is no obvious statutory underpinning is that public law constraints cannot be ignored because a court might rule that the procurement decision fell within the ambit of public law irrespective of whether it is caught by the European procurement regime. This means that caution will be needed when public authorities make their decisions. Conversely, bidders will be able to use the possible applicability of public law principles as a negotiating weapon if the public authority indicates it will act in a way which the tenderer believes will breach those principles.

6.5 PRIVATE COMMON LAW REMEDIES

6.5.1 Public procurement is generally concerned with the process leading up to the award of a public contract. However, where the public body (or any other entity) sets in motion a tendering procedure with a view to awarding a contract, an implied contract may arise at an earlier stage between the awarding body and the tenderers. In *Blackpool and Fylde Aero Club Ltd v Blackpool Borough Council*,[1] the local authority had invited seven parties to submit tenders for a concession to operate pleasure flights from the local airport. The plaintiff submitted its bid before the set deadline but the local authority failed to take it into account because the authority had inadvertently left the bid in their letterbox and subsequently treated it as having been received late. The Court of Appeal held that this refusal to consider the bid amounted to a breach of an implied contract, which gave any party submitting a bid before the deadline a right to have that bid 'considered in conjunction with all other conforming

---

1   [1990] 1 WLR 1195.

tenders' or at least to have that bid 'considered if others are'.[1] The Court did not examine the scope of the contract, leaving it unclear as to whether it will also apply to open tendering procedures where all interested parties, and not just those invited, may bid.

6.5.2 The content of this implied contract was extended in *Fairclough Building Ltd v Borough Council of Port Talbot*.[2] Fairclough was one of a number of firms placed on a list and invited to partake in a two-stage procedure for the award of a contract for the construction of a new civic centre. However, before the first stage of the procedure the Council resolved to remove Fairclough from the list because the local director of Fairclough was married to the Council's Principal Architect and the Council was concerned about a conflict of interest. Although Fairclough's appeal was rejected on the merits, the Court of Appeal accepted that there was an implied contract under which 'what has to be considered is whether the decision was reasonable'.[3] The principle could effectively allow courts to exercise control over the criteria and procedures for considering the bids.[4]

6.5.3 The courts may therefore be willing to ensure procedural fairness in procurement procedures by use of the notion of an implied contract. The above decisions have been criticised on the ground that a tendering procedure merely creates reasonable expectations as to its fair conduct but does not constitute an intended bargain for which consideration is given. The consideration may, however, in a PFI project be the considerable costs which a tenderer will incur in preparing a compliant bid. There remains, however, considerable uncertainty over whether, and to what extent, private law remedies in contract are available in the context of public procurement. It seems likely that there will be an implied contract but the terms of such a contract and whether the contract or some of its terms can be excluded is unclear.

6.5.4 Finally, it was suggested in *Blackpool and Fylde Aero Club v Blackpool Borough Council* that the public authority may owe a duty of care to the Club to ensure that if the Club submitted a tender by the deadline it would be considered along with other tenders. The Court of Appeal did not find it necessary to consider whether a tortious duty of care existed because they had already found the existence of an implied contract, although Bingham LJ was tentatively of the view that the local authority's objections to the imposition of a tortious duty of care were correct.[5] An alternative tort claim could be based on a tortious misrepresentation as to the awarding authority's intentions. However, this would depend on the tenderer proving that a call for tenders involves a representation that the awarding authority will go ahead with a contract.

---

1   Per Bingham LJ at p 1202D.
2   (1992) 62 BLR 82.
3   Per Parker LJ at p 93.
4   Note also *Mass Energy v Birmingham City Council* [1994] Env LR 298 and *Southampton City Council v Academy Cleaning Services* (1993) *The Times*, 11 June.
5   [1990] 1 WLR 1195 at p 1203.

Chapter 7

DESIGN AND CONSTRUCTION ISSUES

7.1 INTRODUCTION

7.1.1 This chapter examines the principal design and construction issues which arise in a PFI project.

7.1.2 Inevitably there will be many issues that are common to any type of construction project, whatever the legal structure adopted. This chapter seeks to highlight the issues which are particular to PFI projects. To put that discussion in context, the parties and principal structures in a traditional construction project are outlined in **7.2**. The PFI approach is outlined in **7.3**. Figures 1 and 2 illustrate the two approaches.

7.2 THE TRADITIONAL CONSTRUCTION PROJECT

7.2.1 In a traditional construction project the awarding authority will employ its own consultants to carry out all its design work. This will involve not only the outline design for the purposes of planning but also every aspect of detailed design. The awarding authority will appoint a construction company to carry out the construction of aspects of the project and the construction company will have no responsibility for design.[1] Alternatively, the awarding authority may choose to appoint a single 'design and build' contractor who will be primarily responsible for the design as well as undertaking the construction. The design and build approach is particularly common where the design needs to be developed during the construction period and the construction company and any specialist sub-consultants or sub-contractors which it may appoint are in a better position to provide the detailed design. The project agreement in a PFI project is much closer in approach to the design and build contract than a contract for construction works alone (with design being undertaken separately by the employer's consultants). Accordingly, it is the former that is described at **7.2.2** to **7.2.5**.

7.2.2 Where the awarding authority is proposing to let a design and build contract it will, normally, with the assistance of its own consultants, develop its brief (the 'employer's requirements') setting out its specific requirements for the facility, in output terms. The design and build contractor responds with its detailed proposals (the 'contractor's proposals') setting out how it proposes to deliver the employer's requirements. As the design and build contractor will only be held responsible for design to the extent that the awarding authority has

---

1   If the size of the contract exceeds the threshold specified under the Public Works Contracts Regulations the appointment will be subject to a competitive tender process. See **3.2.16**.

Figure 1: Design and Build Approach

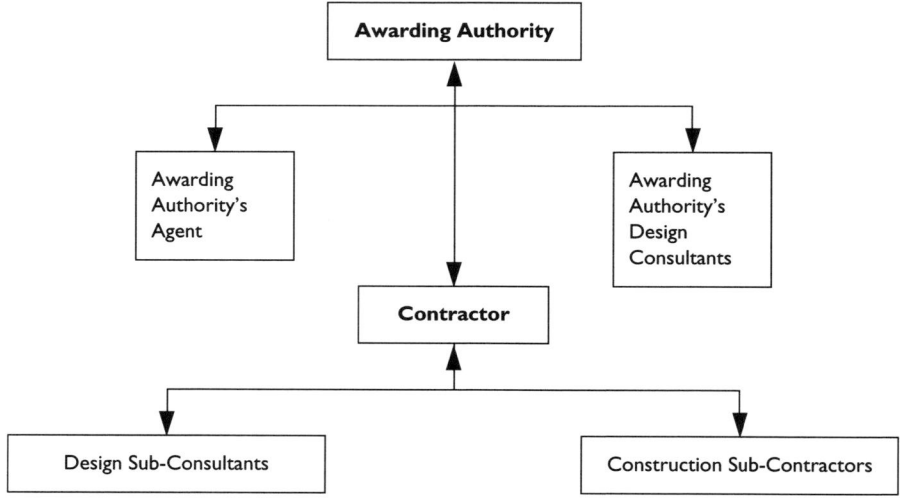

Figure 2: PFI Approach

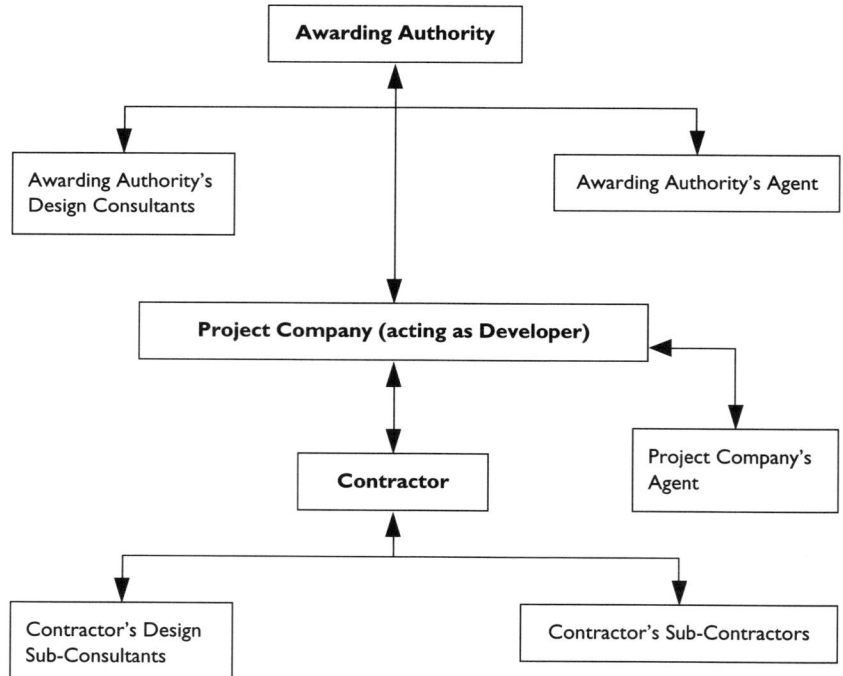

relied upon its skill and judgment and as the construction company's design warranty will only apply to the design proposed, prepared and developed by the design and build contractor as part of the contractor's proposals, any design specified in the employer's requirements is usually kept to a minimum. The awarding authority, as a developer, will usually appoint the design and build contractor pursuant to a standard form of contract such as the JCT Standard Form of Building Contract with Contractor's Design (the 'JCT81'). The employer's requirements and the contractor's proposals will be part of the contract documents forming the JCT81.

7.2.3 Payment to the design and build contractor will typically be made either in stages or by periodic valuation, often monthly in arrears. A certain percentage (3% or 5% is usual) is retained from each payment (the 'retention'). The developer may enter into a finance agreement with a funder to obtain funds to pay the design and build contractor. In the case of a contract let by a public body, the awarding authority would (prior to the advent of the PFI) have funded these payments from its own resources. In a purely private sector development the employer/developer will frequently arrange bank finance to fund these payments and the funders will carry out a due diligence review of the terms and conditions of the JCT81 as this will be a key component of its security package.

7.2.4 The awarding authority, as developer, will traditionally appoint an agent (the 'employer's agent') to administer the JCT81. The role of the employer's agent will include inspecting the works and issuing instructions and certificates on its behalf. The employer's agent may issue instructions to the design and build contractor to change the scope of the works set out in the employer's requirements, which could give rise to an adjustment in the contract price and an extension of the date by which the facilities are required to be completed. Other specific events such as force majeure, exceptionally adverse weather conditions and the threat of terrorism may also entitle the contractor to an extension of time. The employer's agent will issue a written statement that 'practical completion' has been achieved once it is satisfied that the works have been completed in accordance with the terms of the JCT81 contract. The term 'practical completion' connotes that the works have been completed to a stage such that they are fit for occupation and therefore it is recognised that minor defects may exist at the time of practical completion. Such minor defects will be rectified by the contractor during a 'defects liability period' which, for large projects, is normally 12 months. At the end of the period a 'notice of completion of making good defects' is issued. Half the retention is normally released on practical completion and the remainder on the issue of the notice of completion of making good defects.

7.2.5 The contractor will usually be expected to be responsible for any latent defects in the works which are discovered after practical completion for a period of up to 12 years following practical completion. However, the contractor's liability in relation to any economic or consequential losses such as loss of profit, the cost of alternative accommodation and damage to fittings and contents arising as a result of design or works defects is often capped at a certain amount, such as an agreed percentage of the contract sum.[1]

7.2.6 Apart from the limited responsibilities for remedying defects within the agreed periods described in the previous paragraphs, the contractor will have no ongoing maintenance or servicing responsibilities in relation to the facility and the awarding authority will contract for or provide these services separately.

7.3 THE STRUCTURE OF A PFI PROJECT

7.3.1 If the awarding authority decides to procure the development of the facility under the PFI, it will appoint the project company to act, in effect, as the developer pursuant to the project agreement. The project company will have the responsibility for procuring the carrying out of both the design[2] and construction of the facility and, in addition, will have the responsibility for financing these activities up front. It will also have the long-term responsibility for maintaining and servicing the facility throughout the contract term. These additional roles and responsibilities will be priced into the unitary payment charged by the project company. However, as described earlier,[3] such payment will be subject to deductions if the facility or services are not available to the required standards at any time as a result of, for example, latent defects appearing in the works. The project company therefore has a strong incentive to procure that the design and construction of the works carried out during the construction period (and any repairs or additional works carried out during the operating period) are carried out to the requisite standard, particularly as payments to the project company will typically not commence until completion has occurred and the operation of the facility has commenced.

7.3.2 The project company will appoint the construction company pursuant to a construction contract[4] and will seek to pass down to it its design and build obligations under the project agreement. As the terms of the construction contract will normally require the construction company to be paid in stages or by periodic valuations, reference to the project company will have to fund these ongoing costs (using external debt where necessary).

7.3.3 The relationship between the project company and the construction company in a PFI project is therefore similar to that of the developer and construction company under a JCT81. The main difference between the traditional route and a PFI project is that under a PFI project there is an

---

1 However, there is considerable uncertainty over the scope of 'consequential' or 'indirect' loss in the light of *British Sugar Plc v NEI Power Projects Ltd and another* [1997] CLY 1751, CA.
2 See **2.2.7–2.2.10**.
3 See **2.2.20–2.2.25**.
4 The project company may award a single design and build contract to the construction company or may award separate contracts for the design and construction aspects. For the purpose of this and the following paragraphs, the former arrangement is assumed and references to the 'construction company' include that party in its design capacity.

additional party between the awarding authority and the construction company, namely the project company. The project company will, under the terms of the project agreement, undertake to procure the design, construction and maintenance of the facility and, typically, will have direct and sole responsibility to the awarding authority for the facility and related services. However, it, in turn, will pass down many of these responsibilities to the construction company and the operating company.

7.3.4 Whilst the project company will generally seek to pass down to these contractors the same responsibilities as it has undertaken to the awarding authority, there will be some areas of responsibility that those parties may not be prepared to accept. A good example is the responsibility for latent defects. The awarding authority will usually expect the project company to remain responsible for latent defects for the entire contract term. However, the practice in the construction industry, to date, has generally been to limit responsibility for latent defects to a period of 12 years from completion. The project company will be left with the risk (albeit limited) of latent defects arising after this period has expired. This position has generally not proved problematic and debt funders have become comfortable with it.

7.3.5 The tender process leading up to the award of the project agreement is described in Chapter 5. Two of the principal preliminary documents in that process are the document specifying the awarding authority's requirements (the 'output specification') and the designs outlining how the project company proposes to meet those requirements (referred to in this chapter as the 'project company's proposals'). The design and construction aspects of those documents are considered at **7.4** and **7.5**.

7.3.6 Design and construction issues will arise both in the project agreement (between the awarding authority and the project company) and the construction contract (between the project company and the construction company) although naturally these must complement each other and negotiations on one will influence the terms of the other. The project agreement is considered at **7.6** and the construction contract at **7.7**.

7.4. OUTPUT SPECIFICATION

7.4.1 As in the traditional approach, where the developer produces its employer's requirements, in a PFI project the awarding authority will set out its requirements for the facilities including any specific design needs. The approach, however, will be to describe these in functional or 'output-based' terms.[1] The awarding authority's main concerns in relation to design and construction will be to ensure that the project company is fully aware of its requirements and meets these requirements by the required completion date for the price tendered.

7.4.2 However, the awarding authority will need to take care to ensure that its approach to the description of the required facility does not compromise the

---

1   See **1.2.3**.

transfer of design risk to the private sector which is at the heart of the PFI.[1] A delicate balance needs to be struck between, on the one hand, the awarding authority's desire to specify what it requires in sufficient detail and, on the other hand, being seen to provide so much detail that it fetters the project company's freedom to be innovative in meeting such requirements or negates the project company's responsibility for what is produced. The awarding authority will wish the project company to be aware of the awarding authority's requirements for the end product and minimum expectations as to quality and performance. Generally it is inadvisable for the awarding authority to specify detailed design requirements. If a specific design, proposed by the awarding authority, fails to meet the output requirement, a variation will have to be proposed or instructed (which may result in additional time being granted to the project company and/or additional cost being borne by the awarding authority). There may, nevertheless, be certain design requirements which the awarding authority will wish to specify because of the nature of the project, such as lighting and ventilation requirements for operating theatres (for hospitals)[2] or security requirements (for prisons or certain government buildings).

7.4.3 The content of the output specification will include:

– the number of staff to be accommodated;
– space-planning requirements, such as how space is to be split between open-plan and cellular rooms and the width of corridors;
– functional adjacencies;
– preferred locations;
– decanting requirements (if relevant);
– any specific features which will be required, depending on the nature of the project, such as clinical requirements, security requirements, parking, crèche facilities;
– any specific technical requirements;
– any specific materials, goods or finishes required.[3]

7.4.4 The project company will consider the output specification and will be invited to develop solutions to meet the awarding authority's requirements in the most 'economically advantageous' manner. It will then tender its price for the project and produce the project company's proposals.

7.5 PROJECT COMPANY'S PROPOSALS

7.5.1 The project company's proposals will, to the extent they relate to construction, consist of the contractor's proposals prepared by the construction

---

1 See **2.2.7–2.2.10**.
2 The Department of Health has produced extensive guidance (known as Health Technical Memoranda or Health Building Notes) as to the design and construction of health facilities which NHS trusts are expected to comply with. However, de facto observance of these is far from universal and the level of compliance and responsibility for non-compliance can be a difficult area of risk allocation in a PFI project.
3 However, these requirements should be limited for the reasons given at **7.4.2**.

company. The construction company will usually be the principal party in the negotiation of any design and construction issues, particularly technical issues, as it will be the construction company and its sub-consultants and sub-contractors who will develop the design and carry out the construction works.

7.5.2 The project company's proposals typically include outline drawings and plans probably on a scale of 1:500 or 1:200. At this stage, the project company may, if required by the awarding authority, include more detailed drawings in relation to key areas on a scale of 1:50. However, tenderers will be concerned to limit their costs prior to the award of the contract, particularly in the period prior to the selection of a preferred tenderer and the awarding authority will have to temper the scope of its requirements at the bid stage to reflect the anticipated degree of commitment by tenderers. In any event, there are likely to be areas of design development which are not completed until after the award of the contract by the awarding authority.[1]

7.6 CONSTRUCTION-RELATED PROVISIONS IN THE PROJECT AGREEMENT

Project company's design and construction obligations

7.6.1 The provisions of the project agreement defining the project company's design and construction obligations are among the most critical as they ultimately define the product which the project company is required to deliver. They will be linked normally to the output specification and the project company's proposals. The considerations discussed at **7.4** will be relevant in determining the precise form these provisions take, but they will include such matters as the standard of care to be exercised, any required life expectancies and the ongoing performance standards to be met. The provisions may include a 'fitness for purpose' obligation although this tends to be contentious.[2]

7.6.2 The appropriate standards of workmanship and quality of goods and materials to be used will need to be considered carefully so that the project company is aware of and committed to provide the end product required by the awarding authority. Where specific materials, goods or finishes are required by the awarding authority, they should be specified in the output specification (although any such specification should be kept to a minimum). Whilst the aesthetic aspects of materials and finishes are clearly important to the awarding authority, in a PFI project where the project company has the responsibility for the life-cycle costs of facilities for the entire contract term, the awarding authority must be careful not to be prescriptive in areas that are intended to be the project company's risk. A provision may be inserted in the project agreement to provide that if, during the contract term, the project company discovers it cannot obtain a product which has been specified because, for example, it is no longer in production, the project company may use an alternative product

---

1 See **7.6.3–7.6.10**.
2 See **2.2.9**.

provided that it is of a similar standard and quality to the specified product it is intending to replace.

Design development

7.6.3 Because of the reluctance of tenderers to incur significant costs on design work prior to selection of the preferred tenderer, it is inevitable that further design development will need to take place after selection of the preferred bidder and this will continue until the execution of the project agreement and, indeed, beyond.

7.6.4 As a result, meetings will take place between the technical advisers of the project company[1] and the awarding authority, with a view to agreeing the detailed designs and reaching an understanding as to which elements of any design are being approved by the awarding authority. It is important that such understanding is formally documented in the project agreement, even where all the design has been fully developed prior to execution, in case there is any defect in the design. Provisions should be inserted identifying the level of design documents which have been provided by the project company to the awarding authority. For example, prior to the project agreement being executed, the project company may have produced to the awarding authority all of the outline 1:500 drawings and 1:200 drawings with only the 1:50 drawings and detailed scheme drawings remaining to be produced. A provision should be inserted into the project agreement whereby the awarding authority acknowledges that it has received such drawings and, to avoid any future dispute, the drawing numbers should be stated, with the last revision of any drawing submitted to the awarding authority being referred to.

7.6.5 The provisions of the project agreement should also set out clearly which elements of the design documents have been approved by the awarding authority. For example, a design document approved by the awarding authority may have the following effect:

– the awarding authority accepts that the departmental and room relationships and general layout shown in the relevant document meets the output specification; and
– the project company is entitled to proceed to the next stage of design.

The extent to which the awarding authority approves design documents is a critical one: approval (without qualification) connotes acceptance and, consequently, should the design subsequently fail to meet the requirements of the output specification, prior approval would negate the transfer of risk of compliance to the project company. For this reason the awarding authority should strictly limit its approval to elements which are non-controversial and objectively assessable and state that any approval is without prejudice to the obligation of the project company to comply with the output specification. Where any design has been developed by the project company prior to execution of the project agreement, the design documents should be clearly identified and

---

1 For the purposes of this paragraph and **7.6.4** and **7.6.5**, references to the 'project company' include references to the preferred tenderer where applicable.

will form part of the project company's proposals so that the project company accepts liability for such design, the coordination of such design with other design documents and the construction aspects of the facility in accordance with its general obligations regarding workmanship and use of materials.

7.6.6 Where any design document still needs to be developed following the execution of the project agreement, the design development procedure which is to be followed will be set out in the project agreement. In agreeing the design development procedure, the awarding authority will wish to make clear the effect of its approval as referred to in **7.6.5**. The project company will wish to ensure that the awarding authority does not cause the project company any delay in the carrying out of the works as a result of the design development procedure. Accordingly, the project company will require the awarding authority to provide its comments on a design document within a certain time period, failing which the awarding authority's right to comment will lapse but no approval will be deemed to have been given.

7.6.7 As regards detailed scheme drawings such as 1:25 drawings, the project company is likely to argue that the awarding authority should not be entitled to object to such drawings as they will usually contain details not mentioned in or required by the output specification. However, the awarding authority may wish to satisfy itself that the detailed scheme drawings illustrate what the awarding authority expects to be provided on completion of the works. Therefore, by way of compromise, the project company will usually allow the awarding authority to review such drawings and provide comments on them, with the awarding authority acknowledging that it has no right to reject such drawings.

7.6.8 The mechanics of the design development procedure can cause administrative difficulties in practice. The project company will not be able to warrant that it will provide all the design documents within a certain time period as this would unduly fetter its ability to carry out the design at the most appropriate times. A rolling programme is therefore often agreed upon which will usually require the project company to set out periods during which design documents are to be produced and the nature of the design documents to be produced. The project company will be permitted to update the programme from time to time but will be required to provide the awarding authority with the design documents during the relevant periods as identified in the programme. The awarding authority will then be allowed to review the relevant design documents within a specific period and:

- return the document marking it as being rejected if it does not conform with the output specification; or
- return the design document marking 'revisions to be made'; or
- return the document without comment (which should not connote acceptance that it meets the requirements of the output specification); or
- require additional information to be provided in order to satisfy itself that the design document meets the output specification.

7.6.9 The awarding authority will often require the project company to provide more than one copy of a design document when following the design development procedure. The number of copies to be provided will usually be negotiated, depending upon the number of technical advisers who will need to review the document on behalf of the awarding authority, but bearing in mind the cost to the project company in having to provide such copies. Again, design documents approved by the awarding authority under the design development procedure will usually form part of the project company's proposals so that the project company accepts liability as stated at **7.6.5**.

7.6.10 It is also not uncommon for the parties to agree to a design revision procedure which will apply to design documents which have been reviewed by the awarding authority. This procedure requires the project company to notify the awarding authority if it becomes aware at any time that a reviewed design document does not allow the project company to comply with a specific requirement in the output specification, or is inconsistent with a requirement in the output specification or a project company proposal and obliges the project company to provide the awarding authority with its proposed revision and its reasons for requiring to do so. The provisions of the design development procedure enabling the awarding authority to review, reject or require amendments to a design document can then apply equally to such revised design document. The project company should accept the risk of any costs associated with and any delay arising as a result of such revision.

Project company's sub-contractors

7.6.11 The project company will have the primary responsibility for ensuring that the design and construction of the works and any repairs and maintenance works are carried out to the required standards. The awarding authority and the project company's funders will, however, have a strong interest in both the identity of the main contractor and the key sub-contractors and the terms of their appointments. Because the project company is likely to be a special purpose vehicle, the awarding authority and the debt funders will wish to ensure that the project company's obligations under the project agreement are properly passed down the chain of contracts to parties who are technically competent to perform the task and are of adequate financial standing. However, care must be taken to ensure that the awarding authority is not unduly intrusive in these areas (which the project company will typically view as being its business). In any event, the project company's debt funders will inevitably be taking an active interest in these areas to ensure that the sub-contracting arrangements are satisfactory.

7.6.12 In addition to vetting the sub-contracting arrangements, the debt funders will typically require collateral agreements with the main contractors, consultants and, depending on the nature of the project, sub-contractors and sub-consultants, especially those with design input. These collateral agreements will contain 'step-in' rights so that, in the event of project company default, the debt funders can, amongst other things, ensure the facility is completed.[1] The awarding authority may wish to ensure that it has the ability to 'step in' if the debt funders fail to do so and for this reason it may require collateral agreements

---

1   See Chapter 8.

with the main contractors, consultants and even sub-contractors and sub-consultants.[1]

7.6.13 The project company may resist agreeing to procure the provision of collateral agreements from its sub-contractors (as opposed to the main construction and operating contractors) and the sub-consultants in favour of the awarding authority on the basis that they may be difficult to obtain and sometimes the identities of these parties will not be known at the time that the project agreement is signed. One way to overcome this difficulty is to identify certain sub-contractors and sub-consultants before the project agreement is signed and, for those that cannot be identified, to agree a list of pre-approved sub-contractors/sub-consultants. This will allow the project company to permit its contractors to appoint sub-contractors and sub-consultants named on such list without the approval of the awarding authority being required. There will then be an obligation imposed on the project company to procure that only such sub-contractors and sub-consultants are appointed and to obtain collateral agreements from those parties. However, such a list may be so long that it is impractical to use. A compromise is to require the project company to provide the awarding authority with the names of those sub-contractors and sub-consultants it intends to invite to tender for certain elements of the works within an agreed period before the invitations to tender are sent out. The awarding authority will then have a right to approve the names submitted within the agreed period and only those names so approved will be sent an invitation to tender. What is eventually agreed will depend very much on the nature of the project, the identities of the main contractors and the packages of works being carried out by individual sub-contractors and sub-consultants.

7.6.14 If it is agreed that the awarding authority should be entitled to the benefit of collateral agreements, such agreements may be limited to 'step-in' provisions only (instead of containing provisions whereby the sub-contractors and sub-consultants owe a separate duty of care to the awarding authority). However, this assumes that the awarding authority will be satisfied that its regime for deductions from the unitary payment in the event that a defect appears in the facility will be sufficient to cover the losses which the awarding authority may suffer.

7.6.15 As the collateral agreement will contain 'step-in' rights and, in some cases, duty of care obligations whereby the party providing the collateral agreement warrants that it has performed and will continue to perform its duties and obligations as set out in its appointment, the awarding authority will wish to review such appointments to ensure that the obligations of the project company under the project agreement have been passed down adequately. The debt funders will also wish to carry out a due diligence review of these documents and obtain adequate security over them. Both the debt funders and the awarding authority are likely to seek some control over amendments to these contracts.

---

1   See **2.5.6–2.5.8**.

Guarantees and bonds

7.6.16 As already noted, it is probable that the project company will be a special purpose vehicle established purely for the PFI project and will not have any significant assets. The construction company, may itself be a subsidiary of another company. One way of protecting the interests of the awarding authority is to seek a bond or a guarantee, from a company of appropriate standing, of the project company's obligations to construct the facility under the project agreement and/or a parent company guarantee and/or bond in relation to the construction company's obligations under the construction contract. The awarding authority will usually have to justify its request by demonstrating that it has a particular concern given the nature of the project or status of the project company or construction company (as the case may be). There will generally be resistance to giving a guarantee of the project company's obligations particularly as this offends against the limited recourse nature of a special purpose vehicle. The awarding authority should consider carefully the need for such support (particularly in the case of bonds from third parties which will have a direct cost to the project company which will be passed back to the awarding authority via the unitary payment).

7.6.17 There have been a number of PFI projects where the awarding authority has required a bond to be posted in its favour (typically for around 10% of construction costs) to secure performance of the project company's obligations. However, the more usual course is to rely primarily on the awarding authority's other rights and remedies as against the project company (see Chapters 2 and 10) but to take advantage of the guarantees, bonds and retentions which the project company and its debt funders will obtain to protect their own interests. The awarding authority will require these guarantees and bonds to be assignable to it in the event that it 'steps in' and takes over the construction contract pursuant to any collateral agreement entered into by it with the construction company and the project company. However, such rights of assignment will rank in priority behind the corresponding rights of the debt funders. The awarding authority will obtain the benefit of retentions if it 'steps in' and takes over the construction contract. The subject of guarantees, bonds and retentions is discussed further at **7.7.13** to **7.7.17** in the context of the construction contract.

Access and monitoring rights

7.6.18 In a traditional design and build contract, the developer will require that it and its agents have monitoring and access rights during the construction period. The extent to which these monitoring rights should be provided for and exercised in a PFI project should be considered carefully. As in the case of the design procedure, the awarding authority must be careful not to interfere too much. The project company will inevitably argue that it should not be required to take account of comments which may be made by the awarding authority's agent on the progress and quality of the works during construction. Again, a delicate balance must be struck between, on the one hand, the awarding authority's concern to ensure that its output specification is complied with and, on the other hand, interference by the awarding authority in areas that are properly the project company's responsibility and in respect of which it is assuming risk. The awarding authority will, at the very least, wish to have a right to point out any concerns it may have as a result of inspecting the works. This may even extend to a right to request works to be opened up. However, if such a right is granted, then the project company, as under a traditional contract, will normally require an extension of time and reimbursement of proper costs incurred if it is demonstrated that there are no defects in the works which were ordered to be opened up.

Decanting provisions

7.6.19 Some projects will require specific decanting provisions. This may arise where, for example, the facility in question already exists and is occupied by the awarding authority but needs to be refurbished and then maintained by the project company or where existing occupied premises need to be demolished as part of the new development. The reciprocal nature of the parties' obligations in relation to decanting may be complex. The awarding authority may have obligations to ensure that it vacates certain parts of the premises and moves into temporary accommodation at the time specified in the project company's programme (as agreed by the awarding authority) failing which the project company will be entitled to an extension of time and compensation. In turn, the awarding authority will not accept an obligation to occupy temporary accommodation until such time as all necessary services are provided to such temporary accommodation by the project company (where the project company is responsible for preparing such temporary accommodation for use by the awarding authority). Also, if the awarding authority is unable to vacate a part of the premises or move into temporary accommodation at the time agreed because of delay caused by the project company, the awarding authority may incur costs in rearranging its move. The awarding authority will therefore require the project company to indemnify it against such costs. The respective obligations will need to be drafted on a case-by-case basis.

Awarding authority's contractors

7.6.20 In a PFI project it is quite common for the awarding authority to contract with specialist contractors to carry out certain works which are not the responsibility of the project company. For example, the awarding authority may appoint an IT contractor to install IT equipment and hardware prior to completion of the works. The awarding authority will therefore wish to provide under the project agreement that the project company must allow its designated specialist contractors access to the relevant parts of the works, at the appropriate stages of the works, so that they can carry out their works. Whilst the project company will generally accept the principle of this, it will be concerned to ensure that its own programme is not impeded by the presence of third-party contractors on site. An approach is to agree that the awarding authority will be given an agreed number of weeks notice of the anticipated date of practical completion of the works so that the third-party specialist contractors may then enter the site and carry out the agreed works. The scope and duration of these works will be set out in detail in the project agreement.

7.6.21 Provisions relating to liaising, interfacing and co-operation between the project company and the construction company, on the one hand, and the awarding authority's third-party contractors, on the other hand, will be included in the project agreement. Invariably the parties will agree that any damage to the project company's works caused by the awarding authority's third-party contractors will be borne by the awarding authority and any delay caused to the project company's works by the awarding authority's third-party contractors' interference in the works or non-observance of the agreed programme will entitle the project company (and, as a result, the construction company) to an extension of time. By the same token, any damage to the works carried out by the awarding authority's third-party contractors caused by the project company, its contractors and agents should be borne by the project company.

7.6.22 To overcome the interface difficulties that may arise between the different sets of contractors, a solution that is sometimes used where the awarding authority has separate arrangements with third-party contractors is to require the project company to procure that the construction company appoints the awarding authority's third-party contractor as its own sub-contractor (by novating the contracts to the construction company if they have already been entered into). However, both the project company and the construction contractor will wish to have a right to approve the identity and terms of appointment of the relevant contractor and may place limitations on the liability it will accept for the contractor. If this course is followed, the awarding authority may require the project company to procure that the third-party contractor provides the awarding authority with a collateral agreement containing not only 'step-in' rights but also a duty of care obligation from the third-party contractor to the awarding authority. The issue of whether the project company should be placed under an absolute as opposed to a reasonable endeavours obligation to procure such a collateral agreement is entered into in favour of the awarding authority, will depend on whether the contractor has been identified and the form of the collateral agreement agreed, prior to the signing of the project agreement.

Commissioning

7.6.23 The awarding authority may require that all commissioning and testing is carried out as part of the works and that completion of the works will not be considered as having been achieved until it has had an opportunity, with its technical advisers, to test the commissioning and, where appropriate, carry out commissioning itself. Again, interface issues will arise. A solution is for the project company and the awarding authority to agree an inspection and commissioning programme by an agreed date prior to the anticipated completion date. The programme will show the 'windows' during which the project company will be carrying out its own commissioning and testing (which the awarding authority may normally attend and witness) and also the 'windows' during which the awarding authority may have access to the works with its technical advisers to carry out its own commissioning and testing, should this be required.

7.6.24 If, for whatever reason, the 'windows' need to be altered, revised inspection and commissioning programmes will be issued. However, to take account of any difficulties which may occur if a date for commissioning needs to be altered within a very short period, it is advisable that the awarding authority ensures (and the project agreement permits) that its relevant technical advisers are on-site or are available to attend the site near the agreed window dates within a short period, such as 48 hours.

7.6.25 If the commissioning and testing reveals that an element of the works has not been carried out satisfactorily, then the project company will be required to rectify the problem and the works will then be re-commissioned and re-tested.

7.6.26 The awarding authority will normally accept that if it does not attend the relevant part of the works at the agreed date, it forfeits its right to witness the commissioning and testing or carry out its own commissioning and testing and the project company will not be required to re-commission or re-test unless the results of its commissioning and testing show that the works have not been carried out satisfactorily.

Completion

7.6.27 Under traditional construction contracts and design and build contracts it is normally accepted that, notwithstanding practical completion, there may be minor defects which remain to be rectified during the defects liability period. The position is generally no different in PFI projects. However, practical completion is critical in a PFI project as it (together with the test of whether the services at the facility are capable of being delivered) acts as the trigger for the commencement of the unitary payment.

7.6.28 The awarding authority will wish to inspect the works and satisfy itself as regards practical completion and the subsequent making good of minor defects. It will also argue that it should not be bound by certificates as to these matters issued under the construction contract. While the awarding authority will not wish to commence payment until it is completely satisfied that practical completion has taken place (and services are capable of being delivered) the project company and the debt funders will wish to ensure that this is capable of objective determination. It may be agreed that the awarding authority and the project company will jointly issue a completion certificate when they are both satisfied that the works have been carried out and completed in accordance with the project agreement. If no agreement can be reached, the matter can be referred to an independent engineer or dealt with under the disputes resolution procedure in the project agreement.[1] In some cases, as an alternative to joint certification, an independent certifier will be appointed to determine when practical completion occurs.

Responsibility for latent defects

7.6.29 Typically the construction company will seek to limit its liability to the project company for latent defects for a maximum period of 12 years from

---

1   See Chapter 16.

completion. The project company will, however, usually be liable to the awarding authority for defects in the facilities (latent or otherwise) for the entire contract term. As explained at **7.3.4** the project company will be left with the risk that falls between these two obligations. In the event that the defect gives rise to non-availability of the facility the project company will suffer deductions from the unitary payment. Where latent defects emerge but availability of the facilities and delivery of the services is unaffected, the question of whether the project company is nonetheless obliged to remedy the defects will depend on the terms of the project agreement. Where the awarding authority expects to acquire/re-acquire ownership of the facilities at the end of the contract term, it would not be uncommon for the awarding authority to impose on the project company the obligation to remedy all defects (irrespective of whether a defect affects availability).

7.6.30 The cause of the defect concerned may become a contentious issue when attempting to apportion responsibility between the awarding authority, the project company, the construction company and the operating company due to the fact that, while that the defect may be inherent, it may only have arisen as a consequence of improper use of the item concerned or failure to maintain in accordance with the agreed procedures.

Completion to time and to price

7.6.31 The completion date and price tendered may well alter (either upwards or downwards) as a result of a variety of factors including variations to the specification of the works instructed by the awarding authority (or proposed by the project company), changes in law, delay events or relief events. However, consistent with the philosophy of risk transfer, the awarding authority will wish to minimise the opportunities for the completion date and tendered price to be varied (other than as a result of a change in its own requirements). The principal matters which are likely to give rise to an entitlement to a change in the scheduled completion date or an adjustment to the unitary payment are examined in Chapter 10.

Liquidated and ascertained damages[1]

7.6.32 If the completion date (as extended by any time extension) is not achieved, the project company may be liable for loss which the awarding authority may suffer as a result of such delay. If it is anticipated that late completion will result in loss to the awarding authority, the liability of the project company is frequently set at an agreed rate of liquidated and ascertained damages and if the project company accepts a liability for delay it will wish this to be the case in order to avoid being exposed to an open-ended unquantifiable common law claim for unliquidated damages. Careful thought needs to be given by the project company as to how this liability can be passed down to its contractors. The liquidated and ascertained damages payable to the awarding authority must be a genuine pre-estimate of the loss which the awarding

---

1 See **2.2.15**.

authority may suffer as a result of the works not being completed on time,[1] but the project company's loss may be far greater than this. In addition to any amounts the project company may have to pay as damages to the awarding authority, the project company will also suffer increased funding costs and may be liable to other parties. The project company may, for instance, be liable to the operating company for loss which it may suffer as a result of a delay in the completion of the facility and the loss of payments caused by the delay. The construction contract entered into by the project company and the operating contract will need to reflect these matters.

Other issues

7.6.33 Among the many other design and construction issues which will be covered by the project agreement are intellectual property rights, ownership of fossils and antiquities, insurance obligations, and compliance with all necessary consents, laws and regulations affecting the works. This will include compliance, where relevant, with the Construction (Design and Management) Regulations 1994, SI 1994/3140 and Part II of the Housing Grants, Construction and Regeneration Act 1996.

Construction (Design and Management) Regulations 1994

7.6.34 All PFI projects will be affected by the Construction (Design and Management) Regulations 1994 as they apply to any project which includes or is intended to include construction work. The term 'construction work' is widely defined in these Regulations to include site clearance, assembly of prefabricated elements to form a structure and disassembly thereof, demolition, construction, fitting-out and alteration works (which covers works which may be carried out in the construction period of a PFI project) and upkeep, redecoration and other maintenance work (which covers works which may be carried out in the operational phase of a PFI project).

7.6.35 The main duties imposed by the Regulations are imposed on a 'client' and such duties include appointing two professionals being a planning supervisor and a principal contractor. A 'client' is defined in the Regulations[2] as meaning any person for whom a project is carried out, whether it is carried out by another person or is carried out in-house. Accordingly, both the awarding authority and the project company will, in effect, be a 'client' for the purposes of the Regulations. In practice, it is common in PFI projects for the project agreement to provide that the awarding authority appoints the project company as the 'only client' in respect of the project. It may well be that the project company, acting as the 'only client' may decide to appoint a subsidiary company or other party to act as its agent. This is permitted under the provisions of the Regulations, provided that the project company is reasonably satisfied that the person it intends to appoint as its agent has the competence to perform the duties

---

1 This is an order to avoid the damages being unenforceable as a penalty.
2 Regulation 1.

imposed on the 'client' by the Regulations.[1] Provisions to this effect in the project agreement will normally require the project company to provide the awarding authority with a copy of any declaration made to the Health & Safety Executive stating who is to act as the 'client' or its agent for the purposes of the Regulations.

7.6.36 It will be the duty of the 'only client' acting by itself or through its agent (if an agent is appointed) to appoint the planning supervisor and the principal contractor. Again, no person should be appointed as planning supervisor or a principal contractor unless the 'client' is reasonably satisfied that such person has the competence to perform the required functions and has allocated adequate resources to enable it to perform such functions. It is normally the case that the construction company appointed by the project company performs the duty of the principal contractor. The planning supervisor's duties include preparing and maintaining a health and safety file and handing over the file to the 'client' on completion of each structure comprised in the project. It is, therefore, not uncommon for the project agreement to impose an obligation on the project company to procure that a copy of the health and safety file be handed over to the awarding authority on completion of the construction phase, or on termination of the project agreement, whichever is the earlier.

7.6.37 The Regulations do not permit third parties to sue for damages in respect of any injury or death sustained as a result of a breach except in two limited circumstances. Breach of the Regulations will normally result in prosecutions by the Health & Safety Executive through the courts.[2] Directors and responsible executives of the 'client' may be liable to limited fines in the magistrates' courts or, if the matter is taken to the Crown Court, an unlimited fine and/or imprisonment for a maximum term of two years, should the offence consist of contravening a requirement or prohibition imposed by the prohibition notice served by the Health & Safety Executive. Although an indemnity cannot be given for criminal fines, an indemnity may be provided for damages where a civil action is taken in relation to the two exceptions referred to above, or to cover, for example, expenses such as legal costs and the cost of expert witnesses which may be incurred as a result of any prosecutions or court proceedings. Although the Regulations permit a 'client' to appoint another person to act as the 'only client',[3] this only has the effect of transferring the awarding authority's duties under the Construction (Design and Management) Regulations 1994 and not any other responsibilities or duties that the awarding authority may have for health and safety and specific consideration should be given to the effect of the Health and Safety at Work Act 1974 generally.

Housing Grants, Construction and Regeneration Act 1996

7.6.38 Part II of the provisions of the Housing Grants, Construction and Regeneration Act 1996 came into force on 1 May 1998 and applies to contracts

---

1 Regulation 4.
2 Regulation 21.
3 Regulation 4.

for (including arranging for) the carrying out of 'construction operations'.[1] It includes contracts for construction, maintenance and demolition of buildings or structures as well as cleaning and decorating of buildings. The effect of the Act is to give a party to a construction contract the right to refer disputes directly to adjudication.[2] The Act also sets out certain provisions governing terms and dates for payments in construction contracts. For example, parties now have a statutory right to interim payment or stage payment if the contract period is to take 45 days or more.[3] There must also now be an adequate mechanism for fixing the value of each payment and the event which makes the payment due, as well as setting out the final date for payment.[4] A party can no longer withhold sums due under a construction contract without giving notice for what is called a 'prescribed period'[5] before the final date for payment. Also, the payee has the right of suspension of performance if a sum due for payment has not been paid by the final date for payment and no effective withholding notice has been given in relation to such sum.[6] Finally, 'pay when paid' clauses are invalid, although such prohibition does not apply in cases of insolvency and does not prevent payments being made conditional on the occurrence of an unrelated event, such as completion tests, or receipt of certificate, or achievement of a milestone event.[7]

7.7 CONSTRUCTION CONTRACT ISSUES

Typical types of PFI construction contracts
7.7.1 Three different approaches are encountered in drafting construction contracts for PFI projects.

Contract based on JCT81, amended to reflect requirements of the project agreement and the debt funders
7.7.2 The advantage of this approach is that the form of the JCT81 contract is well understood by the construction industry and many of the terms of the JCT81 have been tested in the courts. It is therefore easy to identify any amendments which need to be made to it to reflect those obligations which the project company has undertaken under the project agreement and which it wishes to pass down to the contractor. However, as the JCT81 almost inevitably does not follow, in sequential order, the terms of the project agreement (which is normally drafted first) and the terms of the JCT81 are not always consistent with the terms of the project agreement, a careful review needs to be made of the JCT81 to ensure that all relevant obligations are passed down by the project company to the construction company. Therefore, although from an administrative point of view it may be easier for the construction company to deal with a form of contract based on the JCT81, it is not necessarily easy for the awarding

---

1 Housing Grants, Construction and Regeneration Act 1996, s 105.
2 See **16.6**. The project agreement is excluded from the ambit of the Act. See **16.6.2** and **16.6.3**.
3 Housing Grants, Construction and Regeneration Act 1996, s 109.
4 Housing Grants, Construction and Regeneration Act 1996, s 110.
5 Housing Grants, Construction and Regeneration Act 1996, s 111.
6 Housing Grants, Construction and Regeneration Act 1996, s 112.
7 Housing Grants, Construction and Regeneration Act 1996, s 113.

authority and project company to identify which provision in the construction contract reflects a relevant provision in the project agreement.

7.7.3 In relation to completion, if it is accepted that the construction company will only be entitled to be granted extensions of time in relation to events for which the project company is granted extensions of time, then the construction contract merely needs to state that the contractor will be entitled to claim an extension of time where the project company is entitled to an extension of time under the project agreement and that the time granted to the contractor will be no greater than that granted to the project company under the project agreement.

7.7.4 Provisions incentivising the construction company to accelerate the progress of the works may also be inserted, if commercially acceptable. Such provisions should be considered carefully. If acceleration is tied into a bonus payment (paid for early completion) and a change to the works is then instructed by the project company which delays the time by which completion occurs, the construction company could claim damages against the project company for the loss of the bonus.

7.7.5 As regards payments, the contractor is normally paid a lump-sum fixed price at specified stages throughout the construction period or by periodic valuation as under the JCT81. Stage payments can refer to relevant milestone events. The JCT81 may have to be amended to reflect other payments payable to the contractor. For example, in the case of a DBFO road project, the construction company may be paid a separate fixed fee for site security. Any other sums which the construction company may be entitled to, pursuant to the terms of the construction contract, as a result of changes to the works instructed by the project company, or for the effects of delay events, should normally be restricted to the sums which the project company receives itself under the project agreement.

Stand-alone contract based on project agreement
7.7.6 The advantage of this form of contract is that it can be compared easily to the project agreement so it is easy to identify those provisions under the project agreement which have been passed down to the construction company under the construction contract. A further advantage is that this form of contract is easy to draft as it merely follows the project agreement. Construction companies may have concerns about a stand-alone contract not based on a JCT81, however familiarity with this approach is becoming more widespread. Invariably, the construction company will participate in the negotiation of the project agreement in relation to the design and construction issues and it should therefore not have difficulty in accepting a stand-alone contract based on the project agreement.

'Partnering' contracts
7.7.7 The awarding authority's principal concern will be to ensure that the construction contract clearly identifies the output specification and the project company's proposals, and that the events allowing the construction company an extension of time or an increase in its contract sum are consistent with the project agreement.

7.7.8 The project company's debt funders' concerns will be to ensure certainty, particularly in relation to the contract sum being paid to the construction company. Accordingly, the funders will often expect to see a lump-sum based contract. However, even lump-sum contracts are not 'fixed' in that the sums can be increased or decreased as a result of variations, so the debt funders will wish to review which events can give rise to an increase or decrease in the contract sum or an extension of time. Accordingly, the debt funders will wish to see the construction company being required to take on risks such as unforeseen ground conditions including contamination, adverse weather conditions, strikes, unavailability of materials etc, which cannot be passed back to the awarding authority.

7.7.9 However, the project company may argue that if the risks are placed on the construction company, it will inevitably include a high premium for assuming them in its tendered price which may make the overall bid less competitive. If, on the other hand, the risk remains with the project company, it will only bear the actual cost which arises if the risk becomes a reality and the actual cost may be lower than the premium allowed for by the construction company in its tendered price. In light of this, 'partnering' or 'alliancing' contracts incorporating the concept of a target price are becoming more popular. Under this form of contract the construction company is reimbursed during the course of the contract for actual costs incurred (plus a fee element) rather than at tendered rates. On completion, any overspend or underspend relative to the target price is shared by the parties on a pre-agreed basis. The success of the use of a target price contract is therefore heavily dependent on the way in which the project company (or its project manager) manages all aspects of the works.

7.7.10 A form of contract which adopts this approach is the New Engineering Contract (2nd edition) ('NEC'). This contract is a departure from traditional forms of contracts, such as the JCT81, in that its style is intended to be concise and user-friendly. As a result, the NEC does not contain some of the legal and technical jargon associated with other traditional contracts. However, it is drafted in the present tense which can give rise to difficulties in interpretation and construction and therefore certain amendments or refinements are advisable.

7.7.11 The NEC aims to embody the principle of Sir Michael Latham's report *Constructing the Team* published in July 1994, and foster a spirit of mutual trust and co-operation. The NEC offers six alternative payment options (Options A–F) ranging from lump sum to cost reimbursable payment structures. Option C provides for a 'target price' contract with an activity schedule.

7.7.12 In line with the objective of achieving value for money, the NEC may present a serious alternative to the traditional lump-sum approach for some projects. However, given the uncertainty of the final price, it will clearly only be suitable where adequate flexibility is incorporated into the project company's funding arrangements.

Guarantees, bonds and retentions

7.7.13 It is common for the project company or its debt funders to require that a parent company guarantee be given in favour of the project company in respect of the construction company's obligations under the construction contract.

7.7.14 In addition, the project company and its debt funders may seek a bond, for a percentage of the construction price (commonly in the region of 10%), from a third-party surety to cover any losses or damages sustained by the project company as a result of the default or insolvency of the construction company. Debt funders usually look for a bond that is valid until the issue of the notice of completion of making good defects under the construction contract. The construction company may resist this, arguing that to obtain a bond for this period would be unnecessarily costly. A common compromise is that, upon practical completion, the bond expires but a new bond is issued in its place for the outstanding retention monies held by the project company under the construction contract. The retention will be based on the contract price as increased or decreased (as the case may be) as a result of any variations instructed as at the date of practical completion. This reduced bond will expire on the issue of the notice of completion of making good defects or a fixed date (preferred by bondsmen) which is often a few months after the contractual completion date.

7.7.15 The debt funders may seek an on-demand bond as opposed to a performance bond. An on-demand bond, more commonly available in Europe and other overseas markets, is difficult to obtain in the UK. The main concern a construction company will have in providing an on-demand bond is that such a bond may be called upon irrespective of proof of breach by the construction company under the terms of the construction contract. Also, an on-demand bond precludes the construction company arguing that the amount paid under a bond should be limited to the amount which is adjudged (either by the court or by arbitration) to be due. The project company will include the cost of any bond in its bid price and as the cost of an on-demand bond in the market is usually high it may have an adverse effect on the competitiveness of its bid.

7.7.16 The debt funders may also require a bond for a percentage of the contract price payable to the construction company as such sum is increased from time to time. This, again, is often resisted by the construction company on the basis that a bond for, say, 10% of the contract price will secure the contract price at the date the contract is entered into, so that if, after the first year of construction 50% of the works has been carried out, the 10% bond will still secure the original contract price although the actual amount at risk will be the original contract price less the value of the 50% of the works carried out.

7.7.17 Retentions are normally 3% or 5% but, again, this is a matter of negotiation which is often driven by the debt funders' requirements. Occasionally the retention can be as high as 10%. The debt funders may seek to have the retention charged to them as part of their security but the construction company will resist this and seek to have the retention placed in a separate account and held by the project company as trustee for the construction company (arguing that the retention is its money).

Chapter 8

FINANCING PFI PROJECTS

8.1 INTRODUCTION

8.1.1 One of the fundamental differences between the PFI and traditional forms of public procurement is that the private sector is responsible for financing the project up front and will only receive repayment of that financing if the capital asset meets certain performance criteria (including physical availability and performance of services to requisite standards). As few project sponsors are willing or able to put at risk the increasingly large sums required to fund a PFI project by way of equity investment (irrespective of the fact that the high cost of this would render projects unaffordable for the awarding authority), there is a requirement to obtain third-party finance (usually bank debt) to fund the up front costs of the project. The criteria that funders apply when evaluating PFI projects are not dissimilar from any other project financing transaction: the project must be commercially viable with robust cashflows.

8.1.2 To date, the sources of funding available to finance PFI projects have been predominantly the tried and tested methods generally associated with traditional project financing, although the use of bond financing is becoming more prevalent.[1] The technique of project financing has evolved around the concept of allocation of risk. PFI financing adopts a similar objective, coupled with the concerns of the public sector relating to value for money, affordability and the requisite accounting treatment of the project.[2] The underlying principle of both project financing in general and PFI financing is that recourse of the funders is limited to the cashflow or revenues of the project and, to a limited degree (depending on the nature of the project), the project assets. The extent of the recourse is always a matter for negotiation between the debt funders and the borrower in each transaction.

8.1.3 In the following sections of this chapter, the sources and nature of PFI financings will be reviewed, the debt funders' principal concerns examined and the major terms of the more common funding agreements explored.

8.2 OVERVIEW OF SOURCES OF FINANCE

8.2.1 There are numerous potential sources of finance available to the consortium in order to fund the project, the most common of which are outlined below.

---

1 See **8.2.5–8.2.8**.
2 For a detailed examination of the accounting treatment of PFI projects, see Chapter 17.

Equity

8.2.2 It is usual for PFI projects to be funded, at least in part, by equity investment. Indeed, the contribution of an agreed minimum proportion of equity (commonly between 10% and 15% of the total project costs[1]) may well be a condition of the awarding authority granting the concession (as evidence of the sponsors' level of commitment to the project and in order to enable the necessary level of risk transfer) and a precondition to the availability of third-party funders' debt facilities (in order to cushion the debt funders from the impact of risk assumed by the project company). Investors in the project (commonly the sponsors, although other parties may contribute equity, for example institutional investors, specialist PFI equity houses or funds) will subscribe for equity in the project company. Project sponsors may agree to lend debt to the project company on the basis that it is subordinated to all other borrowings of the project company. Such subordinated lending may be an alternative or in addition to subscription of equity. The degree of equity versus subordinated debt is generally determined by tax considerations and legal restrictions on the payment of dividends.[2]

Bank debt

8.2.3 This has been the most common means of financing PFI projects to date. Generally speaking, loans to finance PFI projects are documented by means of a committed project term loan with a structured drawdown and repayment profile. Depending upon the size of the project and the quantum of funds required, bank debt to a project may be syndicated to a number of commercial banks or financial institutions, each lending upon the same terms and conditions. The advantages of a syndicated project loan are, put simply, that sums may be drawn down when needed to meet costs in the construction phase of the project and the profile of repayments is generally linked to the anticipated project cashflows. In the context of the current PFI market, a syndicated loan agreement is not an unduly complex document being usually in a single currency over a 15- to 20-year period[3] at a floating rate of interest, hedged to provide fixed rate funding. As stated at **8.1.1**, the criteria that funders apply when evaluating PFI projects are not dissimilar from traditional project financing transactions. Accordingly, there is a group of experienced commercial banks in the London market more than adequately versed in the structuring of financing packages for PFI projects.

8.2.4 Finance made available through a syndicated loan will be familiar to most project participants (although perhaps not the awarding authority) and the form and extent of the representations, warranties, covenants, undertakings and events

---

[1] The precise proportion will depend upon the risk profile of the project. A riskier project will require more equity to bear the incremental risk.

[2] The ability to pay dividends to equity funders will be constrained by the distributable profits of the project company which will take some time to build up where the project company is a special purpose vehicle which has not traded (Companies Act 1985, s 263).

[3] However, maturities available in the bank market are increasing rapidly and maturities in excess of 20 years are becoming common.

of default will be negotiated between the debt funders and the project company and will to a large degree depend upon the nature of the project and its risk profile.

Bond issues

8.2.5 Although the issue of Eurobonds is one of the principal financing tools for corporate borrowings, to date there have been relatively few bond financings of PFI projects. However, a trend towards bonds is emerging following the successful bond issues for the A1(M), A419/A417 and M6 DBFO road projects, the Carlisle and Greenwich hospital projects and the extension of the Docklands Light Railway.[1]

8.2.6 One issue which has been a factor in the use of bond financing in PFI projects has been the extent to which the bondholders have been prepared to accept the risks inherent in the construction phase of a project, given that the awarding authority is only obliged to make the unitary payment once construction is complete and operations have commenced. This can be addressed by laying off the risk through the issue of bank guarantees or standby letters of credit, completion guarantees by the project sponsors (for example, the construction contractor) or by the risk being assumed by a monoline insurer which has credit enhanced the bonds. Credit enhancement has been used on most of the PFI project bond issues to date.[2] It involves the monoline insurer guaranteeing repayment of the bonds. The credit rating of the monoline provides a higher rating for the bonds than could be achieved by the project company (which will generally be a special purpose vehicle and highly geared). This improves the marketability of the bonds and, most importantly, reduces the returns required by bondholders.

8.2.7 Some of the perceived advantages of using bonds are:
- the documentation is relatively standardised;
- in general the bond markets provide a cheaper source of funds over a longer period;[3]
- bond documentation contains far less extensive covenants than a PFI credit agreement;
- the bond market provides a much broader investor base than is available in the commercial bank market; and
- bonds are bearer instruments and may be more easily traded than participations in a syndicated term loan facility (notwithstanding the provision of transfer certificates in the latter).

The availability of longer-term cheaper debt can be a key factor in delivering PFI projects which are value for money and, equally importantly, affordable by the awarding authority.

8.2.8 Some of the perceived disadvantages of using bonds are:

1　See also **18.2.5** regarding the proposed bond financing for the Channel Tunnel Rail Link.
2　The Docklands Light Railway and the Greenwich hospital projects are notable exceptions.
3　Although the syndicated debt market is responding to the challenge with finer margins and longer maturities.

- the number of parties involved in a bond issue, including the London Stock Exchange, credit rating agencies, the lead managers, trustees (both security and bond trustees), monoline insurers, depositories and paying agents, as opposed to a single syndicate agent in the case of a syndicated term loan;
- there is usually a single drawdown of bond proceeds rather than the flexibility of staged drawdowns (as under a syndicated term loan facility). This can give rise to a 'negative cost of carry' (ie in the construction period before the project company generates revenue through receipt of the unitary payment, the return on the bond monies invested (prior to being expended on the project) is lower than the returns to be paid to bondholders);
- the procedure for amending project agreements becomes a matter for bondholders in general meetings (which may be time consuming);[1]
- the amount of disclosure required in a bond issue is far more onerous than in the syndicated debt market as it exposes the project financing to the levels of due diligence and disclosure required of a public offering, which invariably raises issues of confidentiality and commercial sensitivity;[2]
- timing issues also arise due principally to the need to adhere to the issuing and marketing timetables required to list and successfully market the bonds;
- the bond markets can be volatile (the latter part of 1998 being an extreme example of this) so the cost of funding – and, indeed, the availability of funding at all – will be less certain than in the case of bank funding;
- it severely limits the scope for refinancing the project once the risky construction phase is completed and an operational track record is established, as large premiums are generally required to repay the issue prior to its scheduled maturity.

Lease financing

8.2.9 In some circumstances, leasing can be used to finance part of the project costs, particularly where major items of capital equipment are required by the project company in order to perform its obligations under the project agreement.[3] Typically, the project company would enter into a finance lease with a leasing company which will finance the capital cost of the leased assets (and own them) and recover that cost over the lease term through the payment of rental by the project company. Such leasing arrangements can be particularly attractive for the project company. As it will not receive any revenue during the construction phase, it will not have taxable profits against which to utilise the capital allowances which would be available were it to acquire the assets itself. The leasing company will have taxable profits and the benefit of the capital

---

1 If the bond issue is credit enhanced the monoline insurer will exercise the bondholder function thus reducing the problem.
2 This may be a particular problem if the PFI project is very sensitive, for example certain defence-related projects.
3 Leasing facilities were utilised in the provision of new Northern Line trains to London Underground and in the Croydon Tramlink Project. Their attraction has, however, diminished due to a reduction in the level of capital allowances available for long life assets from 25% per annum to 6% per annum introduced in the Finance Act 1996. An exception to this is railway assets.

allowances in reducing its taxable profits is passed through to the project company in the level of rental payable. Although leasing has its advantages, one of the difficulties commonly encountered in projects involving a mixture of bank debt and finance leasing is the inevitable competition for priority between the debt funders and the finance lessor. Significant and complicated intercreditor issues often arise, particularly where the finance lessor owns key assets (for example, those necessary for providing the service and generating the project company's revenue). The debt funders other than the finance lessor will wish to avoid the finance lessor effectively holding the project to ransom by threatening to terminate the lease, repossess the assets and sell them to a third party. This is a particular problem if the assets have an easily realisable residual value, less so if they are bespoke. This issue is also of concern to the awarding authority which requires continuity of service provision. Possible solutions involve direct agreements with the debt funders and the awarding authority, enabling the leased assets to be sold to a third party which will continue making them available to the project (without prejudicing the tax treatment of the financing) and the provision of letters of credit to the finance lessor to support the payment of termination sums in the event of a termination of the finance lease. This support inevitably increases the project financing costs and there has been pressure in the project finance market generally, to persuade finance lessors to dispense with letter of credit cover and assume project risk.

Other sources

8.2.10 There are other sources of finance which feature in PFI financings from time to time including investment by institutions such as the European Investment Bank and the European Investment Fund, and, in certain circumstances, government grants, such as capital grants provided for light rail schemes pursuant to s 56 of the Transport Act 1968.

8.3 TYPICAL FUNDING STRUCTURE

8.3.1 Almost all PFI projects have been financed on a limited recourse project finance basis, that is the funders will look only to the revenues of the project and to the project assets to achieve repayment. The exceptions have generally been small projects (eg equipment projects in the NHS) which sponsors (typically equipment manufacturers) have been able to undertake on balance sheet and certain IT projects.

8.3.2 The most common way in which limited recourse has been achieved in PFI projects is by the project company raising the finance being established as a special purpose company which holds no other assets apart from the project assets and which conducts no business other than that contemplated by the project agreement. The debt funders are granted security over all of the project company's assets as security for its obligations under the project documents. In this way, the sponsors' liability is limited to their equity contributions and the obligations which they may owe to the project company under any sub-contract to which they are a party (for example, the construction contract), as the project company's rights under such sub-contract will have been assigned to the debt funders by way of security.

8.3.3 The basic terms and structure of the principal loan, security and associated documents are examined in further detail at **8.5**.

8.4 FUNDERS' COMMON CONCERNS AND OBJECTIVES

8.4.1 To determine whether a project is viable or 'bankable', a detailed analysis of the project and the risks inherent in it is required. Debt funders generally appoint their own independent advisers (including legal, technical, insurance, environmental and other feasibility study advisers) and conduct their own extensive due diligence on the project.

8.4.2 The major considerations to be assessed and evaluated by the debt funders include:

- the project structure (including all project and associated transaction documents) and, in particular, the allocation of risk;
- the covenant of the consortium members and the covenant and capability of sub-contractors responsible for the implementation of the project; and
- the security package available.

8.4.3 In PFI projects, each party is dependent not only upon the performance of its counterparty but also upon the performance of all other parties to the project. The debt funders will wish to be satisfied therefore that each component of the project is compatible with all others and that together they deliver a completed, operational and profitable project. The last thing the debt funders wish to see is a 'domino effect' caused by the failure of one aspect of the project which would or may be likely to result in a failure of the whole project.

Risk allocation

8.4.4 The commercial viability of the project is obviously vital. The debt funders will look to the project cashflows to service the loan. This requires an evaluation and allocation of the various risks present in the project. The nature and extent of these risks varies from project to project. The primary goal of the debt funders will be to ensure that the risks encountered at each stage of the project (pre-construction, construction and post-construction/operation) have been properly analysed and the liability for such risks allocated in such a way as to ensure that few if any risks remain with the project company (for example, by passing them down to sub-contractors or insuring against them). This approach to risk allocation may conflict with the awarding authority's objectives. For example, if the debt funders are not content with the ability of a sub-contractor to bear a particular risk (or the sub-contractor is unwilling to bear it) they may be unwilling to allow the risk to reside with the project company, particularly if it has little equity or subordinated debt. In this situation, there will be pressure on the awarding authority to assume the risk even though the project sponsors were initially prepared to bear it.

8.4.5 Given the multiplicity of sectors promoting PFI projects and the variety of risks from project to project, there is not an exhaustive list of risks which must be assessed. An independent examination of the likely requirements for the successful operation of the particular project is required. Generally speaking, the debt funders' concerns will be the same as those of the consortium when determining the allocation of risks as between the private and public sectors but their appetite will differ from that of the consortium given the limited rewards available to the debt funders relative to those of the equity investors. As the risk profile is of such significance both to the debt funders (in order to achieve a bankable deal) and to the awarding authority (in order to achieve value for money and the correct accounting treatment) it is essential for the debt funders' legitimate interests and concerns to be expressed and addressed at an early stage in the PFI bidding process. The following is representative of those risks which debt funders invariably require to be considered.[1]

Completion risk

8.4.6 Key risk areas are planning, design and construction: until the project is completed no unitary payment is made to the project company from which to service the debt. Completion risk is discussed in detail in Chapters 2 and 7. The key issues for debt funders are that there is appropriate capability and covenant to achieve completion, that the test for completion is objective and that it does not extend to processes which are unfamiliar or untested (for example, commissioning of a bespoke IT system).

Operating risk

8.4.7 This is at the heart of the PFI: payment is made against performance. The ability to operate the project on a continuing basis within acceptable economic and technical parameters will demand a consideration of such factors as the nature and availability of the requisite technology, a competent labour force, an expert operator and skilled management. Equally important will be an analysis of the performance and payment mechanisms, to determine to what extent and how quickly deductions can be made from the unitary payment. These will be important factors in determining the extent to which the risk of such deductions can be passed down to the relevant sub-contractors.[2] In addition, if certain obligations are to remain with the project company (major maintenance, for example) they will require to be satisfied as to the level of reserves built up in the project company to meet such obligations.

Pricing risk

8.4.8 The debt funders will require to be satisfied that the project company's cost estimates, both operating costs and capital expenditure, are realistic and make satisfactory allowances for contingencies. They will wish to be comfort-

---

1 A detailed analysis of the risks encountered in a PFI project is contained in Chapter 2.
2 This is particularly important as many sub-contractors (eg facilities management companies) operate on slender margins and have weak balance sheets, making them suitable repositories for only limited amounts of risk.

able with the pricing of the provision of services. Although any mispricing will generally be borne by the ultimate service provider they may often represent a weak covenant and the debt funders will wish to be satisfied that pricing is robust and the service provider can deliver against the price quoted. As a precondition to most debt financing, the funders will require to see a minimum equity/ subordinated debt commitment from the project sponsors and other equity funders in the project company, to act as a cushion against risk impacting on the debt funders.

Revenue risk

8.4.9 The debt funders will wish to ensure that the unitary payment is made as robust and secure as possible by seeking to minimise and control the extent to which it can be attacked for under-performance by the project company. The debt funders will also seek to protect the project income stream by restricting the possibility of a decrease in the unitary payment as a result of variations to works or services. Equally, the debt funders will wish to control a request for the provision of additional services if their inclusion might change the balance of risk in the project, making subsequent under-performance by the project company more likely.

Awarding authority risk

8.4.10 Associated with the debt funders' evaluation of the payment mechanisms is the strength of the covenant of the awarding authority and whether it has the power to enter into the transaction and perform its obligations. This latter issue is discussed in detail in Chapter 4. Concerns as to the covenant of NHS trusts led to the enactment of the NHS (Residual Liabilities) Act 1996 and the Local Government (Contracts) Act 1997. It was also an issue addressed by the Bates Review.[1]

Change of law risk

8.4.11 The merits and theory of which party should bear change of law risk has given way to developing and emerging market practice. Debt funders are prepared to accept a measure of change of law risk in both the construction and operating phases of the project, subject to limits as to the nature of the change of law and the quantum of its effect.[2]

Land-related risk

8.4.12 The debt funders will wish to be comfortable with the project company's tenure of the project site in relation to its ability to perform the obligations undertaken by it under the project agreement. The land interest in/title to the site will be of particular importance if the project company is accepting any residual value risk as part of the project. The importance of the issue of site conditions will depend upon the risks which the awarding authority

---

1   See **1.3.29**.
2   The issues are discussed at **10.5**.

is seeking to transfer (for example, ground risk, contamination, discovery of fossils and antiquities).[1]

Sponsor/contractor risk

8.4.13 An important, preliminary risk often assessed by debt funders is 'sponsor risk', that is, the financial, management and technical strengths of the sponsors standing behind the project and of other non-sponsor contractors. Even where the revenues of a project are expected to be robust, debt funders may not be prepared to enter into a PFI financing unless the consortium qualifies in terms of certain minimum attributes. Given the limited recourse nature of most PFI financings, they will want to be satisfied that the project company has the qualifications, experience, technical competence and financial resources available to it sufficient to enable it to perform its obligations under the project agreement. The importance of the creditworthiness of the consortium members will be of differing significance depending upon the nature of the recourse available to the debt funders and the reliance placed on the security, completion covenants and other forms of support being provided by consortium members. It is not unusual for the debt funders to prohibit the shareholders in the project company from transferring shares in the project company, at least in the initial years of the project.

Insurance

8.4.14 As with traditional project financings, insurers are often identified as the appropriate and preferred party upon which to lay off certain risks. It is in all participating parties' interests to ensure that the project is adequately and properly insured during the construction and operating phases of the project.[2] It is usual for all of the principal parties, namely the awarding authority, the project company, the main sub-contractors and the funders, to be insured parties for their respective interests. Unfortunately, the awarding authority and the funders often have quite contrary views as to how insurance proceeds should be utilised. Historically, it has been a cardinal principle of project financing that funders have a first call upon insurance proceeds in order to repay their outstanding debt. In PFI financings this has been eclipsed by the recognition of the interests of the awarding authority in ensuring the provision of the service, be it a completed and properly functioning school, hospital, prison etc.

8.4.15 It is not uncommon, therefore, for the project agreement to contain an obligation on the part of the project company to reinstate in the case of damage to or destruction of the project asset. The debt funders will often have no objection to such a reinstatement obligation provided that the project is rebuilt to

---

1   The issues raised by different property structures in PFI projects and environmental liability are addressed in Chapter 11 and at **13.2** respectively.
2   The area of project insurances is a minefield of complex and specialised policies and provisions and, accordingly, a detailed examination of this area is beyond the scope of this chapter.

substantially the original specifications[1] and their debt service is covered during the reinstatement period, commonly through business interruption and loss of revenue insurance. Sometimes an insurance threshold amount may be set, below which the parties acknowledge and agree that the project company will be obliged to reinstate. If the damage caused is above the threshold, an economic test may be invoked and the banking financial model rerun to recalculate the relevant banking ratios (see Annex 1). Should the economic test establish that minimum banking ratios cannot be maintained between the date of calculation and the final debt maturity date, the debt funders would be entitled to receive the insurance proceeds in prepayment of the loans made available to the project company. This is usually one of the more contentious issues for negotiation between the debt funders and the awarding authority with the awarding authority arguing that, provided the facility is rebuilt as originally conceived, no right of application of insurance proceeds should arise.[2]

Default and termination

8.4.16 The debt funders will look carefully at all scenarios which may result in the termination of the project agreement.[3] As the most valuable security held by the debt funders will usually be the contractual rights, powers and remedies of the project company under the project agreement and other project documents (for example, the construction and operating agreements), it is of paramount concern to the debt funders to ensure that they may, if they so choose, keep the project alive. For this reason, restricting the events capable of leading to termination and the debt funders' rights associated with the possibility of termination are of particular interest.

Debt funders' step-in rights

8.4.17 In the case of project company default, the debt funders will commonly negotiate a direct agreement with the awarding authority providing for extended cure periods which will permit the debt funders to remedy defaults or otherwise to 'step in', appoint a receiver or a substitute entity to perform the services or, ultimately sell the project company to a third party as a going concern.[4]

Compensation for early termination

8.4.18 Inextricably linked with the interest debt funders have in events which may trigger early termination, are the provisions dealing with compensation payable to the debt funders and/or project company in the event of early termination.[5] Without satisfactory compensation arrangements, no PFI project

---

1   This is generally required so that the pre-agreed project risk allocation is not significantly disturbed.
2   See Treasury Taskforce draft *Guidance on Project Agreements* (September 1998) section 24.
3   For an examination of the common termination provisions in the project agreement, see **10.7**.
4   The more usual provisions contained in the direct agreement and the rights that debt funders commonly seek vis-à-vis the awarding authority are discussed in Chapter 9.
5   For an examination of the common provisions in the project agreement dealing with the payment by the awarding authority of compensation, see **10.9**.

will be bankable. A major concern of the debt funders is that, as they are contributing the vast majority of the finance required to fund the construction of the asset, in the event of termination the awarding authority should not be entitled to a windfall gain by acquiring a valuable asset for no consideration. They will generally seek repayment of outstanding debt and will achieve this in almost all termination scenarios other than project company default.

Transferability

8.4.19 A crucial issue for debt funders is their ability to transfer their interests under the credit agreement particularly in the context of being able to syndicate the financing. This is generally a legitimate interest recognised and accepted by the awarding authority in the project documents provided it is kept informed from time to time of the identity of the debt funders within the banking syndicate. Most financing agreements will govern the rights of any funder to assign or transfer its rights and/or obligations under those financing agreements. The awarding authority is usually on notice of the conditions attaching to transferability as it will be required to review and approve the financing agreements up front. Restrictions on transferability may be required where the project is of a sensitive nature (for instance, defence-related projects and where interests of national security are paramount).[1]

Value for money reviews

8.4.20 Increasingly, provisions are being included in the project agreement for the periodic monitoring of the level of the unitary payment made by the awarding authority. This has manifested itself through regular market testing or benchmarking of the fees payable for services undertaken by the project company over the operating period, in an attempt to ensure that the cost to the awarding authority does not diverge from market rates over a long contract period. The concern for debt funders will be the effect which such revision of pricing could have on the overall project economics (including banking ratios). Much will depend upon the frequency of such review, whether adjustments are reflected immediately (or banked, with an overall adjustment in the final years of the project agreement) and whether keeping prices in line with the market involves increases in the unitary payment as well as decreases. The issues raised are complex, not least because analysing individual components of the unitary payment against the equivalent market price will be unlikely to reflect how those components fit into the overall funding package and the fact that in a regime which demands payment against performance one cannot lose sight of the importance of the link between cost and quality.

Security issues

8.4.21 In most circumstances, security available to the funders will not include any meaningful security over the primary physical assets of the project, as the project company commonly either has no property rights in the physical assets

---

1   This control of transferability is an issue to be addressed where a bond financing is being considered, given the freely tradable nature of a bearer bond.

(as in the case of DBFO roads) or those which it has (for example, leasehold) will be subject to termination upon default (as in the case of hospitals and prisons).[1] Notwithstanding these obvious limitations, debt funders will seek a fixed and floating charge over all the assets, property and undertaking of the project company, the project revenues, monies deposited in the project bank accounts and the proceeds of the project insurances. Assignments of the contractual rights of the project company under the project agreement and other key project documentation are also essential. In addition, security will be taken over the shares in the project company. The debt funders' primary objective is to maintain the integrity of the project for the life of the loan and to enable them to take management control of the project early if things start to go wrong. In addition to the conventional security package, further control is exercised through direct agreements with the awarding authority and sub-contractors (for example, the construction and operating companies). The direct agreement is viewed by debt funders as being essential but, paradoxically, is one which has rarely, if ever, been used.[2]

8.5 KEY FINANCE DOCUMENTS

Credit agreement

8.5.1 The principal source of funding for a PFI project is likely to be a committed term loan provided by a syndicate of banks which will lend to the project company on the terms set out in a credit agreement. Funds will generally be required to meet costs in the construction phase of the project (when project revenues will be inadequate or non-existent). The loan will begin to be amortised in the operational phase of the project from the project revenues. Accordingly, the typical credit agreement will recognise the two distinct stages in any project, namely the construction or development phase and the operating phase.

8.5.2 Many of the provisions of the credit agreement in a PFI financing will mirror those found in a conventional syndicated term loan agreement for any other sort of project financing. This section examines the following provisions which are of particular importance:

- purpose clause;
- drawdown requirements;
- repayment formulae;
- representations and warranties;
- covenants, both positive and negative;
- default provisions.

---

1   Even if they had meaningful security it is likely that debt funders would be extremely reluctant to enforce given the opprobrium and public and political outcry which would result from foreclosing on a hospital or school.
2   The security package and direct agreements are discussed in Chapter 9.

Purpose

8.5.3 The credit agreement will provide that the application of funds is restricted to the particular purposes of the project. The credit agreement may make provision for the availability of separate facilities, in which case, the borrower will be restricted further in the application of proceeds for each particular facility. Commonly, debt funders will make available:

- a base loan facility required to meet projected costs in the construction phase and other permitted expenditure agreed in advance;
- a standby loan facility which may be called upon in certain limited circumstances such as costs overruns agreed by the funders; and
- other financial accommodation, such as a working capital facility.

8.5.4 The most common purposes for which funds are permitted to be applied include:

- stage payments due and owing by the project company to the construction company under the construction contract;
- the fees and expenses of the architects, engineers and other members of the project design team;
- fees payable to the agent, arrangers and the debt funders in connection with the provision of the banking facilities together with their costs and expenses associated with putting the financing in place (including all advisers' fees incurred in the debt funders' due diligence exercise).

8.5.5 In practice, the debt funders will ensure that funds are restricted to their intended purpose by channelling drawdowns through dedicated project accounts (which may be regulated by a separate account agreement) from which payments may only be made for certain agreed purposes.

Drawdown requirements

8.5.6 The credit agreement will usually specify a drawdown period during which drawings may be made, subject to satisfaction of certain conditions precedent. Conditions precedent may fall into two categories:

- initial general conditions to the availability of funds (ie before the facilities may be considered committed facilities by the debt funders);
- conditions to each drawing.

8.5.7 A credit agreement for a PFI project will contain all the usual conditions precedent to a typical corporate or project loan, including:

- delivery to the agent/funders of all constitutional documentation (ie the certificate of incorporation, memorandum and articles of association etc) of each borrower and obligor providing security or otherwise undertaking obligations in favour of the agent/funders;
- evidence of all corporate and other authorisations necessary or desirable to satisfy the agent/debt funders that the borrower and each obligor has the power, capacity and authority to enter into the finance and other transaction documents;

- delivery of all third-party licences and consents relating to the borrowing and the carrying on of the borrower's business;
- the execution and delivery to the agent/debt funders of all finance documents and security documents required in connection with the loan.

8.5.8 In addition, in a PFI project the agent/debt funders will require:

- a certified copy of the project agreement and all other project documentation (including any lease or licence to occupy the project site, the construction contract and related construction documents, the operating contract or any facilities management agreement and related operational phase documentation) together with evidence that these documents have been duly authorised and entered into by the relevant counterparties and confirmation that they have become unconditional and are legal, valid and binding upon the parties to them and are otherwise in full force and effect;
- all consents required for the design, construction, management, operation, financing and implementation of the project;
- a certificate or report on title (generally from the project company's legal advisers) together with (if required) a special environmental consultant's report;
- reports from all other specialist advisers to the funders including an insurance report, an independent engineer's/technical adviser's report, feasibility studies and an audit of the computer-generated financial model;
- a project budget prepared by the project company and approved by the agent/debt funders itemising the forecast capital and operating expenditure by the project company during the construction phase (to be updated on a regular basis during the operating phase);
- a base banking case demonstrating a satisfactory minimum and average debt service cover ratio, loan life cover ratio (or other applicable ratios);
- evidence that the minimum amount of equity/subordinated debt required by the debt funders has been subscribed and deposited in the project account by the sponsors and any other equity/subordinated debt funders (or if the subordinated debt is to be injected at a later stage, executed bank guarantees or standby letters of credit supporting that obligation);
- evidence that no claims have been made against the awarding authority for breach of the public procurement process in relation to the project.

Conditions to each drawing

8.5.9 Once the initial conditions precedent to availability of the facilities have been satisfied, the project company generally faces other standard conditions to each drawing such as the absence of an event of default or potential event of default and confirmation that the representations and warranties set out in the credit agreement remain true and correct. In addition, the debt funders will generally also require evidence that the proceeds of the drawing are required by the project company for application in or towards meeting permitted payments and where permitted payments comprise payments to the construction company under the construction contract, the debt funders will require their own technical adviser to certify that such payments are properly due and payable and that construction is proceeding in accordance with scheduled milestones, in order that completion will be achieved no later than anticipated in the project budget and financial model. Part of the independent technical adviser's certification will almost always include a certification that the project company has committed and available to it sufficient funds (whether in undrawn amounts under the loan agreement or by way of equity and/or subordinated debt) to enable it to complete construction and achieve operation under the project agreement. During the drawdown period the debt funders will require a prescribed ratio of equity and subordinated debt to senior debt drawings to be maintained.

8.5.10 Where the debt funders agree to provide standby or cost overrun facilities, it is usual that no drawing will be permitted under those facilities unless and until the base loan facility has been fully drawn and the project company has established to the satisfaction of the debt funders the purpose for which the advance will be applied, including delivery of all supporting invoices and other evidence reasonably required by the debt funders. The maintenance of the required debt/equity ratios must also be satisfied in the context of a standby loan facility.

Repayment formulae

8.5.11 As mentioned above, the credit agreement will generally recognise two distinct phases in a PFI project, the construction or development phase and the operating phase. During the construction phase, funds will be drawn down and debt service postponed, either by rolling up interest pending receipt of revenues during the operating phase or by permitting drawdowns to finance interest payments prior to the operating phase. The availability period for drawings under the credit agreement will generally end once the project has been completed and become fully operational. In this situation, when the project company begins to receive revenue to enable it to service the debt, the debt funders generally countenance an initial repayment grace period, sometimes between 6 months and 12 months after the initial commencement of operations. During this period debt service and other reserves will be built up.

8.5.12 Any repayment formula must be structured to reflect the revenues forecast to be received by the project company. The concept of linking repayments to project revenues pervades project financings. Usually, the repayment formula will require the higher of a minimum repayment and a stipulated percentage of project cashflow for the relevant period to be dedicated to amortise the loan facilities. The minimum repayment will be such as to ensure that on a worst case scenario, repayments are sufficient to ensure that the loan is fully repaid within the maximum loan term. The alternate repayment formula – a stipulated percentage of project cashflow – will typically be set at a level where, under a base case scenario, final repayment is achieved with a slight acceleration, for example up to two or three years ahead of final maturity in a 20-year facility. Repayment may also be managed by the implementation of a debt service reserve account (one in which surplus funds build up prior to committed distributions to sponsors) from which funds may be used to top up required amortisation payments where revenues are less than those originally projected.

Representations and warranties

8.5.13 Extensive representations and warranties will be required. In addition to representations as to corporate power, status and due authorisation and enforceability of the finance documentation, there will be a number of project specific representations and warranties required including:

- due authorisation and enforceability of the project agreement and other related project documentation;
- compliance with all laws relating to the implementation of the project and the due issue of all necessary licences, consents and permits;
- the project agreement and all other project documentation are in full force and effect;
- the absence of litigation involving the project company and the project assets;
- the accuracy and completeness of project information given to the funders;
- there has been no breach or default under any agreement (including project agreement);
- there exists no event of default or potential event of default;
- the project company has no assets or liabilities, has not traded and has not incurred any liability or obligation except in connection with the project;
- the project company is solvent;
- the project company has good title to its assets free from any encumbrance save for encumbrances created pursuant to any security document in favour of the debt funders and such security documents are legal, valid and binding and rank first in priority;
- the project company has disclosed all factual information relating to its affairs and the project which could be expected to affect any decision of the debt funders to provide finance and all other information which is of a material nature.

8.5.14 Specific environmental representations and warranties may be included dependent upon the nature of the project site, the results of the environmental consultant's report and the risks to be assumed.

Covenants

8.5.15 The covenants and undertakings given by the project company under the credit agreement are primarily designed to preserve the project, as represented by the project company at the date of the credit agreement, for the life of the loan. Extensive covenants will be required.

8.5.16 Most commonly, the credit agreement will contain detailed obligations to provide the debt funders with information about the project company's finances (and in some cases, the sponsors') and the project itself. The funders will also require detailed information about the progress of the project including:

- regular progress reports during the construction phase specifying the rate at which construction is proceeding, the current status of the works, the forecast completion date, the estimated cost to complete the project and detailing actual or potential cost overruns;

- regular progress reports during the operational phase specifying availability, occupancy, usage, certifying any performance points incurred etc;
- notice of any insurance claims and the receipt of any insurance proceeds;
- information regarding whether or not the construction and operating companies are complying with their respective obligations under the construction and operating contracts; and
- details of any interruption to the construction or operation of the project, including details of delay events, relief events, events of force majeure etc.

8.5.17 Apart from information covenants, the project company will undertake a series of positive covenants aimed at ensuring the maintenance of rights and performance of obligations under the project documents including ensuring that the works are at all times designed, constructed, operated and maintained in good and workmanlike manner and that the services are provided in accordance with good industry practice. The project company may be required to do everything necessary to ensure that no event of default occurs and to notify the debt funders promptly after it becomes aware of any event or matter which may give rise to an event of default. Further, the project company will generally be required to procure that the required insurances are taken out and maintained. Probably the most important of the positive undertakings given by the project company will be the requirement to maintain all authorisations and consents necessary for its business and for the implementation of the project and the observance of its obligations under the finance agreements including compliance with all laws (and, with increasing importance, in particular the environmental laws). The project company will be prohibited from making amendments to or otherwise cancelling, suspending or terminating project agreements, authorisations, consents or licences required for the implementation of the project. To enable the debt funders and their independent advisers to monitor the project throughout its term, the project company will be required to undertake to allow the debt funders and their representatives access to the project site, including the right to attend at site progress meetings during the construction phase.

8.5.18 The usual negative undertakings found in corporate or project loans will also be included, for example a negative pledge prohibiting the creation of encumbrances (other than encumbrances permitted by the debt funders) over the project company or all or any of its interests in the project. The debt funders will usually also restrict the ability of the project company:

- to dispose of any benefit under any project agreement or any interest in the project except in certain limited circumstances;
- to make loans or any other form of credit or financial accommodation except with their consent;
- to incur or permit additional indebtedness to be outstanding;
- to give guarantees;
- to incur capital expenditure other than expenditure incurred in accordance with the project budget;
- to change the nature of its business or abandon or suspend the conduct of the project.

From the debt funders' perspective, it is essential to ensure that they have the right to be intimately involved with all aspects of the project and its operation and any change to the fundamental elements which made up the basis of the credit decision, particularly where the funding is provided on a limited recourse basis. Accordingly, the debt funders will seek to ensure the integrity of the project as represented to them and recorded in the terms of the project documentation. They will prohibit amendments to the project documents without their consent.

Events of default

8.5.19   All loan agreements, whether on a general corporate basis or project finance basis, will include provisions detailing certain events which, should they occur, entitle the debt funders to cancel the facility, accelerate the loan and exercise rights under the security. The usual events of default commonly found in corporate borrowings will be included (for example, monetary defaults, breaches of representations and warranties and failure to perform other obligations, cross-default and cross-acceleration, inability to pay debts, insolvency, illegality, and material adverse effect clauses). In PFI financings, these are usually extended to include a range of project-related matters such as:

- any particular matters referred to in any of the project agreements occurring which would have the effect of threatening the viability of the project for example, construction not having been completed by the long stop date and any other material breaches of the project agreement;
- failure by the sponsors and/or other equity investors to contribute equity at the times and in the proportions agreed with the debt funders;
- government action detrimental to the project, for example nationalisation or a change in the legal status of the awarding authority;
- insolvency of any other project participant which in the opinion of the funders may have a material adverse effect on the project company's ability to observe its obligations under the financing agreements or any other project documents;
- abandonment of the project;
- any strike, industrial action or act of terrorism or sabotage which threatens the continuation of the project; and
- breach of any project ratio such as the loan life cover ratio or debt service cover ratio which are usually required to be maintained on an average and a minimum basis throughout the term of the loan.

Intercreditor agreements

8.5.20   Where there is more than one source of finance provided to fund the project, the debt funders will require some form of subordination or intercreditor agreement to govern the priorities between the various creditors. Negotiation of the intercreditor agreement can sometimes be the most time consuming and complicated element of the total financing package, depending upon the number of creditors involved and their different (and often conflicting) interests in the project, its assets and the risks assumed by each of them. It may involve a renegotiation of established positions which are themselves the product of lengthy negotiations.

8.5.21 The intercreditor agreement will detail the mechanisms and procedures for agreeing to the enforcement of security, acceleration of the relevant debt and the exercise of step in rights under direct agreements. Other issues to be addressed include the procedure for agreeing changes to the project agreement and other project documentation (for example, a variation requested by the awarding authority either to the scope of the asset being constructed or the services being provided). The parties involved in agreeing to a change will depend upon the issue in respect of which approval is being sought (for instance, increasing the margin for the debt funders would require the equity and subordinated debt funders' approval whereas the calling of an event of default would not) and/or the overall protections which individual categories of debt funders have within the project. If, for example, a finance lessor has benefited from letters of credit to support the payment of a termination sum under its finance lease, it might be appropriate for the finance lessor not to have a vote on the basis that it is protected in the event of termination. Similar issues arise if the European Investment Bank is a funder and has the benefit of guarantees or letters of credit.

8.5.22 There will be provisions dealing with the application of project revenues and the proceeds of enforcement and realisation of security. In relation to project revenues there will generally be a payment cascade which addresses the order in which revenues are applied. Payments to sponsors and other equity/subordinated debt funders will be made after scheduled payments to the debt funders (including fees and expenses) payments to fund reserve accounts and to ensure that the operating accounts have sufficient funds to meet scheduled payments (for example, to sub-contractors). They will be permitted only if the banking ratios are being complied with (and will continue to be complied with following payment) and no event of default or potential event of default is outstanding.

8.5.23 As discussed at **8.2.9**, where the finance includes a finance lease, because the finance lessor owns the assets leased to the project company, the other debt funders will be concerned to ensure that the lessor's rights to repossess the assets are controlled and managed in order that key assets (especially those essential to the generation of project revenues) remain available to the project.

8.6 REFINANCING OF PROJECTS

8.6.1 Inevitably, with the relative youth of the PFI as an initiative, there have been few cases of completed projects being refinanced. It is, however, only a matter of time, as the flow of projects reaching completion grows, before an active market in this develops. Depending on the level of any prepayment premiums which have been set by the original debt funders,[1] there may be significant cost savings to be achieved by project companies in refinancing project debt following completion (as has been witnessed in other areas of project finance such as project financing in the independent power sector).

8.6.2 Alive to this prospect, there has for some time been debate within government circles as to whether the awarding authority should be entitled to share in any enhanced profits achieved by the project company following such refinancing. Naturally, the principle of this has been vociferously objected to by project sponsors, who have argued that this is simply one potential upside outcome for the project company and unless the public sector is prepared to share in the pain of downside scenarios, they should not be entitled to share in the benefits when there is an upside scenario. There have also been concerns that, providing for a sharing of benefits by the awarding authority may encourage equity participants to inflate their initial equity returns, in order to achieve their base case return after any refinancing, and also that the requirement to share benefits may inhibit the willingness of sponsors to innovate in their financing structures at the bid stage.

8.6.3 In view of these concerns, the draft Taskforce Guidance on Project Agreements proposes that the awarding authority should only be entitled to share in refinancing benefits 'in strictly limited scenarios'. The scenarios suggested are:

– where competition has been poor (as the bid may have artificially inflated financing costs);
– where there has been a preferred bidder for an extended period (and where, as a result, the unitary payment has effectively been benchmarked to a particular rate of equity return which is higher than the project merits);
– where financing rates remain high in novel markets but are likely to fall as market familiarity develops.[2]

8.6.4 Whatever the merits or otherwise of sharing refinancing savings, the reality is that even where awarding authorities encourage bidders to offer a share of refinancing benefits as part of their initial bid, because such benefits are by their nature contingent, it will be difficult for awarding authorities to attach much, if any, significance to this benefit in their evaluation of tenders.

---

1   Opportunities for achieving these savings are likely to be much more limited where the original financing is through the bond markets where a 'spens clause' is included (which seeks to compensate bondholders for future loss of profits by reference to the yield on a Treasury stock of comparable maturity).
2   See **18.3**. See also Treasury Taskforce draft Guidance on Project Agreements (September 1998) section 14.2.4. This has already been seen in the health sector where there is a downward trend of margins reflecting debt funders' increasing familiarity with the risks associated with projects in this sector.

ANNEX I

Project Life Cover Ratio

This compares the net present value of the future revenues of the project against the debt then outstanding.

Loan Life Cover Ratio

This compares the net present value of the future revenues during the agreed term of the loan with the debt outstanding on the day in question. Accordingly, under the Loan Life Cover Ratio, the project company will not be given the credit for revenues which are forecasted to be received after the final repayment date of the facility.

Drawdown Cover Ratio

This compares the projected peak debt outstanding with the forecast net present value of the project cashflows during the term of the loan

Debt Service Cover Ratio

This is usually a historical test which compares the amount by which the net cashflow for a given period (usually 12 months) has exceeded the debt service requirement (principal plus interest).

Chapter 9

DIRECT AGREEMENTS

9.1 RATIONALE FOR DIRECT AGREEMENTS

Introduction

9.1.1 The direct agreements which will be required by the debt funders form an additional strand of their security in relation to the project. Before looking in detail at some of the more usual provisions to be found in direct agreements, it is worthwhile putting them into the context of the debt funders' overall security package in order to understand why it is that such direct agreements are required over and above the more conventional and wide-ranging forms of security.

Scope of conventional security

9.1.2 Leaving aside direct agreements, the more usual forms of security under English law (referred to in the remainder of this chapter as 'conventional security') will protect the debt funders in two critical respects.

Control over the project company's assets

Following the occurrence of an event of default under the credit agreement, the debt funders will be entitled to exercise their rights of enforcement under conventional security (typically, by way of the appointment of a receiver under a fixed charge or an administrative receiver under a floating charge: in the remainder of this chapter, both will be referred to as a 'receiver' unless otherwise specified). In this way the debt funders will be able to obtain possession and control of the project company's assets to the exclusion of the project company and its other creditors. A receiver appointed by the debt funders will be able to continue to run the business and use the assets or, alternatively, to sell the assets, either to a purchaser who wishes to take them on and run the business or by piecemeal disposal. Obviously, the aim of either course of action is to realise sums which will then be applied towards the receivership expenses and the principal, interest, costs and fees owed by the project company to the debt funders under the credit agreement (the 'bank debt').

Priority over other creditors

By taking conventional security, the debt funders ensure that, as secured creditors, they will rank ahead of other creditors of the project company on a liquidation (subject, in the case of a floating charge, to certain statutorily preferred creditors, for example certain taxes and duties, social security and pension scheme contributions and employees' remuneration).[1]

---

1   Insolvency Act 1986, ss 10 and 11.

Nature of conventional security

9.1.3 In England and Wales, conventional security will normally take the form of fixed and floating charges executed by the project company over the whole of its assets and undertaking. The fixed charges will be likely to include:

- legal or equitable charges over any freehold or leasehold real property;
- fixed charges over bank accounts and book debts;
- assignments by way of security of the project company's rights under all its main contracts, including the project agreement, the consortium contract, the construction and operating agreements and the insurance policies;
- fixed charges over, or assignments of, goodwill and intellectual property rights owned by the project company.

This security can include both assets owned by the project company at the time of execution of the charge and subsequently acquired property.

Floating charges

9.1.4 The conventional security will also include a floating charge over the whole of the project company's assets and undertaking. In addition to providing security over those assets which do not fall within the express fixed charges, it serves a protective purpose: the holder of a floating charge must be notified of any application for the appointment of an administrator and, in effect, usually has the ability to prevent the appointment of an administrator by appointing an administrative receiver under its floating charge.[1] This is important because if an application is made for an administration order, there is a statutory moratorium on the enforcement of security by creditors except with the consent of the administrator or the court. This moratorium continues once an administration order is made, the effect being that the holder of the conventional security will lose control over its enforcement.[2]

Mortgages over shares in the project company

9.1.5 The consortium members will probably be required to execute legal or equitable mortgages over their shares in the project company. These will enable the debt funders to vest ownership of the project company itself in a third-party purchaser upon enforcement following an event of default under the credit agreement. They will thus be able to dispose of the project company itself (albeit subject to all the project company's liabilities). Any provisions in the project agreement regulating changes of control of the project company – which are likely to apply during the construction period at least – must be modified to enable the debt funders to enforce their security in this way. Mortgages over the shares in the project company will not be sufficient security on their own: as such mortgages are created by the shareholders – the consortium members – rather than the project company itself, those mortgages will not cover the assets and undertaking owned by the project company. Therefore, mortgages over the shares in the project company do not give priority over the other creditors of the

---

1   Insolvency Act 1986, s 11.
2   Insolvency Act 1986, ss 10 and 11.

project company itself. Such mortgages will also not provide protection against the appointment of an administrator over the project company that a floating charge created by the project company provides.[1]

The valuable assets

9.1.6 This raft of conventional security is, of course, only as valuable as the assets which it covers. The real worth of the project company, and the principal assets against which the debt funders will make their credit assessment and decision to lend, are the main commercial contracts to which the project company is a party. It is out of the income stream earned pursuant to these contracts that the bank debt will be serviced and repaid. The key contracts will include the project agreement, the construction contract and the operating contract. It is the project agreement that gives the project company the right, and obligation, to construct, operate and maintain the asset at the heart of the project and, in return, the right to receive the unitary payments from the awarding authority. However, the project company may often not obtain any absolute right of ownership of that particular asset, having a right to occupy and use the asset for the purposes of performing the obligations in the project agreement. This right may be granted by way of a lease or other right of occupation by the awarding authority in respect of the land on which the core asset is to be constructed or the premises where the project activity is to be conducted. Such a leasehold interest or other right of occupation will be coterminous with the project agreement unless the project company is taking the residual value risk in the asset, in which case a longer leasehold interest (or even the freehold) will be granted.[2]

Security over contractual rights

9.1.7 The conventional security will charge or assign the benefit of the project company's rights under the project documentation (including any lease or licence to occupy) by way of security to the debt funders. The debt funders will be subject to the same rights possessed by the counterparty against the project company under the relevant project document (for example, rights of termination following the project company's default in performance). It should be noted that the enforcement of conventional security by the appointment of a receiver to the project company does not, in the absence of any agreement to the contrary, prevent the awarding authority from exercising its termination rights under the project agreement, indeed it may well be a term of the project agreement that enforcement of security gives the awarding authority the right to terminate the project agreement. The same is true also of the rights of the counterparties to other project documents.

Preservation of the income stream and risk allocation

9.1.8 It is of critical importance to the debt funders that the income stream of the project is not disrupted. The debt funders will equally be concerned to ensure

---

1 See **9.1.4**.
2 See **11.4**.

that risks which at the outset are not borne by the project company (for instance, design and construction risks which are passed through to the construction company under the construction contract, and obligations as to operation and maintenance which are passed through to the various operating companies through the relevant operating contracts) remain with those third parties and, notwithstanding a default by the project company, do not fall back on the project company as a result of termination of the relevant agreement.

Additional protection and remedy

9.1.9 It is in this area that debt funders require direct agreements in order to give them contractual protections in addition to the widely cast nature of their conventional security package. The direct agreement will include the right of the debt funders to have the project company's rights and obligations under the project agreement assumed by a third-party entity which is willing to take over the project and run it in accordance with the terms of the project documentation. This last element enables the debt funders to sell the project as a going concern to a third-party purchaser and to repay themselves out of the sale proceeds.

Direct agreements with other contractual counterparties

9.1.10 Direct agreements are not the sole preserve of the debt funders. The awarding authority may wish to seek them with counterparties to other significant contracts which the project company has entered into (for example, the construction and operating contracts). In this way the awarding authority can ensure that such contracts continue in full force and effect notwithstanding the project company's default under the relevant contract.[1]

9.2 BASIC STRUCTURE AND EFFECT OF DIRECT AGREEMENTS

Parties

9.2.1 Direct agreements are usually tripartite: obviously the syndicate of debt funders (acting through their agent bank) and the counterparty to the relevant project document will each be parties to the direct agreement relating to their respective project documents. If the project is being financed in the bond market rather than by commercial bank loans, a bondholders' trustee (and also, if applicable, any monoline insurer) will be party rather than an agent bank. The project company will be required to be a party so that it undertakes to enter into, and be bound by, any assumption of its rights and obligations by a third-party purchaser[2] as appointee of the debt funders. Such an assumption will be effected by means of a novation of the relevant project document. (A novation is an agreement by which all the parties to a contract agree that a third party is to stand in the place of one of the original parties. Strictly speaking, this is not a transfer of

---

1   See **2.5.6–2.5.8**.
2   See **9.1.9**.

the original contract but the extinction of the original contract and the creation of a new one: therefore the consent of all parties to the original contract and the new one is required).[1]

9.2.2 The project company also has its own reason to be a party to the direct agreement in that it will want it made clear that, if the debt funders exercise their rights under the direct agreement to step in but do not novate the project to a third-party purchaser, the debt funders are obliged to hand the project back to the original project company once the debt funders have recovered sufficient amounts to pay off the bank debt. This preserves for the project company the equivalent of the 'equity of redemption' in conventional security.

9.2.3 Where the debt funders step-in by way of appointment of a receiver, that receiver has a duty to cease to act as soon as he has repaid (or has sufficient funds to repay) all debts of the project company which he is bound to discharge, all claims which could be made against him in respect of which he is entitled to be indemnified from the secured assets, his own remuneration and all sums secured by the charge pursuant to which he was appointed.[2] If the debt funders step in by way of introducing an entity controlled by them, the direct agreement will provide that such an entity is jointly and severally liable with the original project company. The effect of this will be that, while the original project company is not relieved from its liabilities by the occurrence of such a step in, if the entity owned by the debt funders discharges the bank debt, the project company's liability in respect of that debt is discharged. It will also mean that if the debt funders step out, or the step-in period otherwise comes to an end (other than by virtue of a novation to a third-party purchaser), the remaining undischarged rights and unperformed obligations will remain with the project company. Upon discharge of the bank debt, the step-in period will end and the project will revert to the project company.

Purpose

9.2.4 The basic purpose of any direct agreement will be to provide the debt funders with a breathing space following a material breach by the project company of its obligations under the relevant project document. The debt funders will require, therefore, that any rights of termination or cancellation under the relevant project document which might arise from such a breach are suspended for a limited period while the debt funders decide what they wish to do and then implement their decision. Without this breathing space, the risk is that the counterparties to the project documentation will exercise their rights of termination or cancellation and either leave the project company as a worthless entity (for example, if the awarding authority terminates the project agreement, revoking the right of the project company to run the project and to receive the unitary payments) or throw onto the project company risks which it is not in a position to manage and which have been deliberately passed down to others (for example, under the construction contract or the operating contract).

---

1 See *Chitty on Contracts*, Vol 1, para 19–050 (27th edn, Sweet & Maxwell, 1994).
2 *Rottenberg v Monjack* [1993] BCLC 374.

What is in it for the counterparties?

9.2.5 It will be appreciated from this that the effect of the debt funders' requirement for direct agreements draws third parties into contractual relations with them which would not otherwise arise. It will also be apparent that the nature of those contractual relations is, in essence, that a counterparty to a material project document is being asked to weaken, or at least delay, the rights of redress which it has negotiated with the project company. At first sight, one may well ask why any counterparty would want to make such a concession. The answer is twofold.

9.2.6 First, it will be apparent from what was said at **9.1** that the protections provided by conventional security do not, of themselves, provide adequate protection to the debt funders. Accordingly, over the last ten years or so, debt funders in the project finance market have come to insist on the inclusion of direct agreements in their armoury of remedies. Therefore, market practice means that, without direct agreements, the debt funders will not be prepared to lend to the project at all.

9.2.7 Secondly, all experienced participants in project financing know that the debt funders will require such direct agreements for the reason just explained but will also realise that they can turn the negotiation of the direct agreement to their own advantage so that while, on the face of it, they may be watering down rights they have negotiated with the project company, they benefit in other respects. The whole purpose of direct agreements for the debt funders is to ensure that the project is kept alive, at least for a period while the debt funders determine what they wish to do in the long term. Counterparties to the principal project documents should take the view that, for so long as there is somebody who continues to comply in all material respects with the obligations owed to them and who is exploring ways in which the project can be saved, it is ultimately in their interests to agree to a restriction on the exercise of their strict contractual rights against the project company as the preservation of the project should result in them receiving the return which they originally anticipated. Further, almost all participants in projects are in it not only for financial reward but also to be associated with a successful project and thus generate commercial goodwill and establish a track-record of proven success.

9.3 PRINCIPAL TERMS OF A TYPICAL PFI DEBT FUNDERS' DIRECT AGREEMENT

Introduction

9.3.1 This section deals with some of the more usual provisions of the direct agreement which will be negotiated between the debt funders, the project company and the awarding authority. Obviously, the preservation and continued performance of the project agreement is at the heart of the project. It is also the case that the direct agreement with the awarding authority is likely to be the most detailed and most complicated of the various direct agreements which the debt funders will require. The comments in this chapter reflect experience to date of PFI projects and project financing principles generally.

Notice of intention to terminate

9.3.2 The awarding authority will be required to give a copy of any notice of its intention to terminate the project agreement to the debt funders before or at the same time as (or as soon as possible after) such notice is served on the project company (a 'termination notice'). Except in very extreme circumstances, the project agreement will only be capable of termination after a notice period. The debt funders may well try to broaden the scope of this so as to oblige the awarding authority to copy to the debt funders any notices of breaches (for example, awards of penalty points or rectification notices) which are served on the project company. This will enable the debt funders to monitor the project company's performance more closely and to have advance warning of emerging problems.

9.3.3 Although the credit agreement between the debt funders and the project company will normally contain an express undertaking by the project company to provide the debt funders with a copy of all material notices which it receives from the awarding authority, the debt funders will not wish to rely solely on that undertaking in this situation. In particular, if something so fundamental has occurred which entitles the awarding authority to give a termination notice, timely action will be essential and the debt funders will want to know about it as soon as possible. If the debt funders are dependent upon the project company's performance of its undertaking to pass on notices, there is too much scope for unnecessary delay in the debt funders becoming aware of the termination notice and even the risk that the project company will deliberately fail to notify the debt funders in the hope (possibly misplaced) that it will be able to solve the problem itself in negotiations with the awarding authority.

Step-in notice

9.3.4 The direct agreement will usually provide that, before any termination of the project agreement can become effective, the debt funders have a period within which to appoint a receiver and/or to serve a counter-notice on the awarding authority of their intention to step in (a 'step-in notice'). The service of a step-in notice may not actually oblige the debt funders to step in: it may be merely an indication of intention pending detailed due diligence of the project's problems.

Means of taking over the project

9.3.5 The debt funders can take over the project by:
- running the project themselves or appointing a receiver (or similar officer) over the project company;
- procuring that an entity controlled by the debt funders (a 'substitute entity') takes over the project and duly performs the obligations under the project documentation.

If the project is to be taken over by a substitute entity the awarding authority may require evidence that the substitute entity will have the requisite technical and financial capability to run the project, in order to avoid the risk that step-in merely compounds the problem. Equally, the debt funders are unlikely to go to the trouble of appointing a substitute entity if they do not believe it can address and manage the problem.

Step-in date

9.3.6 The step-in notice will specify a date on which it is intended that the step-in is to take effect (the 'step-in date'). The period between the issue of the step-in notice and step-in becoming effective is to give the debt funders a realistic time to assess what is going wrong with the project, to mobilise whatever resources may be necessary to step in and to obtain any necessary internal approvals (such as credit committee consents) from each of the debt funders. The maximum length of time between the step-in notice and the step-in date will be specified in the direct agreement. There is no standard period, the length depending upon the nature and complexity of the project in question.

Length of step-in period

9.3.7 The period for which the debt funders are permitted to step in (the 'step-in period') will be open to negotiation. The fact that the debt funders elect to step in will not, in itself, extend the contract term. The best position for the debt funders will be for the step-in period to last until the first to occur of:
– the expiry of the contract term;
– the date on which the debt funders have recovered the bank debt in full together with all costs incurred in order to step in and as a consequence of having done so (whether by way of running the project, receivership or novation to a third party).

9.3.8 It is unlikely that such a position will be achieved commercially. The awarding authority may well take the view that the debt funders should only be permitted to step in for long enough to remedy what has gone wrong with the project and to get the project back on track and, if the original project company is not suitable to carry on the project thereafter, to find a third party to whom the project is transferred. The consortium members may also object: they will want the project to revert to the project company once the problems have been resolved so that they can recover their original investments, earn further income by performing under the project agreement and benefit from any long-term increase in value in the project.

Pre-completion step in

9.3.9 The acceptability of any particular length of step-in period will depend on the technical complexity of the project. The debt funders may argue (with justification) that if step-in occurs before the end of the construction period, the step-in period should be longer than if it occurs during the operating period. The rationale for this is that stepping in during the construction period will inevitably

Step in following credit agreement events of default

9.3.10 The debt funders' own credit agreement will contain a raft of detailed events of default following the occurrence of which the debt funders will be entitled to withhold further advances, to demand immediate repayment of money already advanced and to enforce conventional security.[1] These will be far wider in scope than the termination events in the project agreement and are likely to be triggered earlier. Some debt funders seek to obtain the right to step in and take over conduct of the project on the occurrence of an event of default (as stepping in is analogous to the exercise of conventional security, which normally becomes enforceable on the occurrence of an event of default) even if the circumstances triggering the event of default under the credit agreement fall short of those giving rise to a termination event under the project agreement. The awarding authority will argue that the detail of the events of default is largely a matter between the debt funders and the project company and that the occurrence of one of them will give the debt funders sufficient influence over the project company to bring pressure to bear on it to remedy the problem (for example, by making a waiver of the event of default conditional on remedial steps being taken) and that step-in rights are not necessary at that stage and should remain a remedy of last resort.

Credit agreement consequences of a termination notice

9.3.11 Even if there is no pre-existing event of default under the credit agreement, once a termination notice has been served, the debt funders will have a very high degree of influence over the project company. The fact that the awarding authority is entitled to give a termination notice will itself constitute a potential event of default or an event of default under the credit agreement, thereby entitling the debt funders to refuse to disburse any further advances to the project company under the credit agreement, to demand immediate repayment of the bank debt already advanced and to enforce conventional security. The debt funders will, therefore, be in the practical position of being able to influence the project company's conduct.

Risks of going into possession

9.3.12 It is unlikely that the debt funders will wish to take over the running of the project in person. First of all, they are bankers and, although their understanding of the project and its risks will be extremely thorough, they are unlikely to be suitably qualified to run the business on a day-to-day basis. They will also not wish to incur potential liabilities as mortgagees in possession. A mortgagee who goes into possession of the property over which he has a charge is under a duty to account strictly to the mortgagor. The mortgagee in possession will be liable to the mortgagor for gross or wilful negligence resulting in damage

---

1   See **8.5.19**.

to the charged property. He is liable to account to the mortgagor for the rents and profits which he has, or without wilful default might have, received from the time of his possession and this includes profits from the running of the business. If the mortgagee in possession sells the property the subject of the mortgage, he is liable to account for the proceeds of sale which without wilful default he might have received.[1]

Appointment of a receiver

9.3.13 The risk of incurring the potential liabilities of a mortgagee in possession can be avoided if a receiver is appointed. Some awarding authorities have sought to extract an agreement from the debt funders that they will not appoint a receiver over the project company or any of its assets. This is, in most cases, an unjustifiable restraint on the debt funders. First (as noted at **9.1.4**), the debt funders may need to appoint an administrative receiver in order to prevent the making of an administration order (and the consequential statutory moratorium on the enforcement of creditors' rights). Secondly, so long as the material obligations in the project agreement continue to be performed during a receivership or an administration, and the awarding authority retains the ability to terminate if they are not, the debt funders' remedies do not need to be fettered.

9.3.14 Accordingly, the terms of the direct agreement are likely to contain an express acknowledgement that the debt funders are entitled to appoint a receiver or similar officer. A receiver is the agent of the project company, rather than of his appointor (the chargee).[2] The debt funders will not be responsible for what a receiver does for so long as he is the project company's agent, except where the debt funders direct, or interfere with, the receiver's actions.[3] However, in practice, the debt funders will have some influence over the receiver as the receiver may be heavily dependent on the debt funders making further money available in order to be able to continue to run the project while in receivership.

Appointment of a substitute entity

9.3.15 As mentioned at **9.2.3** and **9.3.5**, the debt funders may step in through the medium of a substitute entity. This gives them the protection of a limited liability vehicle between themselves and the liabilities arising from the conduct of the project. A substitute entity will also be directly under the control of the debt funders in a way that a receiver cannot be.

9.3.16 It is important to remember that step in is a right exercisable at the option of the debt funders and not an obligation. If a termination notice is served and it is believed that the project is an irremediable failure, the debt funders can walk away from it, enforce their conventional security to liquidate the assets and write-off the unpaid balance of the bank debt to the extent not discharged by

---

1   In relation to liabilities of mortgagees in possession, see Fisher and Lightwood's *Law of Mortgage* (10th edn, Butterworths, 1988).
2   Insolvency Act 1986, s 44(1) (in the case of an administrative receiver) and Law of Property Act 1925, s 109(2) (in the case of a receiver appointed under statutory power).
3   *Standard Chartered Bank Ltd v Walker* [1982] 3 All ER 938; *American Express International Banking Corporation v Hurley* [1985] 3 All ER 564.

compensation payable by the awarding authority on termination. If the debt funders choose not to exercise their step-in rights, the awarding authority will be entitled to terminate the project agreement in accordance with its terms.

Stepping out

9.3.17 Even if the debt funders do step in, they will not wish to be irrevocably committed to the running of the project no matter what. Therefore, the direct agreement will provide that, once the debt funders have stepped in, they will be entitled to step out (ie to hand back the project) if, for example, it becomes apparent that the project is not viable from the debt funders' point of view.

Step-in undertaking

9.3.18 If the debt funders elect to step in, the awarding authority will require some form of assurance of continued performance during the step-in period. To date, that assurance has often taken the form of an undertaking (a 'step-in undertaking'), given by the debt funders directly to the awarding authority. The debt funders may succeed in persuading the awarding authority to accept a step-in undertaking from their substitute entity. However, from the awarding authority's point of view, a step-in undertaking issued by the substitute entity will be of less value and comfort than one furnished directly by the debt funders. An alternative to a step-in undertaking is for the debt funders to procure that a creditworthy third party (such as another bank) furnishes a bond which the awarding authority can call on for payment if a default occurs during the step-in period (up to an agreed aggregate maximum amount). The third party issuing the bond will require a counter indemnity for reimbursement from the debt funders. However, as outlined at **9.5**, some direct agreements are now being settled without any step-in undertaking at all.

Pre-step in liabilities

9.3.19 One of the first issues to arise in relation to a step-in undertaking will be the extent to which the debt funders are to be liable for any defaults or liabilities of the project company which have accrued before the step-in date. The awarding authority's position (at the start of negotiations at least) is likely to be that it should be in no worse position vis-à-vis the debt funders, their receiver or their substitute entity than it was vis-à-vis the project company. Therefore, the argument goes, step-in should not absolve the parties from the need to remedy any pre-existing defaults and to meet any accrued liabilities. There are a number of counter-arguments to that. First, if they give a step-in undertaking directly, the debt funders will in fact represent a better credit risk than the original project company and the awarding authority will be in a better position (by virtue of the debt funders having deeper pockets than the project company) than it was when it originally awarded the project to the project company. The second argument is that it is unlikely to be acceptable for step-in rights to be exercised if there is a risk that unknown or unquantified liabilities at the time of step-in could subsequently emerge and be the responsibility of the debt funders or a substitute entity.

9.3.20   It is commonly provided that the awarding authority is obliged to notify the debt funders of all unperformed obligations and to identify and quantify all accrued but unpaid financial liabilities which have arisen up to the point of step-in. Until the actual date on which they step in, the debt funders will have the right to decline to step in (including the ability to revoke any step-in notice in the light of the disclosure of such obligations and liabilities).

9.3.21   If the debt funders choose to step in and issue a step-in undertaking (either directly themselves or by means of their substitute entity) or procure the issue of a bond, the awarding authority may have to agree that the pre-step-in date obligations and liabilities are capped at the amounts notified to the debt funders before the step-in date. Alternatively, the amount of such pre-existing obligations and liabilities may not be capped by reference to those already identified at the step-in date but the debt funders may accept responsibility for them (even if not known or notified at the date of step-in) subject to a monetary cap on the aggregate liabilities of such pre-existing liabilities, whenever they become known.

Step-in period liabilities

9.3.22   The debt funders may not accept unlimited liability in respect of obligations and liabilities arising during the step-in period and insist on a monetary cap on those too (in particular, if they are being asked to issue a step-in undertaking directly, rather than through the medium of their substitute entity). Whether or not such a cap is acceptable to the awarding authority will depend on the circumstances and the parties' respective bargaining positions. One compromise is to set a monetary cap but to provide that, if reached, the debt funders will either be obliged to step out and return the project to the awarding authority or to negotiate a further cap. In these circumstances, the direct agreement may contain a mechanism whereby, once the initial cap on liabilities arising during the step-in period has been reached, it thereafter increases by fixed amounts, subject to the debt funders not having served notice that they then wish to step out (in which case their liability will be limited to the level of the monetary cap then prevailing).

Capping liabilities

9.3.23   At present, there is no generally accepted market practice as to whether or not there should be a cap on liabilities which have arisen before the step-in date or liabilities which arise during the step-in period and, if so, how the levels of such caps are to be determined. Awarding authorities are increasingly recognising that some form of limitation on liability will be required although it is not always acknowledged in the initial draft of the direct agreement which the awarding authority offers for discussion.

Nature of debt funders' liabilities

9.3.24   The direct agreement will be entered into by the agent bank on behalf of the debt funders. One issue which may arise is the extent to which the debt funders' obligations under a step-in undertaking are to be several or joint and several. Under the credit agreement, the obligations of the debt funders to advance money in accordance with the credit agreement will be several: each debt funder will be responsible for its own commitment to participate and will not be obliged to advance any further money if another debt funder does not fulfil its commitment to participate for any reason. The debt funders will wish the same principle to apply in respect of their liability under any step-in undertaking. However, the awarding authority may be unwilling to expose itself to the possibility of a failure by one debt funder which would mean that the awarding authority's overall protection under the step-in undertaking will be reduced.

Awarding authority's intervention rights

9.3.25 The awarding authority have its own rights of intervention under the project agreement which will be exercisable in extreme circumstances, for example in cases of emergency or where a breach poses a serious threat to safety. The direct agreement will, therefore, need to set out a clear relationship between these rights exercisable by the awarding authority and the debt funders' rights of step-in. In the absence of provisions regulating competing step-in rights, the debt funders' rights are likely to be subject to the awarding authority's rights of intervention, by virtue of the fact that by stepping in under the project agreement the debt funders will be bound by the terms in the project agreement giving the awarding authority their step-in rights. A key issue will be the extent to which the unitary payments are made during the awarding authority's step-in. If it is a true operational emergency, the unitary payment may well continue, perhaps reduced to reflect the fact that certain services are only paid for on a usage basis (for instance, photocopying or catering). In such a situation, the debt funders ought to be content so long as the unitary payment made covers debt service. Where, however, step-in is triggered by breach by the project company and the need of the awarding authority to ensure continuity of service provision, the issue may become more difficult. The awarding authority may wish to make deductions from the unitary payment for failure to perform and to cover the cost of it stepping in. This may result in a greatly reduced unitary payment which may be insufficient to cover debt service. A solution may be to allow the awarding authority a period during which the reduced unitary payment is made, followed by a period during which deductions are restricted to the awarding authority's costs of stepping in.

Can the project agreement be assigned?

9.3.26 In the absence of a stipulation to the contrary, the rights under a contract are assignable. The courts have recognised circumstances in which an assignee is not permitted to enjoy the benefits assigned to him without also accepting the burdens of the contract.[1] Contracts are not assignable, however, where a party has contracted on the basis of the counterparty's specific personal characteristics. In awarding the project (in particular, after a tender procedure) the awarding authority will have chosen the project company because of its specific merits and

---

1   See *Chitty on Contracts*, Vol 1, paras 19–044 and 19–045 (27th edn, Sweet & Maxwell, 1994).

suitability to undertake the project in accordance with the project agreement's criteria and to deliver value for money in so doing. It is, therefore, arguable that the project agreement is a personal contract and thus not assignable as a matter of general law. In any case the project agreement is likely to prohibit expressly any assignment of rights by the project company or the creation of security over, or transfer of, its interests without the awarding authority's consent.[1]

Transferring the project to a third-party purchaser

9.3.27 The debt funders may find a third party who is willing to take over the project. Given the relatively short time that the debt funders are granted in which to decide whether or not to step-in, it is unlikely that they will find a third-party purchaser who will be able to do all necessary due diligence to take on the project before the step-in date. Therefore, the debt funders will want the ability to transfer the project during the step-in period to a third-party purchaser, by novating the project company's rights and obligations. The project agreement will need to reflect the ability of the debt funders to novate the project to a novatee pursuant to and in accordance with the mechanism set out in the direct agreement.

Identity of novatee

9.3.28 Where the debt funders wish to novate the project to a third-party purchaser, the awarding authority will require the right to satisfy itself as to the technical ability and financial resources available to the proposed novatee, the identity of its shareholders and the amount and structure of its share capital. A novation will only be permitted if the awarding authority has not objected to the novatee. The direct agreement may specify the grounds on which approval may be withheld. The debt funders will want such grounds to be as narrowly drawn, and as objective, as possible.

Sensitive projects

9.3.29 The intrinsic nature of some projects may justify the awarding authority specifying more exacting (or more subjective) criteria to be met by a proposed novatee: for example, defence-related projects or those with a public safety aspect (such as prisons) may give rise to particular concerns about the identity and reputation of the novatee.

Revising the novation proposal

9.3.30 If the details of a proposed novatee are not initially acceptable to the awarding authority, the direct agreement will make provision for a limited time within which the proposed structure of the novatee, or the resources intended to be made available to it, can be revised and resubmitted to the awarding authority

---

1 But see **9.4.2**.

for approval. However, there will be some deadline on this process to prevent it carrying on indefinitely.[1]

The step-in period and novation

9.3.31 Any novation will also be subject to the debt funders having first complied with their obligations under their step-in undertaking. Upon novation occurring, the step-in period will end and the step-in undertaking will be released. Where the project is to be novated, there will need to be provision as to the extent (if any) to which any outstanding defaults or liabilities which have occurred or accrued before such novation are to be passed to the novatee. From the time of such novation, the provisions of the project agreement will apply and the awarding authority's rights of termination will apply in respect of the novatee and its conduct of the project. This is a particular issue if penalty points have accrued during the step-in period, or in respect of penalty points accrued prior to step in which were suspended or ignored during the step-in period.[2] Ideally a novatee will wish to have a clean slate from which to have its performance measured.

How often can step-in occur?

9.3.32 The awarding authority sometimes attempts to limit the number of occasions on which step-in may occur. There have been instances where the awarding authority has started from the position that step-in should only be permitted once. However, given the lengthy contract terms in PFI transactions (25 or 30 years in some cases) and the longer maturities which the debt funders are increasingly willing to provide, this is viewed by banks as an unreasonable restriction. It is possible to envisage circumstances in which, for example, the construction period may give rise to problems requiring step-in, the project may then be constructed in accordance with the project agreement and revert to the original project company but some other problem emerges during the operating period which triggers the step-in rights under the direct agreement. Therefore, direct agreements may provide that there is an initial limit on the number of times step-in can be invoked, for example, once every five years, but that it may be invoked more frequently subject to the debt funders bearing the reasonable costs of the awarding authority in relation to considering the application for step-in and its implementation or paying a fixed fee to the awarding authority.

9.4 OTHER COMMON PROVISIONS

9.4.1 There are a number of other important points which are usually covered in direct agreements, although they generally give rise to less intense negotiation than the provisions governing termination, step-in and novation rights.

---

1   An alternative mechanism adopted in some projects is to allow the debt funders to propose several possible novatees, receive approval for any who are acceptable to the awarding authority and then negotiate with an approved party.
2   See **9.4.4**.

Consent to security

9.4.2 As previously mentioned, the conventional security granted in favour of the debt funders will include an assignment by way of security of the project company's rights under the project documentation. The project agreement is likely to contain a restriction on assignments and the direct agreement will, therefore, provide for an acknowledgement of such assignment and consent by the awarding authority for the creation of security over the project documentation. The debt funders may also seek the awarding authority's confirmation that it has not been notified of any prior assignments or security.

Notification of credit agreement defaults

9.4.3 The awarding authority may require the debt funders to notify it of the occurrence of any potential event of default or event of default under the credit agreement and of the taking of any steps for the enforcement of the debt funders' conventional security. Even though the circumstances giving rise to these may not themselves constitute a breach of the project agreement, the awarding authority may be concerned to have notification of them directly from the debt funders as such events may be an advance warning of problems with the project company.[1]

Extension of remedy periods etc

9.4.4 If remedy periods are already running on the step in date or the project company is close to reaching the limits of penalty points in respect of defaults under the project agreement, the direct agreement may provide for an extension of those remedy periods to allow the debt funders a proper period immediately following step-in to get to grips with the problems. In respect of penalty points accrued up to the step in date, it may provide that penalty points incurred by the project company before step in are ignored or at least suspended during the step-in period. It would clearly be unreasonable, and pointless, if step in were to be given effect to at a time when a remedy period was already running which would expire very shortly after the step-in date, or a penalty points threshold was close to being exceeded thus significantly increasing the likelihood of the awarding authority being able to terminate the project agreement within a short period.

Payment instructions

9.4.5 The direct agreement may also provide that payments by the awarding authority during the step-in period are to be made directly to the debt funders rather than via the project company. The intention of this is to try to protect the debt funders from having to compete with other creditors on an insolvency of the project company.

---

1 This is similar to the motivation of the debt funders in requesting information regarding breaches of the project agreement. See **9.3.2** and **9.3.3**.

9.5 RECENT DEVELOPMENTS

Step-in undertakings

9.5.1 Recently draft direct agreements have been put forward for negotiation in PFI projects (both bank and bond financed) on the basis that there should be no step in undertaking given, whether in respect of pre-existing or future liabilities but which allow the awarding authority to deduct any future liabilities as part of the calculation of the unitary payment made during the step-in period and, assuming the step-in is unsuccessful, to set off any pre-existing or remaining liabilities from compensation payable on termination. Without such an undertaking the debt funders are being given a cure period during which to resolve the problem without undertaking any liability themselves. This may be driven by a concern about the open ended nature of liabilities under a step-in undertaking (although this has been addressed by the use of monetary caps) and the fact that being required to issue a step-in undertaking (or furnish a bond) may in fact discourage the debt funders from ever exercising their step-in rights and, therefore, not add to the chances of preserving or rescuing a project. This approach was taken in the draft direct agreement issued by the Treasury Taskforce for consultation in June 1998. Undoubtedly the existence of the Taskforce draft has conferred an informal endorsement of the approach and hardened banks in their resistance to the traditional more onerous forms of direct agreement.

Bond financing and direct agreements

9.5.2 As noted in Chapter 8, the use of bond financing for PFI projects is on the increase. The use of bond financing raises the issue of whether it is feasible to expect a step-in undertaking to be issued. The potential problem arises from the fact that bonds will be held by a disparate anonymous group of investors from whom it is clearly not practicable to seek a step-in undertaking and bondholder trustees are, by their nature, cautious and clearly will not commit themselves to potential liabilities without being indemnified or funded to their satisfaction. Where a bond is 'wrapped' with a guarantee from a monoline insurer, the monoline insurer may be prepared to give the step-in undertaking itself (either directly or via a step-in vehicle). However, in the case of unwrapped bonds it may be that the approach outlined in the Treasury Taskforce draft direct agreement is the only practical compromise.

9.6 CONCLUSION

It remains to be seen how the issue of step-in undertakings will develop and shape the nature of direct agreements in the future. Although arguments regarding the unwillingness of banks and bondholder trustees to give undertakings cannot be ignored, it is equally the case that the awarding authority should expect a level of protection and comfort for agreeing to defer the exercise of its contractual remedies or, indeed, its right to stepin itself. This is the balance which the Treasury Taskforce draft direct agreement seeks to strike. It remains to be seen how the Taskforce draft direct agreement will be amended in the light of comments made during the consultation period. Undoubtedly, however, the issue of the final form is likely to set the approach going forward.

Chapter 10

NEGOTIATING THE PROJECT AGREEMENT

10.1 INTRODUCTION

10.1.1 The project agreement (sometimes referred to as the 'concession agreement') is the core contractual document in any PFI project. Lying at the heart of the contractual framework,[1] it governs the relationship between the awarding authority and the project company. The role of the project agreement is to set out the core obligations of each of the parties and, in doing so, to establish the allocation of risk between them.

10.1.2 Whilst the negotiation of the project agreement is fundamentally a matter for the contracting parties, neither the awarding authority nor the project company can negotiate in isolation. There is now, in each sector where PFI has application, a body of precedent of previous transactions which will set a backdrop for the negotiations. Quite often what was agreed between the parties on a previous deal will be cited by one side or the other in support of their position on a particular point. In any event, the awarding authority may be subject to the constraints imposed by the need for approval by other governmental bodies: an NHS trust, for example, will require the approval of the NHS Executive and of HM Treasury (where the project is sufficiently large) besides that of its own board of directors. The Treasury Taskforce will oversee the negotiation of the projects which it has identified as 'significant projects'.[2] Those bodies will inevitably have access to all documentation for previous projects and be testing the degree of risk transfer achieved on each new deal against that body of precedent (as well as, where applicable, their own published guidance). The project company, on the other hand, will require approval of its negotiated position by its funders. Likewise, the sub-contractors to the project company must agree to assume the obligations which are to be passed down to them through sub-contracts, before the project company can contract to their performance at the project agreement level.

10.1.3 The result of these often conflicting factors is that the negotiation of the project agreement is more complicated than it may first appear. The number of parties involved and their differing objectives[3] makes the negotiation inherently complex.

10.1.4 The starting point for negotiation of the project agreement is the draft project agreement usually produced on behalf of the awarding authority. The

---

1 See Figures 1 and 2 of Chapter 2.
2 A list of the first 50 significant projects was announced by the Treasury Taskforce in February 1998. A second tranche of 30 further significant projects was announced on 21 October 1998.
3 See Chapter 2.

relative novelty of PFI transactions meant that in the early years, after the launch of the initiative, precedent agreements were not always available. As a result, different PFI sectors have adopted varying approaches. In some sectors, a model form contract which became used for successive deals emerged fairly quickly. In the case of road projects, for example, the Department of Transport developed a model form project agreement which has been successfully used on a number of projects. As groups of this type of project have gone forward, the model form has developed in tandem. Likewise, the project documentation issued on behalf of the Home Office on recent prison projects is a development of the original documents issued for the first two prison schemes at Bridgend and Fazakerley.

10.1.5 In contrast to roads and prisons, NHS hospital projects have been specific to individual NHS trusts rather than common to a single government department. Different trusts have, inevitably, produced different solutions to contractual issues in conjunction with their advisers. Notwithstanding the efforts of the NHS Private Finance Unit to provide centralised guidance, there has been a wide range of different precedents for NHS projects emerging in the market. Undoubtedly this has caused delay and frustration as the wheel has been, to some extent, reinvented across a number of projects. However, the end result has been that the NHS has had the benefit of a broad range of precedents, with their respective solutions for different areas of risk allocation, in developing its centralised guidance and model form contract.

10.1.6 The passage of time and the increasing numbers of PFI projects reaching financial close means that a body of market practice has developed. This assists with the task of preparing a draft model project agreement and, in turn, means that projects in the more established sectors can be delivered more efficiently.

Centralised guidance on project agreements

10.1.7 The need to produce centralised guidance and/or standard form documentation to streamline the production and negotiation of project agreements has been recognised for some time and was highlighted in a number of recommendations in the Bates Review.[1]

10.1.8 A series of publications was issued jointly by the Treasury and the Private Finance Panel with a view to addressing this including:

– *Private Opportunity, Public Benefit – November 1995*;
– *Basic Contractual Terms – October 1996*;
– *Transferability of Equity – October 1996*;
– *Further Contractual Issues – January 1997*.

10.1.9 Whilst these publications (in particular, *Further Contractual Issues*) had some educational value to newcomers to the initiative, in general they did not offer standard wording in the areas that have proved most troublesome in negotiations and the positions espoused on a number of issues were controversial.

---

1   See **1.3.23–1.3.25**.

10.1.10 Recognising the shortcomings of the earlier guidance, the Treasury Taskforce has announced its intention to provide a more comprehensive suite of guidance on project agreements and has embarked on an extensive consultation exercise across both public and private sectors with a view to ensuring that this guidance is balanced. Adrian Montague, Chief Executive of the Treasury Taskforce outlines it as follows:

> 'It is vital that the template accurately reflects market practice, and that we pitch its balance of risk and reward just on the public sector's side of the middle of the road.'[1]

10.1.11 In September 1998, the Taskforce issued, for consultation, preliminary guidance entitled 'Taskforce Guidance on Project Agreements' which was discussed in two conferences held in London on 25 September attended by some 160 leading PFI practitioners from both the private and public sectors. The Taskforce has requested comments on the guidance and, at the time of writing, it is the Taskforce's intention to issue the final guidance in early 1999. The draft guidance issued in September 1998 indicates that the intention is to issue final guidance 'together with drafting of standard provisions where appropriate'. The draft guidance proposes three different forms which the standard provisions may take. First, standard drafting of a whole subject with an ability to make variations as the specifics of a deal demands, with guidance notes. Secondly, standard drafting of parts of a subject with the rest of the subject being dealt with in explanatory notes. Thirdly, a guidance note explaining how a subject should be dealt with in broad terms with a recommended approach to the issue.

10.1.12 In addition to the Taskforce guidance, certain departments (eg the NHS and MoD) are preparing sector specific guidelines in consultation with the Treasury Taskforce. In the case of the NHS, a full model form contract is being produced which the NHS intend to apply to future schemes in the NHS.

10.1.13 The guidance is eagerly awaited by the market. If what emerges is truly balanced and respects the positions that have emerged in the negotiations on recent projects, it will have a major part to play in streamlining the PFI process.

10.2 CORE ISSUES

10.2.1 Whilst project agreements vary depending on the particular category of PFI project and, indeed, between PFI sectors, there are recurring issues and themes. A number of these are considered in the guidance published by the Private Finance Panel and the draft Guidance on Project Agreements issued by the Treasury Taskforce referred to at **10.1.11**. Certain core issues are considered below under the following headings:

- Force Majeure, Compensation Events and Relief Events (**10.3**);
- Payment and Performance (**10.4**);
- Change of Law (**10.5**);
- Variations (**10.6**);
- Termination (**10.7**);

---

1   HM Treasury News Release 171/98, 21 October 1998.

- Effect of Termination (**10.8**);
- Compensation (**10.9**); and
- Step-in (**10.10**).

10.2.2 A large number of other issues will, inevitably, require negotiation in the context of any project agreement. The above issues are only some of the more contentious areas. Many of the other chapters consider issues which will be relevant. In particular, Chapter 7 considers issues of concern to funders, Chapter 8, design and construction issues and Chapter 14, employment law issues.

10.3 FORCE MAJEURE, COMPENSATION EVENTS AND RELIEF EVENTS

10.3.1 The project agreement will need to address the possibility that certain events may occur which will prevent either or both of the parties from performing some or all of their obligations under the project agreement, with the further consequences of possible extensions of time, payment of compensation by the awarding authority and/or termination of the contract. Certain of these events may be insurable (eg a fire) whilst certain events may be uninsurable (eg war). Similarly, certain of the events may be within the control of the parties (eg variations) whilst others may be outside their control (eg legislative change).

10.3.2 These differing strands of cause and effect have led to protracted debate in the negotiation of early PFI projects, with the starting point for the debate being the public sector's approach to the definition of Force Majeure.[1] Other circumstances, besides those which fall within the definition of Force Majeure, have some of the characteristics and consequences referred to above. These events are referred to below as Compensation Events and Relief Events (which is the classification referred to in the draft 'Taskforce Guidance on Project Agreements') depending, in essence, on whether the remedy afforded to the project company is time and money or merely time.

Force Majeure

10.3.3 Force Majeure events are events outside the control of either party, where relief from liability is given to the affected party. The public sector has sought to restrict the scope of Force Majeure in PFI contracts to certain very limited events. This is reflected in the definition of Force Majeure provided in the Private Finance Panel publication, *Basic Contractual Terms*.[2] The definition reads:

(a) war, civil war, armed conflict or terrorist attack arising within and affecting the United Kingdom; or
(b) nuclear, chemical or biological contamination of the Contractor's property arising from any of the events at (a) above.'

---

1   See **10.3.3** et seq.
2   Paragraph 17.1, *Basic Contractual Terms* (HM Treasury and Private Finance Panel) October 1996.

10.3.4 The underlying principle is that Force Majeure risks are those which are generally uninsurable (in absolute terms) or those which may be commercially uninsurable, for example, terrorism. Although the guidance is expressly stated to be non-mandatory, its use 'represents good practice'.[1] The scope of the Force Majeure definition may be subject to some negotiation; for example, it is consistent with the underlying principle for the public sector to accept the risk of nuclear, chemical or biological contamination which does not result from the events in (a) above (and a revised definition of Force Majeure contained in the draft 'Taskforce Guidance on Project Agreements' acknowledges this). Similarly, insurance for damage caused by sonic booms may not be commercially available (and, again, the revised definition contained in the draft 'Taskforce Guidance on Project Agreements' includes this in the Force Majeure definition).

10.3.5 During the life of the project, what is insurable at the time the contract is negotiated may subsequently become uninsurable; either absolutely or commercially. Assuming that project risk has been allocated by reference to whether particular risks are insurable (and that this is reflected in the definition of Force Majeure), the project company may seek provision for review of the definition of Force Majeure during the contract term. This position is being resisted by the Taskforce who take the position that the Government should not act as an insurer of last resort. The draft 'Taskforce Guidance on Project Agreements' proposes a consultation process and that if an uninsurable event subsequently occurs it should be treated as a Relief Event (as to which, see below). In any event, the need to address events which subsequently become uninsurable during the construction period of the project can usually be avoided through the procurement of a project insurance policy by the project company, providing cover for the entire period up to completion.

10.3.6 As to the effects of Force Majeure, a Force Majeure event will suspend the parties' respective obligations to perform. During the construction period, the occurrence of a Force Majeure event will mean that the project company is given further time to complete the relevant works and, typically, the length of the contract term will be preserved.

10.3.7 The issue of compensation is more contentious as neither party is at fault. Where the Force Majeure event does not lead to termination, it is a matter for negotiation as to whether the awarding authority pays compensation to the project company for the costs or losses incurred or whether each party bears its own losses. The draft 'Taskforce Guidance on Project Agreements' takes the line that the awarding authority should only pay for services actually received. However, this position has not been achieved on a number of projects where funders have insisted that a portion of the unitary payment should be paid such that the bank debt (or project bonds) are kept current and do not go into default.

---

1   Explanatory Notes, p 6, *Basic Contractual Terms* (HM Treasury and Private Finance Panel) October 1996.

10.3.8 The question of termination of the project agreement for Force Majeure and the payment of compensation to the project company on termination is considered below.[1]

Compensation events

10.3.9 Compensation Events are uninsurable events which may occur during the pre-completion phase and which give rise to the payment of compensation by the awarding authority. The draft 'Taskforce Guidance on Project Agreements' proposes the following as Compensation Events (although precedents to date have contained a variety of additional items, most commonly Force Majeure):

- variations requested by the awarding authority;
- breach of obligation by the awarding authority; and
- discriminatory or specific changes of law.

10.3.10 In relation to the last event, as discussed below,[2] the risk of change of law will be a matter for detailed negotiation. To the extent that the public sector retains the risk of other legislative change, the project company should similarly be entitled to additional time and money.

10.3.11 The principle underlying payment of compensation by the awarding authority for the occurrence of Compensation Events should be that the project company is held harmless by the awarding authority. However, the methodology of calculating the costs incurred by the project company will require detailed negotiation, although matters such as variations and change of law can be dealt with under the specific provisions of the Agreement dealing with those events.

10.3.12 There are a variety of ways in which the payment of compensation to the project company for a Compensation Event may be made including simply paying the project company's additional costs, adjusting the unitary payment, extending the contract term and commencing the payment of the unitary payment from the original payment commencement date which would have applied but for the delay caused by the Compensation Event. The approach favoured in the draft 'Taskforce Guidance on Project Agreements' is to retain the original contract term and compensate for the project company's loss (which may mean payment of an amount equal to the full unitary payment from the original payment commencement date).

Relief events

10.3.13 As the name suggests, Relief Events lead to the grant of relief for the project company from the performance of its obligations. This means relief during the construction period from its obligation to complete (ie more time) or, during the operating period, relief from its obligation to provide services. The project company will be granted relief in terms of time but not money. When relief is granted during the construction period, the awarding authority may seek

---

1 See **10.7.9** and **10.9.19**.
2 See **10.5**.

to hold the project company to payment of any agreed liquidated damages for late completion (and this is what the current draft of the 'Taskforce Guidance on Project Agreements' recommends).[1] In the operating period, the awarding authority will be relieved from its obligation to pay for services to the extent that they are not being performed.

10.3.14 The key distinction between Compensation Events and Relief Events is that, in the case of Relief Events, the project company bears the financial risks associated with their occurrence. The project company will often manage the risk through insurance. In the case of a fire during construction, for example, the costs of rebuilding can be met through construction all risks insurance and the costs of delay through business interruption insurance. The Taskforce is, however, keen for Relief Events not to be seen as co-extensive with available insurance and it states in its draft guidance that awarding authorities 'should not accept the argument that uninsurable events should inevitably fall within the definition of Force Majeure or equivalent'.

10.3.15 The draft 'Taskforce Guidance on Project Agreements' lists the following as Relief Events but recognises that the list of events should be extended 'where the circumstances warrant':

- fire, explosion, lightning, storm, tempest, flood, bursting or overflowing of water tanks, apparatus or pipes, ionising radiation, earthquakes, riot and civil commotion;
- failure by any statutory undertaker, utility company, local authority or like body to carry out works or provide services;
- any accidental loss or damage to the development or any roads servicing it;
- any failure or shortage of power, fuel or transport;
- any blockade or embargo; and
- any official or unofficial strike, lockout, go slow or other dispute generally affecting the building maintenance or facilities management industry or a significant sector of it (ie general, rather than site specific strikes or strikes just affecting the supplier's staff).

10.3.16 It is generally accepted that Relief Events (unlike Force Majeure) do not give rise to a right of termination. The rationale for this is that termination would not improve the position of the awarding authority as any replacement supplier would be similarly affected and the structure of risk allocation for Relief Events is intended strongly to incentivise the project company to manage the risks in question and resume delivering the service as quickly as possible.

---

1 An alternative approach is to regard the Relief Event as being totally exculpatory in its effect and thus no liquidated damages would arise. Although insurance may be available to meet this liability (see **10.3.14**), it may not represent value for money for the awarding authority to bear that cost.

10.4 PAYMENT AND PERFORMANCE

Payment mechanisms

10.4.1 In the limited category of projects where the private sector recovers its costs through charges to the end-user, payment is essentially driven by demand (albeit that there may be a price regulatory framework to protect the interests of the consumer). However, for most PFI projects, where payments are to be made by the public sector, a detailed payment mechanism will need to be developed. This section examines payment mechanisms of this sort. The guidance in *Further Contactual Issues*, emphasises that the structure of the payment mechanism is 'vital for achieving optimum risk allocation'.[1] The point is illustrated by a number of examples.

Timing

10.4.2 Delay risk is a key risk which the public sector seeks to transfer to the private sector in PFI projects. The risk is transferred by the awarding authority only commencing payments to the project company once the relevant service (the road, the prison, the hospital) becomes available.

Payment elements

10.4.3 Further risk transfer may be achieved through the particular elements which make up overall payment to the project company. These will typically comprise one or more of the following:[2]

- an availability element;
- a performance element; and
- a volume element.

10.4.4 It is likely that part of the payment will be calculated by reference to the availability of the relevant service. Commonly, the availability element is applied to the physical asset provided as part of the service, for example, the hospital buildings and car park. Risk transfer is achieved through payments being conditional on the availability of the physical asset. Whilst 100% availability should lead to 100% of the payment being made, conversely, unavailability generally will lead to a proportionate reduction in the payment. This reflects the guidance in *Further Contractual Issues* which notes that:

> 'The principle should be: if you receive no service, there should be no payment.'[3]

10.4.5 Similarly, the payment mechanism may contain a performance element. Again, 100% performance will lead to 100% of the payment being made. The corollary is that insufficient performance will lead to reductions in the performance element. In this way, performance risk is transferred to the project

---

1 Paragraph 2.2, *Further Contractual Issues* (HM Treasury and Private Finance Panel) January 1997.
2 See **2.2.22**.
3 Paragraph 2.4, *Further Contractual Issues* (HM Treasury and Private Finance Panel) January 1997.

company. This mechanism is frequently applied in the context of individual services (such as cleaning or security) which form part of the overall provision of a fully serviced building. Notwithstanding the philosophical predilection to there being a single unitary payment, in practice, where a number of services are being delivered each service may have its own discrete service fee which, in turn, will be subject to deductions specific to the performance of that service.

10.4.6 Part of the payment may be calculated on the basis of usage of the particular service (eg the number of vehicles using a road). This mechanism achieves the transfer of volume risk to the project company. More vehicles than anticipated will mean a higher level of payment and enhanced returns for the project company. Conversely, fewer vehicles than expected will lead to reduced payments and correspondingly lower returns. Usage or volume risk is more difficult for the project company to manage than, say, the risk of availability of the facility. The project company cannot be certain of the numbers of vehicles that may use the road provided by it. It follows that the project company may seek to limit the volume element of the overall payment. Certainly, the project company's funders will seek as far as possible to achieve certainty of revenue flow to the project company which militates against payment mechanisms which are heavily volume based.[1]

10.4.7 A volume element may also arise in the context of payments for individual services referred to above. Laundry services, for example, may be paid for on a per piece basis. Likewise, payments for waste disposal may be calculated by reference to the quantity of particular types of waste disposed of by the project company. Catering services may attract fees calculated by reference to numbers of meals served and so on.

Amount of payment

10.4.8 Limitations on the variability of the payment agreed between the parties provide a further opportunity for risk transfer. For example, construction risk is transferred by fixing the amount of the payment to the project company regardless of the cost of construction. The project company assumes the risk that construction costs may exceed those budgeted for at the time the project agreement is executed.

10.4.9 The amount by which payments are indexed over the life of the project agreement permits further risk transfer by the awarding authority to the project company. The risk for the project company in agreeing to a particular method of indexation is that a mis-match may arise between the particular index and the project company's cost base. Different indices may be required for different payment elements to avoid unjustified payment increases and to enhance overall risk transfer/value for money (although RPI based indexation will generally be the favoured method).

---

1   In the case of the DBFO road projects, the real likelihood of any significant revenue variability due to fluctuating volumes was mitigated by banded volume payment structures.

10.4.10 Besides indexation, the amount of the unitary payment may be subject to adjustment for matters such as delay or change of law.[1]

Price adjustment and market testing

10.4.11 Given the duration of most projects, the awarding authority may be concerned that the amount of the payment to the project company for the service may become out of line with the cost of similar services in the marketplace and the project company may be concerned that the unitary payment may become out of line with its own cost base. This risk may arise where, for example, the method of indexation chosen for a particular element of the payment proves inappropriate, providing the project company with increases in payments which significantly exceed the relevant increases in its cost base. Whilst the project company may argue that any excesses are an appropriate reward for the risk it assumes in providing services to an agreed price over the term of the contract, the awarding authority will wish to ensure continued value for money in the price it pays for particular services. Obviously, the reverse situation is equally possible when the project company has mispriced and is being under-remunerated.

10.4.12 One method of addressing these concerns is to allow for market testing of aspects of the service during the life of the project. The relevant part of the service is tendered in the marketplace to establish a market price for its provision. The amount paid to the project company in respect of that part of the service will then be subject to adjustment. A good example of this approach is the provision of non-clinical services in NHS hospital projects. Services such as catering, portering, security and car parking may all be subject to market testing procedures.

10.4.13 Inevitably, however, it must be recognised that market testing will be likely to generate a shorter term view by the project company and may not be consistent with life cycle costing for assets with longer lives. For this reason life cycle and asset maintenance services are often excluded from market testing.

10.4.14 Market testing itself raises a whole host of points for negotiation. Amongst these, the parties will need to consider which aspects of the overall services will be subject to market testing. There is then the question of the commencement and frequency of market testing. The awarding authority may wish to market test services first immediately after the construction period. The project company may not wish to be disrupted in its provision of the overall service at a crucial time, namely completion and the commencement of payments to it by the awarding authority. In addition, the operating company may want the opportunity to run services for the project company for a minimum period before they are market tested.

10.4.15 As for the issue of frequency of market testing, the parties will need to balance a number of factors, for example, the public sector's keenness to ensure value for money at all times and the private sector's concerns about disruption and the responsiveness of the marketplace to requests for tenders. Intervals of five years between market testings are common.

---

1 See **10.3** and **10.5**.

10.4.16 There is also the question of the effect of market testing. Should the project company be required to employ the winning tenderer as a service provider or is an adjustment to the payment to the project company reflecting the winning tender price sufficient? Can a robust competitive process be maintained in the marketplace if none of the tenderers is subsequently employed?

10.4.17 The issue of adjustment of the price paid to the project company in respect of the relevant aspect of the service will require negotiation. A key method of transferring risk to the project company is for the project company to agree to price its services for the full term of the contract (subject to adjustment for indexation, change of law etc). If this principle is to be maintained, it would be inappropriate for the payment to the project company to be increased to reflect a higher market tested price, as this would reduce the relevant risk transfer. Conversely, market testing may demonstrate that the market price for the service is lower than that which is being paid by the awarding authority. The relevant saving may be realised as the project company will be able to employ the winning tenderer to provide the particular aspect of the service. The amount of the payment to the project company can then be correspondingly reduced. The project company's starting position will be to resist passing on any saving if it has agreed to price its services for the full contract term. In any event it will wish to negotiate a sharing of the saving with the awarding authority to compensate it for the risk it assumes in agreeing to price its services for the full term of the contract. The most common position agreed is for there to be a symmetrical treatment of cost savings and cost overruns (notwithstanding the reduced risk transfer from the awarding authority's perspective).

10.4.18 An alternative but similar approach to dealing with the issue of payments to the project company being out of line with the cost of similar services in the marketplace, is to provide for benchmarking. At the relevant time, the price paid for a particular aspect of the service is tested against a defined benchmark and payments are adjusted accordingly. Although this is fine in principle, a particular difficulty with adopting benchmarking in PFI projects has been the absence of relevant benchmarks, although this may change as more PFI projects are completed and comparisons can be made between them.

10.4.19 A further area for consideration and negotiation is the question of third-party revenues. Again, the project company may be prepared to accept risk in the context of third-party revenues by factoring them into the price which it charges the awarding authority for the relevant service. The parties may also agree to split the profits arising from any third-party revenues realised during the life of the project. The potential for third-party revenues will depend upon the particular project but could include, in the context of a hospital for example, revenues from the provision of telephones, private beds, pay-per-view television, sports and leisure facilities, car parking and non-patient catering.

Deductions

10.4.20 *Further Contractual Issues* also emphasises that payment mechanisms are 'vital for promoting performance'.[1] In part, a payment mechanism will achieve this through its constituent elements: a well-built prison will continue to be available; an attractive and well-maintained hospital may be used by more patients. The key means of ensuring continuing performance during the life of the contract will, however, be through deductions. This reflects the principle of payment by results.

10.4.21 The scope of deductions will itself be a matter for negotiation. Given the principle that no service means no payment, an awarding authority will seek the right to deduct up to 100% of the particular elements which make up the payment. Besides reflecting this principle, the awarding authority will wish to incentivise the project company to perform to the required level; the absence of an appropriate deduction mechanism may, correspondingly, disincentivise the project company.

Unavailability

10.4.22 Deductions are commonly made where all or part of the relevant service is unavailable. Often, where the PFI project involves the provision of a building, deductions may be made by reference to floor area or particular rooms in the building being unavailable for use. Areas may be graded such that those which are more important attract a higher degree of deduction. It may also be appropriate to make deductions for areas which are consequentially unavailable (ie unavailable as a result of other areas being unavailable).

10.4.23 As an alternative approach, the payment may be structured so that the availability element directly reflects the availability of, for example, prisoner spaces. In these circumstances, the deduction will be implicit. Rather than starting from 100% and deducting for unavailability, the payment starts at 0% and reaches up to 100% through availability.

10.4.24 Regardless of the methodology used, the question of what is or is not available will be a matter for detailed negotiation between the parties. Typically the definition of 'Unavailability' will comprise a list of specific events such as, inadequate access, failure to provide utilities, or failure to meet prescribed environmental standards and this is the approach taken in the draft 'Taskforce Guidance on Project Agreements'. One of the more contentious issues is whether this list is exhaustive or non-exhaustive (ie subject to a catch all that an area must reasonably be capable of occupation and use). The more prevalent approach is the exhaustive list although, self evidently, the non-exhaustive list is far preferable from the awarding authority's perspective as it catches inadvertent omissions and there is certainly precedent for it having been accepted both by sponsors and funders.

---

1   Paragraph 2.4, *Further Contractual Issues* (HM Treasury and Private Finance Panel) January 1997.

10.4.25 The project company will wish to limit the application of deductions where, for example, unavailability arises as a result of the acts of the awarding authority. It may also be reasonable to exclude unavailability arising as a result of:

- planned maintenance;
- failure by statutory undertakings or other bodies;
- inspections by governmental authority;
- variations requested by the awarding authority; or
- acts or omissions of third-party suppliers (eg utility companies).

Besides these, the particular circumstances of the project may lead to the inclusion of further items.

10.4.26 The project company may also seek the right to remedy particular unavailability events before deductions are made. Assuming this principle is agreed, there is further scope for negotiation between the parties in distinguishing between particular areas of the building and the duration of the remedial period that is permitted. In an NHS hospital, for example, the remedial period for an operating theatre may be minimal, say one hour, whilst the period for a car parking space could be 24 hours or more. The project company may also seek to limit unavailability deductions to circumstances where the area in question cannot be or is not used as a consequence. From the awarding authority's perspective, deductions should apply against objective tests irrespective of whether it results in actual non-usage.

Performance points

10.4.27 Deductions will frequently be made by reference to a performance points mechanism. Services will be measured, often monthly, by reference to particular performance standards and marked accordingly. A failure to achieve certain performance standards or, alternatively, the accrual of performance points will lead to deductions from the overall payment to the project company. Whilst the concept is relatively straightforward, a performance points mechanism will give rise to a number of issues for detailed negotiation.

10.4.28 The first issue for resolution will be the identity of the monitor. *Further Contractual Issues* states that:

'Monitoring is the client's responsibility in the PFI partnership.'[1]

Whilst the project company may furnish information to assist in assessing its performance, ordinarily, it should fall to the awarding authority to carry out the task of monitoring. Any information provided by the project company may, itself, be subject to audit by the awarding authority.

10.4.29 A key issue will be the question of what is monitored. *Further Contractual Issues* emphasises that monitoring:

---

1 Paragraph 4.4, *Further Contractual Issues* (HM Treasury and Private Finance Panel) January 1997.

'means confirming the private sector's objective performance against outputs promised under the contract.'[1]

Monitoring should, therefore, focus on what it is that the project company is required to achieve rather than the means by which it achieves its goals, although, inevitably, in assessing an output, a monitor will be reviewing the means of delivering that output; namely, the project company's inputs.

10.4.30 This approach is not only consistent with the PFI philosophy of service delivery against output specifications but also helps address the practical difficulty that, until the building has been designed and constructed, it is difficult to state precisely the means by which any particular service will be provided (not least, since methods of service delivery may change in the intervening period). It follows that the performance mechanism must necessarily be output driven if it is to be included in the project agreement from the outset.

10.4.31 Having established the means of measurement, there is then the question of what constitutes a failure. Although 100% payment suggests 100% performance, the question is what should constitute 100% performance? The parties may recognise that some degree of failure is implicit in the performance of any service. It may, therefore, be appropriate to set the relevant performance standards at a level below the optimum. The project company's performance will, as a result, be tested against a reduced, more realistic standard. An alternative approach to the same issue would be to allow the accumulation of a certain number of penalty points before deductions are made.

10.4.32 The possibility of remedy is a further issue. Assuming a particular output is measured and its performance proves inadequate, should the project company be allowed an opportunity to remedy the relevant failure before it counts for the purposes of deductions? What period of time should be permitted in which to remedy the failure? Just as particular areas of a building may attract a greater level of deduction for unavailability, particular failures in services may attract different weightings, numbers of points or length of remedial period (if any) when calculating the relevant deduction. Again, the attribution of weightings or points to particular breaches will require detailed negotiation; the parties' perceptions of the relative importance of particular aspects of the service may well differ. In any event, deductions should be proportionate to the loss arising from the particular breach or there is a risk that they will be unenforceable as a penalty.

10.4.33 Besides negotiating the scope of deductions, the project company will be concerned to avoid double counting where the same event gives rise to deductions from more than one element of the payment by the awarding authority. For example, a failure to clean part of a building may lead to that part becoming unavailable for use. Should there be a deduction both from the fee payable for the cleaning service and from the availability fee payable for the serviced accommodation?

---

1   Paragraph 4.3, *Further Contractual Issues* (HM Treasury and Private Finance Panel) January 1997.

10.4.34 This raises a further issue in the context of sub-contractors, as the project company will seek to pass on to service providers the consequences of their particular breaches. Whilst a service provider should accept the principle of deductions in payments to it as a result of its failure, its payment is likely to be limited to all or part of the fee payable to the project company for the particular element of the overall service. As a result, the service provider will resist deductions which reflect other deductions suffered by the project company. The service provider would otherwise risk the loss of all or a disproportionate part of its payment for its own, perhaps relatively minor, breach.

10.4.35 Another issue for negotiation will be the scope of any moratorium on deductions allowed to the project company during the period immediately after completion (or, indeed, earlier if there are existing facilities/services which the project company takes over running). The project company may argue that it should be allowed some degree of latitude whilst teething problems are ironed out and services gear up. Similar arguments may be used to justify a moratorium where the project company is required to change a service provider, for example, following market testing of the relevant aspect of the overall service.

10.4.36 Finally, the project company may seek to negotiate further reliefs in relation to performance and deductions, analogous to those listed above for unavailability.[1]

Over-performance

10.4.37 As *Further Contractual Issues* points out, incentives to perform can be two-pronged, being a reduced payment for under-performance and a higher payment for performance in excess of the minimum required.[2] Obviously if there is an element of additional payment for 'super performance' the element must not be open ended and must be affordable.

10.4.38 An alternative approach, which meets the objective of providing an incentive to the project company without requiring the awarding authority to pay any more money than it originally bargained for, is to allow for over-performance by the project company during a particular period to be carried forward and applied against under-performance in subsequent periods. Such a mechanism requires careful negotiation as the awarding authority will not wish the project company to under-perform in relation to one particular service for any significant period and to do so with impunity as a result of over-performance in another service. Because of these difficulties and the fact that awarding authorities generally want to receive the service at the designated level – not better than or worse than that level – awarding authorities are generally circumspect as to the benefits of mechanisms that allow credits in one period to offset debits in another.

---

1 See **10.4.25**.
2 Paragraph 3.5, *Further Contractual Issues* (HM Treasury and Private Finance Panel) January 1997.

10.5 CHANGE OF LAW

10.5.1 The effect of change of law during the life of the project will be a further matter for negotiation between the parties. In essence, from the project company's perspective, the risk is that change of law will increase the cost to the project company of complying with its obligations. As most projects are contracted on a 'fixed price' basis (albeit that all or part of the unitary payment may be indexed), the project company is unable, in principle, to pass on the additional cost to the awarding authority. The issue is, therefore, the extent to which payments to the project company should be adjusted to reflect its increased costs.

10.5.2 The private sector's instinctive reaction to the issue has always been that law is controlled by the Government and, as a result, the public sector should bear the consequences of any change (it being best placed to manage the relevant risk). Conversely, the public sector has argued that all organisations are subject to change of law and that it is commonplace for business to take legislative risk. Furthermore, indexation (for example, by reference to RPI) may mitigate the increased cost to the project resulting from certain changes of law (eg the introduction of a minimum wage) albeit that indexation is only a partial answer to the private sector's concerns as many changes of law could have a disproportionate effect on a project company's economics and not be adequately compensated for by indexation. A further mitigating influence may be the existence of market testing provisions for particular services which will have the effect of rebasing (following a competitive process) part of the unitary payment in the light of changes in costs generally (including any generated by change of law). The draft 'Taskforce Guidance on Project Agreements' points out that: 'Change in law provisions must therefore be read in conjunction with benchmarking, market testing and indexation provisions when assessing the level of risk transfer achieved by a client under a Project Agreement.'[1]

10.5.3 Various approaches have been adopted to resolve these particular issues.

- In certain of the prisons' projects, the project company is compensated for increased costs arising from any change to prison specific and health and safety legislation. There is also provision for compensation if there is a 'significant change' in the project company's underlying costs, resulting from any significant change of circumstances. This would include general change of law.
- In the roads projects, on the other hand, protection for change of law has tended to be restricted to legislation which discriminates specifically against the contract or the road in question – or against DBFO contracts or privately operated roads as a class.
- In projects in the health sector, the emerging practice is for the awarding authority to take the risk in relation to hospital specific legislation but for there to be a distinction drawn in relation to other changes of law between, on the one hand, changes of law which result in the need to incur capital expenditure on the facilities (eg replace an air conditioning system) and, on

---

1   Section 13.1.3 draft Treasury Taskforce Guidance on Project Agreements.

the other hand, changes of law which have a revenue impact (eg the introduction of or a change in minimum wage legislation). In relation to these other changes of law the usual position, at the time of writing, is for the project company to take the entire risk for those changes of law which have a revenue impact and for there to be a sharing of the risk in relation to changes of law with a capital impact (with project company taking the risk during the construction period and, subject to a limit of 2% of the capital cost, 5 years thereafter and with the awarding authority taking the risk beyond this period/amount). The willingness of the private sector to accept the risk of all changes of law with a revenue impact is doubtless in part linked to the fact that, in NHS projects, most services are periodically market tested savings or cost increases being passed back to one awarding authority (either in whole or in part).

- In projects for Government accommodation the practice is very variable but again a sharing of risk is almost always agreed with the basis of sharing being allocated on the basis of a combination of time, amount and the type/impact of the legislation.

10.5.4 The draft 'Taskforce Guidance on Project Agreements' puts forward an alternative approach for sharing change of law risk:

> 'An appropriate approach to sharing [change of law] risk is as follows: in respect of a change in law taking effect during the operational period, risks are shared on a progressive scale so that for example the supplier takes 95% of the first £X of capital expenditure, 75% of the next £Y, 50% of the next £Z and so on. Once a certain amount is reached, the client takes 100% of any amounts above that amount. The figures take into account the size of the project and the impact of other factors such as the likelihood of environmental and health and safety legislation. The client should generally pay such capital costs in accordance with the principles set out in sections 12.2.2.6 for client generated changes that any consequent operating cost increases are borne by the supplier.
> If a change of law requires operational changes then either party should be entitled to require a variation to the project specifications to comply with a change in law and no breach of contract should arise while this is being done. Changes arising in operational costs as a result of a general change in law should be borne by the supplier (subject to section 14 (Price Variation)).'[1]

The intention behind the approach is to arrive at a position whereby the project company, who will be managing the impact of the change in law and therefore best placed to mitigate its effects, is incentivised to minimise the impact of change of law for a greater range (in terms of value) of change of law events before the position is reached where there is a straight cost pass through to the awarding authority.

10.5.5 Whatever basis of sharing is arrived at, it would be normal for the project company to be placed under an obligation to mitigate the impact of the change in law. The draft 'Taskforce Guidance on Project Agreements' points out that there may be a particular linkage between the build up of a life-cycle maintenance reserve and change of law risk allocation. So, for example, the awarding authority

---

1   Sections 13.9.4 and 13.9.5, draft Treasury Taskforce Guidance on Project Agreements.

should not be footing the bill in its entirety for the replacement of an item whose replacement it has already partly funded through the build up of the life-cycle maintenance reserve.

10.5.6 One area of change of law which is usually treated separately is change of law relating to VAT. Unitary payments are always quoted exclusive of VAT and therefore any change in the rate of VAT on supplies made by the project company will be passed on to the awarding authority. The draft 'Taskforce Guidance on Project Agreements' states that any changes in the scope of VAT – in particular, other changes that affect the project company's ability to recover its input VAT – are for the account of the project company unless they result from changes in the VAT status of the service provided by the project company under the project agreement.

10.6 VARIATIONS

10.6.1 The length of PFI contracts make variations in the awarding authority's requirements during the life of the project almost inevitable. In the context of a hospital, for example, given the changing patterns in the delivery of healthcare, it is self-evident that what is built today will need to undergo numerous changes over its lifetime, to enable new technologies and treatments to be delivered. The same will apply in relation to the non-clinical services provided by the project company. Although the need for a general mechanism to deal with change is accepted, various issues will require to be negotiated, including the definition of what is permitted by way of variation, agreement over who will carry it out and how payments to the project company are affected.

10.6.2 In negotiating these general points, the parties will need to have particular regard to the inter-relationship between physical variations, being variations to the works before completion and to the building after completion and variations to the other aspects of the overall provision of the service (for example, the non-clinical services referred to above). A physical variation is likely to affect the provision of other aspects of the service; the addition of a new wing to the building will at the very least give rise to an increase in the quantity of other services which are required to provide a fully serviced building. Likewise, a varation in the output specification for a service may require a physical variation to the building as a consequence.

Restrictions

10.6.3 Whilst the awarding authority should have the right to require variations to the services supplied to it, the project company (and its funders) will seek to restrict the exercise of that right. To an extent, this is consistent with the guidance in *Further Contractual Issues* which extols the virtue of trying, whenever possible, to avoid invoking the change mechanism.[1]

---

1 Paragraph 10.5, *Further Contractual Issues* (HM Treasury and Private Finance Panel) January 1997.

10.6.4 There may be certain absolute restrictions regarding physical variations of the works, as well as on variations to the output specifications for particular services. Typical rights to refuse variations could include where:

- any necessary consents (eg planning) will not be obtainable;
- the variation would adversely affect the design life of the rest of the building or the timing or cost of asset renewals;
- the variation would adversely affect health and safety or give rise to a breach of law; or
- the variation would make insurance unavailable.

In addition, the project company should not be required to effect a physical variation which would give rise to a variation in other aspects of the overall service, where the project company would be entitled to refuse the latter. The same point applies vice versa.

10.6.5 During the construction period, the project company may wish to limit its obligations to effect variations further, to avoid both significant change to the nature of the project or a major delay to the commencement of payments by the awarding authority. Funders will have similar concerns. Besides specifying limits as to the period of delay or the quantum of variations, the parties may agree drop dead dates after which certain elements of the works or the output specifications for particular services may not be varied. Given their concerns, funders are likely to insist upon an express right of approval in relation to variations. The scope of this right will be a matter for negotiation between the parties. The awarding authority, in particular, will be concerned to avoid any blanket right of refusal for funders.

10.6.6 The project company may also seek the right to require variations, for example to ensure compliance with applicable law. Similarly, the project company should be entitled (and even encouraged) to propose beneficial variations. However, there would usually be an absolute discretion for the awarding authority to refuse to agree to these if there is a resulting diminution in the quality of the service.

Implementation

10.6.7 In terms of carrying out a physical variation, it may be appropriate for the project company either to implement the variation itself or for it to procure the variation through its role as facilities manager. For the awarding authority, dealing with a single supplier in the context of procuring the variation may make it difficult to ensure value for money. This point is expressly recognised in *Further Contractual Issues*,[1] although the issue may be addressed through the means of pricing the variation.[2] In relation to variations to other aspects of the overall service, responsibility for effecting the change will inevitably be assumed by the project company.

---

1 Paragraph 10.4, *Further Contractual Issues* (HM Treasury and Private Finance Panel) January 1997.
2 See **10.6.9**.

10.6.8 Involving a third-party supplier in carrying out physical works or providing other services raises other concerns. Understandably, the project company is likely to resist the presence of other suppliers on site during the construction period. Equally, the project company will be reluctant to take responsibility for the actions of third-party suppliers at any time during the term of the contract and may require an indemnity from the awarding authority. Accordingly, these factors tend to point towards the project company carrying out all variations in respect of matters for which the project company is to have a life-cycle responsiblity.

Payment adjustments

10.6.9 The next issue is the funding of the costs of variations and the basis of adjustments to payments to the project company. As a general principle, the project company should be fairly compensated for the additional costs involved. As far as possible, the contract mechanics will need to ensure that those costs are subject to objective measure. During the construction period, this may be achieved in relation to physical variations by referring to a construction cost breakdown. Once the project becomes operational, it may be practicable to ensure value for money by market testing the variation through a tender procedure. Inevitably, there will be an element of agreement to agree, as and when the relevant variation arises and the Dispute Resolution Procedure will apply.

10.6.10 Once the cost of any variation has been determined, future instalments of the unitary payment will need to be adjusted or lump sums paid to reflect those costs. The guidance in *Further Contractual Issues* states that:[1]

> 'in general the payment for the cost of the change should be through an adjustment of the standard payment, rather than through simple "full-cost", or "cost plus" lump sum payments.'

This may not always be possible to achieve, particularly in relation to physical variations and will depend upon the extent to which the project company has financing available to it to fund the up-front cost of the variation.

10.6.11 During the construction period, the project company may agree to make available a standby facility for the costs of variations. This will allow the awarding authority to pay the costs of the variation over time, through the unitary payments made following completion. As the extent of such standby funding will, necessarily, be limited, the variation procedure will need to provide for the alternative of lump-sum payments.[2] During the operating period, it is unrealistic to expect the project company to fund variations by way of a standby facility. This should not preclude funding by the project company by agreement between the parties at the time and it is common to impose on the project

---

1   Paragraph 10.6, *Further Contractual Issues* (HM Treasury and Private Finance Panel) January 1997.
2   The awarding authority will need to consider whether such a standby facility represents value for money, particularly if it has a relatively high degree of confidence of being able to avoid requesting variations during the construction period (see **10.6.3**).

company an obligation to use reasonable endeavours to fund variations. Where the project company is not able to procure funding, the awarding authority will usually pay for physical variations by stage payments as would often be the case under a traditional construction contract.

10.6.12 Where variation costs are to be funded through an adjustment to the unitary payments made after completion, the basis of adjustment to those payments will, itself, require negotiation. The project agreement will need to establish the principles of adjustment, for example, the preservation of a rate of return and certain financial ratios. It may be appropriate for the contract to provide for the adjustment to be calculated through the use of a financial model. It is worth noting that the methodology used for adjusting payments for the purpose of variations may also be applied in calculating adjustments for Compensation Events or for change of law.[1]

10.6.13 It is, of course, possible that a variation will lead to savings for the project company. In this situation, the awarding authority should enjoy the benefit of any savings. As for variation costs, the amount of any savings should be subject to objective measurement. Similarly, savings may be returned to the awarding authority through an adjustment to the unitary payment.

10.7 TERMINATION

10.7.1 The circumstances in which either party will be entitled to terminate the project agreement will need to be negotiated. The following areas will usually be relevant in a PFI project:

– Termination at will;
– Project company default;
– Awarding authority default;
– Occurrence of Force Majeure; and
– Corrupt gifts provisions.

Termination at will

10.7.2 The guidance in *Further Contractual Issues* states that 'Reserving a general right to terminate at will is contrary to the PFI partnership approach'.[2] However, the public sector's position on this seems to be changing and the draft 'Taskforce Guidance on Project Agreements' now recognises that awarding authorities may legitimately wish to reserve a general voluntary termination right and that the project company should not object to this provided it is compensated in full.

10.7.3 In certain areas of PFI, the awarding authority may seek the ability to break the contract at various points during the contract term, without compensation. This may be possible where the project company is prepared to

---

1 See **10.3** and **10.5**.
2 Paragraph 9.3, *Further Contractual Issues* (HM Treasury and Private Finance Panel) January 1997.

accept a 'residual value risk' in relation to the project assets. This will be possible only where the assets in question have some alternative use (for example, government office accommodation in a central city location) and funders to the project will naturally have concerns about lending against an uncertain future value.

10.7.4 The draft 'Taskforce Guidance on Project Agreements' is silent regarding the question of termination of part of the service. For example, an accommodation project will involve the provision of a number of ancillary services as well as the provision and maintenance of the buildings. It may be reasonable to provide in the project agreement for the termination of individual ancillary services by the awarding authority given changing patterns in the use of the building and the requirements of the awarding authority.

10.7.5 Irrespective of the contractual provisions, either party may, effectively, terminate at will by defaulting in the performance of its obligations under the project agreement. However, naturally both sides would be very loath to do this because of political and public relations issues, even if the direct economic effect were acceptable.

Project company default

10.7.6 Termination for default by the project company should only arise as a last resort.[1] Typical events of default will include:

- insolvency events in respect of the project company (which may extend to the insolvency of sub-contractors or guarantors);
- fundamental irremediable breach by the project company of its obligations, for example, abandoning the project or failing to complete the works within a defined period following the date for completion;
- fundamental remediable breach by the project company of its obligations which is not remedied;
- accrual of specified number of performance points/failure to achieve specified performance standards in relation to services over defined periods;
- fundamental obligations of the project company becoming unenforceable (unless they are being performed).

An indicative list of project company events of default is contained in the draft 'Taskforce Guidance on Project Agreements'.

Awarding authority default

10.7.7 As for project company default, default by the awarding authority must be significant before the project company becomes entitled to terminate the project agreement. The obligations of the awarding authority will be different to those of the project company and the termination events will differ accordingly. Common events are:

---

1 Paragraph 9.5, *Further Contractual Issues* (HM Treasury and Private Finance Panel) January 1997 and section 20.2.1 of the draft Treasury Taskforce Guidance on Project Agreements.

- A breach by the awarding authority of obligations to provide access to the site;
- A failure to pay significant amounts for significant periods.

10.7.8 The project company may also require provisions permitting termination where the legal framework constituting the awarding authority is adversely affected. For example, in NHS hospital projects, it took some time and the passage of new primary legislation[1] for the private sector to become comfortable with the issues of NHS trust covenant and vires. As a result, termination events in NHS hospital projects are likely to include changes of law affecting the trust's legal capacity or changes of law affecting the creditworthiness of the trust, in each case, in the absence of appropriate substitute arrangements.

Force Majeure

10.7.9 Ultimately, where the occurrence of Force Majeure affects the parties' ability to perform the contract for a considerable period, the project agreement may be terminated. The relevant period is a matter for negotiation. The project company may also seek to aggregate shorter periods of disruption resulting from Force Majeure for the purposes of termination.

Corrupt gifts

10.7.10 The Private Finance Panel publication, *Basic Contractual Terms*, sets out a corrupt gifts and payments of commission provision which includes the right for the awarding authority to terminate the contract.[2] The draft clause also contemplates the awarding authority acting in a reasonable and proportionate manner and considering action other than termination of the contract, including termination of a sub-contract where the prohibited act is that of a sub-contractor or requiring the dismissal of an employee where the prohibited act is that of the employee concerned. The draft 'Taskforce Guidance' adopts a similar approach with some refinements.

10.7.11 In practice, corrupt gifts provisions have tended to adopt these principles such that termination of the project agreement is only likely to arise in the context of default by the project company itself.

10.8 EFFECT OF TERMINATION

10.8.1 Exercise of termination rights by the awarding authority will usually trigger the rights of funders to step in pursuant to their direct agreement. This issue is considered in detail in Chapter 8.

10.8.2 The parties will also need to consider the treatment of project assets upon termination. This issue is linked to the payment of compensation by the

---

1 National Health Service (Residual Liabilities) Act 1996 and National Health Service (Private Finance) Act 1997.
2 Paragraph 20, *Basic Contractual Terms* (HM Treasury and Private Finance Panel) October 1996.

awarding authority which is considered at **10.9**. Besides the question of compensation, there is the issue of continued provision of the service by the awarding authority or by a new supplier. Project assets (for example, hospital beds) may be essential to the continued performance of the relevant service.

10.9 COMPENSATION

10.9.1 The payment of compensation by the awarding authority on termination of the project agreement is one of the more contentious areas for negotiation. The issue is considered below under the same headings as those for termination.[1]

Termination at will

10.9.2 Save in the relatively rare cases where termination options for the public sector can be structured around a transfer of residual value in the assets (and therefore without a compensation payment), the normal position where a voluntary termination right is included is for the awarding authority to provide full compensation to the project company for its loss of future profits.[2] A detailed formula for calculating these will be included although there are generally two approaches. The first is for the awarding authority to pay out senior debt and third-party creditors and then pay 'market value' for the equity (with an agreed basis for determining 'market value'). The second is for the awarding authority to pay the net present value of the future payment stream (net of costs).

10.9.3 The effect of both these approaches is that if the project company is making 'super profits' the compensation payment will compensate it for loss of these. On occasions, therefore, awarding authorities have succeeded in agreeing provisions where voluntary termination compensation is pre-agreed so that, at the outset, the compensation payment for termination in each year of the contract is known. A variation on this is to provide for compensation payments to be calculated by reference to the return in the project company's original model. The attraction of this from the awarding authority's perspective is that it fixes (and therefore caps) from the outset the costs of unwinding the contract in the future.

Project company default

10.9.4 Perhaps the most difficult issue relating to compensation has been where the project company defaults. The approach across the different sectors of PFI projects has varied, with some projects, for example the roads projects, providing for no compensation to be paid, some, for example prison projects, providing for no compensation until after completion of the facilities and others providing for compensation both pre- and post-completion.

---

1 See **10.8**.
2 It may be that a downward adjustment is made to reflect the fact that the project company can redeploy its capital elsewhere.

10.9.5 There are various arguments for and against the payment of compensation. From the private sector's point of view, where project assets are transferred to the awarding authority on termination of the project agreement, there is a risk of a windfall for the public sector if compensation is not paid. For example, the project company may have constructed buildings on land owned by the awarding authority which will remain vested in the awarding authority after termination of the project agreement. The project company may also argue that the project will not be bankable without payment of compensation, although this argument may not always be justified (see, for example, the roads projects referred to above).

10.9.6 From the public sector's viewpoint, payment of compensation in circumstances of project company default is something which, besides being inherently difficult to come to terms with, raises the more fundamental concern that the project arrangements must provide a keen incentive on the private sector not to default. It follows that any compensation should be limited in its amount rather than full compensation. These principles are reflected in *Further Contractual Issues* and the draft 'Taskforce Guidance on Project Agreements'.[1]

10.9.7 In addition, the public sector will wish to encourage funders to step in under their direct agreement in circumstances of project company default and remedy the relevant default. The incentive to do so will be reduced where substantial compensation is payable on termination.[2]

10.9.8 Assuming some compensation is to be paid, in particular where assets are handed over to the awarding authority, the next issue is the amount of the relevant compensation. When negotiating the amount of compensation payable, a distinction is often drawn between termination pre-completion of the physical works comprising the project and termination after completion, once payments by the awarding authority have commenced.

10.9.9 Prior to completion, where incomplete facilities are handed over to the awarding authority, it may be appropriate to construct a mechanism by which the net value of the project to the awarding authority can be realised. This will need to take into account not only the value of the incomplete facilities but also any losses and costs suffered by the awarding authority (for example, the cost of completion of the facilities).

10.9.10 Where the project agreement terminates after completion, compensation in a number of PFI sectors has been specified as outstanding debt less rectification costs. An alternative approach (used, for example, in certain of the NHS hospital projects) is to provide for continued payment of all or part of the unitary payment to the project company, net of any additional costs incurred by the awarding authority, until an amount equal to outstanding debt has been paid.

10.9.11 What is or is not included within the scope of outstanding debt will itself be a matter for negotiation. Contentious points may be the inclusion of

---

1 Paragraph 9.5, *Further Contractual Issues* (HM Treasury and Private Finance Panel) January 1997 and section 20.2.2.3, draft Treasury Taskforce Guidance on Project Agreements.
2 See Chapter 9.

default interest and other sums which arise or become payable by reason of default. The inclusion of subordinated debt may also be the subject of debate: the awarding authority may resist its inclusion where the debt is provided by the sponsors or is otherwise in substance 'quasi-equity'.

10.9.12 The awarding authority will wish to ensure that what constitutes outstanding debt is net of the proceeds of enforcement of security realised or realisable by the funders and includes only amounts applied in respect of the project. Awarding authorities may seek to cap the amount of outstanding debt by reference to the original repayment profile. This protects the awarding authority against the risk of subsequent refinancings of the project or cost overruns increasing the amount of outstanding debt (and its compensation obligations). However, this is usually strenuously resisted by funders who will argue that the original repayment profile is only indicative.

10.9.13 The draft 'Taskforce Guidance on Project Agreements', recognising the shortcomings of some of the compensation mechanisms agreed to date – in particular, the fact that capping compensation at the amount of senior debt is arbitrary and unfairly discriminates against projects with a greater component of equity funding – has proposed an alternative approach based on 'market value'. The essence of the approach is that, following a termination of the project agreement for project company default, the awarding authority will pay the project company the market value of the unexpired term of the remainder of the project agreement. This has a logical appeal about it in that it avoids a windfall for the public sector but ensures that the awarding authority is not worse off following termination. Also, it does not differentiate between the construction period and the operating period and it does not discriminate arbitrarily between different debt and equity funding structures.

10.9.14 As one would expect, the reaction of equity investors to the proposal has been generally favourable (as under previous formulations the equity investors received no compensation under any circumstances). However, the reaction of lending banks has ranged from cautious sympathy to forceful opposition.

10.9.15 Undoubtedly the market value approach raises a number of practical concerns. Will there be a 'market' at all to take over a distressed project on the basis of a detailed contractual package? Will a subsequent consortium ever be prepared to accept 'warts and all' project documentation negotiated by a third party? How can the outgoing consortium's legitimate interests to prevent a 'fire sale' be protected? As the awarding authority will have to let contracts to ensure continued service provision following termination, what appetite will there be from suppliers to provide such services for a short period prior to a 'market sale' of the project and what appetite will the awarding authority have to go through two separate and time-consuming processes? None of these concerns should prove insuperable but one is left wondering whether the resultant contractual provisions will prove better in practice than previous formulations (such as compensation based on the net present value of the future payment stream less the awarding authority's costs of rectification and securing an alternative supplier).

Awarding authority default

10.9.16 The principle for payment of compensation on default by the awarding authority is that the project company and its funders should be no worse off than if the contract had proceeded as expected. This is recognised in the guidance in *Further Contractual Issues* which states that:[1]

'Full compensation of debt and equity (including anticipated profit) is appropriate.'

10.9.17 The draft 'Taskforce Guidance on Project Agreements' states, at paragraph 20.1.2.2.2, that the level of compensation should be the same as on voluntary termination by the awarding authority and notes that in compensating equity investors there are two approaches: compensation based on the original base case or compensation based on market value at the time of termination.[2]

10.9.18 The project company and its funders may be prepared to accept payment by way of instalments although, given the circumstances of default by the awarding authority, it is unlikely that more than a reasonable period in which to deal with the administration of the payment will be allowed.

Force Majeure

10.9.19 The position is different where termination arises as a result of Force Majeure. The key point is that, by definition, a Force Majeure event is neither party's fault. This suggests that losses should not fall exclusively on one party.

The Private Finance Panel guidance recognises that:[3]

'Termination in a case of Force Majeure will probably involve some (partial) compensation for the supplier; some aspect of the service may have been provided already. But there is no equitable reason for full compensation.'

10.9.20 The detail of the compensation will be a matter for negotiation between the parties although, once again, this is an area where the Treasury Taskforce is seeking to impose a standardised position across all sectors. It is now universally accepted that senior debt (including break costs) should be paid out on a Force Majeure termination. Compensation for equity investors has generally been limited to all or part of the nominal/paid up amount of equity share capital. The draft 'Taskforce Guidance' proposes payment of equity at par and subordinated debt principal and goes on to state that 'sub-contractors break costs should not be paid'.[4]

10.9.21 Again, the project company may allow the awarding authority to pay the compensation by instalments over a relatively short period.

---

1 Paragraph 9.10, *Further Contractual Issues* (HM Treasury and Private Finance Panel) January 1997.
2 See **10.9.3**.
3 Paragraph 9.10, *Further Contractual Issues* (HM Treasury and Private Finance Panel) January 1997.
4 Section 20.3.2.3.3, draft Treasury Taskforce Guidance on Project Agreements.

Corrupt gifts

10.9.22   Assuming the awarding authority retains the right to terminate the project agreement (as described at 10.7.10), there is some logic in providing for payment of compensation by the awarding authority on the same basis as for project company default. This has been the position agreed on some projects where a very limited right of termination for corrupt gifts has existed. However, the more common position to date has been that there is an automatic payout of senior debt in full and this is what the draft 'Taskforce Guidance on Project Agreements' proposes (provided the other range of remedies/sanctions available to the awarding authority have been exhausted).

Set-off

10.9.23   The awarding authority will wish to ensure that amounts payable to it by the project company may be set off against amounts payable in respect of compensation. This point may be the subject of negotiation as some project agreements only permit the awarding authority to exercise rights of set-off against the excess of any compensation over the amount of outstanding debt (ie keeping the banks whole).

10.9.24   The draft 'Taskforce Guidance on Project Agreements' states that the awarding authority should be entitled to set off outstanding claims on a project company default and that these claims should be automatically taken into account in determining 'market value'. However, there should not be set-off in other circumstances as 'termination payments under these circumstances are calculated so as to achieve a particular effect (for instance, payment of senior debt and equity at par on Force Majeure termination) and it would defeat the purpose of the compensation if this amount were then reduced by set-off prior to payment'.

Grossing up of termination payments

10.9.25   A further issue in relation to payments of compensation is the question of gross-up for taxation. The project company and its funders will wish to ensure that the amount of compensation received by the project company is increased to the extent that the project company incurs any liability for taxation in respect of the payment. The intention is that the debt funders and equity funders (where relevant) should receive payment in full, despite the fact that compensation is paid through the project company. The draft 'Taskforce Guidance on Project Agreements' states that 'compensation should be calculated on the basis that there is grossing up of payments (for tax deduction) save in the case of supplier default where a market value payment makes grossing up inappropriate'. This would be the case where the market value was calculated on a pre-tax basis. In relation to grossing up in general, it needs to be borne in mind that, had the project run its full course, tax would have been payable by the project company in any event. Where grossing up is accepted by the awarding authority it should be in relation to compensation amounts which are either calculated on an after-tax basis or where the compensation is capped (for example by reference to senior debt outstanding). In the latter scenario, if the cap operated to limit the amount of compensation payable, grossing up would be appropriate to ensure that the net after-tax amount received by the project company equalled that amount. The awarding authority will inevitably seek some protection to ensure that the project company utilises all available reliefs and allowances flowing from the project to minimise any actual tax charge.

10.10 STEP-IN

10.10.1 Step-in rights will be relevant for both the public sector and the private sector. In the case of the private sector, step-in rights will be a matter for the direct agreement between funders, the awarding authority and the project company. Funder direct agreements are considered in detail in Chapter 9.

10.10.2 Step-in rights for the public sector take two forms. First, as explained in Chapter 2, there may be direct agreements for the awarding authority entitling it to step-in to underlying project company contracts (such as the construction contract between the project company and the construction company). Secondly, step-in rights may be provided, for entitling the awarding authority, as a temporary 'self-help' remedy, to perform or get a third party to perform the project company's obligations under the project agreement in certain circumstances. It is in this sense that 'step-in' is used at 10.10. Unlike step-in rights under direct agreements, the awarding authority's rights will not just be exercisable on termination but may be exercised, from time to time, whilst the project agreement is still continuing.

10.10.3 The guidance in *Further Contractual Issues* states that:[1]

'step-in is not a necessary component of every PFI contract.'

The guidance views step-in as an extreme step which can erode the clear distinction of responsibilities between the awarding authority and the project company. It acknowledges, however, that it is likely to be relevant:

'where the client has a statutory responsibility to ensure the effective delivery at all times of a high profile public service; or where there is an equivalent moral or political responsibility.'[2]

A good example is the running of PFI prisons by the Prisons Service who will not wish the provision of custodial services to be disrupted as a result of breach by the project company of its obligations under the project agreement.

10.10.4 As specified in *Further Contractual Issues*, step-in rights for the public sector should be temporary. They are likely to be exercisable where the project company has failed to remedy a material breach of its obligations or in the context of an emergency. Once the circumstances giving rise to the exercise of the step-in rights have been remedied, the awarding authority's intervention should cease.

---

1 Paragraph 7.4, *Further Contractual Issues* (HM Treasury and Private Finance Panel) January 1997.
2 Paragraph 7.4, *Further Contractual Issues* (HM Treasury and Private Finance Panel) January 1997.

10.10.5 Provisions dealing with step-in rights for the awarding authority should provide for reimbursement of the awarding authority's reasonable costs of stepping-in. Neither party should benefit overall.[1] It follows that any deductions which are made for poor performance by the project company should, where relevant, take account of any monies paid by the project company in reimbursement of the awarding authority's costs: in other words, there should be no double counting.

10.11 CONCLUSION

10.11.1 Although the development of better guidance and more precedent will assist in the task of negotiating future project agreements, the inherent complexity of the arrangements and the unique nature of every project mean that the task will remain one of the key challenges for those concerned with the delivery of a project.

10.11.2 Guidance by its very nature is often generic and cannot answer issues specific to particular projects. It also varies from sector to sector. Likewise, precedent is not a panacea, particularly where different solutions have been adopted for similar projects. Ultimately, the tail should not wag the dog: the essence of the project agreement is consensus between the parties, not rigid adherence to guidance or precedent. The challenge for the contracting parties and their respective advisers is to achieve that consensus in a timely and efficent manner.

---

1   Paragraph 7.8, *Further Contractual Issues* (HM Treasury and Private Finance Panel) January 1997.

Chapter 11

PROPERTY ASPECTS OF PFI PROJECTS

11.1 INTRODUCTION

11.1.1 From a property point of view, the analysis of a PFI project involves many of the same principles as a joint venture/development arrangement in an open commercial environment. The primary commercial issues of control, profit share and commercial viability have parallels in the basic principles of PFI; namely, the transfer of risk, affordability and value for money.

11.1.2 Many private sector development projects involve a degree of public sector participation. At its most basic level this may be simply through the role of the local planning authority in granting necessary planning consents. However, even prior to the development of the PFI, collaborations between the public and private sectors in property development, with direct local authority or central government involvement in an estate interest capacity, were commonplace. Perhaps the main difference between the PFI and the various property-based public/private joint ventures which have preceded it lies in the fact that the PFI is endeavouring to encourage participants to view the arrangements as the delivery of a service. This contrasts with the more traditional institution-led view of regarding the assets *per se* as having intrinsic value.[1]

11.1.3 Many of the issues dealt with in this chapter are those which would be listed for consideration in traditional development projects. The purpose of this chapter is not, therefore, to review in detail each legal issue which may arise in a PFI project but rather to provide an overview of the structures that are typically encountered and to set these in the context of the principles of the PFI.

11.2 THE ROLE OF PROPERTY IN THE PFI CONTEXT

11.2.1 The role of property in the PFI context is fundamentally twofold. First, it ensures that the project is viable from a practical point of view. In the majority of PFI projects (whether, for example, the construction of a hospital, a road, a court house or a school) land is required from or on which the PFI service can be provided. Whilst government guidance is keen to emphasise the difference between traditional capital asset procurement and PFI service procurement, in many cases the presence of a property asset is a physical prerequisite to the carrying out of the service.

11.2.2 Secondly, in the case of many projects that involve an element of surplus land, property disposal or development may play a vital role in establishing affordability and value for money. The sale of surplus property may generate

---

1   See *Risk and Reward in PFI Contracts* (HM Treasury and Private Finance Panel) May 1996.

vital capital to offset and reduce the unitary payment and secure the viability of the project.

11.3 NATURE OF THE PROJECT

Site identification

11.3.1 The logical first step in any project is to consider what property is required for the project. To ensure that the public sector comparator is viable and deliverable, the awarding authority is usually forced to adopt the conservative approach of utilising resources that are readily available to it. Generally this entails the awarding authority's public sector comparator utilising existing properties within its ownership. Inevitably, however, whilst offering certainty of delivery this approach may not produce best value for money. Unless there are overriding reasons to be prescriptive as to location (and there are occasions where there may be legitimate reasons for this) the awarding authority should therefore always invite tenders in a non-prescriptive 'output-based' way. This allows the private sector to come forward with innovative solutions that may involve providing the service from other properties which it has identified as suitable for the project.

11.3.2 Naturally, the development of solutions utilising property in third-party ownership will impact certainty of delivery and, accordingly, the awarding authority will wish to set out in its ITN or ITT what evidence it requires that the solution is deliverable. Recognising the risks that may attach to solutions involving property in third-party ownership, awarding authorities sometimes only permit such solutions to be put forward as a variant bid (accompanying a reference bid based around property already in the awarding authority's ownership or control).

Site risks

11.3.3 Whether the project is to be based on an existing site in the awarding authority's ownership or on a site in third-party ownership, it may be necessary to obtain third-party consents or agreements or address deficiencies in the site to render it suitable for delivery of the service. There are, inevitably, cost and timing implications involved in obtaining these consents or agreements and addressing any deficiencies. The most likely issue will be the need to obtain vacant possession and secure planning consents although other common considerations include addressing restrictive covenants and easements (including, in relation to construction, rights of light and air). The primary question is who should assume the risks of addressing these matters.

11.3.4 Typically, the awarding authority's stance (especially where third-party sites have been introduced by the preferred tenderer) will be that it is up to the preferred tenderer to demonstrate that its solution for the project is deliverable and to deliver it. The reality, however, is that often the risks of delivery are shared. Whilst the responsibility for securing necessary planning permissions or obtaining vacant possession may be placed nominally with the project company, it is likely that the project will remain conditional on these matters being secured (not least because it is likely that funders will make these conditions to the availability of finance). At the end of the day, the awarding authority and the project company are sharing the risk.

11.3.5 Inevitably, a cost will be attributed to the task of obtaining third-party consents or agreements and addressing any deficiencies in the site. The awarding authority may require that all costs associated with the delivery of the service are fixed and guaranteed at the tender stage. Whilst this has the benefit of certainty, the disadvantage from the awarding authority's point of view is that the tenderer may build in contingencies for the worst case scenario and bid an inflated figure to protect it against the risk of being subjected to unbudgeted costs. Where the uncertainties are significant this approach is therefore not likely to produce value for money. In such cases the awarding authority may be better served to deal with certain risks by:

- assuming the risk itself; or
- sharing the risk with the project company (for instance, accepting a lower underwritten value on a surplus site and entering into an overage arrangement to share in upside value generated by the project company).[1] The downside of this is that the ultimate cost of the project to the awarding authority will be uncertain and this may be an untenable position for the awarding authority if affordability is marginal.

11.3.6 The degree to which site risks will be retained by the awarding authority or transferred to the project company can only be determined on a case-by-case basis, but is likely to be influenced by factors such as whether the solution utilises a property already owned by the awarding authority or under the control of another government department,[2] or whether the property has been brought to the project by the project company. If the property was already in the awarding authority's ownership, the degree to which site issues can be fully investigated and evaluated by the project company will be a determining factor in the level of risk transfer (so, for instance, where land is built on, the project company will frequently seek to impose qualifications as to unforeseen ground conditions). The awarding authority may also assume the risk of site delivery in cases where it is intending to acquire the proposed land interest by promoting a compulsory purchase order.[3]

Specific issues

Public body occupiers
11.3.7 It is often the case that the property identified as suitable for the project is occupied by other public bodies or quasi-public bodies. This may range from situations where an NHS trust shares occupation (and often ownership of buildings) with medical, teaching or research establishments or where one government department shares accommodation with another. It is likely that the

---

1   See Chapter 12.
2   See **11.3.7–11.3.12**.
3   See **11.3.13**.

awarding authority will have a better negotiating position to address the occupation issues relating to the other public sector party than the preferred tenderer. Accordingly, it is often preferable for these issues to be addressed by the awarding authority. The situation may be further complicated by the fact that government departments are likely to be bound by the Departmental Estate Occupancy Agreement.

The departmental estate occupancy agreement

11.3.8 The basis on which government departments occupy space owned or leased by another government department is set out in a document known as the Departmental Estate Occupancy Agreement for Crown Bodies (the 'DEOA'). Under the DEOA, the department which owns or leases the space is known as the 'Holder' and the department occupying the space is known as the 'Occupier'.

11.3.9 The DEOA sets out the principal terms on which the Occupier occupies the space. However, these can be varied by agreement between the departments. Where one department occupies space held by another department and no formal agreement relating to the occupation is reached between the departments, the DEOA will automatically apply. Variations to the terms set out in the DEOA and conditions specific to a particular occupation are contained in what is known as a Memorandum of Terms of Occupation and commonly referred to as a 'MOTO'. Since, technically, the Crown is indivisible, the arrangements do not constitute a legal agreement. However, they represent a set of rules and regulations which will be adhered to as between the departments.

11.3.10 Because the Crown is indivisible the DEOA does not grant any legal security of tenure to individual tenants but it does cater for two specific scenarios:

- properties owned by the Holder are let for five-year terms (known as 'Prescribed Terms'). Where a second Occupier goes into occupation half way through a Prescribed Term, it will occupy until the end of the Prescribed Term even though this will be for a period of less than five years. This enables a Holder to plan for the future on a five-yearly cycle;
- in the event that a Holder wishes to obtain vacant possession before the end of a Prescribed Term, it is required under the DEOA to give as much notice as possible to the Occupier. In addition, the Holder may be required to give the Occupier financial assistance towards the cost of relocating to alternative premises. The Holder does not have a right of eviction as regards the Occupier although the Occupier is required to 'co-operate with the Holder wherever possible and deal with occupancy matters in a positive and constructive way'.

11.3.11 Where the Holder sells its reversionary interest to the project company, the DEOA is stated to determine automatically. However, the Occupier will still have the right to remain in occupation notwithstanding the determination of the DEOA. On a strict legal basis, it may be able to argue that there is an implied periodic tenancy based upon the same terms as the DEOA. Given the fact that the project company will be a non-Crown organisation, the

Occupier may also be able to invoke the protection of Part II of the Landlord and Tenant Act 1954 which would result in it having security of tenure.[1]

11.3.12 The awarding authority will wish to manage the arrangements with public body occupiers to introduce certainty and to prevent the preferred tenderer from viewing each arrangement as a significant risk with corresponding financial consequences. For this reason, it would be normal for the awarding authority to take on the responsibility of terminating departmental occupancies or converting MOTOs into legal tenancies as required by the circumstances of the project.

Compulsory purchase order

11.3.13 In order to guarantee delivery of the property with vacant possession (particularly where the property is in third-party ownership), it may be necessary to use compulsory purchase powers. Such powers are not only available to awarding authorities in such obvious cases as highways, transport or urban regeneration projects. Many other awarding authorities have such powers, for instance the Secretary of State for Health has the power to authorise NHS trusts to promote compulsory purchase orders to facilitate land acquisition.[2]

11.4 NATURE OF THE PROPERTY INTEREST TO BE GRANTED: PROPERTY STRUCTURES

Choice of structure

11.4.1 A wide variety of property structures are available and have been adopted in PFI projects. However, as more PFI projects across the different sectors reach financial close, a core of different template structures is emerging. These structures and their respective advantages and disadvantages are considered below.

11.4.2 Generally there are four issues which determine the structure to be adopted.

− Is the awarding authority to be the user/occupier of the property?
− Does the awarding authority need to be able to acquire/reacquire any property interest held by the project company (for instance, on a default by the project company)?
− Does the awarding authority require, or expect to require, ownership of the property at the end of the contract term?
− Is the property structure (when taken together with the totality of the risks transferred) consistent with the assets being off balance sheet from the awarding authority's perspective?[3]

---

1 Occupiers of Crown land (particularly residential occupiers) will not be able to gain security of tenure. See Rent Act 1977 and Housing Act 1988.
2 For further discussion as to the availability of such powers, see **13.3**.
3 See Chapter 17.

11.4.3 The awarding authority's position on each of these issues will often have implications for the value that the tenderers are prepared to ascribe to the property (which will feed through to the unitary payment that they bid).

11.4.4 Whatever structure the awarding authority selects in the light of these considerations, it may be beneficial to allow the tenderers to put forward alternative structures as variant bids where these maximise value for money. One of the features of the PFI, which sets it apart from traditional property development transactions, is that structures can be relatively freely determined by the commercial objectives of the parties rather than constrained by the conventions of what is 'institutionally acceptable'.[1]

Awarding authority as end-user/occupier

11.4.5 Where the awarding authority is to be the end-user/occupier of the property, the property structure for the land associated with the service provision the subject of the project (as distinct from arrangements in respect of any surplus land) is likely to be chosen from one of the following structures:

- the freehold interest in the property is vested in the project company, with a lease back to the awarding authority of that part of the property which the awarding authority needs to occupy;
- the freehold interest remains with the awarding authority, with the grant of a long lease of the property to the project company to allow the provision of a service and with a sub-lease back to the awarding authority of those parts of the site which the awarding authority needs to occupy;
- the freehold interest remains with the awarding authority, with a licence granted to the project company entitling it to enter and exploit the site for the provision of the services.

Project company as end-user/occupier

11.4.6 Where the project company is the end-user/occupier of the property then the structure is likely to be based on one of the following:

- the freehold interest in the property is vested in the project company with no land interest granted to the awarding authority;
- the freehold interest in the property is vested in the project company with a headlease to the awarding authority and a sub-lease back to the project company;
- the freehold interest in the property is vested in the awarding authority and a lease is granted to the project company; or
- the freehold interest in the property is vested in the awarding authority and a licence is granted to the project company entitling the project company to occupy and exploit the property for the agreed purposes.

---

1   See *Financing Projects for Government Accommodation* Jason Fox and Richard Millward, Project Finance International, 6 November, 1996.

Awarding authority as ultimate end-user/occupier: structures

Freehold vested in project company with lease granted back to awarding authority

11.4.7 This structure is likely to be a good starting point in situations where there is nothing inherently unique about the site in question and the awarding authority is not concerned with retaining a long-term property interest beyond the contract term. The structure is most commonly encountered in PFI projects for government accommodation. It was, for instance, used in the case of the DSS Prime Project in relation to all sites which the DSS previously owned as freeholder and occupied. The freehold interest is vested in the project company and a lease, excluded from the relevant security of tenure provisions of the Landlord and Tenant Act 1954, is granted back to the awarding authority. The duration of the lease would, typically, match the contract term.

11.4.8 The commercial relations between the parties would be regulated under the project agreement which would provide for the making of a unitary payment in return for the supply of the various facilities and services.[1] The obligations of the project company under the project agreement and as landlord under the lease would need to be made consistent (and usually this is achieved by the lease cross-referencing the obligations under the other project documents). The lease itself would reserve a peppercorn rent and have nominal obligations on the awarding authority as tenant. Under such a structure, in the event that the project company defaulted or became insolvent, the awarding authority would remain in secure occupation for the remainder of the lease term (because the lease, as an interest in land, could not be disclaimed by a liquidator or receiver of the project company).

11.4.9 The lease would probably also include the traditional landlord's obligations (as appropriate) in relation to repair and services which would be suspended while the project agreement subsisted. This would allow the lease to continue to stand alone from the authority's point of view on the expiry of the project agreement. However, it should be noted that the de facto burden of payment for the maintenance and servicing of the facilities may still fall upon the awarding authority in the event of the project company's default (assuming the project company continued to be the landlord).

11.4.10 In each case, the awarding authority will need to decide whether it wishes to impose a restriction requiring the project company to remain as landlord under the lease throughout the contract term. In most cases, however, it would not be practicable for the reversionary interest to be sold on by the project company during the contract term since the project company would still require a land interest from which to provide the ongoing services. In any event, imposing restrictions on dealing with the reversionary interest is unlikely to have

---

1 The consideration of the structures assumes that relevant controls and obligations in relation to the provision of any service are included within other project documents. Note, however, the need to ensure that the provisions of s 2 of the Law of Property (Miscellaneous Provisions) Act 1989 are observed.

a detrimental effect on the project economics given that the freehold will be subject to a lease to the awarding authority for the contract term at a nominal rent. It is more likely that the project company would wait until the end of the contract term to realise the value in the freehold (though it could, in theory, realise the value earlier by means of a forward sale).

11.4.11 If the property in question is one which was previously in the freehold ownership of the awarding authority and which was transferred to the project company at the outset of the project, difficulties can arise in terms of protecting the awarding authority in the event of a default or insolvency of the project company. If the value of the freehold was to be translated into a lower unitary payment (and therefore spread across the entire contract term), the awarding authority is at risk if the project company defaults or becomes insolvent and the project agreement is terminated early.[1] There are a number of ways in which this risk may be removed or mitigated.

- A cash payment equivalent to the market value of the reversionary interest could be paid by the project company to the awarding authority at the time the freehold is transferred to the project company. However, such a payment would need to be financed by the project company and the cost of this would flow through to the awarding authority by means of a higher unitary payment. The cash payment might equate to the value of the reversion (ie the value of the freehold encumbered by a lease for the contract term for a nominal rent). Clearly, the value of the reversion will be dependent on the length of the lease and is unlikely to be great in most cases as contract terms tend to be upwards of 25 years.
- The reversionary interest could be charged to the awarding authority. This would enable the awarding authority to sell the freehold reversion to a third party (but not to acquire the freehold reversion itself) to realise its value. Clearly, given that the freehold reversion will be encumbered by a non-producing lease in favour of the awarding authority, it may be difficult to market it and the value ascribed by a purchaser in the open market may be less than the value that the awarding authority as the incumbent lessee and occupier would ascribe. The value will, of course, also be influenced by the existence and state of condition of any buildings on the site. If the project entailed a new build or significant refurbishment which had been completed, the value of the reversion at the point of termination should have increased by virtue of the works carried out by the project company.
- The awarding authority could retain an option to reacquire the reversionary interest at a nominal sum. (Provided that the option is registered against the land (or as an estate contract at the Land Charges Registry in the case of unregistered land) even if a liquidator attempted to disclaim the option as an unprofitable contract, the holder of the option may still have the right to

---

1 However, any compensation payable by the awarding authority following termination should reflect the value of land transferred, eg through calculating the net present value of the lower unitary payment (reflecting the value of the freehold transferred).

seek enforcement of the option by applying to the court for an order of specific performance.¹)

11.4.12 A common objective of awarding authorities in PFI projects for office accommodation is to secure flexible arrangements that enable the awarding authority to increase or reduce the amount of accommodation it takes from the project company to meet its changing requirements. Provided the accommodation is general office accommodation (rather than something bespoke to the awarding authority's particular requirements) and depending on the location of the accommodation, it may be possible for the project company to offer the awarding authority options to increase or reduce the area occupied without compromising value for money. Such options can be accommodated in a leasehold structure by making provision for the surrender of designated areas under the lease or, in the case of an option to increase the amount of accommodation, by way of supplemental leases.

11.4.13 It is also possible (and not uncommon) to make provision for the awarding authority to have options to terminate the lease early (perhaps at more than one break point) or to extend the term of the lease (with the contract term under the rest of the project documentation also changing in line with the revised lease term).²

11.4.14 Overall, adopting this structure passes the risk in holding the property and the value in it to the private sector. However, such a wholesale disposal may not always be appropriate and the structure offers limited control in the event of default. Whilst it gives a right of secure occupation for the contract term there is no ability for the awarding authority to take back the property itself. It is possible to attempt to solve this problem by granting the awarding authority an option to buy the freehold in the event of the default of the project company. However, if this is of material concern to the project company the structure described at **11.4.15** to **11.4.25** is likely to be more suitable.

Freehold remains vested in awarding authority and headlease is granted to project company with sub-lease back to awarding authority

11.4.15 This structure is common in PFI projects particularly those involving facilities which the public sector wish to reacquire or to continue to occupy at the end of the initial contract term. It is also used where the awarding authority requires control over the future use of the property at the end of the contract term.

11.4.16 A headlease is granted by the awarding authority to the project company with a sub-lease back to the awarding authority. The duration of the headlease is a commercial decision. At one extreme, the headlease could be granted for such a period that, in economic terms, it amounted to the transfer of

---

1 See Megarry and Wade, *The Law of Real Property* (5th edn) at pages 605 and 623 regarding specific performance of land contracts.
2 It is to be noted that any option arrangements taking effect in situations where the contract term is for a period in excess of 21 years should be included within the lease itself to avoid any possibility of them becoming invalid (Perpetuities and Accumulations Act 1964, s 9).

the freehold. At the other extreme, the headlease may simply be granted for a period equal to the contract term. The key driver will be whether the intention is to transfer residual value in the property to the project company. A sub-lease back to the awarding authority would be granted for the contract term.

11.4.17 Both the sub-lease and the headlease would provide for a nominal rent and the commercial relationship between the parties would, as described at **11.4.8**, be regulated by a project agreement providing for the making of a unitary payment in return for the provision of relevant services.

11.4.18 The headlease is commonly granted over the whole of the property regardless of whether only part of it is used and occupied by the awarding authority. The sub-lease back to the awarding authority would typically be only over those parts which it is actually intending to occupy. The awarding authority would then have the ability, through the terms of the headlease, to control that part of the site which it is not occupying (whether the intention is for the project company to use the remaining area itself, for instance, for occupation by its facilities management personnel, or whether the intention is to let the remaining area to third-party occupiers). Examples include:

– where an awarding authority requiring office accommodation occupies part of a multi-let office building;
– where the awarding authority is an NHS trust which has let a project for a new hospital which contains retail units to be let to third parties.

11.4.19 By virtue of the control it will have under the headlease the awarding authority will be in a position to approve (if necessary) the identity of other occupiers and the nature of their use. Control over identity might be important for security reasons, for instance if the awarding authority was involved in the defence or intelligence services. Control over use would also be relevant where, for example, an NHS trust wanted to ensure that retail units in a hospital were not used for the sale of alcohol, tobacco etc.

11.4.20 A further benefit of the headlease/sub-lease structure is that it provides a level of protection for the awarding authority should it wish to reacquire ownership of the property from the project company by collapsing the structure on a default by the project company. The structure would allow for the collapse of the lease arrangements and the forfeiture of the headlease[1] in the event that there was a default under the project agreement (subject to the usual remedy and step in periods). This would enable the awarding authority to regain control of the whole site and avoid any of the limitations that would result where there was a mere retention of a lease with the awarding authority as the tenant for the remainder of the contract term (as described at **11.4.9**). The result would be that the awarding authority is left enjoying secure occupation in perpetuity (although, again, it would in practical terms thereafter bear the cost of maintaining and servicing the accommodation).

---

1   It is likely that any attempt to introduce a break option triggered by a default under the main project documents instead of a right of re-entry will be treated as an act of forfeiture giving the project company rights of relief.

11.4.21 Typically, the sub-lease would be on similar terms to the lease described at **11.4.7** and **11.4.8** and the same comments would apply.

11.4.22 The terms of the headlease may include the traditional provisions one would expect to find relating principally to repair, alienation and alterations.[1] However, typically these provisions would be suspended for the contract term to allow the project agreement to take precedence. The provisions would therefore only apply at the expiry of the contract term. The awarding authority will be concerned not to impose unnecessary obligations or restrictions as these may have a negative impact on the value of the reversion. However, it is often the case that the awarding authority will seek to ensure that it retains some control over the use of what, in many cases, are sensitive properties both in terms of location and how they are perceived by the public.

11.4.23 It may be the case that the awarding authority will wish to acquire (or reacquire) ownership of the site at the end of the contract term or at least to have the option to do so. There are a variety of ways in which this can be achieved. It will be automatically achieved if the headlease and sub-lease are coterminous (although clearly such a structure would involve no residual value risk transfer to the project company). If, however, a long headlease has been granted, the awarding authority could be given the right to buy out the headlease when the sub-lease expires at the end of the contract term, either at a predetermined value or (more usually) at its then market value (as agreed between the parties or determined by an independent expert).[2] The market value formulation has the benefit of transferring residual value risk to the project company (so, for instance, if the property has been poorly maintained this would be reflected in the price paid by the awarding authority).[3]

11.4.24 The advantage of this structure over that set out at **11.4.7** to **11.4.11**, from the perspective of the awarding authority, is that it gives more security and greater control (particularly on a default by the project company) whilst still achieving residual value risk transfer (if that is the awarding authority's wish). However, the greater degree of control may come at a cost which will be reflected in a higher unitary payment.

Grant of a licence

11.4.25 Leaving aside the question of residual value risk, the simplest and most flexible property structure from the point of view of the awarding authority is not to grant the project company a land interest at all. Depending on the nature of

---

1 In the imposition of any leasehold structure with obligations in the project agreement relating to construction and repair, care must be taken to avoid the vagaries of compensation under the Landlord and Tenant Act 1927 and to ensure that s 18 of that Act together with the Leasehold Property (Repairs) Act 1938 does not prejudice the enforceability of the repair obligations if an obligation is placed on the project company to observe and perform the obligations in the project agreement. See, however, *Rainbow Estates Limited v Tokenhold Limited* [1998] 3 WLR 980.
2 This would only represent value for money if it could be demonstrated that the value has been reflected in a lower unitary payment.
3 As detailed at **11.4.12–11.4.14**, the structure can be modified to accommodate further flexibility for the awarding authority.

the services to be provided, the awarding authority may choose to grant a simple licence to the project company allowing it to occupy the property and carry out the services. This gives the awarding authority the highest degree of control but passes no residual value risk to the project company.

11.4.26   The disadvantages of this structure are:

- because no ownership interest is transferred, the property contributes nothing to the affordability of the project;
- the absence of any transfer of residual value risk will make it more difficult for the project to achieve off balance sheet status from the perspective of the awarding authority;[1]
- reliance on a licence may limit the ability of the project company to derive third-party revenue (it will, for instance, not be in a position to grant leases itself for income generation); and
- certain awarding authorities, such as NHS trusts, may be liable to pay capital charges if they retain ownership of the property and it remains on their balance sheet.
- To the extent that *exclusive* occupation is granted to the project company for the carrying out of its services, then regardless of the licence arrangements, the project company may be able to argue that it is in fact a tenant and may derive security of tenure pursuant to Part II of the Landlord and Tenant Act 1954. As such, the awarding authority will be unable to regain control of those parts of the property occupied by the project company save to the extent that it is able to do so within the confines of that Act which presupposes the grant of a lease.

11.4.27   Because of these disadvantages the structure is rarely used. It was used in the case of the DBFO road projects where, because of the relevant legislative regime, it was not possible to grant the project company an interest in land.

Project company as end-user/occupier: structures[2]

Transfer of freehold interest outright to project company (with no lease back)

11.4.28   Cases where the awarding authority is willing to rely purely on the contractual commitment of the project company to provide the services during the contract term and take no property interest itself will be rare. The covenant status of the project company might be such that the risks of its insolvency or failure to perform are small (for instance, where a large IT supplier contracts directly to provide IT services rather than does so via a special purpose vehicle). However, the political as well as practical ramifications of a failure to provide services in a PFI project mean that an awarding authority is unlikely to consider this option. Its priority will be to ensure that, in the event of default, it can regain control over the provision of the services so as to ensure continuity of service. As

---

1   See Chapter 17.
2   These structures might be applicable where the awarding authority is simply purchasing a service (such as IT service carried out by project company employees) and the awarding authority has no requirement to be in occupation of the property itself.

has been discussed above,[1] where the property is effectively the conduit through which the services are provided the awarding authority is unlikely to consider the outright disposal of the property without retaining an ability to regain control (and ownership) of the property in the event of project company default.

11.4.29 It is possible to envisage a structure involving the outright disposal of the property but with an option for the awarding authority to reacquire the property in the event of default. However, even if the option could be protected from disclaimer by a liquidator or receiver,[2] there could clearly be practical difficulties in ensuring continuity of service.

Freehold is transferred to project company with lease back to awarding authority and sub-lease granted to project company

11.4.30 This arrangement allows the freehold interest to be transferred out of the ownership of the awarding authority (and therefore potentially achieves the transfer of residual value) whilst giving the awarding authority the ability to retain an element of control through a lease and lease back structure. The project company grants a lease, with a duration equal to the contract term, of that part of the property required for the carrying out of the services. The awarding authority, in turn, grants a lease back to the project company of exactly the same demise to allow the project company to fulfil its functions.

11.4.31 The lease to the awarding authority would be on similar terms to that envisaged at **11.4.8**. The sub-lease would be on nominal terms merely granting a legal interest. The awarding authority would be able to determine the sub-lease and take back those parts of the property required for the carrying out of the project functions in the event of a default. This would leave the awarding authority in a similar position to that described at **11.4.9** in the event of default. The disadvantage from both parties' points of view is that the structure will inevitably reduce the value ascribed to the property by the project company and the awarding authority could potentially be left in the embarrassing situation of having disposed of its freehold interest without having received full value for it (unless one of the structures described at **11.4.11** is pursued).

Freehold is vested in awarding authority and project company is granted headlease

11.4.32 This is likely to be the approach favoured by most awarding authorities to whom issues of control and continuity of service are paramount. The lease is purely a mechanism to give the project company control of the site for the contract term. It can allow, through the term of the lease, the awarding authority an ability to control the use of the site (with third-party occupiers if it is a mixed-use site). It also affords the awarding authority the ability to control the future use of the property (if this is a concern). Such a mechanism can also control who is to have responsibility for the site following the expiry of the contract term (since it could cater, by way of an option, for the preferred tenderer to buy the reversionary interest or be granted a longer term). The awarding authority could

---

1 See **11.4.14**.
2 See **11.4.11**.

be offered the relevant protection by allowing for a default under the project agreement to trigger a right of re-entry.[1]

11.4.33 The principal disadvantage of this arrangement is that it prevents the value of the property playing any significant role in reducing the unitary payment unless the lease is a long lease (and not merely coterminous with the contract term) or unless the parties agree an arrangement allowing the freehold to be transferred to the project company at the end of the contract term.

Freehold interest is vested in awarding authority and project company is granted licence

11.4.34 The awarding authority could consider simply granting a licence to the project company to enter and use the property for the provision of the services. The structure here is essentially the same as that described at **11.4.25**, save that here the scope of the licence would be wider, entitling use and occupation by the project company (as required by the nature of the project). The advantages of the awarding authority retaining control and, in the event of default, stepping in to provide continuity of service have already been discussed. The risks to the awarding authority are few although the impact on value for money and affordability may be great. The disadvantages detailed at **11.4.26** apply.

11.5 OTHER MATTERS

Government Circular 6/93

11.5.1 In considering any PFI project which involves the disposal of property, consideration must be given to the provisions of Government Circular 6/93. The Circular states that the disposal of land by local authorities and other public bodies must be at the best obtainable price. There is a corresponding provision in s 123 of the Local Government Act 1972.

11.5.2 It should be emphasised that this does not mean that the awarding authority needs to receive a cash payment for property disposed of by it nor analyse each part of the project in isolation. It may be the case, for instance, that in maximising the value of surplus land, part of a property portfolio is sacrificed to increase the value of the other properties in relation to planning obligations. This would not necessarily mean that the awarding authority would be acting outside its powers in relation to the particular property which has suffered the diminution in value. As long as the property disposals as a whole fulfil the criteria then the requirements of the Circular should be met.

11.5.3 In certain circumstances local authorities will require the consent of the Secretary of State for the Environment, Transport and the Regions for land

---

1 The lease should be excluded from the relevant provisions of the Landlord and Tenant Act 1954 to allow the awarding authority to regain control of the site at the end of the term. This is particularly important if the awarding authority requires the site at the end of the contractual term and the lease term is coterminous.

disposal. If the guidance is not followed, the local authority or officers conducting the disposal could be entering into an *ultra vires* transaction .[1]

The Crichel Down Rules 1992

11.5.4 The Crichel Down Rules 1992 (the 'Rules') are non-statutory government guidelines which aim to compensate former landowners whose land was compulsorily purchased by the government by offering them back their former land holdings. The Rules provide that surplus government land, acquired by or under a threat of compulsion and during certain timeframes, should be offered back to former owners, successors or sitting tenants prior to being disposed of. There are a number of exceptions to this general rule which are examined at **11.5.8**. The detail of the Rules is set out in a publication, *Disposal of Surplus Government Land; Obligation to offer land back to former owners or their successors – The Crichel Down Rules* issued by the Department of the Environment and the Welsh Office on 30 October 1992.

11.5.5 Whether or not the Rules should be considered in the context of a PFI transaction depends on the structure of the project. Where there is to be a freehold disposal of land from a government department to the project company, the Rules will apply. If the structure involves the grant of a long lease of land to the project company with a lease back of those parts of the site which are needed by the government department, the position is less clear cut. The Rules do not address whether a long leasehold disposal falls within the ambit of the Rules. However, the cautious approach must be to assume that it does. This has the following implications:

- those parts of the site (or whole of the site) which are leased back to the government department are, on the basis that the department will remain in occupation, not deemed to be surplus and the Rules should not apply. However, on the expiry of the contract period or earlier determination, it will be surplus if, under the property structure, the project company is left with possession and a property interest at that time. Accordingly, the prudent course must be to make the required offer to former owners at the outset of the arrangements;
- where there is no lease back of land to the government department, the Rules will apply. The possible future impact of the Rules should also be considered if the project company has a later option to buy the freehold.

Where the project involves the grant of a licence to the project company this will fall outside the ambit of the Rules since the government has not disposed of an interest in land.

11.5.6 The Rules apply to all land acquired by or under threat of compulsion. A threat of compulsion will be assumed in the case of a voluntary sale if the power to acquire land compulsorily existed at the time of acquisition. The exception to this assumption is where the land was publicly or privately offered for sale

---

1   See Chapter 4.

immediately prior to negotiations for the acquisition. This may be shown by evidence of offers for sale, for example, estate agent or auction particulars.

11.5.7 The Rules apply only if the acquisition made by the government was within certain timeframes. They apply to:

- agricultural land acquired between 1 January 1935 and 29 October 1992 (inclusive);
- agricultural land acquired on or after 30 October 1992 and disposed of within 25 years of that acquisition; and
- non-agricultural land which becomes available for disposal within 25 years of its acquisition.

The date of acquisition in each case is the date of the conveyance or transfer to the government department. Subsequent transfers (if any) between government departments can be ignored.

11.5.8 A number of exceptions apply to the general obligation to offer back surplus land to former owners. The most relevant in the context of PFI transactions are discussed below, but these are by no means exhaustive and reference should be made to the Rules for a complete list.

- *'Where land has materially changed in character.'* The Rules cite, as an example of material change in character, houses erected on agricultural land. Further examples are where open land has been afforested; offices built on an urban site or where substantial works to an existing building have effectively altered its character. The erection of temporary buildings on land, however, is not deemed to be necessarily a material change. When deciding whether any works have materially altered the character of land, the Rules advise that the disposing government department should consider the likely cost of restoring the land to its original use. The obligation to offer-back will still apply to any part of the land for disposal which has not materially changed in character.
- *'Where small areas of agricultural land would have no satisfactory agricultural use, even when used in conjunction with other agricultural land already in possession of the former owner.'* The application of this exception should be referred to agricultural surveyors for determination.
- *'Where the disposal is execution of government policies for the transfer to the private sector of the functions of providing particular services.'* The relevance of this exception in the context of PFI transactions is self-evident. However, the extent of this exception is untested and if the land that is subject to the PFI transaction is subject to the Rules, the possible application of other exceptions should be examined. It would certainly seem unsafe to seek to rely on this exception in relation to surplus land as that land would not be required for 'the functions of providing particular services'.
- *'Where a disposal is in respect of either*:
    (i) a site for development or redevelopment which comprises two or more previous land holdings; or
    (ii) a site which consists partly of land which has been materially changed in character and part which has not and there is a risk of a fragmented sale of such a site realising substantially less than the best price that can

reasonably be obtained for the site as a whole, ie its market value. In such cases, however, any former owner who has remained in continuous occupation of the whole or part of his or her former property (by virtue of a tenancy or licence) will be given first refusal of that property or part of property, as the case may be.' In the case of (i) above, the Rules state that special consideration will be given where a consortium of former owners has indicated a wish to purchase the land collectively. Determining whether a disposal falls within this exception will be a question for surveyors or valuers. When evaluating the best price that can be obtained for land which is the subject of the disposal they should take into account the obligation on the department disposing the land to obtain planning consent before disposing of land or property with potential for development.

11.5.9 Where the disposal does not fall within any of the exceptions, the procedure for offering back must be followed. The Rules set out timescales for the offer-back process and adequate time should be allowed in the timetable for the PFI transaction to take account of this. Where there is a possibility that the Rules apply, it is useful to ascertain the risk that a former owner will be interested in purchasing the land. It is advisable, early in the PFI transaction, to instruct a genealogist to investigate probate and build up a picture of the former owner's successors.[1] This profile will give an indication as to whether the former owner is likely to want to purchase and whether a former owner or its successors still own land in the vicinity of the disposal land. This will be of relevance when considering the agricultural use exception.

Mixed-use properties

11.5.10 Inevitably, situations will arise in which the property which has been identified as that from which the service is to be provided is part of a larger unit. This will be the situation where the solution envisages the awarding authority occupying part of a multi-let building or where the service being provided by the private sector envisages a complementary activity on site (for example, a hospital with a retail element). A balance needs to be struck between the awarding authority allowing as much flexibility as possible to the project company (the more restrictions placed upon the parts of the property not occupied by the awarding authority the lower the value to the project company) and the risk that, in the event of the failure of the project, the awarding authority takes back a site with unsuitable occupants and/or occupants on unacceptable terms. The level of control and the ability to sever the third-party arrangements from the core service being provided from the property have significant influence on the structure to be imposed. It is easier to exercise relevant controls and positive covenants through a leasehold arrangement rather than through an outright disposal of a property to the private sector.

---

1   'Successor' is defined as the person on whom the property, had it not been acquired, would clearly have devolved under the former owner's will or intestacy, and may include any person who has succeeded, otherwise than by purchase, to adjoining land from which the land was severed by that acquisition.

Other restrictions

11.5.11 In certain cases there may be legal constraints which preclude the awarding authority adopting a particular structure. The most obvious of these is in relation to highways projects where the awarding authority is not empowered to grant a land interest to the project company. Accordingly, such constraints will dictate that the project is based around a bare licence.

11.6 WHEN IS THE PROPERTY STRUCTURE TO BE IMPOSED?

11.6.1 The timing for imposing the property structure will need to be determined on a case-by-case basis. However, in general, where a land interest is to be granted by the awarding authority to the project company to enable or facilitate the provision of the service, it is usual for the awarding authority to delay the grant of the interest until completion of the construction period (which is generally the riskiest phase in any project and is the period during which the project company will be investing capital).

11.6.2 During the construction period the project company (and its sub-contractors) will typically be granted any access rights it needs by way of a licence. Provided that a binding agreement is in place to grant the agreed property interest at an objectively definable point in time (for example, upon certification of 'practical completion' by an independent engineer) this is generally acceptable to the private sector participants and their funders.

11.7 SURPLUS PROPERTY

11.7.1 The approach to the timing of the grant of any property interest in relation to the site(s) from which the services are to be provided contrasts with the approach generally taken in relation to surplus land. The rapid realisation of value of any surplus land can be an important factor in maximising value for money. Typically, the awarding authority will be willing to transfer surplus land as soon as it can be vacated by the awarding authority provided that the issue of ensuring that the authority is not exposed to the risk of not receiving value for the land can be addressed.[1]

11.7.2 One of the aims of the PFI is to utilise private sector expertise to make the provision of public services more cost-effective. In achieving this, it is frequently the case that land interests of the awarding authority can be rationalised and surplus property freed up for disposal. This surplus property may become redundant early in the construction period, at the commencement of the operating period or, in some cases, during the operating period (the latter arising when the need for space to carry out the service or the scope of the service reduces). There is now political recognition that there is no inherent reason why

---

1   See **11.4.11**. The value of any land transferred during the construction period should be deducted from any termination compensation paid by the awarding authority.

the public sector should be an owner of assets and, accordingly, that surplus land can be transferred out of the ownership and control of the awarding authority and any disposal proceeds either paid to the awarding authority or applied in the reduction of the unitary payment or otherwise expended on project costs.[1]

11.7.2 The same considerations detailed elsewhere in the chapter also apply to the disposal of the surplus property. On the part of the awarding authority there is likely to be heightened concern to avoid potential embarrassment by disposing of property for anything less than what is perceived to be the full market price. In particular, there have been recent cases where significant uplift in value has been achieved by the private sector within a short time following disposal of property by the public sector, with consequent concern that assets have been disposed of at an undervalue. Accordingly, it is common for awarding authorities to seek to apply mechanisms to secure a share of unexpected uplifts in value, particularly where there is a delay between the valuation of a property and it becoming available for disposal or where there are significant uncertainties regarding land values.[2]

11.8 CONCLUSION

11.8.1 Overall it can be seen that PFI, rather than providing a restrictive regime in which the private sector and public sector are expected to contract by reference to a rigid set of rules (as is so often the case in other areas of property development), in fact provides an opportunity to develop new structures and new approaches. It encourages the promotion of innovation in investment and development opportunities. This could, in certain spheres, change the focus of how the institution-led market supplies and uses property.

11.8.2 It will be interesting to see, in the coming years, as the influence of PFI grows, the effect that PFI-led advances have on the market as a whole. Already there are signs that private sector occupiers are examining the PFI approach of providing fully serviced and maintained facilities for an agreed price instead of these risks being left with the tenant, as has been the case under traditional full repairing and insuring (FRI) leases.

---

1   Departments are subject to certain limits on the value of land disposals proceeds which can be retained by them. Use of disposal proceeds to reduce the unitary payment will ordinarily be approved as part of the overall approval of the main PFI transaction.
2   A common situation where this arises is where there are uncertainties as to whether planning permissions can be achieved. These issues are discussed further in Chapter 12 and at **13.1.18**.

Chapter 12

OVERAGE/CLAWBACK

12.1 WHAT IS OVERAGE/CLAWBACK?

12.1.1 It is common for PFI projects to involve the vacation of existing land and buildings. This often arises because an accommodation solution involves a consolidation of a number of sites into a smaller number of sites or a move to entirely new premises. Properties vested in an awarding authority may, therefore, become surplus to requirements.

12.1.2 Such surplus properties may have development potential but, for the awarding authority, the retention of such surplus properties until they are vacant (and hence can realise their potential) may represent a risk as the value of the land at the time of vacant possession, often some years in the future, will be uncertain. In such cases the awarding authority may decide to include surplus properties within the PFI project. However, it will need to be satisfied that it is obtaining value for money for the land transferred.

12.1.3 One of the ways in which this is achieved is through an overage or clawback arrangement: if the private sector realises some value on a disposal of the land over and above the value taken into account in the economics of the project, then the awarding authority shares in such additional value. The awarding authority's share is the amount of overage or clawback.

12.1.4 This chapter contains general guidance on the relevant issues relating to overage or clawback.

12.2 HOW DID OVERAGE/CLAWBACK EVOLVE?

12.2.1 Property transactions in the private sector have often included overage arrangements. Usually this arises where it is anticipated that the purchaser will apply for planning permission to develop the land which, if granted, will have a significant impact on the price. As a way of sharing the risk and reward of that planning permission, the property may be sold for a price which reflects the value without the grant of planning permission but the purchaser is required to make a further payment to the vendor if planning permission is granted. Such overage arrangements may result in an obligation to make a payment to the vendor when planning permission is granted but, more commonly, the liability is triggered when the land is actually developed and sold and the profit realised.

12.2.2 A similar concept was introduced into government privatisations where it became known as 'clawback'. The first type of 'clawback' arrangement was seen in the privatisation of the regional electricity companies. The Treasury wanted to be certain that it would realise the inherent value of the land assets. The value of such assets was not reflected in the sale price for the shares in the regional electricity companies except insofar as they were producing a rental income or had an existing use for the business. The value of the shares did not take any account of the development potential of these land interests.

12.2.3 Subsequent privatisations which involved a sale of shares at a price which related to earnings of the relevant company contained a similar clawback regime. These included British Coal, the sale of various ports and British Rail.

12.2.4 Other privatisations involving large property portfolios, such as the sale of the married quarters estate by the Ministry of Defence, have also included clawback provisions. Given the number of properties in the portfolio and the inability to anticipate the development potential of each, the Treasury could not be confident that it had realised the true inherent value of the land on the sale.

12.2.5 In most PFI projects, there is no company sale by the public to the private sector, nor is there a large portfolio of surplus land interests, rather there are a small number of readily identifiable sites the development potential for which can be relatively easily ascertained on or before signing the project documentation. Accordingly, in this chapter, reference will be made to overage rather than to clawback.

12.3 WHY HAVE OVERAGE FOR PFI PROJECTS?

Timing

12.3.1 The main reason why overage is often appropriate in a PFI project is that there will be a significant gap in time between (1) signing the project documentation on the basis of economic assumptions as to the value of land which will become surplus to requirements, and (2) the date on which the land can be released by the awarding authority. In this period, the value of the surplus land may increase significantly.

Property sold without planning permission

12.3.2 In some cases, surplus land is transferred without the benefit of planning permission even though it is considered to have development potential. Under Government Accounting Rule DA011/96, where increased value can be obtained through planning permission it should be sought by the awarding authority before disposal of the relevant land. However, this may not be possible within the timeframe of the project. HM Treasury Disposal Rules, paragraph 19 indicates that:

> 'Where there are, or are likely to be, unusual delays in resolving uncertainties about the planning position of a property which is considered to have development potential, or where there is doubt as to the use which will generate the best price, a department or NDPB [Non-Departmental Public Body] may decide that it should sell that property without the benefit of planning permission, before those uncertainties have been resolved. Where this is the case departments and NDPB

should carefully consider, in the interests of the taxpayer, whether they should seek to secure from the purchaser, by suitable wording of the disposal terms, the whole or at least a substantial part of any increase in value attributable to the grant of planning permission after the disposal terms have been agreed.'

Paragraph 20 of the HM Treasury Disposal Rules suggests that an overage provision should be considered to cover the possibility of the private sector obtaining a significantly improved planning consent to its advantage. It should also be considered where land is sold subject to a planning brief rather than with outline or detailed planning consent.

Windfall gains

12.3.3 There may be other cases where the private sector realises some totally unexpected windfall gain within a relatively short period of taking possession of the property. HM Treasury Disposal Rules recognise the difficulty in gauging the commercial potential of property which has been used in the past for purposes which are key to the public sector and changes in market demand can lead to unforeseen increases in the value of the land after it has been transferred to the private sector. An awarding authority which has transferred a property for an economic benefit which was defensible at the time of transfer may then be criticised later if the property is sold for a higher amount or used for a purpose which suggested that a higher economic benefit could have been obtained. The awarding authority can answer any such criticism by showing that it took all proper steps to secure the highest economic benefit obtainable at the time but an overage regime can provide it with added protection against such criticism.

12.4 THE FORM

General

12.4.1 Where there are specific plans for the development of the surplus sites, then the overage arrangements can be relatively simply defined. The project company or third-party developer can be placed under an obligation to develop the site in a particular way within a specified period and dispose of the land interests in a particular way which will trigger overage payments. Unless appropriate, no account needs to be taken of grants of leases, sales of shares in a company rather than the land interests, or joint venture arrangements. This is the type of overage regime commonly seen in the private sector on the sale of a single property with development potential.

12.4.2 Where the project company or third-party developer is to be given a free hand in developing the land without restriction from the awarding authority, overage arrangements need to be more widely drafted to cater for all possibilities. Their form may therefore need to be closer to some of the clawback regimes seen on government privatisations.

What land interests will overage attach to?

12.4.3 Overage regimes generally apply to land interests which are the original interests acquired by the project company or third-party developer and any other interests in the land the subject of those original interests.

What disposals will trigger overage?

12.4.4 In many cases, the project company which has purchased the surplus land will not itself develop the land but will immediately sell it on to a third party (which may be one of the consortium companies or an affiliate, or a developer unconnected with the project). If a substantial profit is realised by that third party on a subsequent sale by it, the awarding authority will wish to ensure that such disposal is within the scope of the overage regime.

12.4.5 In addition, as mentioned at **12.4.1**, it may be necessary for overage to be triggered on a disposal of an asset which is not itself a land interest but which derives its value from a land interest, such as shares in a company.

12.4.6 It should be noted that, if a termination of the main project agreement takes place, the value of the land transferred to the project company will be taken into account in the calculation of any compensation payable, but overage is not triggered and it is highly unlikely that any notional or deemed overage foregone can be taken into account in the calculation as the development risk is in the control of the third-party purchaser. It is, therefore, important for the awarding authority to have a direct contractual link with the third-party purchaser in respect of overage.

When is overage payable?

Term

12.4.7 The period during which overage payments may be triggered should commence at the time the project company acquires any interest in the land. This might merely be the right to acquire the land on obtaining vacant possession. However, as this is a right that can be dealt in, it is essential that the overage arrangements start from this point.

12.4.8 In privatisations, clawback periods have commonly lasted about ten years from the date of the privatisation. In some circumstances, a longer period may be justified if it is likely that planning permission will be obtained outside that period or the periods link in with the terms of any supply contract with the private sector. However, in the context of a PFI project, a shorter period is more likely to be appropriate given the smaller amount of land involved and the greater certainty in realising the development potential.

Actual disposals

12.4.9 Overage is always triggered where there is an actual disposal of a relevant land interest. This is generally defined in the project documentation by reference to what is a disposal for capital gains tax purposes. This enables regimes to cater for part disposals, grants of leases, deriving a payment for granting an option to acquire the land and other possibilities covered by the capital gains tax rules.

Deemed disposals

12.4.10 Sometimes overage is triggered on the grant of planning permission. This may be resisted on the basis that there may be no actual proceeds available to the project company or third-party developer at that time from which it can finance the payment. More commonly there is only a deemed disposal where the planning permission is still outstanding at the end of the overage period. This broadly prevents deferring the development of the land until after the overage period but obtaining planning permission during that period.

12.4.11 A similar anti-avoidance provision can be incorporated where options and conditional contracts are outstanding at the end of the overage period. In order to prevent a deferral of the date of the disposal until after the end of the overage period, by granting options or conditional contracts over the land, this would be treated as a deemed disposal of the land for the purposes of overage at the end of the overage period.

Small disposals

12.4.12 Clearly, there are a proliferation of circumstances which can be treated as giving rise to a disposal for overage purposes. In order to ease the administrative burden, it may be thought appropriate to make an exemption for small disposals. These could be disposals for a consideration below a specified level with no obligation to share any gain or possibly even to report the disposal to the awarding authority. However, if an exemption is to be given for small disposals, then the regime will almost certainly address what 'associated disposals' need to be taken into account in determining whether the limits for small disposal will apply. This will prevent disposal of the land in a series of small disposals either to the same person or connected persons such that each disposal would otherwise be within the limit for small disposals.

Sale of equity interests

12.4.13 Another important area which may be treated as a disposal of a land interest for the purposes of the overage regime is where there is a sale of shares in a company which owns the land. This may be shares in the original company which acquired the land or, if intra-group transfers of land interests are allowed without triggering an overage charge, shares in a company into which the land has been transferred.

12.4.14 The application of capital gains tax rules (although modified) generally means that where land is specifically hived down to a company in the group and shares in that company are sold, this share sale will be treated as a deemed disposal of the land for the purposes of overage.

How is overage calculated?

12.4.15 A key issue which must be addressed in any regime is how overage is to be calculated. Once again, most overage regimes rely on capital gains tax principles. In essence, the gain is usually calculated by reference to the consideration received less an amount which is equal to the allowable expenditure indexed in line with either the Retail Prices Index or an appropriate property index. In some cases, there may be a threshold which is permitted so that only gains over that threshold are brought into account. This threshold may be permitted to take account of the risk taken by the private sector, the fact that the private sector cannot normally share losses with the public sector and the fact that financing costs are not normally allowable in calculating overage.

12.4.16 The application of capital gains tax principles also requires one to look at the market value of land where a disposal is not at arm's length (including where it is between connected persons) and allows for the possibility of deferred consideration, contingent consideration or consideration being paid in instalments.

12.4.17 The allowable expenditure is generally comprised of three categories: first, the amount which is treated as consideration given for the acquisition of the asset; second, any enhancement expenditure; and third, any incidental costs. The key item will generally be the first category, namely the amount given for the asset.

12.4.18 In most PFI projects the amount treated as given for the asset for these purposes will generally be the value attributed to the land in the project company's financial model for the project. In practice, the awarding authority ought to look for the maximum value to be taken into account up front rather than relying on an uncertain amount of value coming to it through overage.

12.4.19 Any costs are usually indexed in line with the Retail Prices Index or a relevant property index to reach the appropriate figure.

Anti-avoidance

12.4.20 Overage regimes also commonly include a number of measures designed to prevent avoidance through artificial transactions. As any specific provisions are unlikely to be exhaustive, a covenant will generally be included in the regime under which the project company or third-party developer agrees not to enter into any transaction the main purpose or one of the main purposes of which (or the main effect or one of the main effects of which) is to avoid overage.

Administrative provisions

12.4.21 The overage regime will generally include fairly extensive administrative provisions. These will provide for the date on which the benefit of any overage is to be received by the awarding authority. The project company or third-party developer will generally be required to submit a disposal statement periodically giving details of disposals and calculations of overage which will have to be signed off by an auditor and possibly by directors of the project company or third-party developer. The project company or third-party developer will also be obliged to enter into various covenants. As well as the anti-avoidance covenant referred to at **12.4.20** above, there may be covenants requiring the project company or third-party developer to obtain the best price for the property and to provide certain financial information to the awarding authority.

12.5 TAX IMPLICATIONS

12.5.1 A discussion of the UK tax aspects of surplus land disposals generally can be found at **14.6**.

12.5.2 There are broadly three ways in which the benefit of overage may be enjoyed by the awarding authority:

- the overage provisions could be contained in land sale contracts between the awarding authority and the project company. In such a case, they are often mirrored in land sale contracts between the project company and the developer;
- there could be a direct contract (which may or may not be a land sale contract) between the awarding authority and the developer;
- the unitary payment provisions could reflect (by way of reduction) the benefit of any overage payments received by the project company from the developer.

Back-to-back land contracts

12.5.3 Where the surplus land is contracted to be bought by the project company from the awarding authority and contracted to be sold on to the developer on exactly the same terms as to price, including any overage provisions, the tax analysis for the awarding authority and the project company set out at **14.6** should remain unaffected. From the point of view of the developer, the following additional points should be noted.

Chargeable gains
12.5.4 The key issue is whether the overage will be treated as consideration given by the developer for the acquisition of land and will therefore form part of its tax basis in the property. For many developers, overage payments will be deductible as trading expenditure. However, for developers who are investors in land (holding it on capital account), the principles outlined in *Marren v Ingles*[1] will apply. According to this case, if an asset is disposed of in whole or in part for future consideration which is unascertainable at that time, then it is the value of the obligation to pay this future consideration which forms part of the acquiror's base cost in the asset. Any amount paid by the acquiror pursuant to that obligation is not given for the acquisition of the asset but rather is paid pursuant to that contractual obligation. The actual amount paid is not therefore taken into account in calculating any gain or loss on a disposal of the asset. In practice, however, the Revenue do not apply *Marren v Ingles* for the purpose of determining the project company's or third-party developer's base cost in the property. Instead, any overage actually payable is treated as forming part of its base cost in the property.

Stamp duty
12.5.5 The Finance Act 1994, s 242(1) provides that where the consideration or any part of the consideration for the transfer of land cannot be ascertained at the

---

1   [1980] STC 500.

time of the transfer, the consideration for the transfer shall be taken for stamp duty purposes to be the market value of the land immediately before the transfer.

12.5.6 However, if there is a minimum, average or maximum specified amount of overage, s 242(1) would not apply by reason of s 242(3). Section 242(3) provides, basically, that consideration shall not be taken to be unascertainable at any particular time if it could be ascertained on the assumption that any future event mentioned in the instrument in question were or were not to occur. The case law contingency principle applicable to stamp duty then applies such that stamp duty is calculated by reference to the specified amount.

VAT

12.5.7 Whether any VAT is chargeable by the awarding authority will depend upon whether it has elected to waive exemption in respect of the land under para 2 of Sch 10 to the Value Added Tax Act 1994, and whether any VAT is chargeable by the project company will depend upon whether it has so elected.

Direct contract

12.5.8 Where overage is contracted to be paid directly by the developer to the awarding authority, without any provisions being included in the contracts with the project company, the tax analysis discussed at **14.6** is affected as follows.

Chargeable gains

12.5.9 A developer who holds the land as a capital asset may not be able to treat the overage as part of his base cost if the contract is not a land sale contract.

Stamp duty

12.5.10 No stamp duty should be payable on the overage if the contract is not a land sale contract.

VAT

12.5.11 The awarding authority should always charge VAT if the contract is not a land sale contract.

Reduction in unitary payment

12.5.12 Alternatively, overage may be paid by the developer to the project company, but no overage would be paid by the project company to the awarding authority because the economic benefit of the overage would be reflected in a lower unitary payment. The difference this would make to the analysis set out at **14.6** is that, technically, the project company would pay corporation tax on the overage in accordance with the principles outlined in *Marren v Ingles*[1] but of course it would have less corporation tax to pay on the (reduced) unitary payment.

---

1 See **12.5.4**.

Chapter 13

PLANNING, ENVIRONMENTAL AND COMPULSORY PURCHASE ISSUES

13.1 PLANNING

Introduction

13.1.1 The decision whether or not to grant planning permission is taken by local authorities and the Secretary of State for the Environment, Transport and the Regions. For this reason, planning is a political issue. It is always important to remember this in any development transaction and PFI is no exception. There is, at the end of the day, no commercial incentive on the part of the planning authority to grant permission, although regeneration and the need to maintain economic activity can be powerful drivers. However, there may be political pressures, such as local or national elections, which militate against the granting of planning permission. Local authority members are sensitive to the wishes of their electorate and so it follows that there is little incentive to grant planning permission quickly or on terms which involve the planning authority taking risk. In the current climate of the plan-led system, and with planning appeals taking many months to be heard, with inquiries likely to last more than a few days, local planning authorities often have considerable negotiating strength. All parties in a PFI project have to take this into account. Of course, some authorities do move quickly, and many welcome development which will bring or retain employment and prosperity, but even then, there can be many frustrations for project companies and awarding authorities as they negotiate conditions and planning agreements, the latter frequently becoming delayed as professional advisers for applicant and planning authority address the implications of promises made prior to the resolution to grant permission. For these reasons, managing planning risk is something which starts long before the project agreement is signed.

13.1.2 It is important to understand the key elements of planning in structuring a PFI project and few successful projects will progress far without the in-depth involvement of planning consultants, traffic and transportation planners and planning lawyers.

The planning process

13.1.3 The planning process has a number of stages leading to the grant of permission. To begin with, there need to be pre-application discussions with the local planning authority, and often with the highway authority as well. The application is then prepared and submitted by the applicant, accompanied by an environmental statement in certain cases. The local planning authority then carries out consultation, followed by discussion and negotiation of the application between the applicant and the local planning authority which may lead to amendment of the application. The officers of the local planning authority then write a report to the committee with power to decide the application, finishing with a recommendation whether to grant, refuse or defer consideration. If the decision of the committee is to grant, then any planning agreement required to secure positive obligations has to be negotiated with the local planning authority and landowner. When this is settled it is executed and the permission issued. After that, the development may be built, always observing the conditions on the permission and requirements of the planning agreement. Conditions, usually requiring the submission of further drawings and details to be approved by the local planning authority, can deal with phasing and sequence, landscape requirements, drainage, and always impose a time limit, usually five years, on the life of the permission.

13.1.4 Planning applications can be made for outline, full or detailed permission:

- an outline permission is one with no or some reserved matters;[1]
- a full permission is one with no reserved matters;
- a detailed permission is one with all details required pursuant to reserved matters determined.

There is no definition of full or detailed; full, however, is the term used for the converse of an outline permission, and detailed is the term used for the permission which is in place once all 'details' pursuant to all the conditions have been approved. Reserved matters are the siting, design, external appearance, means of access and landscaping of the development.[2] The importance of this lies in the degree of certainty which the awarding authority, the project company and the funders wish to have before committing themselves to the project.

The acceptable planning permission

13.1.5 There are three components of an acceptable permission from the point of view of the project company:

- its scope;
- its conditions; and
- its planning agreement.

This chapter will not discuss scope, save to say that the permission must obviously cover the intended development but will look at the other two components.

Conditions

13.1.6 Commonly in normal land transactions, land will be purchased subject to or with outline planning permission and such a transaction is bankable essentially on the basis that the parties know that development value has been released and that the terms of the permission and any related planning agreement are known. The conditions should be reviewed for deliverability and financial

---

1 Town and Country Planning (Applications) Regulations 1988, SI 1988/1812, reg 2.
2 Town and Country Planning (General Development Procedure) Order 1995, SI 1995/419, art 1.

impact. However, there is case law which supports the proposition that further conditions can be imposed on the grant of approval pursuant to conditions: because this may have financial impact, it is desirable to secure approval to as many conditions as possible prior to the project agreement going unconditional. In practice funders will make the availability of financing conditional upon achieving detailed planning permission.[1]

Planning agreements

13.1.7 Planning permissions are frequently accompanied by a planning agreement which commonly takes considerable time to negotiate as the range of matters it may cover is very great. The powers of planning authorities to enter into such agreements are limited: see *R v Somerset County Council, ex p Dixon*[2] for an example of the restrictiveness of the legislation. If a planning agreement is required by a local authority, then permission will not be issued until the agreement has been completed. The landowner, lessees and mortgagees need to join in to make it bind successors in title.

13.1.8 The range of matters planning agreements may cover is very wide but only matters which are material considerations may be taken into account by the planning authority.[3] They can address non-material considerations.[4] But in such a case the planning authority must not have regard to those in making their decision. What is a material consideration is the subject of considerable case law and articles by both practitioners and academics.[5] Essentially, a material consideration is one which affects the land, and is related to land use planning. The concept allows for degrees of materiality; some matters may be material but *de minimis*; others may be material and given great weight. There are, therefore, relatively few limits to what a planning agreement can require, which means that their negotiation can be a difficult task for the applicant. It is made more difficult because, faced with a planning authority which demands a provision which the applicant feels is unreasonable, the only remedy is to appeal against non-determination of the planning application. In such a case the remit of the appeal is not simply the appropriateness of the provision in dispute but the whole planning application because an appeal requires the Secretary of State to consider the application anew. He can investigate all or any aspects of the application. And even if he does not wish to do so objectors can put before him any material evidence on any issue. Concessions which have been hard won from the planning authority will have to be won again from the Secretary of State. To add to these difficulties for the applicant, the appeal process is currently not fast, with there

---

1   See **2.2.11–2.2.13**.
2   [1997] JPL 1030.
3   *Tesco Stores Ltd v Secretary of State for the Environment and others* [1995] 1 WLR 759; [1995] 2 All ER 636; [1995] JPL 581.
4   *Good v Epping Forest District Council* [1994] 1 WLR 376; [1994] 2 All ER 156; [1993] JPL 127.
5   See Sir Frank Layfield QC 'Material Considerations in Planning: the Law' *The Journal of Planning and Environmental Law Occasional Papers No 17* [1990] p 6; Brock 'Negotiating Planning Agreements after Tesco' [1994] JPL 697; and David Mole QC 'Planning Gain after the Tesco case' [1996] JPL 183.

often being substantial periods of time between lodging the appeal and the holding of an inquiry, and between the inquiry and receiving the decision.[1] For these reasons the minimum level of planning permission that funders are likely to accept is an outline permission and they will often require details to be obtained also.

Preparing the planning application

13.1.9 It is appropriate, therefore, to consider what goes into a planning application in order to be aware of what needs to be done to reach financial close. Assuming that a full permission is being sought, the siting, design, external appearance, means of access and landscaping will all have to be settled. Thus, architects and engineers will have to be commissioned to design the buildings, landscape architects will be needed, and highway access will need to be designed by appropriately experienced engineers. Traffic impact studies will also have to be carried out. Many PFI projects are on a scale which is likely to have significant impact on highways. These impact studies will reveal any need for off-site highway improvements. If any are needed they will, in due course, be the subject of planning agreements. It is commonly a term of such agreements that the development is not to be brought into use until the highway improvements have been carried out. The highway authority will often not do the work itself but will require the developer to undertake it. In such a case the developer will have to secure the land necessary for the works and, if it is necessary to interrupt traffic flows or carry out works on the highway, the highway authority's co-operation will be needed which should be provided for in the planning agreement.

13.1.10 Additionally, a visual impact study is often needed and, in some areas, strategic and local views have protection in the development plan or in other policy guidance. Some developments may need a full environmental statement ('ES') under the Town and Country Planning (Assessment of Environmental Effects) Regulations 1988, SI 1988/1199. These implement EC Directive 85/337/EEC on Environmental Assessment. This Directive has been amended by Directive 97/11/EC which must be implemented by 14 March 1999 and the main effect of this is to make an environmental assessment ('EA') mandatory for a wider range of projects and to require all EAs to address the question of alternative sites.

13.1.11 If an EA is required there are wider consultations and the timescale for deciding the application is in practice extended, as a result of the extra complexity and magnitude of the project. The scope of an ES can be great.

13.1.12 The Directive requires assessment of the impact on human beings, flora, fauna, soil, water, air, climate, the landscape, the interaction between any of these, material assets, and the cultural heritage. Scoping of an ES therefore takes place to establish which of the above list are likely to be affected. This exercise is normally done in co-operation with planning officers and it usually leads to an agreement on the scope of the ES. This agreement, however, is not conclusive;

---

1 The Secretary of State set new performance targets for the Planning Inspectorate in England for 1998–1999. 80% of planning appeals decided by inquiry should be determined within 36 weeks (appeal to final decision, with 7 weeks as the target between inquiry and decision).

there is an objective legal requirement in the Directive to assess all significant effects and failure to do so will mean that the local planning authority may fail to take into account relevant matters.

13.1.13 It is worth considering at this stage the risks which an applicant is taking if he gets anything wrong in a planning application. The decision whether or not to grant planning permission is susceptible to judicial review on the usual grounds. These can be summarised as failure to take relevant matters into account, taking irrelevant matters into account, irrationality, and breach of the rules of natural justice.[1] It follows, therefore, that applicants must ensure that planning authorities have before them all relevant considerations. Planning applications and the negotiation of planning agreements are totally unlike the negotiation of commercial agreements. There is nothing to be gained by taking advantage of some error on the part of the other side for, if this occurs, the planning permission is at risk of being challenged by judicial review. Thus, the project company and awarding authority should err on the side of caution in preparing planning applications. If in doubt, they should be accompanied by appropriate impact studies. Where an ES has to be done, environmental consultants should be discouraged from the practice of not assessing impact simply because this has been agreed in scoping: the consultant should exercise his own professional judgment as to what is needed.

Risk transfer

13.1.14 As explained elsewhere,[2] one of the cardinal tenets of risk transfer is that risk should be borne by the party best able to manage it. What approach should be taken, therefore, to the transfer of planning risk? It will be evident from the uncertainties described above that project companies are unwilling to sign up to an unconditional project agreement (and their funders to make finance available) in advance of obtaining planning permission. Project agreements are usually only signed if permission has been obtained or if they are conditional on its grant. In the case of a conditional contract, what provisions should be included with respect to planning? There will usually be an obligation on the project company to apply for planning permission, in a form approved by the awarding authority and the awarding authority should be kept informed of the progress and negotiation of the application. There should be an obligation on the project company to comply with the terms of the planning permission and any planning agreement, except for any parts which are agreed to be the obligation of the awarding authority. Where, as is frequently the case, the awarding authority is the landowner, it will have to enter into the planning agreement: there will therefore need to be provisions allowing the awarding authority to participate in its drafting and approve what it is asked to sign. In the case of development by government departments there are special procedures and powers.[3]

---

1 *Associated Provincial Picture Houses v Wednesbury Corporation* [1948] 1 KB 223; *Council of Civil Service Unions v Minister for the Civil Service* [1984] 3 WLR 1174, HL.
2 See **1.2.10**.
3 See **13.1.19–13.1.22**.

13.1.15 One of the risk elements in planning which is often specifically recognised, and an attempt made to apportion it, is 'planning gain'. This is not a concept recognised by the law or government planning policy, in fact planning gain is simply an aspect of the flexibility of the planning system and broad scope of the concept of materiality. When planning authorities require, for example, bus subsidies, contributions for public art, traffic calming schemes or the provision of affordable housing on surplus land, these are often considered to be 'planning gain'.

13.1.16 Depending on the circumstances, planning gain requirements may be proper material considerations, whose presence or absence can properly be taken into account. Project companies can find it advantageous to allocate a specific sum in their bids for 'planning gain' or for identified aspects of infrastructure, with the intention of being able to charge the awarding authority through a higher unitary payment if the sum is exceeded. From the awarding authority's point of view, this approach has little to commend it as it removes from the project company any incentive to minimise the cost of the conditions and planning agreements it negotiates (if the budgeted sum will be exceeded). If such an approach is accepted, the awarding authority should satisfy itself that the sum is adequate and that it is sure it knows to what aspects of the planning application it is intended to apply.

13.1.17 There are three basic possibilities as to circumstances in which the project agreement should go unconditional as far as planning is concerned:

– unconditional whenever and whatever planning permission is granted;
– only to go unconditional if the project company approves the planning permission, usually with a requirement that they act reasonably; and
– only to go unconditional if both sides approve the permission, acting reasonably, with a limited period for them to reject the permission.

In practice, the first option is unacceptable as it has too many risks for both parties, the second option is generally unattractive to the awarding authority as it lacks reciprocity and the third option gives both parties an equal position but requires each to accept or reject the permission quickly and is susceptible to some check because of the requirement to act reasonably.

Surplus sites

13.1.18 Both the project company and the awarding authority will need to consider the planning aspects of surplus sites. If the sites are truly surplus, the awarding authority will not be particularly concerned whether or not planning permission has been granted for their development prior to financial close, except in relation to value attributed to them. However, as the development potential of the surplus sites will usually be a significant element of the project company's pricing of its bid the issue will be important to them. Thus, if carrying out development on surplus sites is crucial to the viability of the project, the above comments on planning are equally applicable to it. The awarding authority may also wish to ensure that it obtains a share of any increase in the value of the surplus sites if a permission is obtained after financial close for a more valuable development than that contemplated when the project was priced. This can usually be achieved via an overage agreement.[1]

The special position of government departments in relation to planning

Introduction

13.1.19 The Crown is not bound by and cannot elect to submit to planning control. A number of government legal opinions have concluded that as the Town and Country Planning Act 1990 is not stated to bind the Crown, not only do its enforcement provisions not bite on the Crown, but the Crown (which includes central government departments)[2] may not take advantage of its requirements to obtain permission.[3] Thus, the Crown has its own informal procedure for obtaining approval to its developments set out in Department of the Environment Circular 18/84. This provides for consultation with planning authorities on government developments and 'appeal' to the Secretary of State if the planning authority objects. This informal procedure does not authorise development after the land ceases to be Crown land, or in respect of a private interest in the land. This restriction hindered the Crown in disposing of Crown land. Thus s 299 of the Town and Country Planning Act 1990 was passed which applies the Act to the Crown for the purposes of a development to be carried out after the land ceases to be Crown land, or to the extent of a private interest in such land, and under s 299A, for a planning agreement under s 106 to be entered into, enforceable only against the private interest. The consent of the Crown must be obtained if the agreement is to be enforced against Crown land which is subject to a private interest, such as a lease.[4] The general rule stated in the commentary to s 301 in the *Encyclopaedia of Planning Law and Practice* is that planning permission is not needed for the continuance of a use instituted by the Crown (presumably on the basis that no change of use takes place on continuance). However permission will usually be needed for new development.

Powers and procedures for applications

13.1.20 The Crown's immunity from planning control and the view that it cannot waive the immunity leads to some complications which need to be navigated. In a PFI project the actual construction work will be carried out by the project company, usually before it has a legal interest in the land. At that stage it will as a rule have a licence: this is a private interest in land for the purpose of s 299.[5] Thus, the Crown and the project company can obtain planning permission under s 299 but that will not be usable until the project company is granted the licence (or lease). Any development by the Crown needs to be the subject of the consultation procedure under Circular 18/84. The actual occupation of the buildings created by the project company will often be by the

---

1   See Chapter 12.
2   Note that NHS trusts are not government departments and thus normal planning procedures apply to them.
3   For a fuller discussion of this, see the Commentary in the *Encyclopaedia of Planning Law and Practice*, Vol 2, (Sweet & Maxwell, 1995) pp 299–303.
4   See Town and Country Planning Act 1990, s 299A(5).
5   See Town and Country Planning Act 1990, s 293(1).

awarding authority. That occupation is a change of use which constitutes development under s 55,[1] for which planning permission is necessary. As the development is by the Crown, the consent should technically be sought under Circular 18/84 which leads to the need for two applications, one under s 299 and the other under Circular 18/84. There is an advantage, however, in this because the opportunity can be taken to gain approval under Circular 18/84 for the actual construction by the Crown should it need to take over the project in the case of the project company's default. It might be said that this is a very technical issue and that planning authorities are unlikely to complain about the use of the building for the purpose for which it was constructed, and if they did, the court ought to hold that there was no detriment and refuse relief in the exercise of its discretion. It has been held, however, that Circular 18/84 gives rise to a legitimate expectation of consultation[2] and as there is a small risk of challenge which can be allayed by means of the application under Circular 18/84, it is therefore prudent to make such an application.

13.1.21 The question of whether permission was needed under both procedures was considered in the decision of the Secretary of State on the appeal against refusal of permission for Agecroft prison. In that case, permission was sought under both procedures. It was not known at the time whether development and occupation would be carried out by the Crown or the project company. The use of both procedures seems to have been to allow the Home Office to construct the prison itself if the project company defaulted. The Secretary of State held that the permission was only needed under s 299 and he declined to decide the Circular 18/84 application. Unfortunately, there is no reasoning given and the decision does not record the fact that it was not known whether the occupation would be by the Home Office or the project company. The Secretary of State's refusal to give a decision on the Circular 18/84 application would appear to have been wrong.

Planning agreements with the Crown

13.1.22 The view that the Crown cannot submit to planning control meant that it could not enter into planning agreements pursuant to s 106 of the Town and Country Planning Act 1990. For this reason s 299A was passed in 1991[3] to enable the Crown to enter into planning agreements in anticipation of the disposal of land or creation of a private interest in it. This power does not allow planning authorities to enforce such agreements as long as there is a Crown interest, even

---

1   It should be noted that the permission given by s 75 to use a building for the purpose for which it was constructed is not available to the Crown as a result of the view that the Crown cannot submit to planning control. One effect of this is that it may be that, where a building constructed by a private landlord is first occupied by a tenant which is a government department, a separate consent under Circular 18/84 should be obtained. This is obviously not the normal approach and, in practice, no harm is likely to arise because the planning authority can hardly, in reality, complain that a building is being used for the purpose for which it was constructed simply because the occupier is a government department.
2   *R v Secretary of State for Defence, ex p Camden London Borough Council* [1994] EGCS 33.
3   Inserted by Planning and Compensation Act 1991, s 12, from 25 October 1991 (SI 1991/2272).

in reversion, (as they are normally entitled to do by s 106(6) or by injunction) unless the Crown consents.[1] The planning authority may wish to obtain Crown consent at the time of the agreement but will have to take care not to do so in a way which is a fetter on the Crown's discretion. If the parallel procedure under Circular 18/84 is being pursued, a planning authority which considers it necessary to require a planning agreement for the development proposed may wish to secure the same advantages from the Crown in relation to the Circular 18/84 application, particularly as one of the reasons for that application will usually be to ensure that the Crown can build the development if the project company defaults. This is normally done by making the agreement under s 299A also apply to development under Circular 18/84.

13.2 ENVIRONMENTAL LAW

Introduction

13.2.1 This discussion of environmental law will address common law and statutory liabilities in relation to contaminated land. The project agreement will usually, with little controversy, require the project company to comply with all the other environmental laws and obtain all necessary permits. In special cases, such as waste disposal projects, there will be a much greater emphasis on environmental issues, however, such special cases are beyond the scope of this chapter.

Contaminated land: the problem

13.2.2 Contaminated land has been with us for decades but it is only in recent times that it has emerged as a real source of concern and liability. There are several sources to this problem.

– First, there was a false start in relation to modern statutory liability for contaminated land[2] and a new law on the statute book but not in force and subject to draft guidance only[3] so that it is impossible to tell what its true effect is.
– Secondly, liabilities for contaminated land can both run with the land and be personal. This is because most statutes on the subject make the person who caused or knowingly permitted the state of affairs liable. The person who initially creates the state of affairs is thus liable and, at least arguably, so is the purchaser of polluted land who is or becomes aware of the state of affairs.
– Thirdly, the extent of contamination cannot be discovered definitively until the land is excavated and even then contamination may have wholly or partially migrated off site, reducing apparent levels of contaminants, but in reality contaminating other land and water.

---

1 Section 299A(5).
2 Environmental Protection Act 1990, s 61, repealed 1995.
3 Part IIA, Environmental Protection Act 1990 introduced by Environment Act 1995, s 57.

13.2.3 A detailed review of the sources of liability is beyond the scope of this chapter and is covered in substantial depth in a number of books.[1] It is worth noting the latest proposals for contaminated land liability, namely Part IIA of the Environmental Protection Act 1990. This Part, which is not yet in force, was introduced by s 57 of the Environment Act 1995. It requires guidance from the Secretary of State and this has been subject to public consultation. If the final guidance which is issued is generally in accordance with the consultation draft it will provide for purchasers and long lessees to inherit the liabilities of original polluters for contamination of land. One of the mechanisms by which this is done is for there to be a presumed transfer of liability in arm's length deals where the transferee had the opportunity to carry out a survey prior to acquisition. The guidance is retrospective not simply because land was contaminated in the past but also because there is a presumption that in all transactions since 1990 between large organisations an opportunity to survey was given.[2]

13.2.4 The current position on the draft guidance is that, having been issued by the Conservative administration in 1996, the Labour Government announced on 22 December 1997 that it had concluded its review and was satisfied that the draft guidance and regulations achieved the right result, albeit with the need for some redrafting to tidy up unspecified matters. However, the government did not feel that the funding of local authority and Environment Agency functions under the arrangements was satisfactory and implementation of the new law would be delayed while those aspects were addressed. In July 1998, the Government announced that it would bring Part IIA into force in July 1999.

13.2.5 It is important to appreciate that liability for contaminated land can also arise in tort where the cause of action arises when the damage is caused. This may be many years after the spill which first contaminated the land. The limitation period will thus not begin to run until then and it is therefore not sufficient to establish that no spills have occurred in the last six years, for example.

13.2.6 The cost of removing contaminants is not insignificant in some cases, whether or not there is a risk of liability, and environmental liability should be addressed in PFI transactions.

Transferring risk to the private sector

13.2.7 As in all risk transfer discussions, it is worth reiterating that, from the awarding authority's perspective, the transfer is only worthwhile if it achieves value for money. In addition, there is the principle that particular risks should usually lie with the person best able to manage them. Because it is difficult to quantify the extent of liability for contaminated land where it is known that there is a real risk of existing contamination, it may not always be value for money to transfer the risk to the project company. There has to be a balance, however, as

---

[1] For example *Commercial Environmental Law and Liability* (Sweet & Maxwell, loose-leaf); S Tromans and R Turrall Clarke *Contaminated Land* (Sweet & Maxwell, 1994); Campbell *Conveying Contaminated Land: Developing Issues* (CLT Professional Publishers, 1997).

[2] *Consultation on Draft Statutory Guidance on Contaminated Land*, Vol 1, Draft Chapter 3, para 59(c) DoE.

the project company will be in control of removing the contamination. Thus, the awarding authority should first consider if there is a real contamination issue. If there is not likely to be any problem, it will often be practical to require the project company to take responsibility not only for future contamination, but also present contamination. If there is a likely problem, consideration should be given to carrying out an environmental audit to be made available to the project company and on which it can rely. If disclosed during the bidding process, it can be taken into account in the tenderers' pricing.

13.2.8 The preferred tenderer may be given the opportunity to carry out a survey and this will mean that the transfer of liability provisions envisaged in the draft guidance on contaminated land will take effect. Whilst tenderers would obviously prefer not to have liability transferred to them, it is better to know about a problem so as to be able to deal with it: if it is intended to transfer liability in this way it would be desirable for the project agreement to make it clear that this has occurred.

13.2.9 The project documentation may also need to address specifically responsibility for contamination of land during the contract period. The usual position will be for the project agreement to make each party liable for its own acts and omissions and for special drafting only to be necessary if there is a pre-existing contamination problem. In such a case, liability for expense caused by future spills will need to be debated carefully. There is always the possibility that new contamination triggers a liability in relation to existing contamination which would not otherwise have arisen. Apportionment of cost between the parties may be necessary. Parties may want to give consideration to baseline environmental audits being carried out at the outset of the project and at the end of the contract term. The parties will also need to agree the allocation of risk for contamination by third parties during the contract term: the project company will usually be prepared to accept this risk to the extent that it is insurable

13.3 COMPULSORY PURCHASE IN PFI

Introduction

13.3.1 Compulsory purchase law is a major and complex area of law which encompasses not only administrative and public law, but also land law and valuation. This chapter does not address the whole of CPO law[1] but aims to deal with some aspects which are peculiar to PFI. CPO powers are more or less essential to road and rail schemes and could be advantageous in other schemes to assist in land assembly and the acquisition of land for highway and other off-site improvements likely to be required by planning permission. Sometimes, the use of powers for these purposes will throw up complex valuation issues. The threat of a CPO may significantly speed up and ease negotiations. On some public

---

1   See other texts such as Brand *Encyclopaedia of the Law of Compulsory Purchase* (Sweet & Maxwell, loose-leaf); Boynton's *Guide to Compulsory Purchase and Compensation* (Sweet & Maxwell, 1994).

sector assisted redevelopment projects, a resolution is passed to make a CPO, which is not acted upon, simply to indicate the willingness of the authority to acquire compulsorily if necessary. In many cases the CPO is made. Negotiations on land acquisition proceed against the background of the CPO and it is not unusual for landowners to conclude contracts for the disposal of their interests on the eve of the public inquiry into the CPO. The timescale for the CPO process is a concern; however, the deadline it produces, however distant, is a significant incentive to deals being concluded more quickly.

Issues

Powers

13.3.2 The first issue to address is whether the awarding authority has CPO powers at all. NHS trusts have CPO powers and the Department of the Environment, Transport and the Regions has a wide range of CPO powers at its disposal. Hybrid bills can confer CPO powers, as, for example, in the Channel Tunnel Rail Link Act 1996 and, if works are to be authorised under an order made pursuant to the Transport and Works Act 1992, then the order can confer CPO powers. Secondly, one needs to consider carefully whether the powers can be used for the purpose of the PFI project in hand. This is a question of construing the relevant statute. Care should be taken if land is to be acquired for transfer to the project company, for example as surplus land as, in addition to *vires* problems arising, there may be Crichel Down issues in such cases.[1]

Valuation

13.3.3 On the purchase of land under CPO powers the general rule is that market value is paid, but that the underlying scheme is ignored in calculating that value. In a number of cases the question of what is the underlying scheme has been debated, and whether that means that the landowner is entitled to a share of the development value of the land released by the acquisition of his land. This is commonly termed 'ransom value'. Avoiding the ransom problem is a question of establishing a sufficiently wide scheme to support the CPO.[2] Thus, the CPO and all its supporting papers need careful drafting.

Contractual provisions where a CPO is to be used

13.3.4 The project agreement should require the project company to give the awarding authority a complete indemnity against CPO costs, which will include, of course, the compensation, legal fees and all other professional fees. The project agreement would normally be conditional on the making of the CPO with no land excluded. The project company will want to examine closely all the heads of compensation it is accepting in the indemnity. The project company will usually wish to be in control of the CPO process, thus the agreement should provide for it to do this.

---

1   See **11.5.4–11.5.9**.
2   In this way the land in question will form part of the scheme and its underlying value is ignored.

Chapter 14

TAX ISSUES

14.1 INTRODUCTION

14.1.1 In many ways, the tax issues arising in the context of a PFI project are the same as those arising in any project. How can whatever direct tax reliefs are available for initial expenditure be utilised to the maximum extent possible at the earliest opportunity? How can irrecoverable VAT be avoided and any cashflow cost of VAT be minimised? Will any stamp duty be payable and, if so, how can it be avoided and/or minimised?

14.1.2 The purpose of this chapter is not to describe in detail all of the general rules affecting PFI projects, rather it is to outline which of those rules are more significant in the PFI context and to explain some of the special provisions which apply to many participating public sector bodies.

14.2 PFI PROJECT STRUCTURE

14.2.1 As discussed in Chapter 1, the most prevalent form of PFI project will involve the private sector being responsible for the construction of a facility at their own cost and, once construction has been completed, supplying over a specified period a fully serviced and managed asset to an awarding authority such as a government department, NHS trust, local authority etc in return for a unitary payment.

14.2.2 In tax terms, this will involve the following payments and receipts:
- start-up costs of the consortium and/or the project company;
- construction costs;
- financing costs;
- the unitary payment (comprising availability and service elements).

14.2.3 It is also possible that an interest in land will be transferred, assigned and/or granted by or to the awarding authority and/or the project company for which capital sums and/or rents will be paid. For example, in some projects land surplus to requirements will be disposed of by the awarding authority in such a way that its economic value is reflected in the unitary payment paid by the awarding authority.

14.2.4 Many PFI projects involve the consortium members forming a joint venture project company (often on a limited recourse basis) to contract with the awarding authority. There are, of course, other types of joint venture structure but these are less commonly used in the context of a PFI project. In this chapter, it will be assumed for ease of discussion that a limited recourse joint venture company structure has been adopted.

14.3 DIRECT TAX

Public sector perspective

14.3.1 Government departments are not within the charge to income tax, corporation tax or capital gains tax because the Crown and servants of the Crown (acting in that capacity) are immune from all Acts of Parliament including the Tax Acts.[1] In addition, the following exemptions from direct taxes are available to awarding authorities which are technically potentially within a charge to direct tax:

- local authorities and local authority associations are exempt from income tax, corporation tax and capital gains tax;[2]
- health service bodies (including NHS trusts) are exempt from income tax, corporation tax and capital gains tax;[3]
- charities and other bodies which apply their profits or gains for charitable purposes only are (subject to certain limits) exempt from income tax and corporation tax[4] and from capital gains tax.[5]

14.3.2 It follows that most awarding authorities need not concern themselves with any direct tax planning for their own account. In particular, they are not generally concerned with obtaining relief for any unitary payment, nor is direct tax an issue for them on any disposal of surplus land.

14.3.3 Of course, direct tax issues for private sector bodies can (and do) have an indirect impact for the awarding authority to the extent that the project documentation seeks to impose on the awarding authority the economic cost of any tax inefficiencies. What is discussed below in relation to the private sector's perspective may therefore be relevant for the awarding authority.

Private sector perspective

14.3.4 From the private sector's perspective, significant expenditure will be incurred before any income is received. The key issues which therefore arise are:

- what type of expenditure is incurred, capital or revenue?
- what reliefs are available?
- how and when can the reliefs be used?

14.3.5 As mentioned at **14.2.2**, the main types of costs are start-up costs, construction costs and financing costs and each of these is considered in turn.

---

1 *The Case of the Master and Fellows of Magdalen College in Cambridge* (1/615) 11 Co Rep 66B at 68b; *Madras Electricity Supply Corporation Ltd v Boarland* [1955] AC 667.
2 Income and Corporation Taxes Act 1988, s 519 and Taxation of Chargeable Gains Act 1992, s 271(3).
3 Income and Corporation Taxes Act 1988, s 519A and Taxation of Chargeable Gains Act 1992, s 271(3).
4 Income and Corporation Taxes Act 1988, s 505, Schs A, D and F.
5 Taxation of Chargeable Gains Act 1992, s 256.

Start-up costs

14.3.6 Most start-up costs are capital in nature and attract no direct tax relief.[1] There are, however, two particular ways in which some relief may be available in the context of a PFI project.

14.3.7 First, professional fees incurred in connection with construction works may be treated as part of the expenditure which qualifies for capital allowances.[2] A more detailed discussion of the potential availability of capital allowances in the context of a PFI project is set out at **14.3.9** to **14.3.20**. Secondly, some expenditure incurred before a trade has commenced may be treated as expenditure incurred wholly and exclusively for the purposes of the trade and allowable as a deduction from income under Schedule D, Case I principles when the trade is commenced.[3]

Construction costs

14.3.8 As with start-up costs, construction costs are mainly of a capital nature. However, unlike start-up costs such as professional fees on setting up the corporate joint venture structure, construction costs attract capital allowances to the extent they are incurred on industrial buildings or structures or on the provision of plant and machinery wholly and exclusively for the purposes of a trade.[4]

Industrial buildings or structures

14.3.9 Capital allowances for expenditure on industrial buildings or structures are mainly relevant in the context of infrastructure projects (roads, bridges etc). A straight-line allowance of 4% per year for 25 years is available in respect of expenditure on a building or structure where:

- the person who incurred that expenditure is, at the end of his chargeable period for tax purposes, entitled to an interest in a building or structure;
- that building or structure is, at the end of that chargeable period, an industrial building or structure; and
- the interest to which that person is entitled is the 'relevant interest' in relation to the expenditure incurred on the construction of that building or structure.[5]

14.3.10 In the context of PFI projects, buildings or structures in use for the purposes of the following undertakings are regarded as industrial buildings or structures:

- transport, dock, inland navigation, water, sewerage, electricity or hydraulic power undertakings;[6]

---

1 *City of Dublin Steam Packet Co v O'Brien* (1912) 6 TC 101.
2 *Inland Revenue Manual on Capital Allowances*, paras CA 1035 and CA 1505.
3 Income and Corporation Taxes Act 1988, s 401 and the *Inland Revenue Inspector's Manual*, Vol 1, IM 940.
4 Capital Allowances Act 1990, ss 1–3 and 22–24.
5 Capital Allowances Act 1990, s 3.
6 Capital Allowances Act 1990, s 18(1)(b).

- tunnel undertakings;[1]
- bridge undertakings;[2] and
- highway undertakings.[3]

14.3.11 An interest in an industrial building or structure is a 'relevant interest' if it is the one to which the person who incurred the expenditure was entitled when he incurred that expenditure.[4] It should be noted that, in the context of a road project, a highway concession in respect of that road is an interest in the road[5] which is a relevant interest for a person if he was entitled to it (but not to any other land interest in the road) when he incurred the expenditure in question.[6] For a more detailed discussion of this topic, reference should be made to *Simon's Direct Tax Service*, Division B2.

Plant and machinery

14.3.12 Allowances for capital expenditure incurred by a person on plant and machinery are available at the rate of either 6% (in respect of long-life assets)[7] or 25% (in respect of all other plant and machinery)[8] on a reducing balance basis (namely 6% or 25% of the full expenditure in year one and 6% or 25% of 94% or 75% of the expenditure (as the case may be) in year two and so on) where the following conditions are satisfied:

- the person carries on a trade;
- the expenditure is on the provision of machinery or plant;
- that machinery or plant is provided wholly and exclusively for the purposes of the trade; and
- in consequence of incurring the expenditure the machinery or plant belongs to that person.[9]

14.3.13 In the context of PFI projects, the first three conditions mentioned at **14.3.12** rarely give rise to any difficulties. However, the fourth condition (that in consequence of a person incurring expenditure on the provision of machinery or plant that machinery or plant belongs to him) requires further examination.

14.3.14 An asset 'belongs' to a person if he has an unlimited interest in it and if he is, in law or equity, the absolute owner of it.[10] As a basic proposition, therefore, any limit on a project company's right to use or otherwise deal with an asset may give rise to a technical problem in relation to the claiming of capital allowances.

14.3.15 In addition, as a matter of property law, any machinery or plant which is so fixed to a building or land that to remove it would cause serious damage,

---

1 Capital Allowances Act 1990, s 18(1)(c).
2 Capital Allowances Act 1990, s 18(1)(d).
3 Capital Allowances Act 1990, s 18(1)(da).
4 Capital Allowances Act 1990, s 20.
5 Capital Allowances Act 1990, s 3(5).
6 Capital Allowances Act 1990, s 20(6).
7 Capital Allowances Act 1990, s 38F(1).
8 Capital Allowances Act 1990, s 24(2).
9 Capital Allowances Act 1990, ss 24 and 38F.
10 *Stokes v Costain Property Investments Ltd* [1984] STC 204 at 209; *Melluish (Inspector of Taxes) v BMI (No 3) Ltd* [1995] STC 964 at 974.

belongs to the holder of the freehold interest.[1] Without more, therefore, any fixture would belong to the freeholder (often the awarding authority) and no other person and, unless the project company paying for an item of machinery or plant held the freehold interest at the time that item became a fixture, the 'belonging' condition would not be satisfied.

14.3.16 That said, tax law has long recognised that a strict application of property law principles to the legislation permitting allowances for capital expenditure incurred on fixtures would artificially and unnecessarily restrict the availability of allowances. Accordingly, there are special rules which override the property law rules and apply to determine to whom fixtures are deemed to belong for tax purposes.[2]

14.3.17 In essence, an item of machinery or plant which is bought by a trader and becomes a fixture will be deemed to belong to him for capital allowances purposes if, at the time it becomes a fixture, he has an interest in the relevant land.[3] For this purpose, an interest in land means:

- the fee simple estate in the land or an agreement to acquire that estate;
- in Scotland, the estate or interest of the proprietor of the *dominium utile* (or, in the case of property other than feudal property, of the owner) and any agreement to acquire such an estate or interest;
- any leasehold estate in, or in Scotland lease of, the land (whether in the nature of a headlease, sub-lease or underlease) and any agreement to acquire such an estate or, in Scotland, lease;
- an easement or servitude or any agreement to acquire an easement or servitude; and
- a licence to occupy land.[4]

14.3.18 To ensure that the belonging condition is satisfied, the project company could take either a transfer of the freehold, or a new lease subject to a lease back to the awarding authority, or a non-exclusive licence to occupy the relevant building or structure. Of course, commercial and other considerations may restrict what can be done in any given project (see, for example, the discussion on public sector powers in Chapter 4). Often, the awarding authority's requirement is that the project company obtains as inferior an interest in land (for property law purposes) as possible to ensure that the awarding authority retains the ultimate right to the land or building.

14.3.19 Assuming that a transfer of the freehold by the awarding authority is out of the question (see Chapter 11 for reasons why this may be the case) one solution is for the awarding authority to grant the project company a non-exclusive licence to occupy the land in question. This has the merit of providing the project company with a sufficient interest in land for tax purposes without necessarily being an interest in land for property law purposes (a mere licence to occupy being a personal right (*in personam*) rather than a proprietary

---

1   *Wake v Hall* (1883) App Cas 195.
2   Capital Allowances Act 1990, Chapter VI, Part II.
3   Capital Allowances Act 1990, s 52.
4   Capital Allowances Act 1990, s 51(3).

right (*in rem*)[1]). It is, of course, important to ensure that what purports to be a licence to occupy land is exactly that and is not merely a licence to enter land. It is a well-known legal principle (particularly in relation to property law) that the nature of the relationship created by the parties to that relationship must be determined according to the effect of what is actually written and intended and not merely by reference to convenient labels.[2] In other words, writing a document called a licence to occupy land and repeating that phrase throughout the document does not of itself prove that a licence to occupy land has been created.

14.3.20 Another solution is for the awarding authority to grant the project or operating company a lease subject to a lease back to the awarding authority. Whilst this is helpful in the capital allowances context, it raises further questions regarding utilisation of direct tax reliefs, VAT and stamp duty. These are discussed at **14.3.26, 14.4** and **14.5**.

Financing costs

14.3.21 In most PFI projects, although some equity funding is injected by the consortium members, the major part of the finance required is provided by way of loans of one description or another from the debt funders to the project company. The interest cost for the borrower will give rise to a deduction from Schedule D, Case I trading income if it is a relationship to which the borrower is a party for the purposes of a trade carried on by it. In all other cases the interest will give rise to a deduction from Schedule D, Case III income.[3]

14.3.22 Whether financing costs are of a capital or revenue nature is no longer relevant since the introduction of the new code for dealing with 'loan relationships' in the Finance Act 1996. A full discussion of this new code is outside the scope of this chapter. For further details, reference should be made to *Simon's Direct Tax Service*, Division B3.19.

Other costs

14.3.23 Apart from start-up, construction and financing costs discussed above, a project company will incur miscellaneous costs such as compliance costs. The general principles which apply to determine whether such costs are revenue or capital in nature and, if revenue, the extent to which they are deductible for trading or investment companies, are dealt with in *Simon's Direct Tax Service*, Divisions A1, D2 and D4.4.

Timing of reliefs

14.3.24 To recap, the following direct tax reliefs are available in the context of PFI projects:

---

1 *Cowell v Rosehill Racecourse Co Ltd* (1937) 56 CLR 605.
2 See, for example, *Street v Mountford* [1985] AC 809.
3 Finance Act 1996, s 82.

- relief by way of deduction from income under Schedule D, Case I for some initial expenditure and most ongoing expenditure incurred once the completed building or structure is up and running;[1]
- relief by way of deduction from income under Schedule D, Case I for capital expenditure on industrial buildings at the rate of 4% per year (unless the person incurring the expenditure leases the building or structure in which case relief is given by way of discharge or repayment of tax and must first be used to reduce tax payable on rental income under Schedule A);[2]
- relief by way of deduction from income under Schedule D, Case I for capital expenditure on machinery or plant at the rate of 6% (for long-life assets) or 25% per year (unless the person incurring the expenditure leases the building or structure in which the machinery or plant is used in which case relief is given by way of discharge or repayment of tax and must first be used to reduce tax payable on rental income under Schedule A);[3]
- relief by way of deduction from income under Schedule D, Case I for financing costs incurred on a borrowing made for the purposes of a trade;[4]
- relief by way of deduction from income under Schedule D, Case III for financing costs incurred on a borrowing made otherwise than for the purposes of a trade;[5]
- relief by way of deduction from income under Schedule D, Case I for expenditure wholly and exclusively laid out for the purposes of a trade;[6]
- relief by way of deduction from any income of an investment company for expenses of management.[7]

14.3.25 These reliefs are available at the following times:

- relief for pre-trading expenditure is given in the year in which the trade is commenced;[8]
- allowances for capital expenditure on industrial buildings or structures are given over a 25-year period beginning with the period in which the expenditure is incurred or, if later, the year in which the trade commences;[9]
- allowances for capital expenditure on machinery or plant are given in the year for which they are claimed,[10] or, if later, in the year in which the trade commences;[11]
- relief for deficits on loan relationships is generally given for the year in which the deficit accrues on authorised accruals principles of accounting (unless it is incurred before a trade is commenced which would be a trading

---

1   Income and Corporation Taxes Act 1988, s 74 and see *Simon's Direct Tax Service*, Division B3.12–14.
2   Capital Allowances Act 1990, s 9.
3   Capital Allowances Act 1990, s 73.
4   Finance Act 1996, s 82(2).
5   Finance Act 1996, s 82(3) and (4).
6   See Income and Corporation Taxes Act 1988, s 74.
7   See Income and Corporation Taxes Act 1988, s 75.
8   Income and Corporation Taxes Act 1988, s 401.
9   Capital Allowances Act 1990, s 3.
10 Capital Allowances Act 1990, s 24(3).
11 Capital Allowances Act 1990, s 83(2).

deficit if it had accrued after the trade had commenced and an election is made to treat it as a trading deficit when the trade commences);[1]
- generally, expenditure which is laid out or expended wholly and exclusively for the purposes of a trade gives rise to relief in the year in which it is so laid out, but it may also be deductible in the year in which it is sufficiently certain and quantifiable (even though not actually laid out or expended);[2]
- for investment companies, expenses of management give rise to relief in periods for which they are disbursed.[3]

14.3.26 It is apparent from the above description of the reliefs available and when they can be given that, in the context of a PFI project, significant reliefs may be available before the project is up and running and before any income is generated from the project. Of course, the earlier these reliefs can be utilised, the better, but there are three potential limiting factors which need to be addressed.

- Expenditure which is deductible from trading income under Schedule D, Case I but is incurred before trading commences, does not give rise to any relief until the trade is commenced. In the context of a PFI project in which a new special purpose vehicle is used, it will not commence trading until it acquires a source of trading income. This may not be until the relevant building or structure has been completed, but it is possible (if required) that the project documentation could provide for a relevant income stream to be generated for the project company at an earlier stage.
- Expenditure which is deductible trading expenditure but is in excess of any income or gains for the year in which it is deductible (and cannot be surrendered by way of group or consortium relief[4]) will create a trading loss for that year. Such a loss can be:
    - carried back to set off against any profits of whatever description for a period of 12 months before the start of the accounting period for tax purposes in which the loss is incurred;[5] and
    - carried forward to set off against income from the trade in which the loss is incurred for any succeeding accounting periods for tax purposes.[6]

The limit here is that carried forward trading losses cannot be used to shelter any income other than income from the same trade and, in this connection, the Inland Revenue has been known to argue that at least some part of the availability element of the unitary payment which the project company charges the awarding authority for making available the completed building or structure is Schedule A income (and thus not capable of being sheltered by carried forward trading losses) in cases in which the project company has

---

1 Income and Corporation Taxes Act 1988, s 401(1AB) (see also Finance Act 1996, Sch 9, para 2(2), where the lender and borrower are connected for the purposes of the Finance Act 1996, s 87).
2 See *Simon's Direct Tax Service*, para B3.916.
3 Income and Corporation Taxes Act 1988, s 75(1).
4 See **14.3.27**.
5 Income and Corporation Taxes Act 1988, s 393A(1)(b) and (2), and see transitional provisions in the Finance (No 2) Act 1997, s 39(9).
6 Income and Corporation Taxes Act 1988, s 393.

an interest in land. For this reason, it may be preferable for a project company not to be granted any interest in land, although it will almost inevitably require a licence to occupy land to preserve its ability to claim capital allowances for expenditure on machinery or plant which will become a fixture.[1] It should also be noted that, in the early years of a project, allowances for capital expenditure on machinery or plant need not be claimed to the extent that they cannot immediately be utilised either by the project company or by surrender by way of group/consortium relief. This would minimise any trading losses to be carried forward and, as and when those allowances are subsequently claimed, they could generate current year losses in the year of claim which could then be utilised to shelter profits of any description in that year.

– It has also been suggested that some of the income which a project company will receive may be treated not as trading income but as miscellaneous income charged to tax under Schedule D, Case VI, which would also be incapable of shelter through the use of carried forward trading losses. This suggestion goes to the very core of what is a trade, a full discussion of which is outside the scope of this chapter but can be found in *Simon's Direct Tax Service*, Division B3.2. However, it is suggested that the correct view is that the income which a project company derives from making available and managing completed buildings or structures and everything in them will almost inevitably be trading income.

14.3.27 Assuming that a trade is commenced and that the expenditure incurred in the early years of a project exceeds the income generated, trading losses (including trading deficits on loan relationships), charges on income (if any) and non-trading deficits on loan relationships may be surrendered by the project company to its shareholders (or members of the shareholders' groups).[2] These provisions are complex and a good basic description of how they apply to corporate joint ventures can be found in Nigel Doran, *Taxation of Corporate Joint Ventures* (2nd edn, Butterworths, 1996).

14.4 INDIRECT TAX: VAT

Private sector perspective

14.4.1 VAT is rarely ever an absolute cost for the project companies. Almost every supply made by the project company to the awarding authority is or can be standard rated for VAT purposes. It follows that almost all input VAT incurred by a project company is or can be made to be recoverable, any cost being cashflow only.

14.4.2 The one supply made by the project company to the awarding authority which may be an exempt supply is the grant of an interest in land, such a supply being generally exempt but subject to any election made by the project company

---

1   See **14.3.19**. But see also **11.4.26** for the disadvantages of following a licence route.
2   Income and Corporation Taxes Act 1988, Chapter IV, Part X.

to waive exemption and treat that supply as standard rated.[1] If any such exempt supplies are made, any related input VAT is irrecoverable. In practice, however, and particularly following a beneficial change in law for government departments in April 1996,[2] most project companies which make any such supplies elect to waive exemption to ensure that all related input VAT remains recoverable.

14.4.3 However, if the project company's election is prevented from applying, this means that the project company will suffer irrecoverable VAT on the whole or part of the capital cost of construction of the project building or structure and no doubt the additional economic cost so arising for the project company would be passed on to the awarding authority through increased unitary payment. This could occur in cases in which the awarding authority which will occupy the new building or structure directly or indirectly provides funds for meeting the whole or any part of the project company's cost of developing the land[3] and the awarding authority providing the funds is not a s 33 body or a s 41 body as described at **14.4.5** to **14.4.7**.[4] In this context HM Customs & Excise interpret the meaning of 'providing funds' very widely, but there is some doubt whether their interpretation of the law is correct.

Public sector perspective

14.4.4 By contrast with the private sector in which VAT does not pose any significant economic difficulties, an awarding authority's main tax concern is with VAT (assuming, of course, that one regards HM Treasury as distinct from the awarding authority participating in the relevant PFI project).

14.4.5 The VAT issues for an awarding authority participating in a PFI project vary by reference to the type of body. In this connection, there are essentially three types of body:

- Value Added Tax Act 1994, s 33 bodies (local authorities and other specified bodies);
- Value Added Tax Act 1994, s 41 bodies (government departments including NHS trusts);
- other bodies to which those sections do not apply (such as universities and housing associations).

14.4.6 Section 33 bodies are listed in Annex 1 to this chapter and enjoy a more beneficial position than s 41 and other bodies. They are able to recover all input VAT on supplies which are made to them otherwise than for business purposes, whatever the nature of the supplies.[5] Where supplies are made partly for business and partly for non-business purposes, a proportion of the VAT is recoverable.[6]

---

1   Value Added Tax Act 1994, Item 1, Group 1, Sch 9 and Sch 10, para 2.
2   See **14.4.7** and **14.4.8**.
3   Value Added Tax Act 1994, Item 1, Group 1, Sch 9 and Sch 10, para 2(3AA) as inserted by the Finance Act 1995, s 37(2).
4   Value Added Tax Act 1994, para 3A(10), Sch 10 as inserted by the Finance Act 1997, s 37 (3).
5   Value Added Tax Act 1994, s 33(1).
6   Value Added Tax Act 1994, s 33(2).

In practice, the relevant proportion is agreed with HM Customs & Excise in any given case.

14.4.7 Section 41 bodies are listed in Part 1 of Annex 2 to this chapter and are almost (but not quite) as well treated as s 33 bodies. They are able to recover input VAT on supplies of particular types as listed in Part 2 of Annex 2 which are used by them otherwise than for business purposes.[1] As with s 33 bodies, proportional recovery of VAT is allowed in appropriate cases.

14.4.8 In the context of PFI projects, the more tightly drawn rules applying to government departments give rise to two important concerns.

– VAT on rents or other consideration (for example, possibly, the availability element of the unitary payment) for grants of interests in land to government departments is recoverable only if the rent or other consideration so mentioned is paid under a lease of more than 21 years in length which is granted as part of one or more of the supplies listed in Part 2 of Annex 2. Until April 1996, such VAT was not recoverable by government departments but it became so recoverable from then by virtue of an extension to the rules made under the Value Added Tax Act 1994, s 41(3), as amended from time to time and published in *The London Gazette*.
– VAT on supplies of construction goods and services remains irrecoverable by government departments because those supplies are not contained in the list at Part 2 of Annex 2. It is therefore imperative for any s 41 body that it does not receive any such supplies. Normally, this is readily achievable because such supplies are made to the project company and not to the awarding authority (it being the essence of a PFI project that construction costs are borne by the private sector), but difficulties can arise where surplus land is to be sold and the sale proceeds are to be applied towards defraying part of the capital cost of the project.[2]

14.4.9 Other awarding authorities not falling within the scope of either the Value Added Tax Act 1994, s 33 or 41, such as universities and housing associations, must rely on the general law. For many such bodies, this causes significant difficulties because the supplies they make are often mainly exempt. In particular, education is an exempt supply. If they take supplies of construction goods and services, the VAT will be mainly irrecoverable. Similarly, if facilities and the management of those facilities are supplied to them, the VAT will be mainly irrecoverable.

---

1 See *The London Gazette*, 12 September 1997.
2 The tax issues arising in connection with surplus land are discussed at **14.6** below.

14.5 STAMP DUTY[1]

Public sector perspective

14.5.1 Following the Finance (No 2) Act 1997, the rate of ad valorem stamp duty on premiums of over £500,000 for transfers of interests in land and grants of leases increased from 1% to 2%.[2] It increased further to 3% for transfers or leases executed on or after 24 March 1998 (unless executed pursuant to a contract made before 17 March 1998) following the enactment of s 149 of the Finance Act 1998. The rate of ad valorem duty on rents payable under leases remained unchanged and is as set out in Annex 3 to this chapter.

14.5.2 For many awarding authorities participating in PFI projects, stamp duty is not an issue as they are exempt from ad valorem stamp duty by virtue of general or specific provisions. These are as follows:

- Finance Act 1982, s 129 (bodies established solely for charitable purposes);
- Finance Act 1987, s 55 (Ministers of the Crown);
- National Health Service and Community Care Act 1990, s 61(3) (NHS trusts).

It should be noted, however, that 'Ministers of the Crown' has a technical meaning in this context and does not include, for example, local authorities.

Private sector perspective

14.5.3 Private sector bodies which are not established solely for charitable purposes do not enjoy any exemption. Accordingly, to the extent that they take transfers of interests in land or are granted leases and any premiums or rents are payable, ad valorem stamp duty is an issue.

14.5.4 In connection with land, it is important to have regard to the provisions of the Finance Act 1994, ss 241 and 242.

- Section 241 essentially provides that, where an interest in land is transferred or granted for a non-monetary consideration which has not been given any monetary value, ad valorem stamp duty is calculated by reference to the market value of the non-monetary consideration as it was immediately before the stampable document is executed. For this purpose, the market value of property at any time is the price which it might reasonably be expected to fetch on a sale at that time in the open market (s 241(2)).
- Section 242 deals with the case in which the consideration for a transfer of an interest in land or grant of a lease is unascertainable at the time the stampable document is executed and provides that, in such a case, duty shall be calculated by reference to the market value of the relevant interest in land or market rent of the lease as it was immediately before the stampable document is executed. For this purpose, market value is the same as for s 241

---

1 A detailed examination of stamp duty planning principles can be found in *Munroe & Nock on the Law of Stamp Duties*, Part D (Sweet & Maxwell).
2 Finance (No 2) Act 1997, s 47.

and market rent at any time is the rent which the lease might reasonably be expected to fetch at that time in the open market (s 242(3)).[1]

14.5.5 These provisions need to be considered in the context of any PFI project which involves land transfers or leases to project companies because, although it is often the case that no premiums or rents are payable by project companies, it is arguable that either:

– non-monetary consideration is given in the form of a lease back by the project or operating company to the awarding authority (which would need to be valued); or
– the consideration given cannot be ascertained because it takes the form of a contractual promise by the project company to spend significant sums of money on constructing a building or structure on land which may revert to the awarding authority at the end of the life of the project, thus giving rise to a requirement to value the interest transferred or lease granted to the project company.

14.5.6 There are, however, counter arguments which it is suggested are the better view:

– In relation to s 241, it is generally the case that the awarding authority never disposes of any interest in land or grants any lease other than a fettered interest or lease, the fetter being that the interest or lease granted is subject to a lease back to the awarding authority. The lease back to the awarding authority is not consideration for the interest transferred or lease granted to the project company, rather it is an inherent part of that interest or lease. Such an interpretation is consistent with the view taken in practice by the Inland Revenue in the context of taxation of chargeable gains.[2]
– Section 242 is more readily applicable to situations such as arose in the case of *LM Tenancies 1 plc v IRC* [1996] STC 880 where a monetary consideration was payable but the basis on which it was to be calculated could not be ascertained at the date of execution of the stampable document. (In that case, the High Court ruled that a price to be calculated by reference to a specified gilt price 30 days after the execution of the stampable document was in fact ascertainable at that date because gilt prices do not fluctuate to any significant degree. No doubt the answer would have been different had the contracting parties in this case used a different yardstick by which to determine the price which could fluctuate, although presumably that would have been regarded by the seller as too risky.) By contrast, in the context of a PFI project a promise to construct a building or structure which will revert to the awarding authority at the end of the life of the project is clearly not a monetary price that can be calculated at some point in the future. In any event, even if such a value can be so calculated, it is arguable that the market value of the building or structure at the end of the life of the project is likely to be small, having reached the end of its useful economic life.

---

1 See also *Inland Revenue Tax Bulletin*, Issue 18, August 1995, p 235.
2 See *Inland Revenue Manual on Capital Gains*, para CG70774.

14.5.7 It is possible to deal with these potential stamp duty costs by avoiding a transfer of an interest in land or the grant of a lease to the project company and relying instead on the grant of a licence to occupy land (which is not an interest in land to which s 241 or 242 can apply) to preserve the ability of the project company to obtain allowances for capital expenditure on machinery or plant which become fixtures.[1]

14.6 SURPLUS LAND

14.6.1 In some PFI projects, land vested in the awarding authority is surplus to requirements. Whereas many awarding authorities which make a profit on the sale of land must give part of that profit back to central government under certain specified rules (consideration of which is outside the scope of this chapter), no such charge arises where surplus land is disposed of in the context of a PFI project and the value of that land is taken into account in the economics of the project.

14.6.2 The tax issue arising in relation to surplus land disposals is how to ensure as far as possible that the value of the land is not in any way reduced when it is passed from the awarding authority to the project company and that the cash payments derived from the land disposals are available to the project company to meet the project capital expenditure. For the project company, this means eliminating or minimising direct tax and for the awarding authority it means ensuring that no irrecoverable VAT is generated.

14.6.3 If the value of the land is passed to the project company as advance consideration for the facilities being made available and managed, it will be subject to tax in full under Schedule D, Case I as trading income in the hands of the project company. If it is passed as a capital contribution towards construction costs, it may reduce the capital allowances available to the project company and may give rise to irrecoverable VAT for the participating public sector body if it is not a Value Added Tax Act 1994, s 33 body.[2]

14.6.4 Capital contributions towards capital costs of the project company (including, for example, certain construction costs and professional fees) can be non-taxable capital receipts for the project or operating company which would either not give rise to any VAT (because they are indemnity payments and are not made as consideration for any supplies of goods or services by the project or operating company to the awarding authority) or do give rise to VAT which is recoverable by Value Added Tax Act 1994, ss 33 and 41 bodies.[3]

14.6.5 Another possibility is that the awarding authority sells the land to the project company for a consideration which specifically takes the form of a contractual promise by the project company to fulfil its obligations under the project documentation: including, in particular, a promise to make the facilities

---

1　See **14.3.19**. But see also **11.4.26** for the disadvantages of following a licence route.
2　See **14.4.6**.
3　See **14.4.6** and **14.4.7**.

available and to provide services in return for the unitary payment (which will reflect the economic value of the surplus land which has been invested in the project). From the project company's point of view, the value of the non-monetary consideration given by it for the land is equal to the cash consideration received by it on its on-sale of the land.[1] Once the project is up and running, an amount equal to surplus land proceeds spread over the project period is subject to tax in the project company's hands as additional consideration for the provision of the facility. With regard to VAT, even if it is chargeable by the project company, it would be recoverable for the awarding authority if it is a s 33 or s 41 body as described above. Stamp duty should arise only once for the developer and no stamp duty should be payable by the project company by virtue of sub-sale relief under the Stamp Act 1891, s 58.

14.6.6 A further alternative structure is as follows:

- the awarding authority contracts to sell the surplus land to the project company and the project company contracts to sell the land on to the developer, both contracts containing identical price terms;
- when the facility to be used by the awarding authority is practically completed, a headlease for a term of more than 50 years[2] is granted by the awarding authority to the project company at a nil premium and a peppercorn rent, but an underlease for the same term less one day is granted back by the project company to the awarding authority at a premium equal to the surplus site proceeds and the peppercorn rent.

14.6.7 In direct tax terms, the project company makes no gain or loss on the purchase and sale of the surplus land and, when it receives the premium on the grant of the underlease to the awarding authority, it may technically make a loss by virtue of the part-disposal provisions contained in the Taxation of Chargeable Gains Act 1992, s 42, depending upon the value of the consideration given for the underlease (which should be the premium paid) and the residual value of the land interest retained by the project company after the grant (which is arguably nil or minimal). With regard to VAT, any VAT chargeable by the project company to the awarding authority on the premium payable for the underlease should be recoverable under the special rules published in *The London Gazette*, as described above. In addition, there would be no stamp duty cost for any awarding authority which benefits from an exemption.[3]

14.7 TERMINATION PAYMENTS

14.7.1 Any PFI project will provide for the possibility that the project may be terminated before the end of the project period is reached and that, on such termination (whether by reason of awarding authority default, project company default or certain non-fault events) certain compensating payments will be made

---

1   See the Taxation of Chargeable Gains Act 1992, s 17.
2   See the Income and Corporation Taxes Act 1988 for the treatment of premiums paid for leases with terms of 50 years or less.
3   See **14.5.2**.

depending on the time at which the termination occurs. Such termination payment provisions vary from project to project, but what is set out below is a broad description of the likely tax consequences of termination payments under current law.

14.7.2 If termination occurs during the construction period, termination payments are generally made by the awarding authority to reflect the fact that the project company has incurred expenditure on a partly constructed building or structure from which that project company will forfeit the right to derive any income. The payment is therefore, in essence, made for construction goods and services and may give rise to balancing charges or allowances for the project company and irrecoverable VAT for the awarding authority if it is not a Value Added Tax Act 1994, s 33 body.

14.7.3 By contrast, if termination occurs after the facilities have been completed and at a time when they are being made available and services provided, the termination payment is generally in effect a final payment in lieu of the unitary payment that would have been charged. As such, the termination payment should be treated as Schedule D, Case I trading income for the project company and it would attract VAT which should be recoverable by any Value Added Tax Act 1994, s 33 or s 41 body.

14.7.4 In some cases, rents may continue to be payable by the awarding authority under leases granted by the project company. This will often give rise to VAT for the awarding authority which will be recoverable by it only if it is a Value Added Tax Act 1994, s 41 body which continues to receive one or more of the services listed in Part 2 of Annex 2 and the lease is part of those supplies, or if it is a s 33 body.

14.7.5 It may be that any termination payment will need to be 'grossed up' in certain circumstances, particularly if there has been an adverse change of law between the execution of the project agreement and the termination. The details of grossing up clauses need to be tailored to each specific project by reference to the overall project economics. The issues associated with grossing up of termination payments are discussed at **10.9.25**.

ANNEX I

Section 33 Bodies

(a) a local authority;
(b) a river purification board established under s 135 of the Local Government (Scotland) Act 1973, and a water development board within the meaning of s 109 of the Water (Scotland) Act 1980;
(c) an internal drainage board;
(d) a passenger transport authority or executive within the meaning of Part II of the Transport Act 1968;
(e) a port health authority within the meaning of the Public Health (Control of Disease) Act 1984, and a port local authority and joint port local authority constituted under Part X of the Public Health (Scotland) Act 1897;
(f) a police authority and the Receiver for the Metropolitan Police District;
(g) a development corporation within the meaning of the New Towns Act 1981 or the New Towns (Scotland) Act 1968, a new town commission within the meaning of the New Towns Act (Northern Ireland) 1965 and the Commission for the New Towns;
(h) a general lighthouse authority within the meaning of Part XI of the Merchant Shipping Act 1894;
(i) the British Broadcasting Corporation;
(j) a nominated news provider, as defined in s 31(3) of the Broadcasting Act 1990; and
(k) any body specified for the purposes of this section by an order made by the Treasury.

ANNEX 2

Part 1
Section 41 Bodies

Advisory, conciliation and Arbitration Service
Ministry of Agriculture, Fisheries and food Cabinet Office
CCTA (The Central Computer and Telecommunications Agency)
Charity Commission
Crown Office (Scotland)
Crown Prosecution Service
Department for Culture, Media and Sports
HM Customs & Excise
Ministry of Defence
Department for Education and Employment
Employment Service
Department of the Environment, Transport and the Regions
Department of the Environment, Transport and the Regions – Queen Elizabeth II Conference Centre
Foreign and Commonwealth Office
Government Actuary's Department
Government Communications Bureau
HM Government Communications Centre
Government Communications Headquarters
Health Authorities, Special Health Authorities, Special Health Boards (Scotland), National Health Service Trusts, Area Health Boards (Scotland), The Common Services Agency (Scotland), The Welsh Common Services Agency
Health and Safety Executive
Department of Health
Historic Royal Palaces
Historic Scotland
Home Office
Inland Revenue
Department for International Development
Intervention Board
National Investment and Loans Office
Land Registry
Lord Chancellor's Department
National Savings
Northern Ireland Court Service
Northern Ireland Office
Office for Standards in Education (England)
Office of Electricity Regulation
Office of Fair Trading
Office of Gas Supply
Office of Her Majesty's Chief Inspector of Schools in Wales
Office of National Lottery
Office for National Statistics
Office of Passenger Rail Franchising
Office of Public Service
Office of The Rail Regulator
Office of Telecommunications
Office of Water Services
Property Advisers to The Civil Estate
Privy Council Office
Public Record office
General Register Office for Scotland
Registers of Scotland
Register of Friendly Societies
Royal Parks Agency
Department of Social Security
Department of Trade and Industry
HM Treasury
Secret Intelligence Service
Security Facilities Executive
Security Service
Scottish Courts Administration
Scottish Office Administration
Scottish Prison Service
Scottish Record Office
Serious Fraud Office
The Treasury Solicitor's Department
Welsh Office

Part 2
Relevant Services

1. Accounting, invoicing and related services.
2. Administration of the following
    Career development loans
    Government support payments to the Railway Industry Pension funds
    Grants and awards
    Services supplied under the Companies Acts and the Patent and Trademark Acts
    Teacher's Superannuation Scheme
    Vehicle Excise Duty refunds.
3. Administration and collection of toll charges.
4. Aerial photographic surveys and aerial surveillance.
5. Agricultural services of the kind normally carried out by the Agricultural Development and Advisory Service.
6. Alteration, repair and maintenance of road schemes, except (a) any works carried out pursuant to an agreement made under section 278 of the Highways Act 1980 or (b) works involving construction on land not already used for road schemes.
7. Broadcast monitoring services.
8. Cartographic services
9. Cash in transit services.
10. Catering.
11. Ceremonial services.
12. Childcare services.
13. Collection, delivery and distribution services.
14. Computer services in connection with the collection, preparation and processing of data.
15. Conference and exhibition services.
16. Debt collection.
17. Departmental staff records and payroll systems including administration and payment of pensions.
18. Employment advisory services as directed by the Race Relations Act 1976.
19. Engineering and related process services.
20. Environmental research and protection services of the kind normally carried out for the Department of the Environment, Transport and the Regions.
21. Estate management services.
22. Export intelligence services.
23. Filming, audio-visual and production services.
24. Health promotion activities.
25. Hire of reprographic equipment including repair and maintenance.
26. Hire of vehicles including repair and maintenance.
27. Insolvency services.
28. Interpretation and translation services.
29. Issue of documents to, and control of, bingo halls and off-course bookmakers.
30. Issue of documents under Wireless and Telegraphy Act.
31. Laboratory services.
32. Laundry services.
33. Library services.
34. Maintenance and care of livestock and fauna in connection with the Royal Parks.
35. Maintenance, non-structural repair nd cleaning of buildings.
36. Maintenance and repair of civil engineering works.
37. Maintenance, repair and cleaning of equipment, plant, vehicles and vessels.

38 Maintenance and repair of statues, monuments and works of art.
39 Medical and social surveys.
40 Messenger, portering and reception services.
41 Nursing services.
42 Office removals.
43 Operation and maintenance of static test facilities, engineering and support services and test range industrial support and security/safety services inlcuding those acquired for the purposes of research and development.
44 Operating and maintenance of stores depots.
45 Operation of hospitals, health care establishments and health care facilities and the provision of any related services.
46 Operation of prisons, detention centres and remand centres, including medical services.
47 Passenger transport services.
48 Pest control services.
49 Photographic, reprographic, graphics and design services.
50 Preparation and despatch of forms.
51 Press cutting services.
52 Professional services, including those of any manager, adviser, expert, specialist or consultant.
53 Provision and management of accommodation, including leased accommodation, for office use or as part of any other listed service.
54 Publicity services.
55 Purchasing and procurement services.
56 Radio services.
57 Recruitment and relocation of staff and other related services.
58 Research, testing, inspection, certification and approval work for the Health and Safety Executive.
59 Scientific research of the kind normally carried out for the Ministry of Agriculture, Fisheries and Food.
60 Security Services.
61 Services of printing, copying, reproducing or mailing any documents or publications, including typesetting services.
62 Share Registry Survey.
63 Storage, distribution and goods disposal services.
64 Surveying, certification and registration in connection with ships and relevant record-keeping and verification, issue of certification, cards, discharge books and campaign medals to seamen.
65 Training, tuition or education.
66 Transport research of the kind normally carried out for the Department of the Environment, Transport and the Regions.
67 Travel services, excluding hotel accommodation and fares.
68 Travel and transport surveys, including traffic census counts.
69 Typing, secretarial telephonist and clerical services.
70 Waste disposal services.
71 Welfare services.

[1 September 1997]

ANNEX 3

AD Valorem Stamp Duty on Rents

	If the term does not exceed 7 years or is indefinite		If the term exceeds 7 years but does not exceed 35 years		If the terms exceeds 35 years but does not exceed 100 years		If the term exceeds 100 years	
	£	p	£	p	£	p	£	p
Not exceeeding £5 per annum	Nil		0.10		0.60		1.20	
Exceeding £5 and not exceeding £10	Nil		0.20		1.20		2.40	
Exceeding £10 and not exceeding £15	Nil		0.30		1.80		3.60	
Exceeding £15 and not exceeding £20	Nil		0.40		2.40		4.80	
Exceeding £20 and not exceeding £25	Nil		0.50		3.00		6.00	
Exceeding £25 and not exceeding £50	Nil		1.00		6.00		12.00	
Exceeding £50 and not exceeding £75	Nil		1.50		9.00		18.00	
Exceeding £75 and not exceeding £100	Nil		2.00		12.00		24.00	
not exceeding £150	Nil		3.00		18.00		36.00	
Exceeding £150 and not exceeding £200	Nil		4.00		24.00		48.00	
Exceeding £200 and not exceeding £250	Nil		5.00		30.00		60.00	
not exceeding £300	Nil		6.00		36.00		72.00	
Exceeding £300 and not exceeding £350	Nil		7.00		42.00		84.00	
Exceeding £350 and not exceeding £400	Nil		8.00		48.00		96.00	
Exceeding £400 and not exceeding £450	Nil		9.00		54.00		108.00	
Exceeding £450 and not exceeding £500	Nil		10.00		60.00		120.00	
Exceeding £500; for any full sum of £50 and also for any fractional part thereof		0.50	1.00		6.00		12.00	

Chapter 15

EMPLOYMENT LAW ISSUES

15.1 INTRODUCTION

15.1.1 This chapter deals with the employment issues arising in the context of PFI projects. The main issues arise from the potential application of the Transfer of Undertakings (Protection of Employment) Regulations 1981, SI 1981/1794 ('the Transfer Regulations') to a situation where the provision of a service changes hands. Employment issues also arise during the provision of the services themselves.

15.1.2 The first topic is by far the more complex: there is a considerable legal content due to the ever-changing judicial interpretation of the Transfer Regulations (and the Acquired Rights Directive, Council Directive 77/187 ('the Directive') on which they are based), in particular by the ultimate arbiter, the European Court of Justice ('the ECJ'). The Transfer Regulations have been applied increasingly to different types of transactions since they took effect in 1982 and have become an extremely important factor in outsourcing and PFI projects. They impact heavily on the freedom of the private sector to provide services more cheaply and efficiently than the public sector. This chapter addresses the application and consequences of the Transfer Regulations and suggests how the potential problems can be alleviated in practice. The principal difficulty is the need to anticipate future changes in a rapidly developing area, given that transfers of services often do not take place until several years after the project documentation is signed and the fact that the services themselves are often to last for many years.

15.1.3 The Transfer Regulations are by definition relevant principally to those PFI projects which involve the transfer of services with an existing workforce, such as a facilities management contract for large premises. By contrast, the Transfer Regulations may have little, if any, impact on a project starting from scratch, such as road building.

15.2 THE TRANSFER REGULATIONS

The effect of the Transfer Regulations

15.2.1 The Transfer Regulations enacted the Directive into English legislation. Their purpose is to protect employees who are affected by a transfer of the undertaking (or part of the undertaking) in which they are employed. Where there is any ambiguity, the Transfer Regulations are to be construed to give effect to this purpose.

15.2.2 The principal effects of the Transfer Regulations can be summarised as follows:

- employees of the undertaking transfer to the transferee on their existing terms and with continuity of service;
- if either the transferor or the transferee dismisses employees for a reason connected with the transfer there are usually financial penalties;
- employee representatives must be informed in advance about the transfer and how it will affect the workforce.

15.2.3 All employees employed wholly or substantially in the undertaking transferred must be taken on by the new operator of the undertaking ('the transferee'). (In the PFI context, a transferee may be either the project company itself, if it is to employ staff, or, more likely, the sub-contractors who will actually provide the various services: for simplicity, references in this chapter are predominantly to the project company). The intention is to prevent the transferee from simply replacing the transferor's employees with its own new staff. Where employees only spend some of their time working in the undertaking which is transferring, this can give rise to difficulties in assessing whether they should transfer. Ultimately, it is a question of degree.

15.2.4 The transferee must honour all existing terms and conditions of employment. In effect, the transferee is substituted for the transferor in the employees' contracts. There are severe constraints on the transferee's ability to make detrimental changes to the employees' terms. The employees also transfer with any accrued rights and liabilities. Any claim that formerly lay against the transferor will be against the transferee (although criminal liabilities do not transfer). At present, rights under occupational pension schemes are specifically excluded from the automatic transfer by regulation 7 of the Transfer Regulations,[1] but the Directive has been amended to allow Member States to end this exclusion.

15.2.5 Union recognition agreements pass to the transferee but they are usually not legally binding (although the government's Fairness at Work White Paper[2] proposes compulsory union recognition if certain conditions are met). The transferee could therefore de-recognise the union and withdraw from collective bargaining arrangements with legal impunity (but with the risk of an adverse impact on industrial relations). However, if any terms of the union recognition agreement have been incorporated into employees' contracts (such as those relating to pay rates[3]) those terms would transfer.

15.2.6 The employees' statutory continuity of service is preserved and redundancy payments are not payable to the employees. P45s are, however, issued by the transferor because the employees' employment with the transferor will be terminated by operation of law.

15.2.7 Any dismissal for a reason connected with the transfer will, on the face of it, be automatically 'unfair' whether it occurs before or after the transfer. There is no formal limit in time to when a dismissal is 'connected with' the transfer; it is the reason that is important, not the timing. In practice, the longer

---

1 See **15.10.1**.
2 Fairness at Work White Paper – Cm 3968, DTI, May 1998.
3 See **15.9.10**.

the period of time between the dismissal and the transfer, the more likely it is that the dismissal can be shown to be for a reason not connected with the transfer.

15.2.8 If a dismissal is for an 'economic, technical or organisational reason entailing a change in the workforce' it will not be *automatically* unfair. Such a reason is termed an ETO and basically means a genuine redundancy or one which results from a change of function. However, the dismissal may still be unfair according to the general principles governing the fairness of a dismissal set out in the Employment Rights Act 1996. In these circumstances, a redundancy payment (and possibly unfair dismissal compensation) would be payable (assuming the qualifying conditions of service for each were satisfied). Liability for an automatically unfair dismissal made before the transfer will pass to the transferee but, although this is not beyond doubt, liability for an ETO dismissal pre-transfer will remain with the transferor. The importance (and number) of unfair dismissal claims is set to increase because the government is going to raise the current statutory compensation limit of £12,000 to £50,000 during 1999.

15.2.9 The transferor and the transferee must provide information to, and in certain circumstances consult with, representatives of all the employees who may be affected by the transfer. In the public sector, recognised trade union officials will usually be the representatives for this purpose. However, where there are no recognised trade unions, or where they do not represent all classes of employees who may be affected by the transfer, the transferor and transferee must invite members of their respective workforces to elect representatives. Sufficient time before the transfer must be allowed both for the elections to be held and for meaningful consultation to take place. Some organisations (particularly those regularly involved in transfers covered by the Transfer Regulations) have set up standing committees of employee representatives to avoid the need for elections before each transfer.

15.2.10 There is an added incentive to establish such committees because there must be similar consultation on redundancy programmes involving 20 or more employees at one establishment over a period of 90 days or less.[1]

15.2.11 Employees have the right to object to the transfer of their employment. However, this is largely theoretical since, by exercising that right, they are deemed to have resigned from their employment without any right to compensation. More pertinent is their right to resign and claim constructive dismissal (with a right to compensation) if a substantial detrimental change is made to their employment terms or working conditions as a result of the transfer (without their consent) or to argue that the change is invalid because it is for a transfer-connected reason.

---

1   Section 188 of the Trade Union and Labour Relations (Consolidation) Act 1992.

15.3 THE APPLICATION OF THE TRANSFER REGULATIONS

15.3.1   The Transfer Regulations apply whenever there is a 'relevant transfer'. A relevant transfer occurs on a transfer of an undertaking (or a part of one) situated immediately before the transfer in the United Kingdom. 'Undertaking' is simply defined as including 'any trade or business'. 'Transfer' is not defined and was also not defined in the Directive. However, in the amended Directive which came into force on 17 July 1998, a transfer is defined as:

> 'a transfer of an economic entity which retains its identity, meaning an organised group of resources which has the objective of pursuing an economic activity, whether or not that activity is central or ancillary'.

This definition reflects language used by the ECJ in case-law and is an attempt to introduce some certainty into the long-running debate as to what constitutes a 'transfer' and an 'undertaking'. Member States have until 17 July 2001 to incorporate the amendments to the Directive into national legislation (it is expected that the UK will do so during 1999). In the meantime, it will be up to courts and tribunals to give effect to the amended Directive in their interpretation of existing national law.

15.3.2   The background to the definition in the amended Directive is that creative judicial interpretation (largely by the ECJ) of an 'undertaking' has extended its meaning from a traditional commercial business (for example, the manufacture and sale of products) to any kind of economic activity or function (for example, the provision of a service such as cleaning or catering). In addition, the test of whether there was a transfer of an undertaking also developed. Courts and tribunals began no longer to look simply at whether there was a transfer of a business as a going concern, but rather whether there was a 'change of operator of an identifiable economic unit or activity, which continues to operate in substantially the same way after such a change'.[1] It became immaterial whether the ownership of any assets was transferred and there was no need for a contractual relationship between the new and the old operators of the undertaking.

15.3.3   The application of this test saw the Transfer Regulations operate in virtually any outsourcing operation (and any reversion of a service in-house), as well as on the replacement of one contractor by another. In one case, the ECJ held that an undertaking comprised only a single cleaner working a few hours a day to clean a particular building and that there was a relevant transfer when that cleaning work was contracted out.[2]

15.3.4   Following this decision, the position was reached that any incoming contractor taking over the provision of a service from either an in-house provider or a third-party contractor usually had to take on all the previous provider's employees who were assigned to the service. This would be the case whether or

---

1 *Rask and Christensen v ISS Kantineservice A/S* C-209/91 [1993] IRLR 133, ECJ.
2 *Schmidt v Spar und Leihkasse der Fruheren Amter Bordesholm, Kiel und Cronshagen* C-392/92 [1994] IRLR 302, ECJ.

not the new contractor had jobs for them to do and regardless of whether any assets or other hallmarks of a business such as goodwill were transferring to it. The one advantage of this position was, however, that there was at least certainty: not everyone agreed with the result but they could plan accordingly. Tenderers and awarding authorities generally learned how to deal with the Transfer Regulations and means were found by which their impact could be accommodated.

15.3.5 However, this situation led many to question whether the Transfer Regulations had moved far beyond the circumstances for which they were originally intended. In particular, the Conservative Government's Compulsory Competitive Tendering programme was affected and some doubt was cast over prospects for the PFI. If the private sector employer is obliged to take on all the existing public sector employees on their same terms and conditions of employment with protection against dismissal, the scope for cost-savings and risk transfer can be substantially lessened.

15.3.6 As a result, the UK government (along with some European partners, in particular Germany) lobbied to amend the Directive to reduce the impact on contracting-out exercises. Those efforts stalled but the baton was taken up (ironically) by the ECJ itself. As will be seen below in the discussion of the *Suzen*[1] case, the ECJ applied a brake to the seemingly inexorable progress of the Directive by tightening the circumstances in which there could be a relevant transfer. However, in doing so it caused further confusion because of the dramatic effects of its decision on existing contracts for the provision of services and the uncertainty that returned to the law. Partly because of this uncertainty, the amended Directive included a specific statement that the Directive did in principle apply to contracting out, both first and second generation. The UK government is consulting about its proposed amendments to the Transfer Regulations with the TUPE Forum (which represents public bodies, contractors and trade unions). The TUPE Forum apparently favours the application of the Transfer Regulations to the contracting out of public services as a general rule, except where in reality there is no transfer of the same service to a new contractor.

15.4 THE *SUZEN* DECISION

15.4.1 The ECJ's judgment in the *Suzen* case delivered on 11 March 1997 halted the ever-widening application of the Directive. Whilst it was still relatively clear after the decision that the Transfer Regulations applied to a sale of a traditional 'business', there was renewed uncertainty over their application to the contracting out of services (and, consequently, many PFI projects).

15.4.2 In *Suzen*, a contract to clean a school was terminated and a new contractor was engaged. The cleaners employed by the previous contractor were dismissed because there was no longer any work for them to do. The cleaning

---

1   *Ayse Suzen v Zehnacker Gebaudereinigung GmbH Krankenhausservice and Lefarth GmbH* C-13/95 [1997] IRLR 255, ECJ.

supervisor, Mrs Suzen, claimed that the change of contractor was a transfer of an undertaking and therefore she should be employed by the new contractor.

15.4.3 The German courts referred the case to the ECJ for a decision on whether the Directive applied. On the basis of the law as it then stood, it should have been a fairly routine application of the Directive. However, the ECJ found that there was no transfer of an undertaking and, in so doing, reaffirmed the principles laid down in the *Spijkers*[1] decision in 1986. The Court held that the Directive would not apply unless there was a:

> 'concomitant transfer from one undertaking to the other of significant tangible or intangible assets or [the] taking over by the new employer of a major part of the workforce, in terms of their numbers and skills, assigned by his predecessor to the performance of the contract.'

15.4.4 The mere switch of a contract did not of itself mean that an undertaking was transferred and the Court observed that an entity could not be reduced to the activity carried on by it. The Court said that an undertaking was a stable economic entity, comprising:

> 'an organised grouping of persons and assets facilitating the exercise of an economic entity which pursues a specific objective.'

15.4.5 As for when there was a relevant transfer of an undertaking, the Court held that:

> 'The decisive criterion for establishing the existence of a transfer within the meaning of the Directive is whether the entity in question retains its identity, as indicated *inter alia* by the fact that its operation is actually continued or resumed.'

15.4.6 However, the similarity between the services carried on by successive contractors was only one factor to take into account; it was not, of itself, conclusive.

15.4.7 The explanation for this change in the interpretation of the Directive is unclear, although the ECJ seemed to be heavily influenced by the severe effects on competition caused by earlier cases. It may well be that *Suzen* reverted to an interpretation of the Directive which was much closer to the one originally intended. The difficulty was that the element of certainty developed by the courts was lost. As a result of *Suzen*, there had to be a more careful analysis on a service-by-service basis of whether there is a relevant transfer. It is a particular problem where there are several services changing hands, as is the case with most PFI projects.

15.4.8 In addition, two further problems were created. First, the emphasis on whether a major part of the workforce was taken on by the new contractor for there to be a relevant transfer of an undertaking placed the new contractor in a potentially powerful position because its decision as to whether or not it wanted to take on a major part of the workforce would largely govern whether the Transfer Regulations applied. (The circularity of the test established by the ECJ was, at best, confusing and, at worst, open to abuse.) Second, contractors who

---

1   *Spijkers v Gebroeders Benedik Abattoir CV and another* C–24/85 [1986] ECR 1119.

inherited a workforce when winning a contract could not be sure that they would be able to pass it on if they lost the contract. They would usually have tendered for, and priced, the contract on the basis that they had no choice but to inherit staff under the Transfer Regulations, expecting to be able to transfer on their staff if they were replaced by new contractors. If that was not the case, they would have a redundancy liability in respect of those employees who could not be redeployed, for which they were unlikely to have budgeted.

15.4.9 The impact of *Suzen* was immediately demonstrated by the Court of Appeal decision in *Betts*,[1] later in March 1997. The case involved contracts for the provision of helicopter services to oil rigs in the North Sea. KLM took over one contract from Brintel but did not take over any of Brintel's helicopters or equipment and deliberately chose not to engage any of Brintel's staff. The Court of Appeal allowed an appeal by KLM and held that although there was an undertaking, there was no relevant transfer because KLM did not take on significant assets or staff. The Court specifically applied the reasoning in *Suzen* (which had been decided after the High Court decision in *Betts*, which had reached the opposite result). Lord Justice Kennedy observed:

> 'I accept that the decision in Suzen does represent a shift of emphasis, or at least a clarification of the law, and that some of the reasoning of earlier decisions, if not the decisions themselves, may have to be reconsidered.'

15.4.10 The Court also indicated that although both *Betts* and *Suzen* involved a second generation change of contractor, the reasoning would apply equally to an initial contracting out. This must be right: the issues are much the same and the test should be the same. (However, in *Suzen* itself, the existence of a contract between a transferor and a transferee was not discounted as a factor, so it may have some reference to the analysis.)

15.4.11 *Betts* emphasised the point made in *Suzen* that there was a distinction to be drawn between labour-intensive undertakings (such as cleaning services) and other types of undertaking. Where a service comprises a large number of cleaners using few assets other than their mops and buckets, there is little point looking for a transfer of significant assets to establish whether there is a transfer of an undertaking if the service changes hands. However, there could be a relevant transfer indicated simply by the continuation of the service with substantially the same staff and nothing more. The ECJ in *Suzen* had made the point that, effectively, employees could be the assets of the undertaking.

15.4.12 However, for other types of undertaking where assets are also important, a more wide-ranging enquiry should take place, looking at all the relevant circumstances (as in *Spijkers*) including whether tangible or intangible assets are transferred, whether employees are taken on, whether customers are transferred and the degree of similarity between activities carried on before and after the transfer.

---

1   *Betts and others v Brintel Helicopters Limited and KLM ERA Helicopters (UK) Limited* [1997] IRLR 361, CA.

15.5 DEVELOPMENTS POST - *SUZEN*

15.5.1 The consequence of *Suzen* was that the Transfer Regulations seemed less likely to apply to changes of contractor than had previously been the case. However, the question is still one of fact for Employment Tribunals to determine and there are signs that they (and the EAT) are attempting to mitigate the effects of *Suzen* (in particular the fact that it seemed that a new contractor could choose not to take on employees (or assets) and thereby reduce the likelihood of being obliged to do so).

15.5.2 This issue was addressed by the EAT in the *ECM* case in June 1998.[1] A company called Axial Limited had a contract with VAG Limited to transport and deliver Audi and Volkswagen cars from Grimsby and Folkestone docks to car dealers. The northern part of the contract was lost to ECM and as a result, Axial made redundant 19 drivers and 5 yard men. The redundant employees then indicated to ECM that they wished to be employed by ECM and that if they were not taken on, they would claim unfair dismissal against ECM on the basis that there had been a relevant transfer under the Transfer Regulations. None of them was taken on by ECM.

15.5.3 If a significant number of the ex-Axial employees had been employed by ECM, the second limb of the *Suzen* test would have been satisfied and the Transfer Regulations would have applied. However, the fact that none of them was employed by ECM suggested the Transfer Regulations should not apply for the same reason. This was not a result that either the Employment Tribunal or the EAT was prepared to allow.

15.5.4 In the EAT's judgment, Mr Justice Morrison quoted extensively from *Suzen*, observing that *Suzen* reaffirmed earlier decisions of the ECJ although recognising that there may have been a change in emphasis (as Lord Justice Kennedy had observed in *Betts*). He noted that the ECJ in *Suzen* had not dealt expressly with a situation where there was a deliberate decision not to take on employees to try to avoid the application of the Transfer Regulations. The Employment Tribunal in *ECM* had specifically found that the Managing Director of ECM had refused to take on the applicants because they had threatened proceedings based on there being a relevant transfer.

15.5.5 Mr Justice Morrison dealt with the point by stating:

> 'It seems to us that we should adopt a purposive approach to the interpretation of the Regulations so as to give effect to the Government's obligations thereunder. We cannot and do not accept that it would be proper for a transferee to be able to control the extent of his obligations by refusing to comply with them in the first place. There is nothing in the *Suzen* decision which requires us to adopt that course.'

15.5.6 Although in this respect the EAT in *ECM* attempted to address one of the problems created by *Suzen*, difficulties still exist, such as the circumstances in which a new contractor can decide for proper business reasons that he does not require any of his predecessor's staff and if he does have an improper motive, the need to be able to prove it.

---

1   *ECM (Vehicle Delivery Services) Limited v B Cox & others* [1998] ICR 631, EAT.

15.5.7 The EAT in *ECM* also analysed the difference between an 'economic entity' and a 'mere activity'. It held that the applicants were conditioned to the VAG contract in that their continued employment depended on the contract. This was demonstrated by the large number of employees made redundant by Axial when the contract was lost. Therefore, the VAG contract and associated activities were an economic entity not a mere activity; the EAT observed that the Employment Tribunal had correctly distinguished between the loss of a business to which employees were dedicated and the loss of a single customer.

15.5.8 There was also an argument in *ECM* that even if there was an economic entity, there was not a relevant transfer because the entity was organised in a different way by ECM and so did not retain its identity. The EAT recognised the differences but took a broad approach, deciding that the entity did retain its identity because the customers were essentially the same and the work done was essentially the same.

15.5.9 As well as the issue with most labour-intensive activities of whether the incoming contractor chooses (or can be obliged) to take on a major part of the workforce of the outgoing contractor, the following are further situations where the Transfer Regulations may not apply:

- on the construction of a new building to replace an existing building or on the refurbishment of a building (with employees being redeployed in the meantime), there will not necessarily be a relevant transfer when services eventually come to be provided by a new operator in the new or refurbished building. It could depend on the extent to which the particular service is specific to the building rather than being part of the overall undertaking of the awarding authority;
- on the completion by a third party of a relatively small part of a contract to provide a service because it does not constitute a 'stable economic entity'.[1] This will no doubt give rise to questions of degree;
- on a division between separate geographical sites of services previously carried on at a central location, where employees may not have been assigned to each service (or part of a service).

15.6 DOCUMENTING THE IMPACT OF THE TRANSFER REGULATIONS

15.6.1 Given the uncertainty in the law, the awarding authority and the project company must decide how to deal with the application of the Transfer Regulations in the project documentation. There are basically two options:

- to impose a contractual obligation on all parties to act as if the Transfer Regulations applied (whether or not in fact they do apply at law); or

---

1 *Rygaard Ledernes Hovedorganisation v Dansk Arbejdsgiverforening* C-48/94 [1996] IRLR 51, ECJ.

- to leave it to the state of the law at the time of the change of service provider to determine whether the Transfer Regulations apply and only if they do to act in accordance with their provisions.

15.6.2 The latter approach has the immediate attraction of matching the parties' obligations in the contract with their obligations in law but creates uncertainty for all concerned. In practice, most awarding authorities try to oblige tenderers to act as if the Transfer Regulations apply in any event. This creates greater certainty and has the major advantage for the awarding authority that it can reassure its employee representatives and the staff themselves that they will be protected.

15.6.3 However, there is no guarantee that the employees concerned will necessarily take the same line. An employee could argue that the Transfer Regulations did not apply and seek a redundancy payment from his existing employer (perhaps because a move to the private sector was particularly unattractive and because of the generous public sector redundancy benefits, particularly for older, long-serving employees). The risk of such a claim should ideally be addressed in the project documentation.

15.6.4 In practice, with labour-intensive services such as cleaning, if the project company does agree to take on a significant number of employees, then the Transfer Regulations are very likely to apply for that reason. However, if the service is not labour-intensive, then even if the project company agrees to employ most or all of the employees, the Transfer Regulations *may* still not apply (as was pointed out in *Betts*).

15.6.5 Any clause requiring the project company to take on the employees should make clear that all the requirements of the Transfer Regulations must be honoured. The project company will no doubt require comfort in relation to accrued liabilities which it might inherit.

15.6.6 The issue of what may happen on a subsequent market-testing, on expiry of the contract or on any early termination should also be addressed. The project company may well seek an assurance that future tenderers will be obliged to accept a similar obligation to act as if the Transfer Regulations applied (including the awarding authority if it takes a service back in-house). If the issue is simply left to the law at the time of the change of service provider, then the project company should seek an indemnity from the awarding authority against redundancy costs which it may have to bear if the Transfer Regulations do not apply or else provide for that risk by higher pricing during the term of the contract. The advantage of the indemnity is that it may never be called upon; the project company may not lose the contract because it successfully re-tenders or, if it does lose the contract, the Transfer Regulations may apply. Higher pricing during the contract would result in the project company making money at the awarding authority's expense if in fact it did not incur any redundancy liability. Despite this, PFU guidance for health service projects is currently against trying to provide in the project documentation that the Transfer Regulations will apply on subsequent changes of service provider and is also not in favour of indemnities in respect of redundancy costs (implicitly accepting the risk of higher pricing during the contract).

15.6.7 One disadvantage of a blanket indemnity against redundancy costs on termination of the contract is that it would not provide any incentive for the project company to manage the workforce with a view to minimising potential redundancy liability (although a specific obligation to do so could be included in the project documentation). There would also be the issue as to which employees should be covered by the indemnity: should it be all employees employed by the project company at the time of termination of the contract or only those who were formerly employed by the awarding authority? Over time, the numbers in the latter category will diminish as employees retire or leave for other reasons. The indemnity could be limited only to that element of a redundancy payment which is attributable to the employee's service with the awarding authority. In that scenario, the awarding authority's liability would be at its greatest immediately following the initial transfer of its employees to the project company (and could be accurately quantified).

15.6.8 New employees joining the project company during the term of a contract could be recruited on the project company's own terms of employment and there would be no need, for example, for them to be entitled to such favourable enhanced redundancy terms as the former awarding authority's employees. This would lessen the potential redundancy liability on the loss of a contract. (Such a situation could, however, create industrial relations problems and possible equal pay claims between the different categories of employees, although the project company's defence to any such claims would be that the difference in terms was because of the need to comply with the Transfer Regulations, ie a genuine material factor other than sex.)

15.6.9 There is also the issue of employees inherited by the project company from existing third-party contractors. The awarding authority will wish to exclude these employees from the scope of any indemnity which it does agree to give (although there would then be the same issue as to whether the project company would price into its contract the potential redundancy risk for these employees). Generally, the whole issue of whether the awarding authority takes any responsibility for third-party employees needs to be addressed and is usually a major concern for the project company. The extent to which the awarding authority is prepared to include employees of existing contractors within the scope of, for example, any indemnity against pre-transfer employment liabilities will depend on factors such as the number of employees, whether there are any relevant terms in the existing service provision contract (such as any relevant indemnities) and whether it is possible to obtain comfort from the contractor in any other way (perhaps as a term in any renewed contract).

15.6.10 If a redundancy indemnity is agreed in principle, it may depend on the circumstances in which the contract is lost (for example, not applying if the contractor is in default). It could also be agreed that there should be no indemnity on the expiry of a contract through effluxion of time because the project company will know the position at the beginning of the contract and will have at least some opportunity to make plans to minimise its liability on the expiry of the contract. The awarding authority may agree to an indemnity if *it* voluntarily terminates the contract or if the project company terminates because the awarding authority is in default of its obligations. If such an early termination resulted from a breach by the awarding authority of its obligations, resulting redundancy costs would probably in any event form part of a claim for damages by the project company. However, an indemnity should be easier to enforce.

15.6.11 An indemnity against redundancy costs on a market testing or expiry of a contract also carries the risk that the project company may seek to redeploy some employees (perhaps the better-performing or younger employees) away from the service which is coming up for renewal, particularly if the project company suspects that it will not succeed on a re-tender (or perhaps simply does not wish to re-tender). If this happened and the Transfer Regulations did apply, the new service provider would inherit the less able or older employees. If, on the other hand, the Transfer Regulations did not apply, the redundancy payments could be higher than they needed to be because the long-serving and therefore expensive employees had been left working on the contract whilst their younger colleagues with shorter lengths of service had been moved elsewhere. Again, suitably drafted contractual provisions could address the problem but for them to achieve their purpose requires considerable vigilance by the awarding authority.

15.6.12 There is also the possibility of the incumbent employer at the time of a future change of service provider taking action, for whatever reason, to the detriment of his successor (such as improving rates of pay immediately prior to termination or expiry of his contract, which would have to be inherited under the Transfer Regulations). A provision of the project documentation could be that no changes to employment terms can be made within, say, six months prior to expiry or a market test (or, if shorter, once notice to terminate had been served for any reason). The absence of such a provision can deter future tenderers on a subsequent market test, particularly if the outgoing contractor has a bad track record of doing this sort of thing. It is also useful to be able to require the provision of employment information by the project company to potential new employers prior to subsequent market tests. The amended Directive allows Member States to require transferors to provide information about their employees to potential transferees.

15.6.13 In all these discussions about the effect of the Transfer Regulations and any indemnities which may be negotiated, it is particularly important to remember that the project company will probably use its own sub-contractors to provide the various services. In reality, the question of whether the Transfer Regulations apply is really to be answered with reference to the onward transfer to the sub-contractors, as well as questions of any indemnities to be given. Whatever is included in the project documentation is likely to be reflected in the sub-contracting agreements on a 'back-to-back' basis.

15.7 TRANSFER REGULATIONS COSTS

15.7.1 If the Transfer Regulations do not apply to a change of service provider the position of the relevant parties is relatively simple and is capable of fairly accurate costing (existing staff would have to be redeployed or made redundant and new staff could be recruited on the new service provider's own terms). When the Transfer Regulations do apply, the project company will often seek to be indemnified against costs arising directly from the application of the Transfer Regulations. It is important to be able to define what those costs actually are. Ultimately, this will be a question for negotiation, but the principal costs could include the following:

- costs incurred in connection with dismissals arising out of the transfer including:
  - dismissals by reason of redundancy (either redundancies implemented by the transferee after the transfer or, potentially, redundancies at the point of transfer if the PFI project involves a relocation from one site to another);
  - constructive dismissals resulting from any transfer-related change to the contracts of transferring employees;
  (Costs relating to dismissal could include statutory redundancy payments, enhanced redundancy payments (including, arguably, enhanced pension benefits for some public sector employees aged 50 or over), unfair dismissal liability, payments in lieu of notice/wrongful dismissal liability (if notice is not given), unlawful discrimination claims and legal costs.)
  - non-transfer-related dismissals which occur in the future but which are more expensive because of the inherited service and terms of employment of the transferred employees; and
  - costs of dismissing inherited employees for incompetence, misconduct or incapability (based on the argument that the project company might inherit a number of unsuitable employees under the Transfer Regulations);
- costs incurred in relation to alleged unlawful deductions from wages if the transferring employees' financial terms and conditions are not maintained;
- sex, race or disability discrimination claims which could relate to changes in working conditions, environment or terms and conditions following the transfer;
- costs incurred in buying out terms and conditions (including non-cash benefits) previously enjoyed by inherited employees which the new employer is not able to provide;
- costs involved if a recognised trade union is de-recognised or an inherited collective agreement is terminated and strike or disruptive action results;
- costs incurred because of any change to the Transfer Regulations or the Directive (including any repeal) or any change in their judicial interpretation (for example, a change to when the Transfer Regulations apply or a change in relation to the pension benefits to be made available to the inherited employees, which could prove an expensive liability);[1]
- costs in relation to any accrued liabilities to the transferring employees which were incurred pre-transfer (including, for example, personal injury);

---

1   See the proposals for pension law reform at **15.13**.

– costs relating to any claims brought by employees of the awarding authority who are not the specified transferring employees if they allege that their employment should have transferred under the Transfer Regulations.

15.7.2 Clearly, the project company will wish to include as wide a definition of Transfer Regulations costs as possible, with the awarding authority taking the opposite approach. The general principle should be that a Transfer Regulations cost is something which makes an employee more expensive to employ, or to dismiss, than an employee recruited off the street who starts with a clean slate. A definitive and agreed list of costs is often the subject of protracted negotiations. An alternative approach is not to have an indemnity but for tenderers to be provided with complete employment information so that they can price into their tenders the additional costs that they perceive would result from the application of the Transfer Regulations. The awarding authority may wish to see this separately identified.

15.7.3 There are often arguments as to which terms and conditions of employment do actually transfer under the Transfer Regulations. The enhanced redundancy benefits provided through the NHS Pension Scheme for employees aged 50 or over are, depending on who is advising (and who is being advised), regarded as either part of terms and conditions and therefore transfer, or are part of the benefits provided under an occupational pension scheme and are therefore subject to the 'Regulation 7' exclusion.[1] Often the best course is to try to clarify any ambiguity in the project documentation, particularly if it is important to the awarding authority to be able to demonstrate to unions and employees alike that it is doing everything it can to protect their interests in the process.

15.7.4 There are also certain benefits provided by the public sector which it is very difficult for the private sector to match. For example, the NHS Injury Benefit Scheme makes generous provision for employees who suffer an injury at work. The private sector has found that to provide a comparable level of cover through an employer's insurance liability scheme is prohibitively expensive. If the benefit is part of terms and conditions, then it would transfer and an employer who did not provide the benefit could face claims by transferring employees. However, an Employment Tribunal has considered the point and held that the benefit did not transfer; it was in effect a social security scheme funded by the Secretary of State and was not therefore an obligation of the employer (a Health Authority) which would transfer under the Transfer Regulations to a new employer.[2] On the basis of that decision, an awarding authority wishing to demonstrate its determination to protect its employees' interests may seek a contractual obligation on the private sector to match the benefit or else use best endeavours to provide something as close as possible to it.

15.7.5 A point which is becoming increasingly important concerns the possible future impact of equal pay claims on the terms of employees who transfer to the private sector. There are currently a number of claims by NHS staff (usually backed by UNISON) that different categories of employees in the health service

---

1   See further discussion at **15.10** and **15.12**.
2   *Fry v Three C's (Lewisham) Limited* Employment Tribunal, 2300189/98, unreported.

who are doing work of equal value are being paid differing amounts, with women usually suffering the lower pay rates. The argument raised by the private sector is that if those claims are successful and, as a result, the disadvantaged categories of employees have their pay rates increased through the Whitley Council[1] mechanism to achieve equality, then those increases will have to be matched by the private sector (provided they still have employees who remain on the Whitley Council terms of employment on which they originally transferred from the health service).

15.7.6 Indemnities are being sought against this risk but they are complicated to draft and it is often difficult to agree exactly what they are supposed to cover. Because of the length of time equal pay claims tend to take, the project company will usually seek protection for a period of many years. The various risks which could be covered by such an indemnity include:

- the retrospective effect of awards for those employees who were formerly public sector staff[2];
- the ongoing costs of implementing the awards for those staff in the future;
- the possible impact on the pay rates of other employees of the project company because of the need to maintain equality within its own workforce, whether inherited from a third-party contractor or recruited from elsewhere; and
- the effect on maintaining differentials between employees of different grades.

15.7.7 Future market testing of services will have a bearing because, at that point, there would usually be a revision to the base employment costs for the service which would then reflect any increases to those costs which had been required because of successful equal pay claims. It may be therefore that any indemnity which is agreed should last only until the first market testing at the latest.

15.7.8 It seems clear that the whole area of indemnities and contributions from any party in a PFI project will become increasingly complex as those involved in PFI become more sophisticated in their approach and more alive to the issues. Precedents are being set and then quoted on other projects to justify particular stances both by the awarding authorities and the project companies. The central role of the Treasury Taskforce and the PFUs in trying to achieve some consistency of approach by awarding authorities, at least within sectors, is of particular importance in the employment field.

---

1   Whitley Councils for the Health Service (Great Britain) General Council Conditions of Service.

15.8 COLLECTIVE OBLIGATIONS

15.8.1 Regulation 10 of the Transfer Regulations imposes obligations on a transferor and a transferee to provide information to, and in certain circumstances consult with, representatives of all affected employees prior to a relevant transfer. The obligation falls primarily on the transferor since its staff will be most affected by the transfer because of the change in their employer. However, the transferee itself must also consider whether any of its existing employees will be affected by the transfer (for example, the influx of new employees may affect working practices or even lead to redundancies). In addition, it must supply certain information to the transferor about its proposals for the employees it is to inherit.

15.8.2 The representatives of the employees may be either recognised trade union officials or employee representatives elected by the affected employees for the specific purpose of consultation (although as part of a general consultation exercise on amendments to the collective consultation regime, the government has proposed that if there is a recognised trade union, it must be consulted; the employer should not be able to choose to consult elected employee representatives instead). On the initial move from the public to the private sector, there will usually be an established union presence. However, not all affected employees may be covered by the particular union recognition agreements and there may well not be any significant union presence in a transfer involving two contractors. In those situations, the employer must invite the relevant staff to elect representatives.[1]

15.8.3 Once the employee representatives are in place, the employer must provide them with certain specified categories of information. These are set out in regulation 10(2) of the Transfer Regulations:

- the fact that the relevant transfer is to take place, when (approximately) it is to take place and the reasons for it;
- the legal, economic and social implications of the transfer for the affected employees;
- the 'measures' (if any) which the employer envisages it will take in relation to those employees in connection with the transfer;
- if the employer is the transferor, the 'measures' (if any) which the transferee envisages it will take after the transfer in relation to the transferring employees (this is usually the most important issue).

15.8.4 This information must be provided 'long enough before a relevant transfer' to allow consultation to take place. This is the only requirement so far as timing is concerned, unlike the formal time limits for consultation before redundancies. A practical view must be taken about the length of the process, bearing in mind the obligation that any consultation must be meaningful and 'with a view to seeking [the representatives'] agreement to measures to be taken'.[2]

---

1 The election process itself is outside the scope of this chapter.
2 Transfer Regulations, regulation 10(5).

15.8.5 The duty to consult only arises where the transferor (or the transferee in relation to its own existing workforce) envisages taking 'measures' in connection with the transfer. 'Measures' are not defined but would include, for example, any material change of terms (including pension entitlement), relocation, redundancies and de-recognition of trade unions. 'Envisages' also has no definition but implies a firm proposal to take a step even if a final decision has not been taken. There is no duty on a transferor to consult about measures which the transferee envisages taking; the transferor's duty is simply to pass on the information as to what they would be. There is also no obligation on the transferee to consult with representatives of the transferor's staff. In practice, it will usually be in all parties' interests (particularly where trade unions are involved) for some form of voluntary consultation to take place with the representatives of the transferor's workforce which involves a representative of the transferee.

15.8.6 If only a few employees will be affected by a relevant transfer and/or the transferee has confirmed that he will employ all the employees on their existing terms and conditions with continuity of service, then there will be little about which to consult. In those circumstances, only a few weeks before the relevant transfer may be long enough for the consultation process. The required information would be provided and there may be a meeting between management and employee representatives to discuss it, but that may be all both sides consider necessary. At the other extreme, if large numbers of employees are likely to be affected by a transfer and substantial redundancies or other changes are envisaged then a more lengthy period of several months may well be appropriate.

15.8.7 It is sometimes difficult to assess at what point the obligation to inform and consult arises. It seems reasonably certain that it would be difficult for 'meaningful' consultation to begin until, at the earliest, a preferred tenderer has been identified. The argument on behalf of the trade unions is that the Transfer Regulations give them the right to be consulted about the selection of the preferred tenderer. However, the better argument is probably that it is only once that selection has been made that the transferor could comply with its obligation under regulation 10(2) to provide details to the employee representatives about the measures which the transferee envisages it will take (only then would there be a definite transferee which could comply with its obligation under regulation 10(3) to provide that information). It could also be argued that until a preferred tenderer is selected, it is not certain that there will be a transfer at all. Even when a preferred tenderer is chosen, the obligation to inform and consult would not automatically arise at that point because a later date may still be long enough before the transfer to allow meaningful consultation to take place. However, once the decision on the preferred tenderer is taken and becomes known to employees (and particularly to any unions involved), there are likely to be calls for talks. The duty to provide information is a continuing one and it could involve provision of information on several occasions as matters develop.

15.8.8 The liability for a failure properly to inform and consult is currently a maximum of four weeks' pay per affected employee (although the government is proposing to increase this to 90 days' pay per affected employee). A claim would be heard in an Employment Tribunal and must be made by one of the employee representatives within three months of the transfer. There is a defence for an employer if it can show that there were special circumstances which meant that it was not reasonably practicable for it to comply. However, this is unlikely ever to be applicable in the case of a PFI project, mainly because of the normally lengthy timescale for negotiations between the awarding authority and the project company.

15.8.9 Agreements with recognised trade unions may contain procedures for consultation before a relevant transfer which impose obligations over and above the requirements of the Transfer Regulations. Public sector unions have increasingly sought to agree specific consultation procedures for Compulsory Competitive Tendering or PFI projects. They would usually specify when information should be provided and consultation should start, as well as laying down the periods of time during which consultation must take place before the next step in the tendering or PFI process can take place. An awarding authority would be at risk if it ignored any such agreed procedure, both from an industrial relations perspective and, if the agreement is intended to be legally binding, because of possible legal action to halt the project until the procedures had been followed. The latter would, however, be very rare since the vast majority of collective agreements are not intended to be legally binding.

15.8.10 In one particular case involving University College Hospital, London ('UCH'), UNISON held a strike ballot because, principally, UCH had refused to seek from the private sector a guarantee that employment terms of transferring staff would not be changed for the 30-year life of the PFI contract. UCH obtained an injunction preventing strike action on the basis that the reasons for their proposed action put forward by UNISON did not constitute a trade dispute. This injunction was upheld by the Court of Appeal. There were special factors present in the case because UCH is in the constitutency of the current Health Secretary, Frank Dobson, and this added a political dimension which perhaps explains why UNISON took the action they did. Nevertheless, the case is a useful reminder of the possibility of disruptive action if unions are not happy with what is proposed in a particular project (and the options open to the awarding authority to take legal action in response).

15.8.11 Although the Transfer Regulations provide some protection for recognised trade unions and their continued role with a transferee after a transfer, often there will be a specific commitment in the project documentation that the project company will continue to recognise the unions which had been recognised by the awarding authority, for the same purposes and on the same basis. This can become an issue depending on the extent to which the private sector companies involved are used to dealing with recognised trade unions (in particular, for the purpose of collective bargaining) but proposed reforms to the law governing union recognition in the Fairness at Work Bill may in effect require this result in any event.

15.8.12 The whole issue of providing information and engaging in consultation should be addressed early on in the project. Often the perceived need for confidentiality will be the dominant concern but it will be in the interests of all involved to keep staff and unions 'on side' as much as possible. The prospect of moving from the public to private sector causes uncertainty amongst employees, which is only accentuated by a lack of information and any impression of being kept in the dark. The whole process should be portrayed in as positive a light as possible, emphasising whatever benefits will result. Definite information should be provided wherever possible since ambiguity will inevitably be construed unfavourably. Regular bulletins to staff are useful and often a 'question and answer' brief should be prepared to arm management with the appropriate responses to the most common questions.

15.8.13 The current government seems to be in favour of giving unions a role in the process of selecting a preferred tenderer and in the subsequent negotiations over the project documentation. Whether this remains at the level of ministerial pronouncement or is reflected in legislation remains to be seen, but it is likely that it will lead to union demands for greater, and earlier, involvement in PFI projects.

15.9 CHANGING TERMS AND CONDITIONS OF EMPLOYMENT AFTER A TRANSFER

15.9.1 It was the intention behind the Transfer Regulations to place the transferee in the same position as the transferor vis-à-vis the employees in the undertaking; no more, no less. For example, if the transferor either had the right to make changes to terms and conditions or could do so with the employees' agreement, then so could the transferee. It is a crucial issue for contractors taking on staff under the Transfer Regulations. They may wish to implement changes for the sake of efficiency (to provide services to the required specifications), to achieve cost-saving, to harmonise terms with those of their existing workforce or because certain public sector benefits cannot practically be matched by the private sector.[1] However, the ability of the transferee to implement changes to employment terms in the context of a relevant transfer has been cast into doubt.

15.9.2 In *Wilson* and *Meade*,[2] the House of Lords heard together two appeals dealing with the circumstances in which new terms and conditions of employment could be introduced after a transfer. Both cases involved dismissals of employees in the context of a relevant transfer, followed by engagement by the transferee on less favourable terms and conditions. The issue was the fact that the Directive and the Transfer Regulations make void any attempt to contract out of their provisions. The ECJ has often stressed the public policy of protection of employees but has also made clear that this would not prevent agreement with an employee to vary terms if this was allowed by the domestic law of the member state *provided that the transfer was not the reason for the change*.[3] The meaning

---

1 See **15.7.4**.
2 *Wilson and others v St Helens Borough Council*; *Meade and Baxendale v British Fuels Ltd* [1998] IRLR 706, HL.
3 *Foreningen af Arbejdsledere i Danmark v Daddy's Dance Hall A/S* 324/86 [1988] IRLR 315, ECJ.

of these final words and the degree of freedom they actually gave to the transferee to effect changes to terms and conditions have not been clear.

15.9.3 Two approaches to this problem could be identified. The first 'absolutist' approach stressed the protection of the employees and their vulnerability on moving to a new employer. On this view, any attempt to change terms because of the transfer would be unlawful and any purported agreement reached would be invalid and could be set aside. The second more pragmatic view sought to place the transferee in the same position as the transferor and would regard most such agreements as valid provided, for instance, that no pressure was exerted on the employee to consent to the change.

15.9.4 The House of Lords in *Wilson* and *Meade* managed to avoid having to choose between these two approaches, commenting that if it had been necessary to determine which was right, they would have referred the point to the ECJ. Their Lordships concentrated on the fact that, in both *Wilson* and *Meade*, the employees concerned had been dismissed by the transferor and then taken on by the transferee. They decided that the real issue was the status of those dismissals. They held that the dismissals were effective (not void, as the Court of Appeal had held) and that the new contracts were also effective, even if they contained less favourable terms. The protection for the employees lay in their right to seek a remedy for unfair dismissal against their former employer; dismissals for a reason connected with a relevant transfer would be automatically unfair unless the 'ETO' defence[1] could be upheld (which would presumably be unlikely for those employees who were re-employed to do much the same job). Their Lordships accepted that, effectively, the employees' previous contracts could be 'bought out' by this route. They were essentially agreeing with the reasoning of Mr Justice Morrison in an EAT decision delivered between the time of the Court of Appeal judgment and the House of Lords' hearing, where he had questioned the concept of a dismissal being a nullity.[2]

15.9.5 Once the cap on unfair dismissal compensation is increased, the route of dismissal followed by new employment may become less attractive. However, presumably earnings from the new employment, albeit perhaps lower than from the previous employment, will be taken into account when compensation is assessed.

15.9.6 As a result of *Wilson* and *Meade*, where there is no dismissal but rather an agreement to accept new terms, it seem that this will be void as an attempt to contract out of the Transfer Regulations provided the reason for the change in terms is the transfer itself. An employee's consent to any adverse change to terms of employment, even in return for consideration, would be ineffective. Because of the wide approach currently taken to deciding when a transfer is the reason for any changes to terms, a transferee would have to delay any changes for a considerable period of time before it could be reasonably confident of convincing a court or tribunal that there was some reason for the change other than the transfer. This issue will no doubt be litigated in the courts but it is likely that only the ECJ will feel able to determine it, so the uncertainty of the current position will last for some time.

---

1 See **15.2.8**.
2 *Cornwall County Care Limited v Brightman and others* [1998] IRLR 656, EAT.

15.9.7 The decision could have the consequence that a private sector contractor wishing to cut costs could be more likely to consider redundancies than to preserve the existing workforce but on lower pay. Although such dismissals would risk being automatically 'unfair', there is the possibility of arguing the ETO defence which may be preferable to the uncertainty of agreeing changes to terms across the board only to have them challenged subsequently by employees.

15.9.8 The transferee could perhaps go one stage further and ensure that the employees take independent legal advice before giving their consent, by way of analogy with the system of Compromise Agreements under s 203 of the Employment Rights Act 1996 (by which employees can effectively waive their statutory rights to bring claims). However, this is untested by the courts and there can be no guarantee that it would be successful. In labour-intensive services, it could also be a costly administrative exercise. There is also, as ever, the practical point that most employees who agree to changes to their terms of employment will probably regard themselves as bound by their agreement and will not subsequently challenge what has happened.

15.9.9 As another variant on *Wilson* and *Meade*, the EAT has held that changes to less favourable terms and conditions made to assist an NHS trust to submit a more competitive tender to retain a contract in-house were valid, even in circumstances where the changes were agreed with a trade union representing the employees rather than with the employees themselves.[1] The *Wilson* and *Meade* problem was finessed by a finding that an in-house bid is not covered by the Transfer Regulations because the identity of the employer does not change. If that is right, an in-house bid has an advantage over a bid from an external tenderer; the former can bid on the basis that it can introduce less favourable terms and conditions, the latter cannot.

15.9.10 The desire to change terms and conditions of employees may be all the more pressing because of another decision of the EAT.[2] Where an individual's remuneration is stated in his employment contract to be set according to a national pay bargaining process between trade unions and a management body, that process will continue to govern the individual's remuneration after a transfer to the private sector (although not if the incorporation of the national award is subject to the employer's approval, since 'the employer' will become the transferee).[3] In *Whent*, a private sector employer who had inherited such a term in employees' contracts of employment had to implement future pay awards resulting from the national collective bargaining process, despite having no input into or influence over the negotiations that led to the awards. This could, in theory, continue ad infinitum, unless the private sector employer negotiated a change to an employee's contract so that pay became a matter to be determined solely between the employee and the new employer. However, in agreeing any such change, the employer would have to bear in mind *Wilson* and *Meade*.

---

1   *Burke v Royal Liverpool University Hospital Trust* [1997] ICR 730.
2   *Whent v T Cartledge Ltd* [1997] IRLR 153.
3   *Glendale Grounds Management v Bradley* [1998] EAT, unreported.

15.9.11 There is no easy solution to the problems thrown up by *Wilson* and *Meade*. Either the dismissal route will have to be followed or contractors will have to seek to agree changes and hold their breath over any future legal challenge. Apart from the untested Compromise Agreement approach, one further possible option is simply to 'red circle' the inherited employees and to deny them any pay or benefit increases until they have been matched by the rest of the workforce. However, this is not foolproof (particularly if the employees have an express or implied right to pay increases) and could cause industrial relations problems, including widespread disincentivisation.

15.9.12 As part of the general consultation exercise following the amendments to the Directive, the DTI is specifically considering the merits of amending the Transfer Regulations to allow transfer-related variations to terms and conditions to be agreed between employers and trade unions (or appropriate employee representatives), but only in connection with transfers from insolvent employers. An extension of that approach may provide the solution that is obviously needed but that is only likely to come from the ECJ.

15.10 THE 'REGULATION 7' PENSION EXCLUSION

15.10.1 On a relevant transfer, employees and their terms and conditions of employment will transfer automatically to the project company (or relevant service provider) under the Transfer Regulations, except for those terms and conditions relating to an occupational pension scheme (regulation 7 of the Transfer Regulations). Regulation 7 is based on Article 3(3) of the Directive, which states that the automatic transfer principle:

> 'shall not cover employees' rights to old-age, invalidity or survivors' benefits under supplementary company or inter-company pension schemes outside the statutory social security schemes in Member States.'

15.10.2 The question of whether the contractual rights excluded by regulation 7 (the 'excluded rights') will remain with the transferor or simply disappear has caused much concern. The Court of Appeal[1] has affirmed that the exclusion in Article 3(3) of the Directive (and, by implication, regulation 7) should be interpreted as applying to all contractual pension rights in relation to occupational pension schemes (both in respect of past and future service). In the first instance decision which the Court of Appeal upheld, Mr Justice Robert Walker observed (obiter) that the excluded rights would not remain with the transferor as a result of the Directive. He said that they would only do so if the employment contract so provided and that the existence of such an obligation would be very unusual.

15.10.3 When a relevant transfer occurs, it is clear that all contractual pension rights (for example, to have contributions made to a personal pension arrangement) will automatically pass to the project company, apart from the

---

1 *Adams v Lancashire County Council and BET Catering Services Limited* [1997] IRLR 436.

excluded rights. However, the most common contractual pension rights, particularly in the public sector, are to membership of an occupational pension scheme and will therefore be excluded rights. Assuming that there is nothing in the employees' contracts of employment to suggest otherwise, it can reasonably be assumed that the excluded rights will not remain with the previous employer. In any event, the employees' contracts of employment are likely to provide that they are only entitled to active membership of the relevant public sector scheme in accordance with its terms and conditions from time to time; the rules of the relevant scheme will usually provide that a person may only continue to be an active member so long as he is employed by a participating employer in the scheme.

15.10.4 Therefore, following a relevant transfer, even if employees' contractual occupational pension scheme rights were to remain with the previous employer, such contractual rights are very unlikely still to confer an entitlement to membership of the previous employer's pension scheme (because the relevant employees would no longer be employed by an employer participating in the scheme). However, the government has taken the view that it faces the risk of constructive dismissal claims from the relevant employees if it fails to ensure that the project company provides comparable pension provision for them in the future. This is based on the assumption that the government will have breached its duty, implied into every contract of employment, to act in good faith towards its employees. The government appears to take this view even if (as explained above) the relevant employees' contractual pension rights do not give them any entitlement to membership of the relevant government pension scheme after the transfer and even, apparently, if their contracts of employment do not confer upon them the right to membership of the relevant government pension scheme prior to the transfer.

15.10.5 This argument appears highly debatable. If correct, then it would in effect negate regulation 7. Lord Johnston in the EAT[1] has stated that where an employee's current contractual terms appeared to be in danger after the contemplated transfer, the duty of good faith owed by the employer to its employee would not be breached (and the employee would not therefore be able to resign and claim constructive dismissal):

> 'because [the Transfer Regulations] provide an absolute answer by way of remedy to any attempt by the transferee to alter those terms unlawfully after the transfer.'

15.10.6 His Lordship also added that:

> 'We do not consider that the conduct of an employer ... can be regarded as sufficiently drastic with regard to the obligation of mutual trust and goodwill, if it does nothing to alter the remedies available to the employee upon transfer.'

15.10.7 He observed that the duty of good faith could only be breached by an employer proposing to transfer his employees to a third party 'in the rarest of cases', where 'there is no other remedy than that the employee must resign in his own interests'. Therefore, where the prospective transferee is proposing to alter

---

1 *Sita v Burton* [1997] IRLR 501.

terms of employment in relation to occupational pension scheme benefits or is proposing not to provide comparable pension provision, this would not appear to justify a claim of constructive dismissal against the transferor for arranging the transfer to that transferee. A much more important consideration is the fact that if the awarding authority makes no effort to ensure that the project company provides a certain level of future pension provision, there are likely to be adverse employee relations consequences.

15.11 COMPARABLE PENSION ARRANGEMENTS

15.11.1 The protection traditionally sought by awarding authorities is an obligation on the project company to admit the relevant employees to pension arrangements which are broadly comparable with the relevant public sector pension arrangements. The 'broadly comparable' test does not require identical benefits to be provided, indeed public sector pension arrangements usually differ significantly in detail from those in the private sector. Public sector arrangements provide full index-linking (whereas private pension schemes generally provide lower pension increases), but only a 1/80th pension accrual basis (whereas private pension schemes often have a 1/60th pension accrual basis). The protection may extend to seeking to bind the project company to undertake to maintain or not to alter such pension arrangements in the future but this is usually resisted (the project company may alternatively try to obtain an undertaking from the awarding authority to meet all or part of the cost of funding such benefits – particularly where, were it not for the awarding authority's insistence, the project company would not be offering the relevant employees comparable pension provision).

15.11.2 It is now common practice for the project company to be required to obtain a certificate (a 'GAD certificate') from the Government Actuary's Department confirming comparability between the public and private sector schemes. Either a formal certificate can be issued following examination of the project company's pension arrangements after it has submitted a tender, or else a 'passport' certificate can be issued if the project company submits details of its pension arrangements to the Government Actuary for examination before it submits the tender. There is a fee payable for the GAD Certificate and it is normally sufficiently substantial for a tenderer to be reluctant to have to incur the cost until it achieves the status of preferred tenderer.

15.11.3 In issuing its Certificate, the GAD will take into account the entire remuneration package offered by the project company and will seek to ensure that no identifiable individual or group is disadvantaged. If there was a regulation 7 liability risk, the fact that the project company was providing more favourable benefits in other respects would not absolve the awarding authority from liability for ensuring continued comparable pension provision. However, the government considers that the issue of a GAD Certificate will provide added protection against any constructive dismissal risk (which, if such a risk exists, seems likely to be the case).

15.11.4 Also, provided the remuneration package as a whole is equally favourable, the risk of an adverse impact on employee relations ought to be slight, although some employees will regard pension provision as rather more important than others, depending on their personal circumstances. As an additional selling point to employees and unions, the awarding authority may also consider trying to obtain an undertaking from the project company that the provision of broadly comparable pension arrangements (or other protection of employees' pension position) should be a condition of any future market testing of services by the project company. However, it should be noted that even if the project company's pension arrangements are broadly comparable, this will not ensure that the relevant employees' accrued pension rights (ie in relation to their past service at the date of transfer) are fully protected.[1]

15.12 ENHANCED PENSION BENEFITS ON REDUNDANCY AND ACCRUED PENSION RIGHTS

15.12.1 As members of the relevant public sector pension scheme, employees aged 50 or over may well have had an entitlement to enhanced pension benefits on redundancy (for example, under section 46 of the General Whitley Council terms and conditions). The government's view has been that such entitlement automatically passes to the project company following the transfer because it is part of the employees' terms and conditions of employment and therefore passes under the Transfer Regulations. Accordingly, such entitlement does not need to be taken into account for the purpose of the GAD Certificate. However, in the *Frankling* case,[2] the EAT held that even if the right to enhanced pension benefits on redundancy arose under the contract of employment (which it did not), such a right would fall within the regulation 7 exclusion.

15.12.2 In particular, the EAT first held that the right to enhanced pension benefits contained in section 46 of the General Whitley Council terms and conditions was not part of the obligations of an employer which could be transferred under the Transfer Regulations; the benefits were instead enjoyed by virtue of statute. This was essentially the same point as in the NHS Injury Benefit Scheme case.[3] The EAT also went on to consider whether such benefits fell within the regulation 7 exclusion. They held that they did, because the fact of early payment in the event of redundancy did not change the nature of the benefits; they were still benefits relating to old age. The court did note, however, that the employees were treated as retirees in order to give them the benefits under the statutory scheme. If they could have been paid the benefits without being retirees, then the position might have been different.

15.12.3 Again, this is a major issue for the unions. Long-serving public sector staff can be eligible for substantial payments under these arrangements and they are often among the most hotly debated topics in a PFI project. The methods of

---

1   See **15.12.5**.
2   *Frankling v BPS Public Sector Limited*, EAT 442/98.
3   See **15.7.5**.

calculating the benefits are complex and there can be arguments about whether payments must be made at the same time as they would have been in the public sector, as well as to the same value. Because of the uncertainty, unions have usually urged the awarding authority to obtain a contractual commitment from the project company to continue to provide the enhanced redundancy benefits (and in the light of the *Frankling* case, this will be all the more necessary). Most private sector pension schemes will not provide such benefits and honouring this commitment could be a major potential cost to the project company. One of the points often made by the awarding authority is that it is only a contingent cost, since the project company could choose not to make redundant any employee aged 50 or over to whom the enhanced terms applied.

15.12.4 The project company may also seek to secure protection against its potential pension liabilities. Its main concern will probably be that if it loses its contract on a future market testing, the Transfer Regulations may not apply and therefore it will face redundancy claims from its employees. If it has committed to honouring the enhanced redundancy benefits for those aged 50 and over, this could be an expensive process. It may try to seek an indemnity from the public sector against any costs it may incur in providing enhanced pension rights on redundancy even prior to any future market testing. The project company may also be concerned that even if there is a transfer under the Transfer Regulations on a future market testing, there is the regulation 7 risk[1] (albeit small).

15.12.5 At the time of a relevant transfer, the transferring employees will have accrued pension rights arising from their membership of the awarding authority's pension scheme. A 'bulk transfer payment' may be made from the awarding authority to the project company's pension scheme, representing the accrued pension rights of such of the relevant employees who wish those rights to transfer. The bulk transfer payment will be calculated on an enhanced basis to that which would otherwise be used to calculate individual transfer payments. This would be in return for the project company undertaking to provide such of the relevant employees in respect of whom the payment is made with 'transfer credits' comparable to those pension rights which they have accrued in the public sector pension scheme. The government view is that if the tenderer is not prepared to accept a bulk transfer payment on 'value for money terms to the taxpayer', this should be considered a 'significant disadvantage' of the tender. However, a bulk transfer is not always made and the awarding authority will only consider negotiating such a payment if various pre-conditions are satisfied.

15.12.6 If a suitable bulk transfer payment is not made, then the relevant employees may be disadvantaged in respect of their accrued pension rights, because if they retain their rights in the public sector pension scheme they will lose the link between those rights and any future increased salary they receive. If they choose to take an individual (non-enhanced) transfer payment to the project company, the 'transfer credits' they are awarded may not be as favourable as those pension rights they had previously accrued.

---

1   See **15.10**.

15.13 PROPOSALS FOR PENSION LAW REFORM

15.13.1 Article 3(3)(B) of the Directive provides that:

'Member States shall adopt the measures necessary to protect the interests of employees and of persons no longer employed in the transferor's business at the time of the transfer in respect of rights conferring on them immediate or prospective entitlement to old-age benefits ...'.

15.13.2 It has been suggested that the UK government has failed to comply with this provision. The European Union has, however, amended the Directive to enable Member States to apply the automatic transfer principle to rights under occupational pension schemes. Also, a Select Committee of the House of Lords has recommended removing the regulation 7 exclusion and it seems likely that the government will act on this recommendation.[1] It remains to be seen what action the UK government takes once it has completed its current deliberations over changes to the Transfer Regulations.

15.14 PROVISION OF INFORMATION

15.14.1 During the tendering process, there is always an issue as to how much information about employees and their terms and conditions should be supplied to the various tenderers. Here a distinction must be drawn between employees of the awarding authority itself and employees of any existing private sector contractors. The awarding authority will have access to the former information, but is unlikely to have access to the latter. Sometimes, with a considerable degree of foresight, the awarding authority may have inserted into a contract a requirement for the contractor to supply information concerning its employees for the purposes of any subsequent market testing or other replacement of the contractor, but this is by no means common with current contracts. It is certainly something that should be included in future outsourcing agreements and, in particular, in the project documentation with the project company.[2]

15.14.2 Given this constraint in relation to third-party contractors' employees, the most the awarding authority may be able to do is give an approximate idea of the number of staff engaged in the provision of a particular service and, perhaps, their total wage bill if this is identifiable from the fees paid for the service. The actual terms and conditions and rates of pay of existing contractors' employees may not be known in any detail, but competing contractors in the same industry ought to have a reasonable feel for the terms on which particular categories of employee are likely to be employed. As the market develops further, many contractors will find that they have inherited employees under the Transfer Regulations from their competitors, and vice versa, resulting in the wide dissemination of information concerning particular contractors' terms and conditions and rates of pay.

---

1 House of Lords Select Committee on the European Communities – Transfer of Undertakings; Acquired Rights, Session 95/96, Fifth report.
2 See **15.6.12**.

15.14.3 In the provision of information, there is also the issue of the employer's duty of confidence to its employees. This is a very grey area of the law with little, if any, guidance from the courts and could well vary according to the type of information: for example, details of a medical problem disclosed by an employee could well be said to have been disclosed in confidence whereas details of many terms and conditions of employment in practice are not treated (even by the employee) as confidential. Some employers adopt a robust approach and disclose all such information on the basis that employees are unlikely to challenge the decision. Others are conscious of potential industrial relations problems, particularly if the specific PFI project may in any event be likely to cause problems with morale amongst the workforce, and try to ensure that information is provided on an anonymous basis.

15.14.4 This can be achieved with varying degrees of generality: on the simplest level, the total number of employees and the aggregate cost of their salaries/wages and other benefits could be disclosed, along with copies of standard statements of terms and conditions of employment for different categories of employee. If more specific information is required, there could be a list of employees drawn up in which employees are not identified by name but rather by the allocation of individual numbers, with details being provided of each anonymous numbered employee's individual pay, benefits and length of service. In addition, consideration must be given to the position of the awarding authority under the Data Protection Act 1998 and the protection which that Act affords to employees.

15.14.5 It has become clear in many projects that the early provision of accurate information can avoid a number of problems. Such information is valuable to tenderers so that they can evaluate the costs of employment (and of termination) of employees whom they are to inherit under the Transfer Regulations. Whilst there may be uncertainty over whether the Transfer Regulations will actually apply in the first place, this is unlikely to affect the need for tenderers to assess the existing workforce; even if they do not inherit employees under the Transfer Regulations, they may wish to offer employment to some of the staff and knowledge of their existing terms would be useful in formulating those offers. Problems often result if vague, inaccurate or out-of-date information is provided to tenderers because, when calculating the potential 'Transfer Regulations costs', they are bound to err on the side of caution if in any doubt, resulting in an estimate which may be far higher than necessary. Sometimes a deliberately high estimate is given with the explanation that it has resulted from unsatisfactory information being provided, in the interests of trying to persuade the awarding authority to improve the quality and detail of the information which is made available.

15.14.6 The current government consultation exercise concerning possible amendments to the Transfer Regulations includes a proposal to make a transferor employer provide to tenderers comprehensive and accurate information about the size and terms and conditions of employment of its workforce. Until that happens, there will be continued discussion about the information to be provided, with the project company seeking warranties from the awarding authority as to the completeness and accuracy of the information and the awarding authority trying to limit its exposure on any such warranty.

15.15 INFORMATION CONCERNING MEASURES TO BE TAKEN BY THE PROJECT COMPANY

15.15.1 As explained above, there is an obligation on the transferee under the Transfer Regulations to provide to the transferor details of the measures, if any, which it envisages it will take in relation to the transferring employees.[1] Clearly, if the Transfer Regulations apply, that obligation will exist independently of any documentation between the parties. However, it is advisable if there is any doubt over the application of the Transfer Regulations, even if both parties are agreeing to act as if they apply, specifically to state that the project company will provide to the awarding authority details of any measures which it envisages that it (or its sub-contractors) will be taking.

15.15.2 Furthermore, since liability for a failure to comply with these provisions of the Transfer Regulations falls in the first instance on the transferor, an indemnity against any failure to provide details of measures will also often be sought by the awarding authority (although under the Transfer Regulations themselves the awarding authority could seek to pass on some or all of any such liability to the transferee if it had failed to provide the information in good time to enable the awarding authority to comply with its obligations).[2]

15.16 TRAINING AND COMPETENCE

15.16.1 In the documentation concerning the provision of services, the awarding authority will often seek to impose an obligation on the project company to ensure that the workforce it employs in the provision of the services is properly trained and competent for the work in question. If specific skills are required, the project company may be obliged to ensure that the necessary skilled staff will be available. There will also often be an obligation to provide sufficient numbers of appropriate staff, including reserves to cover for absence due to holidays or sickness or any other reason. The project company may resist these requirements on the basis that they consider them unnecessary; the adequate performance of the services will generally be dealt with elsewhere in the project documentation in the service level specifications, along with the consequences of a failure to perform.

15.16.2 Where the project company is inheriting staff under the Transfer Regulations, it will not be in a position to give any sort of undertaking as to the training, competence and skill of the employees it inherits as from the date of transfer and this may well have to be made an exception to the general undertaking. However, a period may be agreed during which the project

---

1 See **15.8.1**.
2 Transfer Regulations, regulations 11(3) and 11(4).

company is to ensure that the staff it has inherited are of the necessary standard (again, the extent and quality of the information provided about the staff before the transfer is important). Alternatively, the awarding authority may agree to provide a warranty about the competence of its staff as at the point of transfer.

15.16.3 An obligation would normally be imposed on the project company to ensure that all staff comply with all relevant procedures as if they had continued in the public sector. This may also require staff to attend ongoing training; the project company would want the nature of the training to be specified as accurately as possible, whereas the awarding authority may wish to keep the reference deliberately flexible, to allow for future developments in training requirements. The project company may also argue that the awarding authority should meet the costs of training any staff who transfer without having received mandatory (or recommended) training during their employment with the awarding authority (such as hygiene requirements).

15.17 STAFF AND CONVICTIONS

15.17.1 If the duties of private sector employees will involve contact with vulnerable classes of people (for example, patients in a hospital or children), the awarding authority will usually seek to impose an obligation on the project company to ensure that all potential staff should be questioned about previous convictions for any offences. This would usually exclude the employees inherited under the Transfer Regulations because the awarding authority should have already carried out the exercise. Convictions would include any 'spent' convictions as defined by the Rehabilitation of Offenders Act 1974. The Act essentially allows people who are convicted of criminal offences and given certain types of sentence to become 'rehabilitated' after a fixed period of time (the conviction does not disappear but, for certain purposes, the individual is no longer tainted by it). Rehabilitation under the Act can only take place if the sentence imposed was no worse than a custodial sentence of 30 months or less.

15.17.2 However, there are a large number of exceptions under the Act which require a person to disclose a conviction even if it is spent. Such exceptions include employees who may have access to people in receipt of medical treatment or who may be involved with the provision to persons aged under 18 of a wide range of facilities, including schooling. The awarding authority will want to ensure that no person who discloses any such conviction is employed without the awarding authority's prior consent. Furthermore, there may well be an extension of this provision to the effect that if a member of staff is subsequently convicted of an offence which is material in the context of the service in which that person is employed (or whose previous undisclosed conviction becomes known), that person should be dismissed immediately by the project company or, at least, removed from the relevant service.

15.18 DISCIPLINARY ACTION

15.18.1 Where private sector employees will be working on premises still owned by the awarding authority, it would be usual for the authority to have some right to require disciplinary action by the project company against any of its employees, certainly for misconduct and sometimes for poor performance. The awarding authority would usually want to have the right to dictate what that action should be, leading up to and including dismissal, but the project company would normally resist giving up ultimate control of its disciplinary procedures to a third party. One compromise is for the parties to reach agreement at the outset on the disciplinary procedures to be operated by the project company and for the awarding authority to be able to require an investigation if there is a disciplinary issue, whilst the ultimate decision as to what action to take remains with the project company. There may be a general statement of principles agreed between the parties with the project company being obliged to take action in the spirit of those principles.

15.18.2 If the project company does agree that the awarding authority should have the right to dictate disciplinary action, this might be on the condition that it should indemnify the project company against any claims which may result (for example, for unfair dismissal or unlawful discrimination). Where disciplinary procedures are part of an employee's contract of employment, failure to follow them correctly could also expose the employer to a claim for breach of contract and they could not simply be ignored in favour of new procedures agreed between the awarding authority and the project company. Where such new procedures represent a change in the employee's contract, the issues discussed in relation to *Wilson* and *Meade* would be relevant.[1]

15.18.3 As well as input into disciplinary action to be taken against existing employees, the awarding authority may seek input into the project company's recruitment of new staff. This could either be by way of an opportunity to recommend whether or not a particular applicant should be employed or, perhaps, the right to refuse a particular individual if, for example, they had previously been engaged in the provision of a service or employed directly by the awarding authority and had performed unsatisfactorily. Generally, however, such involvement is seen to be intrusive and not consistent with PFI philosophy.

---

1   See **15.9.2–15.9.6**.

Chapter 16

DISPUTE RESOLUTION PROCEDURES

16.1 INTRODUCTION

16.1.1 Despite the efforts of lawyers to document the agreed position between the parties in a PFI transaction, disputes will inevitably arise (particularly over lengthy contract periods where the parties are being required to assume risks on a predetermined basis) and procedures for resolving disputes are an important element of any PFI transaction. Dispute resolution takes many different forms and should be tailored to the specific requirements of the project documentation and, in particular, the long-term relationship between the parties to the project. In general, the different forms of dispute resolution can be categorised as follows:

- Panels/Dispute Review Boards;
- Alternative Dispute Resolution;
- Expert Resolution;
- Adjudication;
- Arbitration;
- Litigation.

16.1.2 When the parties consider the form of the dispute resolution provision, the first and most obvious point is that the provision must provide a machinery whereby any dispute is finally resolved by imposing a binding decision on the parties. The dispute resolution provision must also be sufficiently robust to regulate a dispute which might threaten the existence of the commercial relationship between the parties and properly serve their legitimate commercial interests. This requires, ultimately, a clause providing for a tribunal capable of imposing a final and binding decision that resolves the dispute.

16.1.3 There are many different forms of project and the project documentation will reflect the particular nature and commercial requirements of the project concerned. As a consequence, it might be appropriate simply to refer disputes immediately for resolution to the High Court in London which will give a binding decision. However, issues such as confidentiality which may be of particular interest to the parties, as is often the case with PFI projects, or the existence of an international element, might dictate that as an alternative to litigation in the High Court, the dispute resolution provision may refer the dispute to immediate arbitration which will also give a binding decision. On the other hand, the ongoing commercial relationship between the parties may suggest that a gradualist form of escalating dispute resolution procedure might assist to maintain good commercial and personal relations for the benefit of the project as a whole. The dispute resolution provision may provide for the dispute first to be referred to an informal form of dispute resolution and thereafter to escalate through subsequent stages to litigation or arbitration that will impose a binding decision resolving the dispute. This approach has found favour with parties in many PFI projects.

16.1.4 The approach to adopt when drafting a dispute resolution provision is decisively influenced by the nature of the project, the project documentation, whether the project is domestic or international in scope and whether statute imposes any obligations in relation to dispute resolution, such as the Housing Grants, Construction and Regeneration Act 1996. Therefore, when drafting a dispute resolution provision, the following issues must be considered:

- is the provision to include a gradualist/escalating process through various stages towards obtaining a binding decision?
- does the intervention of statute require consideration?
- does the form of dispute resolution procedure inspire confidence in the impartiality and quality of the tribunal to decide the dispute?
- does the provision achieve speed in resolving the dispute?
- is the procedure cost-effective?

Where a PFI project is performed overseas so that the project is international, additional issues will need to be addressed, such as the fact that the parties may well prefer to adopt international arbitration as a means of resolving disputes rather than to submit those disputes to the jurisdiction of local courts.[1]

16.1.5 Wherever a project involves an ongoing relationship between the parties, as is the case in PFI projects, there is much to be said for adopting a gradualist/escalating form of procedure which may commence by referring the dispute to a panel of individuals, sometimes referred to as a dispute review board. In the event that the dispute is not resolved at that level, it may then be referred to some form of alternative dispute resolution procedure, thereafter, perhaps, to adjudication, and then, only after failure of those stages, to arbitration or perhaps litigation, both of which will impose a binding decision on the parties resolving the dispute.

16.1.6 Many projects adopt this gradualist/escalating form of referral simply because it provides a means of resolving disputes at a lower, more relaxed level in the first instance, without the hostility often associated with the immediate issue of a writ in respect of a dispute which could be resolved at a commercial level. This form of procedure also provides flexibility to deal quickly and cheaply with disputes, in the first instance by those closest to the issues raised by the project and by suitably qualified personnel, and provides an opportunity to resolve disputes without having to proceed through the whole process to final arbitration or litigation in the High Court.

16.1.7 Use of the gradualist/escalating system of panel, alternative dispute resolution, perhaps adjudication and ultimately arbitration may require the parties to identify suitably qualified individuals to constitute the appropriate panel, or mediator in the alternative dispute resolution process, and even the arbitrator. There exists a large number of alternative dispute resolution and

---

1   See Chapter 18.

arbitration institutions available to assist in this process, or alternatively to act as appointing authorities to nominate suitable individuals where the parties agree.

16.1.8 The disadvantages of the gradualist approach is that it may take longer for a final resolution of the dispute to be achieved (if a dispute runs through several tiers of the resolution process before resolution is achieved). Accordingly, it is not uncommon to find provision made for a 'fast track' dispute resolution procedure which will be applied to the resolution of certain types of dispute within the project documents. Typically, this will be applied to minor disputes or to disputes where delay in the resolution would impede the project as a whole (for example, disputes over design matters in the construction period). It is to address this latter concern in the context of construction projects generally that the Housing Grants, Construction and Regeneration Act 1996 was passed.[1]

16.2 THE PANEL OR DISPUTE REVIEW BOARD

16.2.1 This first level of dispute resolution procedure may involve a dispute review board which may merely comprise a liaison panel to provide a mechanism where all matters relating to the project can be discussed between the parties with the intention of ensuring the successful and efficient operation of the project and avoidance of disputes. It acts as a means of identifying potential difficulties before they elevate into a dispute. There are many different forms of dispute review board, some of which are of a general nature and some of which are very specific and occasionally vested with considerable power to resolve disputes pending final resolution by arbitration or litigation.

16.3 ALTERNATIVE DISPUTE RESOLUTION

16.3.1 Alternative dispute resolution is generally understood as a dispute resolution procedure which has the potential to resolve a dispute without immediate recourse to the two main forms of dispute resolution, namely arbitration and litigation. Unlike arbitration and litigation, most forms of alternative dispute resolution will not necessarily lead to a decision resolving the dispute which is binding upon the parties. In alternative dispute resolution, no third party is vested with the power to impose a binding decision on the parties in dispute. The reason for this lies in the main purpose of alternative dispute resolution which is to create a forum where a 'neutral' seeks to facilitate a settlement. The 'neutral' does so by encouraging the parties in dispute to identify mutual interests which they are brought to recognise may form the basis of an agreed settlement.

16.3.2 The intention is to ensure the parties in dispute retain control of the dispute by dispensing with concepts of conflict and the complex procedures associated with arbitration and litigation. This is achieved in part by the fact that

---

1   See **7.6.38** and **16.6**.

in general the 'neutral's' role is not to make and impose a binding decision, but instead to create an environment in which the parties seek to achieve a settlement.

16.3.3 There are many different forms of alternative dispute resolution procedure. There is the 'executive tribunal', sometimes referred to as 'mini-trial', often involving a panel which consists of senior management representatives from each of the parties in dispute and a neutral third party chosen by the parties. Short presentations are made to senior management by way of direct presentation followed by negotiation, usually assisted by the neutral third party. 'Conciliation' involves the appointment by the parties of a neutral third party to act as conciliator to make suggestions to the parties as to what may constitute a reasonable settlement proposal on a fair assessment of the dispute. However, by far the most common form of alternative dispute resolution practised within the United Kingdom is 'mediation' where the parties appoint a neutral third-party mediator who will not seek to propose a solution but, having heard both parties together make their respective presentations, will meet each party individually in private in an attempt to facilitate a settlement.

16.3.4 The advantages of a successful alternative dispute resolution is the saving in costs, resulting in a speedy resolution of the dispute, preserving the commercial relationship between the parties within a private and confidential environment.

16.4 ARBITRATION

16.4.1 Neither the dispute review board panel nor alternative dispute resolution procedures fulfil the ultimate requirement of every dispute resolution clause, which is to provide for a tribunal with power to impose a binding and final decision upon the parties. Arbitration is designed to decide on the merits of the dispute and resolve the dispute by imposing such a binding decision on the parties and it is for that reason that the next stage in a gradualist/escalating form of dispute resolution provision is to refer the dispute to arbitration or to litigation.

16.4.2 All common law countries treat arbitration as part of private law created and largely regulated by an agreement between the parties to refer any dispute between them to a mutual third-party arbitrator for a decision. English legal principles have for a long period supported the concept of disputes being resolved outside the courts by a third party who is knowledgeable in the field in which the dispute has arisen. As a consequence, the third-party arbitrator is given power to make a binding decision between the parties in dispute. The courts encourage the parties' use of arbitration by assisting that process and by regulating that process so as to avoid abuse. As a result, the law of arbitration is concerned with the agreement to arbitrate and the relationship between the courts and the process of arbitration. In England the sources of the law of arbitration are found within the common law and the Arbitration Act 1996. The Arbitration Act 1996 grants the courts specific powers to require the parties to comply with an arbitration agreement and many procedural powers in support of an arbitration.

16.4.3 The general principles of the Arbitration Act 1996 are set out in s 1:

'The provisions of this Part are founded on the following principles, and shall be construed accordingly –

(a) the object of arbitration is to obtain the fair resolution of disputes by an impartial Tribunal without unnecessary delay or expense;
(b) the parties should be free to agree how their disputes are resolved, subject only to such safeguards as are necessary in the public interest;
(c) in matters governed by this Part the Court should not intervene except as provided by this Part.'

16.4.4 As will be apparent, arbitration and alternative dispute resolution are distinct concepts underpinned by their respective distinct legal principles. Alternative dispute resolution does not make a decision between the parties, it cannot generally bind the parties and need not be conducted according to any particular legal process: the parties are free to search for a compromise however they may choose and a mediator has no power to impose a decision. In contrast, an arbitrator is empowered to bind the parties and many arbitrations follow a generally accepted format, although the parties are free to agree a procedure in arbitration best suited to the resolution of the dispute.

16.4.5 The most crucial distinction between alternative dispute resolution and arbitration lies in the fact that arbitration is a process which will decide a dispute on the merits according to law and will therefore generally identify where the merits of the dispute lie with precision, unlike an alternative dispute resolution process where the sole object is to achieve a compromise of the dispute. It follows that there will be certain forms of dispute which can only be finally resolved by arbitration, being those forms of dispute where it is important to the parties to resolve the dispute with precision, for example a difference of view arising over the proper interpretation of the project documentation during the operating period where the consequences of such a decision will continue for many years.

16.5 EXPERT DETERMINATION

16.5.1 There are many projects where it may be appropriate to provide for the appointment of an expert to make decisions which are final and binding on the parties in respect of a particular category of dispute arising in a particularly complex or highly technical area such as the determination of the market value of the equity share capital of the project company.[1] The individual selected to act as expert is invariably one who is a recognised authority in the particular area of concern and the procedure may be by way of either written exchange of submissions alone or written submissions combined with oral presentations to the expert whose decision is generally made final and binding by the terms of the dispute resolution clause. The procedure to be adopted must be set out in the clause referring these disputes for expert resolution.

---

1   This is frequently one of the components in the calculation of the compensation payable to the project company in the event of awarding authority default.

16.6 ADJUDICATION

16.6.1 Statute has intervened by the Housing Grants, Construction and Regeneration Act 1996 (the 'Construction Act') to impose certain provisions in respect of agreements which fall within the definition of 'construction contracts' which means an agreement with a person for any of the following:

'(a) the carrying out of construction operations;
(b) arranging for the carrying out of construction operations by others, whether under sub-contract to him or otherwise;
(c) providing his own labour, or the labour of others, for the carrying out of construction operations.'[1]

16.6.2 Partly as a consequence of this definition and the definition of 'construction operations' in s 105 of the Construction Act,[2] it applies to a large number of agreements which might not in the first instance be thought of as 'construction contracts'. The Construction Contracts (England and Wales) Exclusion Order 1998, SI 1998/648, excludes certain agreements that would otherwise be 'construction contracts' for the purposes of the Construction Act and in particular:

> 'A Construction Contract is excluded from the operation of Part II if it is a Contract entered into under the Private Finance Initiative (within the meaning given).'

16.6.3 The Construction Contracts (England and Wales) Exclusion Order 1998 will exclude the operation of the Construction Act from the project agreement between the awarding authority and the project company, but will not apply so as to exclude the Construction Act in respect of other agreements entered into by the project company which fall within the definition of 'construction contracts'.

16.6.4 In summary, the Construction Act provides that 'construction contracts' between the project company and 'construction companies' must enable a party to give notice at any time of its intention to refer a dispute to adjudication, an adjudicator must be appointed within seven days of notice of the dispute and, generally, the adjudicator must reach a decision within 28 days of referral of the dispute. The decision of the adjudicator is binding upon the parties usually on an interim basis, and must be implemented immediately, although there is a right thereafter to refer the dispute either to arbitration or to the High Court for final determination.

16.6.5 The Construction Act merely provides the outline for the referral of disputes to adjudication and 'construction contracts' must provide a suitable procedure which complies with the basic framework set out in the Construction Act. Should the 'construction contract' fail to do so, then the parties are bound to comply with the adjudication provisions contained in the 'Scheme for Construction Contracts' implemented under the provisions of the Construction Act and

---

1 Housing Grants, Construction and Regeneration Act 1996, s 104(1). See generally, ibid, ss 104–107.
2 See also **7.6.38**.

which sets out detailed procedures for the appointment, replacement and decision-making process for the adjudication.

16.6.6 Each party to a 'construction contract' has a statutory right to refer disputes to adjudication which cannot be excluded or waived by contract and therefore every 'construction contract' must contemplate adjudication. Therefore, adjudication provisions must be inserted into these 'construction contracts' in a coherent fashion so as to operate within the procedure of the overall dispute resolution process. Because parties are entitled to refer disputes to adjudication 'at any time' difficult situations may arise where parties to a 'construction contract' first seek to refer disputes to a dispute review board and thereafter to alternative dispute resolution procedures, since the adjudication process may be commenced at any time and may disrupt these other processes designed to resolve the dispute amicably.

16.6.7 Certainly one of the most important issues is the speed with which the adjudication process must conclude and the consequences such decisions may have in the context of the project as a whole, particularly during the construction phase. The potential difficulty arises where an adjudicator speedily makes a decision of a technical nature (for example, concerning the quality of structural foundations) which allows the construction process for the project to proceed, but which is found to be in error by subsequent arbitration or litigation, thereby prejudicing the success of the project.

16.7 JOINDER OF PARTIES

16.7.1 Any PFI project will involve a large number of organisations including the awarding authority, the project company, the funders, the construction company, the operating company, suppliers and sub-contractors and many more. As a result, there are a large number of separate contracts any one or more of which has the capability of impinging upon the proper discharge of another contract. There will always be a large number of interlocking contractual obligations involving a number of different parties, each of whom must satisfactorily perform its own respective contractual obligations so as to secure the success of the project. In these circumstances, it is often the prudent course to include a joinder provision in the dispute resolution process requiring any dispute between two of the parties to be referred for a decision to the same tribunal that decides a linking dispute between one of those parties and a third party. For this to be achieved, there must be a joinder provision written into the appropriate contracts referring all linking disputes to the same dispute resolution process.

16.7.2 The concept of joinder avoids duplication of parallel claims before different tribunals with the possible adverse consequence of inconsistent findings of fact and law. However, unlike a dispute resolution provision which refers all disputes to litigation in the High Court, only the persons who are parties to the contract are the persons who are bound by the dispute resolution process of the dispute review board panel, alternative dispute resolution and arbitration, and only their rights and obligations are in issue and only they are bound by the decision: that is why joinder must be dealt with expressly as a contractual term.

16.8 CONCLUSION

16.8.1 A dispute resolution provision is like any other contractual term and must satisfy the usual rules relating to contract. In the context of a domestic PFI project, the drivers that will govern the choice of procedure are likely to be the need for the relatively large numbers of minor disputes that may arise in the course of the project to be settled in a swift and cost-effective manner, and concerns of confidentiality.

16.8.2 When considering a dispute resolution clause in the international context, a number of additional legal issues arise. The express proper law of the contract will govern the underlying contract in which the dispute resolution provision exists, but there will also be a law which governs the agreement to submit disputes to arbitration (if applicable) which is usually, but not always, the same as the law governing the underlying contract, and there will also be the procedural law governing the conduct of the arbitration which will be mainly governed by the law of the place where the arbitration occurs.

Chapter 17

ACCOUNTING FOR PFI TRANSACTIONS

17.1 INTRODUCTION

17.1.1 Rarely has there been so much confusion and concern as to how transactions should be accounted for as in the case of PFI contracts. This chapter sets out the background to the debate, focusing on the key accounting question 'Should the transaction be accounted for on the balance sheet of the *public sector*?' It is this issue which has dogged the progress of many PFI projects over the last few years, and which only recently has been tackled seriously. The current position is summarised, with some observations as to how the final stages of the debate might move forward to resolution. The most significant consequence of the accounting consideration is not so much how the item should be disclosed or quantified (if the transaction is 'on balance sheet'), but whether it should be accounted for 'on balance sheet' at all. This chapter therefore only deals with matters relevant to this decision; accounting disclosure matters are not covered.

17.2 WHY ACCOUNTING TREATMENT IS IMPORTANT

17.2.1 Central government departments do not presently produce commercial style accounts, which begs the question why accounting treatment of PFI projects is at all relevant to the public sector. The matter comes down to approval by the Treasury, and the requirement for approval that PFI schemes should be accounted for 'off balance sheet' (that is, were the projects to be accounted for on a commercial basis, payments under the project agreement would be shown as revenue charges in the year to which they relate, rather than as an asset, and a corresponding liability, being accounted for when the project is entered into).

17.2.2 Failure to meet this requirement would mean that the awarding authority concerned would be required to provide out of its annual expenditure budgets, for the *entire value of the capital asset involved in the project*, most probably during the first year or so of the contract. In most cases, this amount would be well beyond the available resources of the awarding authority in these early years. The consequence, in all likelihood, is that the project would not go forward.

17.2.3 This requirement is not unique to PFI transactions; similar conditions apply to government departments entering finance leases. These types of transactions are viewed as poor value for money, as they involve little, if any, risk transfer greater than government borrowing, but at a higher cost. This concern extends to PFI transactions; because they can take many forms, there is a risk that, if poorly defined or negotiated, they might in effect be little more than finance leases. Consequently, the relevance of the accounting test is not whether the transaction is *de facto* borrowing, but whether it represents good value for money.

17.2.4 The Treasury recognises that an accounting test is not designed primarily as a measure of value for money, and that 'good' PFI transactions (that is, those offering value for money and other benefits) might be accounted for 'on balance sheet'. For this reason, HM Treasury is willing to make exceptions to the rule. Nevertheless, there is a presumption that 'off balance sheet' means good value for money and vice versa. To avoid the difficulty of proving otherwise, it is the aim of the awarding authority in every PFI project to structure and negotiate the deal so that it is off balance sheet.

17.3 THE ACCOUNTING CONTEXT

17.3.1 As noted above, the critical accounting question from the awarding authority's standpoint is whether the PFI transaction is off balance sheet. Similar considerations have been the focus of accounting debate in the private sector ever since financing structures more sophisticated than simple corporate borrowing became commonplace. The growth of the finance leasing industry in the 1970s eventually gave rise to the accounting standard SSAP 21, issued in 1984 after long debate. This standard was written very much with traditional finance leases and similar forms of financing transactions in mind, and lays down prescriptive rules as to how such transactions should be analysed to determine accounting treatment.

17.3.2 A 'line in the sand' quantitative test, such as in SSAP 21, whilst having the advantages of being objective and relatively simple to determine, becomes an obvious target to beat. After SSAP 21, the leasing industry developed ever more sophisticated off balance sheet financing schemes which, arguably, were borrowing in substance, but which technically did not require to be accounted for as finance leases.

17.3.3 The Accounting Standards Board ('ASB') responded in 1994 with the issue of *FRS 5: Reporting the Substance of Transactions* ('FRS 5'). FRS 5 differs from SSAP 21 in two fundamentally important aspects:

- the reporting standard offers a broad conceptual framework applicable to most types of transactions; and
- emphasis is placed on determination through professional judgement, based on the balance of evidence available, not prescriptive tests.

The aim of FRS 5 is to avoid abuse of the spirit of accounting standards such as SSAP 21, not least by making the 'target to beat' less certain.

17.3.4 Both SSAP 21 and FRS 5 were developed before PFI transactions became commonplace. Neither offers specific guidance on the complexities involved in such schemes, such as novel payment mechanisms for performance and availability, or project financing issues. Efforts to interpret the standards have challenged accountants leading to many different approaches. The inevitable consequence has been delay and confusion.

17.3.5 Faced with a growing appreciation of this difficulty, the ASB published an Application Note, *Amendment to FRS 5 'Reporting the Substance of Transactions': The Private Finance Initiative and similar contracts* (the 'Application Note') in September 1998, interpreting the general principles of FRS 5 in the context of PFI transactions, and proposing how the public sector should account for them. The approach suggested is described at **17.5**.

17.4 TREASURY GUIDANCE

17.4.1 In the early days of PFI, the accounting test was addressed relatively informally, often based on in-house accounting advice available to spending departments and HM Treasury. When the flow of projects started to increase, more robust tests were required, typically requiring comfort from the awarding authority's auditor (generally, either the National Audit Office, the District Auditor or a professional firm). At this stage, the potential for inconsistency in the absence of guidance became clear, culminating in late 1997 with the Treasury producing its own guidance on the interpretation of FRS 5 to accounting for PFI transactions ('Treasury Guidance').[1]

17.4.2 Whilst based on the principles contained in FRS 5, the Treasury Guidance was developed from existing precedent at the time, and attempted to produce as focused a framework as possible whilst at the same time being generally applicable to a wide range of PFI projects. The principal test that the Treasury Guidance applies is the impact of variability of net revenue on equity return to the private sector, one measure of risk indicative of future economic benefits which FRS 5 associates with recognition of an asset.

17.4.3 How the Treasury Guidance can be applied in detail is described at **17.6**.

17.5 THE APPLICATION NOTE APPROACH

17.5.1 Two fundamental concepts upon which the FRS 5 framework is based are:

– an asset is defined as the '… rights or other access to future economic benefits controlled by an entity as a result of past transactions or events …'.[2] This goes much deeper than most accounting definitions; not only would assets generally recognised as fixed and monetary assets be included, but assets dedicated to the provision of long-term service contracts or supply commitments, such as outsourcing arrangements or power purchase agreements could also be caught;

---

1   Technical Note No 1 *How to Account for PFI Transactions* (Treasury Taskforce) September 1997.
2   FRS 5, paragraph 2.

- FRS 5 states that '... Evidence that an entity has rights or other access to benefits (and hence has an asset) is given if the entity is exposed to the risks inherent in the benefits, taking account of the likelihood of those risks having a commercial effect in practice ...'.[1]

17.5.2 According to FRS 5 therefore, the existence of an asset is closely linked to the exposure of economic benefits to risk and the genuine likelihood of occurrence of that risk. Further guidance is included in FRS 5 which emphasises the need fully to understand the commercial effect of the arrangements in reaching an accounting decision.

17.5.3 Commercial transactions are often complex and may not be discretely 'packaged'; the totality of the transaction needs to be examined in order to make a properly informed judgement as to its accounting treatment. Paragraph 47 of FRS 5 explicitly recognises that:

- legal title may not be indicative of accounting treatment, where the rights or other access to the principal future economic benefits are separated from legal ownership;[2] and
- transactions may need to be linked with others and considered as a whole in order for the overall commercial effect to be understood.[3]

Paragraph 51 provides further guidance to considering the totality of a series of transactions recognising that if a transaction appears to lack commercial logic, this could be indicative that not all related parts of the transaction have been identified or properly considered.

17.5.4 The emphasis on commercial effect is taken further in paragraph 52 where motives and expectations, together with the expected returns, are regarded as important evidence as to where risks and economic benefits (and hence assets) lie. In applying these principles to PFI transactions, the Application Note emphasises the following:

- the genuine commercial nature of the transaction is exposed through considering which, if any, elements of the PFI arrangements are separable, and hence should be considered independently from an accounting standpoint; and
- for each non-separable element, those risks that are germane to the accounting treatment, and the extent to which they evidence the existence of an asset or otherwise, should form the basis of the accounting decision. Judgement plays a large part in this process.

17.5.5 Paragraph F10 of the Application Note states that a contract may be separable where in the following circumstances:

- an element of a payment stream varies according to the availability of the property itself and another element varies according to usage or performance of certain services;

---

1 FRS 5 paragraph 17.
2 FRS 5, paragraph 47(b).
3 FRS 5, paragraph 47(c).

- different parts of the contract run for different periods or can be terminated separately;
- different parts of the contract can be renegotiated separately.

'Separability' is evidenced by any of these circumstances, but it is not limited to them. In addition, how separable elements of the contract and associated payments are precisely identified is not dealt with in any detail.

17.5.6 To the extent that a separated element is, in substance, no more than a stand-alone lease, the Application Note requires that the accounting treatment should be determined by applying SSAP 21, as these payments are akin to a lease.[1] Where a lease may be an element of a larger arrangement, the principles of FRS 5 as set out in the Application Note should be applied to the overall scheme. As discussed earlier, this will depend principally on 'access to benefits', evidenced by exposure to risk, measured by which party bears variations in profits or losses.[2]

17.5.7 The Application Note makes a clear distinction as to which risks (and hence variations in profits and losses) are relevant. The key requirement is that they must flow from features of the property. To the extent that profit variations relate purely to a service, such as deductions for sub-standard performance in catering, then these variations would not be considered relevant.[3] The principal risk factors that could be relevant, are:[4]

- demand risk;
- third-party revenues;
- variations arising from poor performance or non-availability;
- changes in relevant operating costs;
- who determines the nature of the property;
- obsolescence and effects of changes in technology; and
- arrangements at the end of the project and residual value risk.

Paragraph F21 of the Application Note proposes that the relevance and scale of each of these risks be considered, and weighted according to its likely commercial effect overall on the transaction.

17.5.8 Following the principle outlined earlier, paragraph F50 also suggests that the underlying motives of each party to the transaction be considered as further evidence of the genuine commercial nature of the transaction.

17.5.9 The likely factors under each of the categories listed above which give rise to variations in revenue and costs are presumed to be largely self-explanatory; the Application Note covers these in some detail in paragraphs F24 to F80. Of particular note, however, is the relevance of 'determining the nature of the asset' covered in paragraphs F35 to F37. The Application Note here embraces the concept that genuine PFI projects are truly output driven. The private sector should have substantial, if not complete, freedom to decide how the property should be built and maintained, and assume the cost risks of these decisions over

---

1　See Application Note, paragraphs F11 and F12.
2　See Application Note, paragraph F19.
3　See Application Note, paragraphs F17 and F20.
4　See Application Note, paragraph F22.

the life of the project. However, the Application Note only recognises certain consequences of these decisions; construction risk is differentiated from design risk (and subsequent operating risk) and is explicitly excluded from the analysis as it '... normally has no impact during the property's operational life ...'.[1] This is highly questionable in the context of many PFI transactions and this and other difficulties in the practical application of this guidance are discussed at **17.7**.

17.5.10 Once relevant risks have been identified, weighted and evaluated, the Application Note proposes that the property should be recognised by the party that bears the greater proportion of these risks. This concept recognises that many relevant risks will not lie wholly with one party or the other and so an overall view can only be reached by looking at where the majority of relevant, property related risks lie.

17.5.11 The Application Note clearly shows how the principles of FRS 5 support the approach proposed. As explained earlier,[2] FRS 5 provides a framework within which professional judgement can be exercised; the same applies for the Application Note. The benefit is that judgment can be applied flexibly to ensure that the spirit of FRS 5 is met at all times; the inevitable compromise, however, is that predictability and consistency may be lost. Within the wide commercial context that FRS 5 is intended to apply, this compromise is probably acceptable, but consistency of treatment is essential for the accounting test of PFI transactions. By way of contrast, the Treasury Guidance, whilst based on FRS 5 principles, was developed to provide as objective as possible an approach to accounting for PFI transactions.

17.6 THE TREASURY GUIDANCE APPROACH

17.6.1 As with the Application Note, the Treasury Guidance recognises that, in substance, a PFI arrangement may be more than one transaction and a 'separability test' should be applied. However, although the criteria for separability appear similar at first glance, the test differs significantly in how the conditions apply. In the Treasury Guidance, elements of the contract should be treated separately *only* where:

- the service payment is separable, such that elements of the service payment operate independently from each other *and* the cost of different elements of the service or the underlying asset can be identified; *and*
- the contract is separable such that separate elements of the contract run for different periods or can be terminated/renegotiated.

This is very different in effect to the test proposed in the Application Note even though the conditions tested look superficially similar. The consequences of this difference are discussed in more detail at **17.7.2**.

17.6.2 Not featured in the Application Note are *de minimis* thresholds which the Treasury Guidance has established on grounds of practicality. Where the

---

1 See Application Note, paragraph F37.
2 See **17.3.3**.

initial capital cost of the asset forming part of the PFI arrangements (or the separated element) is either less than 10% or more than 90%, the component should be treated respectively as either a contract for services, or be subject to analysis according to SSAP 21. No further risk-based analysis is proposed in either situation. For all other transactions (or separable elements) falling between the *de minimis* thresholds, the Treasury Guidance then describes two further steps to be followed sequentially:

- analysis of key risks in the transaction; *then*
- assessing if the risk analysis is consistent with other supporting evidence.

17.6.3 Distinct from the Application Note, the Treasury Guidance requires that relevant risks to the accounting treatment should not only be identified, but that their combined potential financial effect on the project should be considered. The risks to be considered are broadly similar to those set out in the Application Note, and are listed in paragraphs 15 and 16 of the Treasury Guidance. They include:

- demand risk;
- availability and performance risk;
- pricing risk (that is, the extent to which payments for the PFI service vary from the underlying costs incurred in delivering the service);
- residual value risk;
- operating cost risk (that is, the extent to which major changes in the operating cost base can change over time, affecting the return to the project); and
- design risk, equivalent to the Exposure Draft[1] condition regarding which entity dictates the nature of the asset.

In common with the Application Note, 'pure' construction risk is not considered relevant.[2]

17.6.4 The Treasury Guidance then proposes measurement of the combined impact of the financial risks by reference to the likely effect on *equity return* to the project. What constitutes 'equity' is outlined in paragraph 28 (although this analysis overlooks the consequence on the capital structure of a project where risk is substantially passed on to sub-contractors, thereby exposing sub-contractor equity to risks of the project, but not necessarily evident from the capital structure of the project company itself).

17.6.5 The Treasury Guidance also recognises that transfer of real commercial risk by definition will result in uncertainty of outcome and looks for evidence of risk in the *range of likely outcomes* (or 'spread', as described in the Treasury Guidance), and the extent to which the 'worst case' results in equity return being less than 'lender's return' (defined by reference to the awarding authority's marginal cost of borrowing). The Treasury Guidance suggests that 'worst case' be taken as the 5 percentile downside point on the distribution of possible

---

1   An earlier version of the Application Note was published in draft in December 1997 as an Exposure Draft for public consultation.
2   Treasury Guidance, paragraph 26.

outcomes for equity return. Should the 'spread' be sufficiently wide, and 'worst case' equity return meet or fall short of 'lender's return', then the transaction is considered, prima facie, 'off balance sheet'. Determining sufficiency of risk transfer by reference to the potential variation in equity return provides some form of objective measure which, in theory, should apply to most, if not all, types of PFI transactions. In this respect, the Treasury Guidance goes further than the Application Note in setting out a determinable method for the accounting test, although it is recognised that professional judgement still plays an important part, particularly as any quantitative analysis dealing with evaluation of risk relies heavily on assumptions and data derived from the effect of similar risks in other transactions. There is also a divergence in approach between the ASB and the Treasury. The Treasury Guidance looks only to the question of risk assumed by the private sector as the basis for the accounting determination. As noted earlier, the Application Note requires the level of risk attributable to both the public and the private sector to be considered.[1]

17.6.6 The next step in the Treasury Guidance is a 'sense check' on the outcome of the analysis described above, recognising that mechanical analysis alone cannot always be relied upon to provide the right answer. However, there is a presumption that the quantification of risk transfer will provide a robust basis for the decision; only if the answer is inconsistent with supporting evidence is further investigation proposed. Factors which the Treasury Guidance suggests should be considered at this stage include:

- the intention of the awarding authority (that is, whether the real underlying purpose is to acquire an asset, or to acquire an infrastructure or accommodation service);
- the intention of the operator (that is, whether the real underlying purpose is to provide a long-term service or just to build an asset);
- the nature of funding: highly geared projects are seen as indicative of low risk transfer (although this conclusion can be misleading if consideration is not given to the level of risk transferred on to sub-contractors or covered by insurance);[2]
- the extent of control of the awarding authority over the asset: how it is designed and built, how it can be used and so on;
- the consequences of change: does the cost consequence always flow through to the awarding authority or not; and
- the consequences of termination of the contract and events of default: how much risk is genuinely taken by the operator and its funders in these circumstances.

17.6.7 This stage requires qualitative consideration of certain risk factors already subject to quantitative analysis in the previous stage, and also covers factors which are not easily evaluated in a quantitative manner, for example, aspects such as control over the nature and purpose of the asset. Only if supporting evidence strongly contradicts the conclusion reached through the quantitative analysis is any further action proposed. This takes the form of

---

1 See **17.5.9**.
2 See **17.6.4**.

'further investigation' (to resolve the contradiction); it does not necessarily mean reversing the accounting decision.

17.7 DIFFERENCES AND SIMILARITIES

17.7.1 There are therefore, at present, two streams of advice on accounting for PFI contracts. Before considering which one applies in any particular situation, it is worth considering whether it matters: will there be any real difference in the outcome if one approach is taken rather than the other? To a large degree, the Application Note and the Treasury Guidance cover common ground. They both consider, by and large, that the same risks count (although the Application Note explicitly dismisses cost and revenue variation not attributable to the property).[1] The FRS 5 principles of considering the totality of the arrangements in context and weighting risks according to the likelihood of their occurrence and impact is common to both approaches.

17.7.2 There are, however, a small number of fundamental differences which in practice will lead to different results possibly for a wide range of PFI schemes. First is the approach taken to 'separating' the arrangements. The Treasury Guidance presumes PFI contracts are integral and requires several conditions to be demonstrated before the contract can be separated. Not only must different parts of the contract be capable of termination or renegotiation at different times, but the payments must be explicitly separable and matched to underlying costs. The Application Note sets out three circumstances giving rise to separability[2] and also a more general condition that separability will apply where elements of the payment operate independently of each other,[3] any of which, in theory, could lead to the contract being separated. As described earlier, there is also a difference in view as to which elements of risk are relevant to the analysis; the Application Note allows only variations arising from features of the property, the Treasury Guidance makes no distinction. Finally, the approach to evaluating risk in order to reach a view on where the property asset should be recognised is different: the Treasury Guidance takes a detailed quantitative approach which considers the impact on private sector returns, the Application Note requires an evaluation and comparison of the relevant risks affecting both parties but offers no detailed guidance on the method of evaluation.

17.7.3 The differences are not academic. Take, for example, the separability conditions. A common feature of PFI schemes is to allow certain parts of the contract to be repriced periodically, by requiring that the project company market test or benchmark sub-contracts for certain parts of the service. The purpose of this mechanism is not to pull the contract apart at the earliest opportunity, but to secure value for money over time for aspects of the service where the private sector is not offering good value for money through long-term fixed prices. The obligations of the service provider in the prime contract do not change, even if a sub-contractor is replaced; all that changes is price. Transfer of

---

1   See **17.5.7**.
2   Application Note, paragraph F10 and **17.5.5**.
3   See Application Note, paragraph F6.

long-term pricing risk is therefore limited, but only where it fails to offer demonstrable value for money at the outset. Apply the Treasury Guidance, and this mechanism, of itself, will not lead to separation of the contract for accounting purposes (nor should it, if the overall contractual obligation of the service provider to the public sector entity does not change). Apply the Application Note, and the answer is less clear. As there is no clear guidance as to how to separate a contract under these conditions (there may be no obvious split in the payment stream which can be identified with costs), the consequence of separation under such circumstances could lead to a wide range of accounting decisions, varying from 'off balance sheet' to capitalisation of 'property assets' of widely differing values.

17.7.4 The consequence of this particular example highlights the real problem of inconsistency of outcome between the two approaches. But does *either* the Treasury Guidance *or* the Application Note consistently lead to the 'right' answer (where 'right' means that PFI transactions which offer demonstrably good value for money and appropriate risk transfer will end up passing the accounting test)? The answer is that both are deficient to some degree.

Achieving consistency

17.7.5 The Application Note sets out a framework, but no detailed guidance on method. There is still too much room for judgment to lead to quite different accounting conclusions for the same transaction. This arises in particular from treatment of demand and residual value risk; the Application Note places emphasis on these two aspects above all else, certainly in terms of pages devoted to their description. Yet, for many PFI schemes, the economic significance of these two risks is much less than for other relevant risks. The balance of risk, and hence the accounting decision, could very easily turn on the qualitative views of the person interpreting the guidance, just the situation that guidance on PFI accounting needs to avoid.

17.7.6 The Treasury Guidance at least has the benefit of a clear method which forces a judgment to be made by reference to a quantitative test. But the 'equity return' measure is itself an arbitrary test. As noted earlier, equity explicitly contributed to a project is not necessarily an accurate basis for quantifying risk transferred in a PFI scheme.[1] Equity, and its likely range of variation in return, needs to be considered in the context of how much 'equity risk' has been assumed by sub-contractors, for example, through providing extensive liquidated damages and/or underwriting their obligations through performance bonds, performance guarantees and so on. In addition, the range of likely return is likely to increase as a consequence of higher project gearing, even though this may mean no overall change in the risk being assumed in the project company. There is a growing voice arguing that, whilst a well developed quantitative method is a helpful tool for the accounting determination, *project return* (rather than equity return), and its likely range of variation, is likely to be a more consistent approach. In any event, this approach does not fit easily with the

---

1   See **17.6.4**.

requirement in the Application Note for both public and private sector risks to be considered.

Exclusion of construction risk

17.7.7 Both sources disregard construction risk from the accounting analysis, and yet recognise both design and operation risks as relevant. The Application Note argues that construction risk should be ignored as it has no effect on the ongoing operation of the asset/service. This appears to deny the underlying economic rationale of the PFI; that focusing responsibility for all aspects of the delivery of an 'infrastructure service', from design, through construction, to operation will deliver innovation in all aspects of the process, resulting in lower overall costs of the delivery of the service over the life of the project.

17.7.8 This process has been shown very clearly to deliver value for money, with the private sector considering the overall risk profile of the project in order to determine lowest cost. The potential service provider does not specifically 'ring-fence' construction; it is just one of the many risks that have to be optimised in aggregate. This begs the question, if the underlying commercial approach adopted in the formulation of a PFI project is the substance of the transaction, why is construction risk ignored arbitrarily in the analysis?

17.7.9 This might be less of a concern if consistency could be assured even if construction risk is ignored. However, the consequence of innovation is often very different risk profiles, some with much higher construction risk than others, but all delivering much the same outputs over the life of a project. The classic example of such polarisation is the choice between high quality initial build cost, linked with low cost operation and maintenance, and lower quality build with higher subsequent costs. It is illogical, and very dangerous to the development of the PFI, that certain approaches to delivery of a PFI project deriving from genuine innovation, may fall foul of the accounting test because of an arbitrary exclusion of risks.

Presumptions about 'service performance' failures

17.7.10 The Application Note requires that variations in payments '... for reasons that clearly relate purely to a service...' should be regarded separately, even though they may give rise to a significant loss. This view seems to presume that there will always be a match between the consequences of a service performance failure and the underlying costs of providing that service, for example, reductions for poor catering services will flow through as lower costs for the provision of catering.

17.7.11 There is no reason why this should be the case. A major move forward in PFI has been to link reductions, as far as possible, to the loss of benefit to the public sector, and not be directly concerned about the effect on the underlying cost base of the project company and its sub-contractors. Major reductions in charges are negotiated successfully in PFI projects for facilities not being available for many reasons, some of which could be failure to clean to an acceptable standard, or failure to deliver a catering service. In such cases, because the facilities cannot be used, the level of reduction will be significant, nearly always much more than the cost of simply providing the cleaning or catering service. Because there is no 'ring fencing' of reductions of charges to underlying costs in many PFI schemes, it is inappropriate, and arbitrary, to attempt to separate out certain reductions and associate them with particular costs; this will quite possibly understate the genuine impact of these reductions on other parts of the revenue stream.

17.7.12   There is, of course, no reason why the accounting test should always identify 'good' PFI schemes. The ASB's aim has been to interpret FRS 5 for these types of transaction purely from an accounting perspective; there is no belief on its part that off balance sheet treatment necessarily corresponds with better value for money. However, for the purpose they need to serve, both the Application Note and the Treasury Guidance only have any value for the public sector if they facilitate a properly informed analysis of complex PFI transactions and achieve, as far as possible, consistency in accounting treatment. The Treasury Guidance, whilst not perfect, provides a more focused approach and a detailed method, with the likelihood of more predictable results.

17.8 THE FUTURE

17.8.1   The Treasury Guidance has been in place since late 1997 and, by and large, has proved to be workable. The Treasury is aware of its deficiencies, some of which have been pointed out in this chapter, and has committed to refining the guidance in light of the developing body of precedent. The Application Note was only published in Autumn 1998 and hence contradictions between the ASB's interpretation of FRS 5 and that of the Treasury have only recently become apparent. That said, the Treasury is keen to refine its approach in a way that accords with the Application Note and is endeavouring to issue revised guidance in early 1999. Until then, for projects advanced to Best and Final Offer stage, the existing Treasury Guidance continues to apply.

17.8.2   It remains to be seen how the Treasury will interpret the Application Note, particularly given the clear differences that exist between its preferred approach and that of the ASB. The Treasury Guidance, with its emphasis on a detailed methodology could complement the higher level approach set out in the Application Note, but only if the differences can be satisfactorily reconciled.

17.8.3   The Treasury still has options open to it even if the difference in approach remains. There is no obligation on central government to follow commercial accounting practice, although the recent thrust has been to take the public sector in this direction and pressure to do so will increase with the introduction of Resource Accounting and Budgeting for central government departments, in the near future. To account on a different, arguably more lenient, basis ignoring accounting guidance put forward by the ASB would undoubtedly be embarrassing for both sides, but is not impossible. An alternative would be for the Treasury to decouple the approval test, which could continue to be based on its own guidance, from the accounting decision, which could follow the amended

FRS 5. After all, the approval test's primary purpose is to discriminate between 'good' and 'bad' PFI schemes, based on risk transfer and value for money; accounting treatment is only the means to the end. However, were this course of action to be taken, another problem surfaces; what are the public expenditure consequences for 'good' schemes which are 'on balance sheet'? If money needs to be provided up front to meet the underlying capital cost of the project, there is neither an incentive nor, probably, the funds, to allow more than the occasional PFI scheme to proceed whatever the potential benefits of the project. And if this control on public expenditure does not apply, what could be put in its place?

17.8.4 Most likely, the Treasury will find a way of reconciling the Application Note and its revised guidance with the Application Note. If this happens, there is an understandable concern that PFI schemes will have to be structured, or restructured, in a way that attempts to transfer unacceptable levels of risk to the private sector. There are some encouraging signs that this need not be the case:

- payment mechanisms are now being developed, which transfer acceptable levels of risk to the private sector, and which will not fall foul of the separability conditions in the Application Note;
- for many PFI schemes, the key relevant risks which are not transferred to the private sector relate to demand and residual value. For a well planned, long-term PFI scheme the economic impact of such risks will often be minimal, as their incidence is unlikely to arise for many years into the future; and
- close scrutiny of well structured PFI schemes, where full responsibility for the cost of ongoing services, maintenance and asset replacement is integrally linked to the design approach taken, shows that a wide and disparate range of variations in profits and losses will arise as 'features of the property'

Above all, there is a clear understanding in the Treasury of which conditions and allocation of risk give rise to PFI schemes that are deliverable and offer value for money. The current Treasury Guidance was developed with the clear aim of allowing 'good' PFI schemes to pass the test and, in most instances, this has proved to be the case. There is every reason to believe that this remains the utmost priority in developing the Treasury's revised guidance.

Chapter 18

THE FUTURE PROSPECTS FOR THE PRIVATE FINANCE INITIATIVE

18.1 INTRODUCTION

Since its launch in 1992, the PFI has been in a state of constant development and evolution. A creation of the Conservative Government, it has survived and been renewed and reinvigorated by the Labour Government elected in 1997. As discussed in Chapter 1,[1] the Bates Review in 1997 proposed various recommendations for breathing new life into the PFI and its processes. Those recommendations were accepted by the Labour Government and have in the main been implemented. This chapter looks at future developments in the PFI both domestically and internationally.

18.2 PUBLIC/PRIVATE PARTNERSHIPS

18.2.1 While endorsing the PFI enthusiastically, the Labour Government has been careful in its choice of words. The Bates Review makes it clear that, when handled properly, the PFI can work as one method of conducting successful public/private partnerships. This was reinforced by the Chancellor of the Exchequer, Gordon Brown in his foreword to the Treasury Taskforce publication *Partnerships for Prosperity* where he stated:

> 'We are keen to see the Private Finance Initiative and other public/private partnerships succeed in delivering the necessary investment the country needs on terms it can afford.'

18.2.2 What other forms of public/private partnership does the government have in mind? At present, there are no signals suggesting any particular preferred variant to the PFI being established. In early 1998, it was announced that private sector involvement in London Underground would be taken forward. The structure proposed is for separate concessions for the provision and maintenance of track, signalling and other infrastructure and rolling stock. The operation of the Tube will, however, remain in the public sector. The focus is on achieving investment while at the same time recognising a requirement (albeit a political one) to maintain public sector involvement. The provider/purchaser relationship is still there but, in addition, a separate role exists in the enterprise for the public sector.

18.2.3 However, the same issues will arise in relation to London Underground as in any PFI project. The private sector investment must be paid for, it must deliver value for money, it must be off balance sheet for the public sector and

---

1   See **1.3.17–1.3.36**.

consequently, there must be risk transfer. By creating separate private sector concessions and retaining a key function within the public sector, the allocation of risk among the relevant 'partners' will be the subject of long and complex negotiations, particularly the basis upon which the interface risk between the partners is to be apportioned.

18.2.4 The approach to investment in the London Underground reflects a desire within the Labour Government to utilise the skills of the private sector, subject to certain politically driven limitations. This is no different to the approach adopted by the Conservative Government in its application of the PFI to the NHS. In the early formulation of schemes in the NHS, much debate took place over the extent to which the services to be provided under a PFI scheme should include clinical services or those on the borderline (such as pathology). It was eventually decided that no clinical services should form part of the range of PFI services.

18.2.5 The Channel Tunnel Rail Link, a flagship PFI transaction promoted by the Conservative Government, hit funding problems and, early in 1998, the Labour Government was asked to increase its subsidy to the project. The Deputy Prime Minister, John Prescott, refused to agree to the increase and a revised plan was proposed. The approach being adopted by government in relation to this project is instructive. The centre piece of the revised financial proposal is a £3.8bn bond issue which the government has agreed to guarantee. By so doing the cost of capital for the project has been significantly reduced, which in turn has reduced the level of additional subsidy required. On the face of it, this appears to offend against one of the basic tenets of the PFI, that the financing should be off balance sheet for the government. The generally accepted convention is that such a guarantee by government would have to score against the public sector borrowing requirement. However, in this case as the risk of default is assessed at less than 20% there is no such requirement. In return for the guarantee the government is entitled to a share of future profits and a stake in Eurostar the company which was originally transferred from public sector ownership to the private sector promoter of the project.

18.2.6 Although these arrangements are driven by the particular circumstances in which the project found itself and the inclusion of a government guarantee is viewed as a 'one off', they do display an approach which focuses the participation of government on sharing in certain risks in return for a share of future rewards. This participative approach is in marked contrast to the injection of public money in projects by way of capital grant[1] where there is no return on the investment should the project prove to be successful.[2] In the same way that the transfer of risk to the private sector under a PFI transaction has a price, so the assumption of risk by the public sector in this situation has its price. The desire for the public sector to receive a return for its contribution to the project may have wider application in PFI transactions in future.

---

1   For example, grants under the Transport Act 1968, s 56.
2   As the decision to make the grant will presumably be predicated upon a successful project, it seems logical that the government should extract a future return.

18.3 REFINANCING OF PROJECTS

18.3.1 As discussed in Chapter 1,[1] the early PFI transactions may well have delivered sub-optimal solutions either because of a lack of risk transfer or because of the premium attaching to the risks transferred (reflecting the unfamiliarity of the private sector with the risks in question). As PFI transactions develop the premium attaching to certain risks ought to reduce and thus the price payable by the awarding authority should also reduce. This has already resulted in a reduction in bank margins on NHS PFI financings. Once PFI transactions have successfully completed the testing and construction phase, a large risk element will have been removed but one which was reflected in the original pricing of the transaction including, in particular, the cost of raising finance. It is therefore highly likely that PFI projects will be refinanced to obtain cheaper funding, reflecting the reduced risk profile once the project has successfully entered the operating phase. Without any repricing of the payment stream from the awarding authority this has the effect of creating incremental profitability in which the awarding authority does not share. There has been an increasing focus on the extent to which the public sector should share in any refinancing gains.

18.3.2 A variety of methods have been proposed as a basis for sharing, such as allowing the awarding authority to share in the upside once the rate of return to the private sector from the project reaches a pre-determined level (calculated by reference to an agreed set of assumptions) or applying a ceiling to the private sector's rate of return in order to avoid excessive super profits. The extent to which government should share in the successful execution of a project is bound to be a contentious and complex issue. Why, for example, should the awarding authority share in any upside if it is not also sharing in the downside risk? Equally, however, the hindsight of the National Audit Office and the Public Accounts Committee cannot lightly be ignored. Much will depend upon the extent to which the negotiation of the initial risk allocation and pricing is regarded by the awarding authority as being robust and offering best value for money.[2]

18.4 THE PFI PROCESS

18.4.1 Much focus continues to fall on the extent to which the PFI process can be speeded up. As discussed in Chapter 1, the Bates Review recommended the standardisation of contracts and the Treasury Taskforce has this within its remit.[3] However, it must be borne in mind that PFI transactions are complex, involving not only the construction of a capital asset but the related services and the financing for the project. While standardisation of certain key commercial issues can and should be achieved (which will help to reduce the time from project inception to financial close) there is likely to be an irreducible minimum period

---

1 See **1.3.13**.
2 See draft Treasury Taskforce Guidance on Project Agreements, section 14.2.4.
3 See draft Treasury Taskforce Guidance on Project Agreements.

of time required for a PFI procurement.[1] In addition, the experience of project financing in the private sector (and other supposedly mature products such as finance leasing) is that each project or transaction has its own individual problems or issues and, unless this is accepted, a significant measure of frustration will arise from a belief that a standardised commodity product can deliver PFI contracts which merely require the parties to fill in the blanks. Long-term partnership contracts which involve significant risk transfer are not to be entered into lightly.

18.4.2 To an extent, the issue of the length of time taken to close PFI transactions can be addressed through an imaginative approach to the initial packaging of the project. Grouping or bundling of individual projects not only helps to create the critical mass necessary to attract finance, it can also allow a series of projects to be taken forward together under one procurement more quickly than if the projects were taken forward individually. Perhaps the most successful example of this is the DSS 'Prime' Project. However, it is important for there to be a logic to the bundling otherwise shoehorning a group of disparate projects into one package will lead to complications and delay.

18.4.3 Upon coming to power the Labour Government instituted a review of the asset holdings of government in what was styled a 1990s Domesday Book. The product, the National Asset Register, was published in November 1997 and details existing assets with a view to determining which are surplus to requirement and can be disposed of. The aim of these disposals is to raise cash for public investment. In addition, a new Investing in Britain Fund has been established which will allocate new public capital investment according to government priorities. Part of this fund will be overseen by the Treasury and will be available to departments either as additional capital or to fund PFI projects. Access to the fund will depend upon bids made by departments which will be assessed against certain criteria, including best value for money for the proposed use of funds.[2] It is anticipated that this will result in the PFI continuing to be the preferred route for capital investment where it delivers value for money, while at the same time enabling government to co-invest capital in public/private partnership projects. The commitment of the government to the PFI has been reinforced by the role identified for it as part of the comprehensive spending review conducted by the government in July 1998 which projected PFI investment of £7.7bn in the period to the year 2000.[3]

18.4.4 In specific areas, a shift in emphasis and approach can be seen. In the NHS, the second wave of general hospital projects are being developed on the basis of pre-determined commercial terms (and, eventually, a standard contract). In addition, a possible shift towards PFI transactions involving only design build, finance and management of hospitals is being discussed.[4] This would

---

1 The Chief Executive of the Treasury Taskforce has suggested that this is in the order of 12 months (*Financial Times*, July 24 1998).
2 This part of the fund is known as the Capital Modernisation Fund.
3 Modern Public Services for Britain: Investing in Reform (Comprehensive Spending Review White Paper – Cm 40, July 1998), paragraph 2.30.
4 *Health Service Journal*, 30 July 1998, p 10.

remove the service provision element from the PFI process, leaving it to be separately procured by the NHS trust. This would be a significant move away from the focus on service provision identified in the Bates Review.[1] However, the approach may have some merit given the approach adopted by the Accounting Standards Board to accounting for PFI transactions (with its view that the service provision element should largely be ignored)[2] and the difficulty of laying off risk to FM service providers which are in many cases weakly capitalised companies operating on slender margins.

18.4.5 In addition, health ministers have ambitious plans for the PFI to focus on capital developments which respond to a local area's health and social needs involving a combination of health and educational facilities. Given the cross-departmental involvement in the procurement process which this would require, and the fact that the Education and Health sectors are at different stages in the PFI learning curve, this is a development which may take some time to realise its potential.

18.4.6 As discussed in Chapter 1, one of the recommendations of the Bates Review was that the Treasury Taskforce projects arm should have a limited life of 2 years (having been established in August 1997). In November 1998, the then Paymaster General, Geoffrey Robinson, asked Sir Malcolm Bates to conduct a further review to determine what should happen to the Treasury Taskforce projects arm following its scheduled demise in August 1999.[3] It remains to be seen what the outcome of that review will propose and whether a successor body emerges with a strategic role more focused on the wider development of public/private partnerships rather than PFI. Much will depend upon the way in which the government wishes public/private partnerships to develop.[4] If, for example, it is tempted to make strategic investments in such partnerships, there might well be a useful role for a body to determine the basis upon which such investments were to be made and to be responsible for making and managing such investments.[5]

18.5 INTERNATIONAL PFI DEVELOPMENTS

18.5.1 The use of private finance to provide public infrastructure and services is not the exclusive preserve of the UK. The development of the PFI has attracted interest worldwide. The UK government has been visited by countries such as Australia, Brazil, China, Finland, Hungary, Iceland, Japan, Korea, Lithuania, Morocco, New Zealand, South Africa, Sweden, Taiwan and the United Arab Emirates as well as European countries, all wishing to understand and explore

---

1   Bates Review, Recommendation No 14.
2   See **17.5.7**.
3   HM Treasury News Release 187/98.
4   See HM Treasury publication *Selling Government Services into Wider Markets, Policy and Guidance Note* (Enterprise and Growth Unit) which is referred to in the second Bates Review terms of reference.
5   See **18.5.5** regarding the approach adopted by the Netherlands.

the benefits of the PFI.[1] The reasons for this are broadly similar to those driving the PFI in the UK.

18.5.2 Australia has been using PFI techniques for several years in relation to the procurement of public infrastructure. The projects have been developed at State level with individual States adopting differing approaches to implementation. In South Africa, prisons are being developed using contract structures based on those developed by HM Prison Service. In addition, toll road projects are being developed and there is interest in health projects and projects in government property and local government services. Italy, the Netherlands and Ireland are considering forming bodies, similar to the Treasury Taskforce, to assist in the development of their own versions of the PFI.

18.5.3 In Italy, a Public Works Authority (Autorita per le infrastrutture) is proposed under a new draft law which is intended to create a legal framework for the project financing of public works. It would comprise a president and four members with skill and experience in the public works sector. The role of the Authority would be to:

- monitor the award of contracts;
- publicise the terms of contracts;
- suggest ways in which legislation could be improved to facilitate the development of such financing.

18.5.4 In Japan a draft law relating to the PFI is also progressing through the Japanese parliament and the Japanese equivalent of the CBI has published a report regarding the implementation of the PFI in the UK and its potential application to Japan.

18.5.5 In the Netherlands, the approach to PFI style projects has been for government to become a shareholder in the project rather than the UK model of an arm's length contract between the public and private sectors with the public sector investment being in the form of grants, subsidies or contribution of assets.[2]

18.5.6 In August 1998, following completion of a report by Chesterton and Farrell Grant Sparks & Goodbody,[3] the Irish Government announced its intention to establish a dedicated unit within the Department of Finance to identify suitable projects for public/private partnerships and progress the initiative on the basis of a number of pilot projects. One of the first such projects, a public/private partnership to provide a new light rail system for Dublin is now being prepared for tender by the Department of Public Enterprise.

18.5.7 The development of PFI as an exportable product worldwide has the potential to be at least as successful as the export of privatisation. The worldwide

---

1   HM Treasury News Release 26/98.
2   But see **19.2.5** regarding the government's approach to the Channel Tunnel Rail Link Project.
3   A Report to the Inter-Departmental Group in relation to: Public Private Partnerships, July 1998. See also *Filling the Gap*. The Nature, Scale and Costs of Ireland's Infrastructural Deficit by Fitzpatrick Associates, Economic Consultants (Irish Business and Employers Confederation, April 1998).

demand for investment in public infrastructure shows no signs of diminishing (although the economic crisis in South East Asia may have slowed its pace). Up to date, efficient infrastructure is a pre-requisite for a competitive economy and the need to compete in a global marketplace exposes all countries to that pressure. That coupled with a generally accepted political desire not to increase taxation makes the PFI model, while not the only show in town, one that looks set for a long run.

BIBLIOGRAPHY AND USEFUL ADDRESSES

1. PFI PUBLICATIONS

The following is a list (according to department, sector or body) of some recent PFI-related publications.

HM TREASURY

General

Taskforce Guidance on Project Agreements: Consultation Draft
Treasury Taskforce, October 1998

Private Finance and IT: A Practical Guide
Treasury Taskforce/Cabinet Office Central IT Unit, November 1998

Partnerships for Prosperity
Treasury Taskforce, November 1997

Taking Forward PFI in Local Government
Treasury Taskforce, September 1997

A Step-by-Step Guide to the PFI Procurement Process
Treasury Taskforce, Revised April 1998

VAT on PFI Service Payments
HM Treasury and Private Finance Panel, March 1997

Further Contractual Issues
HM Treasury and Private Finance Panel, January 1997

PFI in Government Accommodation
HM Treasury and Private Finance Panel, October 1996

Basic Contractual Terms
HM Treasury and Private Finance Panel, October 1996

Writing an Output Specification
HM Treasury and Private Finance Panel, October 1996

Transferability of Equity
HM Treasury and Private Finance Panel, October 1996

5 Steps to the Appointment of Advisers
HM Treasury and Private Finance Panel, May 1996

Risk and Reward in PFI Contract
HM Treasury and Private Finance Panel, May 1996

Guidelines for Smoothing the Procurement Process
HM Treasury and Private Finance Panel, April 1996

The Private Finance Initiative and Government IS/IT: Evaluation
HM Treasury and Private Finance Panel, February 1996

The Private Finance Initiative and Government IS/IT: Report on the NIRS2 project
HM Treasury and Private Finance Panel, September 1995

The Private Finance Initiative and Government IS/IT: Risk
HM Treasury and Private Finance Panel, March 1995

Private Opportunity, Public Benefit
HM Treasury and Private Finance Panel, November 1995

The Private Finance Initiative and Government IS/IT (Management Briefing)
HM Treasury and Private Finance Panel, December 1994

Policy statements and technical notes

POLICY STATEMENT No 1: PFI and Public Expenditure Allocations
Treasury Taskforce, October 1997

POLICY STATEMENT No 2: Public Sector Comparators and Value for Money
Treasury Taskforce, March 1998

POLICY STATEMENT No 3: PFI and Public Expenditure Allocations for Non-Departmental Public Bodies
Treasury Taskforce, August 1998

POLICY STATEMENT No 4: Disclosure of Information and Consultation with Staff and other Interested Parties
Treasury Taskforce, November 1998

TECHNICAL NOTE No 1: How to Account for PFI Transactions
Treasury Taskforce, September 1997

TECHNICAL NOTE No 2: How to Follow EC Procurement Procedure and Advertise in the OJEC
Treasury Taskforce, June 1998

TECHNICAL NOTE No 3: How to Appoint and Manage Advisers
Treasury Taskforce, August 1998

Case study material

Colfox School, Dorset: A Case Study on the First DBFO School Project
Treasury Taskforce/DfEE/4PS, March 1998

Private Finance and IS/IT: CASE STUDY – TAFMIS ... and after
Treasury Taskforce/CITU/Ministry of Defence, March 1998

DBFO – Value in Roads
March 1997

OSIRIS' – Private Finance and IS/IT case study: Office Systems Infrastructure Review and Implementation Strategy for the Welsh Office
September 1996

Private Finance and IS/IT: The IND caseworking programme
October 1996

Report on the Procurement of Custodial Services for the DCMF Prisons at Bridgend and Fazakerley
HM Prison Service/Private Finance Panel, April 1996

Lowdham Grange Prison Services

Lewisham Extension to Docklands Light Railway

DEPARTMENT OF CULTURE, MEDIA AND SPORT

Private Finance and the National Lottery

MINISTRY OF DEFENCE

The Ministry of Defence publishes some of its guidance and information on projects at its web site: **www.mod.uk/pfu/database.htm**

DEPARTMENT FOR EDUCATION AND EMPLOYMENT

General

Investing for Excellence: Business Opportunities in Education and Employment
DfEE, February 1998

Investing for Excellence: Guide to the Structure and Financing of the Education and Employment Sectors
DfEE, February 1998

Education PFI Projects List: Projects considering PFI options in further education, higher education and schools
DfEE

Voluntary Aided Schools PFI Projects: Q & A Guidance
DfEE, June 1997

LMS and County Schools PFI Projects: Guidance for LEAs
DfEE, April 1997

Case Studies

Colfox School, Dorset: A Case Study
Treasury Taskforce/DfEE/4Ps, March 1998

(Copies available from DfEE. Tel: 0171 925 6222; Fax: 0171 925 5113)

Higher Education Funding Council for England

Practical Guide to PFI for Higher Education Institutions
HEFCE, November 1997

Private Investment in Higher Education
HEFCE, April 1998

Circular Letter 8/98: PFI Projects – Arrangements for 'signing off'
HEFCE, April 1998

Circular Letter 9/98: Bids for Pathfinder Funding
HEFCE, April 1998

(Copies available from HEFCE Private Finance Unit. Tel: 0117 931 7227; Fax: 0117 931 7203)

Further Education Funding Council

PPP Prospects in Further Education
A register of projects and services which colleges may require from potential private sector providers
FEFC, August 1998

(Copies available from FEFC. Tel: 01203 863211; Fax: 01203 863220)

EFFICIENCY AND EFFECTIVENESS

12 Guiding Principles in using Market Testing and Contracting Out
November 1997

Better Quality Services
July 1998

DEPARTMENT OF THE ENVIRONMENT, TRANSPORT AND THE REGIONS

From the DETR Free Literature
PO Box 236, Wetherby, L23 7NB Tel 0870 1226236; Fax 0870 1226237:

Local Government and the Private Finance Initiative
An explanatory note on PFI and encouraging Public/Private Partnerships in local government
September 1998
Also accessible on the Department's local government website: **www.detr.local.gov.uk**

The Local Government Capital Finance system
A Guide to Recent Changes
February 1997

Energy services for the public sector
A Working Guide
revised in 1997

From DETR Publication Sales Centre
Unit 21, Goldthorpe Industrial Estate, Rotherham S63 9BL. Tel 01709 891318; Fax 01709 881673

Local Authorities' Involvement in Companies
Findings of Research
November 1997

Local Authorities' Involvement in Companies
Good Practice Guide
November 1997

Also from DETR

Integrated Transport White Paper
A New Deal for Transport
July 1998
Available from The Stationery Office (ISBN 0 101395027) and on the DETR website: www.detr.gov.uk

Other materials in this sector:

Options Appraisal and the Outline Business Case (Local Government)
1998

A Guide to the Local Government (Contracts) Act 1997: A practical guide to the provisions and their effect
January 1998

DEPARTMENT OF HEALTH

Health Service Guidelines (HSG)

HSG(94)31 Capital Investment in the NHS: the Capital Investment Manual
June 1994

HSG(95)15 Private Finance and Capital Investment Projects
March 1995

HSG(95)48 Information Management and Technology (IM&T) Procurement and Private Finance
November 1995

Forthcoming guidance

The NHS Executive is due to publish a comprehensive new PFI guidance manual.

HOME OFFICE

Implementing a Full Design/Finance/Build/Operate Package
(HM Prison Service)
3 November 1997

The International Scene – UK Trends and Perspectives
(A presentation by the Head of Contracts and Competition Group, HM Prison Service)
16 September 1997

The United Kingdom Experience
(A paper on the UK's experience of private sector provision of custodial services by the Head of Contracts and Competition, HM Prison Service)

LORD CHANCELLOR'S DEPARTMENT

The Lord Chancellor's Department plans to produce a general information booklet about opportunities within the courts sector and to make available documentation once schemes have been completed.

SCOTTISH OFFICE

Public Services and Private Finance: A Partnership for Scotland
May 1996

The Scottish Office Private Finance Unit: Occasional Paper No 3 – the Private Financing Initiative – Financing Issues
December 1996

The Scottish Office also publishes a regular newsletter on PFI in Scotland.

WELSH OFFICE

Private Finance and Public Projects in Wales 1995

The Private Finance Initiative and Local Authorities
a joint publication between the Welsh Office and Department of Environment

Private Finance and IS/IT: Case Study
a joint publication between the Welsh Office, Private Finance Panel, Cabinet Office and Central Computer and Telecommunications Agency (CCTA)

ACCOUNTING STANDARDS BOARD

Amendment to FRS 5 – 'Reporting the Substance of Transactions': Private Finance Initiative and Similar Contracts
ASB, September 1998

NATIONAL AUDIT OFFICE

The Contract to Develop and Operate the Replacement National Insurance Recording System
May 1997

The Skye Bridge
May 1997

Bridgend and Fazakerley Prisons
October 1997

The Private Finance Initiative: The First Four DBFO Roads Contracts
January 1998

2. PRESS RELEASES AND OTHER MATERIAL

RECOMMENDATIONS TO REINVIGORATE PFI – SEPTEMBER DEADLINES ARE MET
Press Release 115/97
30 September 1997

INTERIM GUIDANCE ON THE APPLICATION OF FRS 5 TO ACCOUNTING FOR PFI TRANSACTIONS IN PUBLIC SECTOR ACCOUNTS
Treasury Taskforce, September 1997

TAKING FORWARD PFI IN LOCAL GOVERNMENT
Treasury Taskforce, September 1997

BATES RECOMMENDATION 10 – TREASURY TASKFORCE APPROACH TO MODEL CONTRACTS
Treasury Taskforce, November 1997

PARTNERSHIPS FOR PROSPERITY – A NEW FRAMEWORK FOR THE PFI
Press Release 132/97
4 November 1997

PFI CONFERENCE PROGRAMME LAUNCHED
167/97
22 December 1997

SIGNIFICANT PROJECTS LIST PUBLISHED
17/98
10 February 1998

TASKFORCE PFI TRAINING PROGRAMME LAUNCHED
60/98
24 April 1998

MORE LOCAL GOVERNMENT PFI PROJECTS GET GREEN LIGHT
DETR News Release 517

GEOFFREY ROBINSON UNVEILS SECOND SIGNIFICANT
PROJECTS LIST
Press Release 171/98
21 October 1998

3. ACTS AND WHITE PAPERS

The National Health Service (Private Finance) Act 1997

Local Government (Contracts) Act 1997

Modern Local Government: In Touch with the People
White Paper, July 1998

A New Deal for Transport: Better For Everyone
White Paper, July 1998

Modern Public Services for Britain: Investing in Reform
White Paper, July 1998

4. PFI CONTACTS IN GOVERNMENT

The following is a list of useful Government contacts:

HM TREASURY TASKFORCE

Chief Executive Projects
Adrian Montague
Chief Executive Projects
Room 22/G
Parliament Street
London SW1P 3AG
Tel: 0171 270 4701
Fax: 0171 270 5760

Head of Private Finance Policy Team
Tim Wilson
Room 20/G
Parliament Street
London SW1P 3AG
Tel: 0171 270 4702
Fax: 0171 389 9739

Policy Helpdesk
Nick Crowther
Room 19/G
Parliament Street
London SW1P 3AG
Tel: 0171 270 5527
Fax: 0171 389 9739

PRIVATE FINANCE UNITS

Defence – PPPU
Peter Ryan
Head of the Public/Private
Partnership Unit (PFI and CFQ)
Ministry of Defence
Room G4
Metropole Building
Northumberland Avenue
London WC2N 5BL
Tel: 0171 218 0985
Fax: 0171 218 0055

Agriculture
William Arnott
Head of Financial Policy Division C
Agriculture, Fisheries and Food
Room 311
Whitehall Place (West Block)
Tel: 0171 270 8423
Fax: 0171 270 8436

Customs and Excise
Phil Bennett
Efficiency and Private Finance Unit
HM Customs and Excise
New Kings Beam House
22 Upperground
London SE1 9PJ
Tel: 0171 865 5748
Fax: 0171 865 5700

Culture, Media and Sport
Miss Alex Stewart
Director of Finance
Department of Culture,
Media and Sport
2–4 Cockspur Street
London SW1Y 5DH
Tel: 0171 211 6217 (Mark Brookfield 211 6501)
Fax: 0171 211 6227

Education and Employment
Stephen Burt
Head of Private Finance Division
Department for Education and Employment
Room 5.10, Sanctuary Building
Great Smith Street
London SW1P 3BT
Tel: 0171 925 6087
Fax: 0171 925 5113

Defence – PE PFU
Owain Ellis
Head of Procurement Executive
Private Finance Unit
Birch 2c
#234 MoD Abbey Wood
Bristol BS34 8JH
Tel: 0117 91 32368
Fax: 0117 91 32944

Education and Employment (Schools)
Richard Wilkinson
Department of Education and Employment
Room 3.09
Sanctuary Buildings
Great Smith Street
London SW1P 3BT
Tel: 0171 925 6566
Fax: 0171 925 6987

Foreign and Commonwealth
Richard Kinchen
Head of Resource Planning
Foreign and Commonwealth Office
Room 4.2.16
1 Palace Street
London SW1E 5HE
Tel: 0171 238 4016
Fax: 0171 238 4004

Health
Peter Coates
Private Finance Unit
NHS Executive, Department of Health
Quarry House, Quarry Hill
Leeds LS2 7UE
Tel: 01132 545 487
Fax: 01132 545 406

Efficiency & Effectiveness Group
Brian Avery
1 Horse Guards Road
London SW1P 3AL
Tel: 0171 270 5255
Fax: 0171 270 5846

Environment, Transport and the Regions
Crispin Tuckley
Private Finance Unit
Ashdown House
123 Victoria Street
London SW1E 6DE
Tel: 0171 890 5014
(or Robert Gregory × 5015)
Fax: 0171 890 5009

Inland Revenue
Jerry Page
Head of Private Finance Unit
Inland Revenue
Somerset House
Strand
London WC2 1LB
Tel: 0171 438 7294
Fax: 0171 438 7663

International Development
Richard Manning
Director General, Resources
94 Victoria Street
London SW1E 5JL
Tel: 0171 917 0439
Fax: 0171 917 0694

Home Office
Polly Leithead
Home Office Procurement Unit
Room 965B
50 Queen Anne's Gate
London SW1H 9AT
Tel: 0171 273 3480
Fax: 0171 273 3949

Northern Ireland Civil Service
Derek Smith
Appropriation and Resource Control Division (ARCD)
Department of Finance and Personnel
Rathgael House
Balloo Road
Bangor BT19 7NA
Tel: 01247 858602
Fax: 01247 858202

Public Service
Pat Pattenden
Cabinet Office/Office of Public Services
Procurement Policy Unit
Room 407, Queen Anne's Chambers
28 Broadway
London SW1H 9JS
Tel: 0171 210 0578
Fax: 0171 210 0591

Trade and Industry
David Fincham
Finance and Resource
Management Directorate
Department of Trade and Industry
Room 3.H.18
1 Victoria Street
London SW1H 0ET
Tel: 0171 215 6832
Fax: 0171 215 6739

Lord Chancellor's Department
Richard Atkinson
PFI/LCD HQ Aramis Unit
Lord Chancellor's Department
Room 9.05
Selbourne House
54–60 Victoria Street
London SW1E 6QB
Tel: 0171 210 8631
Fax: 0171 210 8606

Scotland
John Henderson
Head of Private Finance Unit (FFB)
Scottish Office
323C Victoria Quay
Edinburgh EH6 6QQ
Tel: 0131 244 7497
Fax: 0131 244 7499

Social Security
Sue Joseph
Supply Management Group
Department of Social Security
Room 509B
Norcross
Blackpool FY5 3TA
Tel: 01253 333 183
Fax: 01253 333 616

Welsh Office
Emyr Roberts
Private Finance Unit
Welsh Office
Cathay's Park
Cardiff CF1 3NQ
Tel: 01222 823765
Fax: 01222 823700

THE 4Ps (PUBLIC PRIVATE PARTNERSHIPS PROGRAMME LIMITED)
35 Great Smith Street, Westminster, London SW1P 3BJ
Tel: 0171 664 3145; Fax: 0171 664 3178

The Board
Councillor Tony Colman MP
(Chairman)
Councillor Theresa Stewart
Councillor John Jenkins
Councillor Richard Arthur
Councillor Keith Whitmore

Councillor Chris Marriage
Councillor Rita Taylor
Judith Mayhew
Gren Folwell

The Executive
Peter Fanning (Chief Executive)
Tel: 0171 664 3142
Media and Housing

Martin Lipson
Tel: 0171 664 3149
Schools Refurbishment, Property matters and Leisure

Fred Portnell
Tel: 0171 664 3141
Home Office projects, Waste Management and IS/IT schemes

Sue Sanders
Tel: 0171 664 3146
Education and Social Services

Rob Hann
Tel: 0171 664 3140
Legal and regulatory issues
and Public Transport

David Locke
Tel: 0171 664 3140
Transport

Steve Trueman
Tel: 0171 664 3147
Housing

Huw Zachariah
Tel: 0171 664 3150
Welsh projects, Heating Schemes,
Waste Management and IS/IT schemes

Ian Paterson
Tel: 0171 664 3143
IT, Technology and New Working Practice Projects

5. INTERNET ADDRESSES AND WEB SITES

The following is a list of useful internet addresses and web sites:

Ministry of Defence (Public/Private Partnership Unit):

- pfu@dgics.mod.uk (the P/PPU also has a website which can be accessed via the MoD website set out below)
- www.mod.uk/

Department of the Environment, Transport and the Regions:

- Local Government – www.detr.local.gov.uk
- General – www.detr.gov.uk

HM Treasury:

www.hm-treasury.gov.uk

Treasury Taskforce:

www.treasury-projects-taskforce.gov.uk

Cabinet Office – Central IT Unit:

pfi@citu.gov.uk

CCTA Government Information Service:

www.open.gov.uk/

6. PFI LIBRARY

The Treasury Taskforce maintains a PFI Library containing Contract Documentation, Business Cases, Case Studies and Post-implementation Reviews (including NAO/PAC Reports), Central Guidance, Departmental/Sector Specific Guidance, Press Releases/Cuttings, Parliamentary Questions on PFI, Periodicals and Contract Award Notices. The Treasury Taskforce should be contacted for access details (access restrictions apply to private sector bodies in respect of Contract Documentation and Business Cases). An index to the PFI Library is maintained at the Treasury Taskforce web site mentioned above.

INDEX

References are to paragraph numbers.

Access
  inadequate   10.4.24
  planning permission, for   13.1.9
Access to site/works   7.6.18, 7.6.23, 8.5.17
  breach of obligation by authority   10.7.7
Accommodation project, *see* Government (central)
Accounting   17.1 *et seq*
  Accounting Standards Board view   1.2.4, 1.3.28
  Bates Review   1.3.17
  early tests for PFI   17.4.1
  FRS 5 amendment (Application Note)   17.3.5, 17.5, *see also* **Balance sheet treatment**
  finance lease, *see* **Finance lease**
  public sector   17.1.1, 17.8.3
    balance sheet, *see* **Balance sheet treatment**
  services   3.3.1, *see also* **Services contract**
Adjudication   16.1.1, 16.6, *see also* **Dispute**
Administrator/administrative receiver *see also* **Receiver**
  notification of appointment to charge holder   9.1.4
Advertisement
  OJ, in, *see* **European Union**
Advertising services   3.3.1, *see also* **Services contract**
Agreement, *see* **Contract**
Agricultural land   11.5.8, 11.5.9
Aims   1.2.1–1.2.4, 11.7.2
Alternative dispute resolution   16.1.1, 16.3
Antiquities   7.6.33
Arbitration   16.1.1, 16.4
Architectural/engineering services   3.3.1
Asset
  accounting test   17.5.1, 17.5.2
  charge on, *see* **Charge**
  damage/destruction   8.4.15, *see also* **Insurance**
  duration   1.2.6
  land, *see* **Land**; **Site**
  leasing finance   8.2.9, 8.5.23
  legal title to   2.2.34
    warranty on   8.5.13
  maintenance, *see* **Maintenance**
  National Asset Register   18.4.3
  non-fixed, charge, etc, to protect   2.2.34
  plant and machinery, *see* **Capital allowances**
  private sector responsibility   1.2.2–1.2.6, 1.2.9, 1.2.15
  property, project subject, *see* **Property issues**
  residual value, *see* **Residual value risk**
  transfer of, whether transfer of undertaking, *see* **Transfer of undertaking**
Assignment
  contract rights, of   9.3.26, 9.4.2
  sub-contract   8.3.2
Audit Commission
  EU public procurement rules apply   3.2.2
Authorisation, *see* **Consent**
Awarding authority   2.2
  act creating service unavailability   10.4.25, *see also* **Deduction**
  agreement with project company, *see* **Project agreement**
  bid evaluation, *see* **Bid**
  breach/default by
    compensating event, as   10.3.9
    termination, giving entitlement to   10.7.1, 10.7.7, 10.7.8
    see also **Judicial review**; **Tender**; **Vires**
  change in legal framework of   10.7.8
  change in requirements, *see* **Variation**
  collateral agreement for   2.5.6–2.5 8, 7.6.12–7.6.15, 7.6.22
  contractors for   7.6.20–7.6.22
    damage caused by   7.6.21

Awarding authority – *cont*
  design document approval   7.6.5
  developer, as   7.2.2, 7.2.3, 7.2.4
  direct agreement, use of   9.1.10
  discretion, fettering of   4.2.22–4.2.24, *see also* **Vires**
  EU rules for, *see* **Public procurement rules (EU)**
  financial contribution prior to completion   2.2.31
    delaying   2.2.32
  financial security, circumstances when has   2.2.30
  inspection   7.6.18, 7.6.28
  key risks to be transferred   2.2.5–2.2.35, *see also* **Risk allocation**
  legal compliance obligation   7.6.33
  monitoring   7.6.18
  objectives   2.2.3, 2.2.4, 2.2.40, *see also* **Risk allocation; Value for money**
  outline business case   5.6.21, 5.6.22, *see also* **Public sector comparator**
  output specification, *see* **Output specification**
  pension rights, 'bulk transfer payment' to protect   15.12.5
  powers, *see* **Vires**
  preferred tenderer, dealings with   5.7.8–5.7.14, *see also* **Bid**
  property ownership issues, *see* **Property issues**
  protection of interests   7.6.16, 7.6.17, *see also* **Step-in**
  public procurement, compliance, *see also* **Public procurement rules (EU)**
  refinancing profits, share in   8.6.2–8.6.4, 18.3
  rights on default/insolvency, *see* **Default; Insolvency (of project company)**
  step-in rights, notice etc, *see* **Step-in**
  surplus land etc disposal, *see* **Surplus site/property**
  tender process, *see* **Tender**
  VAT issues   14.4.4–14.4.9, *see also* **VAT**

Balance sheet treatment   1.2.4, 1.2.13, 1.5, 2.2.24, 17.1 *et seq*

  Application Note (FRS 5 amendment)   17.3.5, 17.5, 17.7, 17.8.1
  'asset'   17.5.1, 17.5.2
  commercial effect   17.5.3, 17.5.4
  deficiencies of   17.7.4, 17.7.5
  demand risk   17.5.7, 17.7.5
  lease as element   17.5.6
  motives of parties   17.5.8
  residual value risk   17.5.7, 17.7.5
  risks, relevance of   1.2.13, 17.5.7–17.5.10, 17.6.5
  separable contract   17.5.5, 17.5.6, 17.7.2, 17.7.3
  spirit of FRS 5, meeting   17.5.11
  totality of transaction/series   17.5.3
  Treasury guidance distinguished   17.7
  construction risk exclusion   17.5.9, 17.6.3, 17.7.7–17.7.9
  projects falling foul of   17.7.9
  'off balance sheet'   17.2
    awarding authority, importance for   2.2.40, 17.2.4, 17.3.1
    effect of   17.2.1
  property structure, consistency with   11.4.2
  'on balance sheet'   17.2.4
  service payment variations   17.7.10–17.7.12
    reduction in charge   17.7.10, 17.7.11
  Treasury approval, and   17.2.1
    failure to meet   17.2.2
  Treasury guidance   17.4.2, 17.4.3, 17.5.11, 17.6, 17.7, 17.8.1
    Application Note distinguished   17.7
    de minimis thresholds   17.6.2
    deficiencies of   17.7.4, 17.7.6
    equity return, likely effect of risks on   17.6.4, 17.6.5, 17.7.6
    more focused approach in   17.7.12
    revision likely   17.8.1–17.8.4
    risks, and combined impact of   17.6.2–17.6.5
    'sense check' on risk transfer, and factors for   17.6.6, 17.6.7
  'separability test'   17.6.1, 17.7.2, 17.7.3

Balance sheet treatment – *cont*
  value for money   17.2.4, 17.7.4, 17.7.8, 17.7.12
Bank, *see* **Debt funder; Funding**
Bankability   2.3.5, 2.4.1, *see also* **Funding**
Bates Review   1.3.17–1.3.19, 18.1
  acceptance of   1.3.36, 1.4.2
  OJ notice, wording standardisation   3.3.16
  outcomes   1.3.20–1.3.36
    bid costs   1.3.35
    improvements to process   1.3.23–1.3.30, 18.4
    institutional structure   1.3.20–1.3.22
    lessons and training   1.3.31–1.3.34
    standard form agreement   1.3.23, 10.1.7, 18.4.1
Benchmarking   10.4.18, 10.5.2
Bid
  comparing   2.2.37
  costs   5.6.2, 5.6.11
    compensation for, after tender breach   6.2.6
    minimising   2.3.2
    refund, recommendation   1.3.35
  evaluation   5.7
    competitive environment, prolonging   5.7.9–5.7.14
    consistency   5.7.4–5.7.6
    criteria   5.7.1, 5.7.2, 5.7.3, 5.7.7
    methodology   5.7.3
    minimum requirements   5.7.3
    more than one/variants   5.7.4, 11.4.4
    'most economically advantageous' preferred   3.3.45, 5.7.2
    commitment evidence   5.7.14
    deliverability, assessment of   5.7.12, 5.7.13
    negotiations with   5.7.8–5.7.14, 5.8
    price reduction/affordability requirements   5.7.15
  public procurement rules, *see* **Public procurement rules (EU)**
  refusal to consider   6.5.1
  reserve   5.7.11
  standard of reference   5.7.4–5.7.6
  submission   5.7
    deadline   5.5.5, 6.5.1, 6.5.4

  guidance   5.6.17, 5.7.6
  see also **'evaluation'** *above*
  transfer of undertakings issues   15.9.9
Boilerplate contract clauses   1.3.11
Bond (financing)   1.3.27, 8.1.2, 8.2.5–8.2.8
  advantages of use   8.2.7
  credit enhancement   8.2.6
  direct agreement   9.5.2
  disadvantages   8.2.8
  Eurobond   8.2.5
  examples of use   8.2.5
  risks   8.2.6
  trustee, party to direct agreement   9.2.1
Bond (performance), *see* **Performance bond**
Bond, 'on-demand'   7.7.15
Breach
  Construction (Design and Management) Regs 1994, of   7.6.33
  project agreement, of   8.5.19, 9.2.4, 10.7.6, *see also* **Default; Direct agreement; Termination**
  public procurement process, of, *see* **Public procurement rules (EU)**
  tender process, *see* **Tender**
Bridge   1.2.15, 1.3.3, 3.2.12, 14.3.9, 14.3.10
Budget   8.5.8
Building
  see also **Construction contract; Land; Service; Services contract**
  decanting   7.6.19
  industrial, *see* **Capital allowances**
  new to replace existing, transfer of undertaking issues   15.5.9
  project, subject of, *see* **Property issues**
  unavailable rooms   10.4.22
  variation to   10.6.2

Capital allowances   14.3.7–14.3.20
  industrial building/structure   14.3.9–14.3.11
    conditions for   14.3.9
    'industrial building or structure'   14.3.10
    rate   14.3.9
    'relevant interest'   14.3.11

Capital allowances – *cont*
  industrial building/structure – *cont*
    road or bridge, relevance to 14.3.9
    plant and machinery   14.3.12–14.3.20, 14.5.7
      'belongs' to   14.3.14, 14.3.18
      conditions   14.3.12, 14.3.13
      fixtures   14.3.15–14.3.17
      interest in land, and   14.3.17–14.3.20
      rate   14.3.12
    professional fees   14.3.7
    reduction of   14.6.3
    time for relief   14.3.25
Capital finance regime, *see* **Local authority**
Capital gains tax
  overage, and
    developer, position of   12.5.4, 12.5.9
    disposal defined by rules   12.4.9, 12.4.14, 12.4.15–12.4.17
    project company, and   14.6.5, 14.6.6
Catering   10.4.7, *see also* **Service; Services contract**
Change in law, *see* **Law, change in**
Channel Tunnel   1.3.3
  bond issue   18.2.5
  compulsory purchase for   13.3.2
Channel Tunnel Rail Link   3.2.13
Charge
  credit agreement prohibition   8.5.18
  equipment etc, protecting   2.2.34
  fixed   8.4.21, 9.1.2, 9.1.3
  floating   8.4.21, 9.1.2–9.1.4
  notification of administrator's appointment, right   9.1.4, 9.1.5
Checklist   1.5–1.6
Civil engineering contract, *see* **Construction contract**
Clawback, *see* **Overage**
Cleaning
  see also **Contractor; Service; Services contract**
  transfer of undertaking issues   15.4.2–15.4.8, 15.5, 15.6.4
Collateral agreement   2.5, 7.6.12–7.6.15
Collateral warranty   2.5.12, 7.6.15
Commencement   1.3.1, 1.3.5

Commission
  termination right   10.7.10, 10.7.11
Commissioning   7.6.23–7.6.26
Company
  construction   7.6.33, *see also* **Construction contract**
  operating   7.3.3, 9.1.6
  project, *see* **Project company**
  special vehicle, *see* **Special vehicle company**
Compensation
  see also **Crichel Down Rules; Damages**
  events   10.3.9–10.3.12
    calculation of   10.3.11, 10.3.12
    meaning   10.3.9
    negotiation on   10.3.10, 10.3.11
  force majeure, for   10.3.7, 10.3.8, 10.9.19–10.9.21
  grossing up   10.9.25, 14.7.5
  instalments   10.9.18, 10.9.21
  negative figure, where   2.5.12
  performance not possible   2.2.21, 2.2.32, 8.4.18
  set-off   10.9.23, 10.9.24
  termination, on, *see* **Default; Tax; Termination**
Competition
  tender process, in   5.2.3
    competitive negotiated procedure   3.3.7–3.3.21, 3.3.30
Completion   2.2.14–2.2.19, 7.6.27
  certificate   7.6.28
  'completion to time'   2.2.15, 2.2.16, 7.6.31
    late completion   2.2.15
  cost, completing to   2.2.17
    adjustment events   2.2.17, 10.6.9
  date, alteration to   2.2.16, 7.6.31, 10.3.6, 10.3.12
  defects liability period   7.2.4, 7.6.27
  defects, minor   7.6.27, 7.6.28
  disputed   7.6.28
  early
    aim of authority   2.2.40
    bonus payment   7.7.4
  extension of time, events allowing 2.2.16
    construction contract, in   7.7.3
    grant of land interest, time for 11.6.1
  late   2.2.15, 7.6.32

Completion – *cont*
  late – *cont*
    damages for loss   2.2.15, 7.6.32, 7.7.4, 10.3.13
    liquidated damages, cost of imposition   2.2.15
  notice of completion of making good defects   7.7.14
  overspend/underspend adjustment   7.7.9
  payment obligations, and   2.2.19, 2.2.29, 7.6.27, 7.6.28
  post-completion termination   10.9.8, 10.9.10
  practical   7.2.4, 7.6.27, 11.6.1
    objective determination   7.6.28
  pre-completion phase   2.2.19, 10.3.9
    step-in during   9.3.9
  pre-completion termination   10.9.8, 10.9.9
  progress reports on   8.5.16
  quality, to   2.2.18, 2.2.19
  risk aspects   2.2.14–2.2.19, 8.4.6
Compulsory purchase   11.3.6, 11.3.13, 13.3
  awarding authority, powers as to   13.3.2
  compensation, *see* **Crichel Down Rules**
  incentive to conclusion of deals   13.3.1
  indemnity for awarding authority costs   13.3.4
  valuation   13.3.3
Computer services   3.3.1, *see also* **Services contract**
Concession agreement   10.1, *see also* **Project agreement**
Conciliation   16.3.3
Confidentiality   5.6.17, 5.6.19, 5.6.20, 5.6.25, 5.6.27
Consent   7.6.33, 8.5.8
  covenant as to   8.5.17
  planning, *see* **Planning permission**
  security, to   9.4.2
Consideration
  see also **Payment**
  fettering of discretion as part of   4.2.23
  stamp duty on   12.5.5, 12.5.6, 14.5
  surplus land as part of, *see* **Surplus site/property**

Consortium   2.3
  see also **Contractor; Joint venture; Sponsor**
  alteration to, after pre-qualification   5.5.14, 5.6.20
  credit-worthiness of members   8.4.13
  funding, *see* **Funding**
  investment, selling on   2.3.7, 2.3.8
  mortgage of shares   9.1.5
  objectives   2.3.2–2.3.8
    limiting exposure   2.3.6
  step-in by debt funders, view on   9.3.8
Construction contract   7.7
  adjudication, meaning for   16.6.1–16.6.4
  breach or default   7.7.14–7.7.17
  construction works alone   7.2.1
  DBFO, *see* **Design, build, finance and operate (DBFO)**
  'design and build', *see* **Design and build contract**
  EU rules   3.2.1, *see also* **Public procurement rules (EU); Works contract**
  guaranteeing   7.7.13
  JCT81, based on   7.7.1–7.7.5
    acceleration provision   7.7.4
    consistency with project agreement   7.7.2
    extension of time events   7.7.3
    payments   7.7.5
  'partnering'   7.7.7–7.7.12
    cost reimbursement   7.7.9
    extension of time/increase in contract sum   7.7.7, 7.7.8
    lump-sum, based   7.7.8
    overspend/underspend adjustment   7.7.9
  payments under, debt funders' check on   8.5.9
  retention under   7.7.14, 7.7.17
  stand-alone, based on project agreement   7.7.6
  target price contract   7.7.9–7.7.12
    payment options   7.7.11
  types of   7.7, *see also* **Works contract**
Construction costs
  taxation aspects   14.3.8–14.3.20

Construction issues 7.1 *et seq*, *see also* **Construction contract; Project agreement**
Construction operation
  definition (1996 Act) 7.6.33, 16.6.2
Construction period 8.5.1, 8.5.11, 9.1.5, 9.3.32
  force majeure during 10.3.6
  land interest grant after 11.6.1
  relief event during 10.3.13
  risk becoming uninsurable during 10.3.5
  termination during, tax 14.7.2
  variation during 10.6.8, 10.6.11
Construction risk 10.4.8
  accounting treatment 17.5.9, 17.6.3, 17.7.7–17.7.9
Construction work
  definition (1994 Regs) 7.6.33
Constructive dismissal 15.2.11, 15.10.4–15.10.7
Consultation 15.8.5–15.8.9
Contaminated land 13.2
  cost of clean up 13.2.6
  environmental audit 13.2.7
  legislative position 13.2.2, 13.2.4
  liability for 13.2.2, 13.2.3
    contamination during contract period 13.2.9
    long lessee 13.2.3
    tort, in 13.2.5
  risk transfer 13.2.7–13.2.9
    project company responsibility 13.2.7
    tenderer's position 13.2.7, 13.2.8
Contract
  awarding authority with project company, *see* **Project agreement**
  breach, *see* **Breach; Default; Termination**
  breaking, *see* **Termination**
  categories, public procurement rules, *see* **Services contract; Supplies contract; Works contract**
  direct contract, *see* **Direct agreement**
  implied in tender process, breach claim 6.5.1–6.5.3
  income stream from 9.1.6–9.1.9
  operating 7.3.3, 9.1.6
  project company with construction company, *see* **Construction contract**

security over rights 9.1.6–9.1.9
separability for accounting purposes 17.5.5, *see also* **Balance sheet treatment**
standardisation 1.3.23, 10.1.7, 18.4.1
structure 2.5
sub-, *see* **Sub-contractor**
target price 7.7.9–7.7.11
Contracting out 4.2.19, 4.2.20
  transfer of undertakings, position on 15.3.3–15.3.6, 15.4, 15.5
Contractor
  see also **Construction contract**
  agreeing prior to project agreement 7.6.13
  awarding authority, for 7.6.20–7.6.22
  collateral agreement from 7.6.22
  design and build 7.2
  duty of care 7.6.22
  employees of, information on 15.14
  interface difficulties 7.6.22
  principal, for compliance duties 7.6.33
  risk associated with 8.4.13
  sub-, *see* **Sub-contractor**
  transfer of undertaking, position on 15.3.3–15.3.6, 15.4
Cost(s)
  base 10.4.11
  bid, refunding of 1.3.35
  completion to cost 2.2.17
  compliance costs 14.3.23
  construction 14.3.8
  design, of, minimising pre-selection 7.6.3
  due diligence, of 5.7.8
  estimates 8.4.8, *see also* **Price**
  financing 14.2.2, 14.3.5, 14.3.21, 14.3.22
  increase, from change in law 10.5
  late completion, and 7.6.32
  public sector benefits, of matching 15.7.3–15.7.5, 15.12.3, *see also* **Pension rights**
  redundancy, indemnity for, *see* **Indemnity**
  refinancing savings 8.6.1
  'significant change' 10.5.3
  start-up 14.2.2, 14.3.6, 14.3.7
  tax, arising for 14.2.2, 14.3.5
  Transfer of Undertakings Regulations, arising from 15.7.1

Counterparty, *see* **Third party**
Covenants
  awarding authority powers, *see* **Vires**
  project company   8.5.15–8.5.18
    information   8.5.16, 9.3.3
    negative   8.5.18
    positive   8.5.17
Credit agreement   8.5.1–8.5.19
  advancement obligation   9.3.24
  clauses   8.5.2 *et seq*
  covenants and undertakings   8.5.15–8.5.18, 9.3.3
    consents, etc, as to   8.5.17
    information, as to provision   8.5.16, 9.3.3
    prohibition against charges and encumbrances   8.5.18
    workmanship   8.5.17
  default events   9.3.10, 9.3.11
    notification of   9.4.3
  drawing   8.5.11
    conditions to each   8.5.9
    stand-by facility   8.5.10
  phases   8.5.1, 8.5.11
  purpose clause   8.5.3–8.5.5
    application of funds   8.5.4
    conditions precedent   8.5.7
    drawdowns   8.5.5–8.5.9, *see also* **Drawdown**
  repayment
    formula   8.5.12
    grace period   8.5.11
  representations and warranties   8.5.13, 8.5.14
Creditor, *see* **Credit agreement; Debt funder; Funding; Intercreditor agreement; Security; Subordinated lending**
Crichel Down Rules   11.5.4–11.5.9
  application   11.5.5–11.5.7, 11.5.9, 13.3.2
  exceptions   11.5.8
  leaseback, and   11.5.5
  licence, and   11.5.5
  outline   11.5.4
  procedure for offer back   11.5.9
  relevance of   11.5.5
Criminal conviction
  employee, of   15.17.1, 15.17.2
Crown   11.3.9, 11.3.10, 13.1.19–13.1.22, *see also* Government (central); **Planning permission**

Damages
  breach of tender process   6.2.5, 6.2.6
  late completion, *see* **Completion**
Debt/equity ratios   8.5.8, 8.5.9, 8.5.10, 8.6.4
  breach of   8.5.19
Debt funder   2.4, 2.3.7, *see also* **Funding**
  agreement, tripartite   2.5.5, 5.7.8
  bond requirements   2.5.11, 7.7.14–7.7.17
  collateral agreements   7.6.12
  construction contract, interest in   7.7.8
  direct agreement requirements, *see* **Direct agreement**
  documentation
    drawdown requirements   8.5.6–8.5.8
    intercreditor agreement   8.5.20–8.5.23, *see also* **Credit agreement**
  due diligence, *see* Due diligence
  evidence of commitment from   5.7.14
  finance lessor, priority difficulties with   8.2.9, 8.5.23
  objectives   2.4.1–2.4.6
  receiver, appointment of, *see* **Receiver**
  risk, and   2.4.2, 2.4.3, 8.4.4 *et seq*, *see also* **Risk allocation**
  sale of project as going concern   9.1.9, *see also* **Direct agreement**
  security for, *see* **Security**
  step-in rights, *see* **Step-in**
  step-out   9.3.17
  sub-contractors, and   7.6.11, 7.6.12
  taking over project   9.2.3, 9.3.5, 9.3.12
    mortgagee in possession, as   9.3.12, 9.3.13
  termination, early notice of   2.4.6, 2.5.5, 9.3.2, 9.3.3
  transfer of interest   8.4.19
Decanting provisions   7.6.19
Decision of public body
  validity challenge, heads for   4.2.1, *see also* **Vires**
Decoration   7.6.34
Deduction   7.6.14, 7.6.29, 9.3.25, 9.5.1, 10.4.20–10.4.36

Deduction – *cont*
  excluded events   10.4.25
  negotiating mechanism for   10.4.21
  performance points mechanisms
    10.4.27–10.4.36
    double counting   10.4.33
    'failure'   10.4.31
    further reliefs   10.4.36
    monitoring   10.4.28, 10.4.29
    moratorium after completion
      10.4.35
    output driven   10.4.30
    proportionate deduction   10.4.32
    remedying   10.4.32
    sub-contractors   10.4.34
  principle of payment by results
    10.4.20 *et seq*
  'unavailability'   10.4.24
    payment methods   10.4.22, 10.4.23
    remedying   10.4.26
Deduction (tax relief)   14.3.24
Default   2.2.19, 2.2.30, 8.4.16
  awarding authority, by   10.7.1, 10.7.7, 10.7.8
    termination compensation
      10.9.16–10.9.18
  bond for   7.7.14
  contractual provisions for   2.2.32, 8.4.17, 8.5.19
    list of usual events   8.5.19
  covenant against   8.5.17
  credit agreement provisions for
    9.3.10
  effect of   8.5.19, 10.9.4 *et seq*
  pre-step-in   9.3.19–9.3.21
  project company, termination
    compensation   10.9.4–10.9.15
    amount of   10.9.8–10.9.12
    approaches to   10.9.4–10.9.7
    'market value' approach   10.9.13–10.9.15
    'outstanding debt' method
      10.9.10–10.9.12
    post-completion event   10.9.8, 10.9.10
    pre-completion event   10.9.8, 10.9.9
  protection from, *see* **Direct agreement**
  set-off rights   10.9.23, 10.9.24
Defect
  see also **Operational risk**

  bond covering   7.7.14, *see also* **Bond (financing)**
  commissioning revealing   7.6.25
  completion, and   7.6.27, 7.6.28
  deduction from unitary payment
    7.6.14, 7.6.29, 9.3.25
  'defects liability period'   7.2.4, 7.6.27
  facility affected by   7.6.29
  latent   7.3.4, 7.6.29, 7.6.30
  liability for   7.3.4, 7.6.29
    disputed   7.6.30
  penalty limit   9.4.4
  time limit   7.2.5, 7.3.4, 7.6.29
Delay
  see also **Completion**
  notice of   8.5.16
  risk of   10.4.2
Delegation   4.2.16–4.2.21, *see also* **Vires**
Demand risk
  accounting treatment   17.5.7, 17.7.5
Demolition   7.6.19, 7.6.33
Departmental estate occupancy agreement   11.3.8–11.3.12
  application and effect   11.3.9
  'holder'   11.3.8
  sale of interest to project company   11.3.11
  Memorandum of Terms of Occupation (MOTO)   11.3.9, 11.3.12
  'occupier'   11.3.8, 11.3.11
  scenarios catered for   11.3.10
  termination   11.3.11, 11.3.12
  terms of occupation   11.3.9
Design and build contract   7.2.1–7.2.5
  PFI project
    awarding authority   7.3.1, 7.3.3
    construction company   7.3.2, 7.3.3
    design risk, *see* **Design risk**
    developer company   7.3.1, 7.3.3
    latent defects   7.3.4, *see also* **Operational risk**
    monitoring rights   7.6.18
    output specification, *see* **Output specification**
    payment and funding   7.3.1, 7.3.2
    project company's proposals   7.3.5
    responsibilities   7.3.3, 7.3.4
    traditional approach   7.2, 7.6.18

Design and build contract – *cont*
  traditional approach – *cont*
    agent for authority   7.2.4
    contractor's liability   7.2.5, 7.2.6
    'defects liability period'   7.2.4,
      7.6.27
    developer authority   7.2.2, 7.2.3,
      7.2.4
    extension of time   7.2.4, 7.6.18
    maintenance and repairs   7.2.6
    output specification and response
      to   7.2.2
    payment and funding   7.2.3
    'practical completion'   7.2.4
    retention   7.2.3, 7.2.4
    standard contract for contractor
      appointment   7.2.2

Design, build, finance and operate (DBFO)   1.2.7, 2.2.8
  capital finance rules   4.3.3
  contracting out to project company   4.2.20
  EU rules, and, 3.2.6
  licence, use of   11.4.27
  performance bond   2.5.10
  residual value risk, and   2.2.27
  volume-related payment mechanism   2.2.25, *see also* **Payment**

Design contest   3.3.1
Design document approval   7.6.5, *see also* **Project agreement**
Design issues, *see* **Project agreement**
Design risk   2.2.7–2.2.10
  transfer of
    fitness for purpose   2.2.9, 7.6.1
    planning risk, relationship with   2.2.10
    private sector freedom central   2.2.7
    specifications prescribed, effect of   2.2.8, 7.4.2

Developer
  design and build contract
    awarding authority as   7.2.2–7.2.4
    project company as   7.3.1, 7.3.3
  overage, and   12.4.4, 12.4.6, 12.4.10, 12.4.21, 12.5.2
    direct contract with, tax   12.5.8–12.5.11
  third party, *see* **Third party**

Direct agreement   9.1 *et seq*
  advance notice of termination 9.3.2–9.3.3
  awarding authority
    debt funders', with   9.3.1 *et seq*
    developer with, and overage   12.5.2, 12.5.8–12.5.11
    use by   9.1.10, 10.10.2
  consent to security   9.4.2
  counterparty, position of   9.2.5–9.2.7
  credit agreement default notification   9.4.3
  debt funders' need for   9.1.8, 9.1.9, 9.2.6
  draft, by Taskforce   9.5.1, 9.6
  novation provisions, *see* **Novation agreement**
  parties   9.2.1–9.2.3
    agent bank for debt funders   9.3.24
  payment instructions   9.4.5
  pre-completion step-in   9.3.9
  project company, position of   9.2.1–9.2.3
  purpose of   9.2.4
  receiver, right to appoint   9.3.14., *see also* **Receiver**
  remedy period extension   9.4.4
  security aspect of   9.1.1, 9.1.9, 9.3.1
  step-in/out clauses, *see* **Step-in**
  terms, debt-funders' agreement   9 3
  transfer of project, *see* **Third party: taking over project**
  undertaking, *see* **Undertaking (step-in)**
  undertaking, alternative to   9.5

Director
  liability   7.6.33
Disciplinary action   15.18
  awarding authority right to control   15.18.1, 15.18.2
  indemnity for claims   15.18.2
Disclaimer   5.6.17, 5.6.23
Discretion, fettering of   4.2.22–4.2.24
  consideration, fetter as part of   4.2.23
  express wording   4.2.22
  Secretary of State's planning functions   4.2.24
Discrimination, *see* **Unfair discrimination**
Dismissal
  constructive, *see* **Constructive dismissal**
  indemnity for claims   15.18.2
  offence, for   15.17.2
  transfer of undertakings, and, *see* **Transfer of undertaking**

Dispute   7.6.28, 7.6.30, 16.1 *et seq*
  adjudication reference   7.6.33, 16.1.1, 16.6
    'construction contract'   16.6.1–16.6.4
    decision later found to be wrong   16.6.7
    excluded agreements   16.6.2, 16.6.3
    procedure   16.6.5
    speed of   16.6.7
    statutory right of parties   16.6.6
  alternative dispute resolution   16.1.1, 16.1.7, 16.3, 16.4.4, 16.6.6
    advantages of   16.3.4
    forms of   16.3.3
    forum for settlement   16.3.1, 16.4.5
    'neutral' person   16.3.1, 16.3.2
  arbitration   16.1.1, 16.1.7, 16.4
    ADR contrasted   16.4.4, 16.4.5
    binding decision   16.4.1, 16.4.5
    court assistance and regulation   16.4.2
    principles   16.4.3
  conciliation   16.3.3
  contract term for   16.7, 16.8
  dispute review board or panel   16.1.1, 16.1.5, 16.2, 16.6.6
  expert determination   16.1.1, 16.5
  forms for resolution   16.1.1
    binding decision needed   16.1.2
    factors for choice   16.1.3, 16.1.4
    fast track   16.1.8
    informal through to formal   16.1.3, 16.1.5–16.1.8
    overseas element   16.1.4, 16.8.2
  joinder of parties provision   16.7.1, 16.7.2
  mediation   16.3.3
  same form for all contracts   16.7.1
Drawdown   8.5.5–8.5.9, 8.5.11
  conditions precedent   8.5.6, 8.5.7
  conditions to each drawing   8.5.9
  dedicated project account for   8.5.5
  period   8.5.6, 8.5.9
  requirements   8.5.6–8.5.8
Due diligence   5.7.8, 5.7.14, 7.2.3, 7.6.15, 8.4.1
Duration   9.3.32
  effect of   10.4.11, 10.6.1

Education   1.3.24, 1.3.26
  health facilities combined with   18.4.5
Employee   15.1 *et seq*
  see also **Transfer of undertaking; Workmanship**
  claims by, indemnity for   15.18.2
  contractors', information on   15.14, *see also* **Transfer of undertaking**
  disciplinary action   15.18
  dismissal, *see* **Transfer of undertaking**
  misconduct   15.18
  pay after transfer to private sector, case   15.9.10
  pension, *see* **Pension rights**
  previous convictions   15.17.1, 15.17.2
  recruitment   15.18.3
  training   15.16
Employment contract
  change to, after transfer, *see* **Transfer of undertaking**
Environmental audit   13.2.7
Environmental law   13.2, *see also* **Contaminated land**
Environmental standards   10.4.24
Environmental statement
  planning application, for   13.1.10–13.1.12
Equal pay claims   15.7.5
Equipment
  see also **Asset; Capital allowances**
  capital, and lease financing   8.2.9, 8.5.23
  charge protecting   2.2.34
  project funding   8.3.1
  purchase or hire contract, rules   3.2.1, 3.2.6, 3.2.16
Equity investment   8.2.2
Equity return   17.6.4, 17.6.5, 17.7.6
Eurobond   8.2.5
European Commission
  complaint to, breach of tender process   6.3
    infringement proceedings against government   6.3.1
    interim order   6.3.1
    risk and effect of   6.3.2
European Investment Bank/Fund   8.2.10, 8.5.21
European Union
  acquired rights Directive   15.1.2, 15.2.1

Index

European Union – *cont*
  acquired rights Directive – *cont*
    amendments   15.3.1, 15.3.6
  Community Product Classification
    3.2.21
  Maastricht convergence criteria
    1.4.1
  Official Journal of the European
    Communities, advert in   1.3.23,
    3.2.11
    negotiated procedure, for   3.3.7–
    3.3.20, 5.4.1
    notice of award   3.3.48
    public works concession, of
    3.2.14
    see also **Public procurement rules
    (EU)**
  public procurement rules, *see* **Public
    procurement rules (EU)**
Event of default, *see* **Default**
Expenditure
  see also **Cost(s)**
  allocation   1.3.30
  allowances for, *see* **Capital allowances**
  deductibility for tax   14.3.24–
    14.3.26, *see also* **Taxation**
Expert determination   16.5
  procedure   16.5.1
  selection of expert   16.5.1

Facilities
  availability, and payment   2.2.22,
    10.4.4
  ownership option for awarding
    authority   2.2.28
    defect remedy, and   7.6.29
Fairness   6.5.3, *see also* **Natural
  justice; Unfair discrimination; Vires**
Fairness at Work   15.2.5, 15.8.11
Fees   8.5.4, 14.3.7
Finance lease   8.5.21, 17.2.3
  accounting standard   17.3.2, 17.3.4
  FRS   17.3.2, 17.3.4
    amendment   17.3.5
Financial services contract   3.3.1, *see
  also* **Services contract**
Financially free-standing project
  1.2.15
Financing agreement, *see* **Funding;
  Refinancing**
Fire   10.3.14, *see also* **Relief event**

Fire authority   3.2.2
Fitness for purpose   2.2.9, 7.6.1
Force majeure   2.2.16, 2.2.21, 7.2.4,
  10.3.3–10.3.8
  compensation   10.3.7, 10.3.8,
    10.9.19–10.9.21
    standardised position sought
    10.9.20
  definition   10.3.3–10.3.5
  effect of   10.3.6–10.3.8
  extension of time   10.3.6
  notice of   8.5.16
  Taskforce guidance on   10.3.4,
    10.3.5
  termination   10.3.8, 10.7.9
  uninsurable risks   10.3.4
    becoming, during construction
    period 10.3.5
Fossils   7.6.33
Freehold
  see also **Property issues**
  sale by project company   11.4.10
  transfer to project company
    11.4.28, 11.4.29
  risk mitigation   11.4.11
Funding   8.1 *et seq*
  agreement   2.5.4
  background and criteria for   8.1
  bank debt   8.2.3, 8.2.4
    documentation   8.2.3
    negotiating   8.2.4
  base loan facility   8.5.3
  bond, *see* **Bond (financing)**
  charge, fixed or floating   8.4.21
  costs, tax aspects   14.2.2, 14.3.5,
    14.3.21, 14.3.22
  debt funders' considerations   8.4.2,
    8.4.3
  detailed planning permission as
    condition   13.1.6
  documentation   8.5
    credit agreement, *see* **Credit
    agreement**
    intercreditor   8.5.20–8.5.23
  domino effect   8.4.3
  due diligence, *see* **Due diligence**
  equity   8.2.2, 8.5.8
  European Investment Bank/Fund
    8.2.10
  grants   8.2.10
  interest costs, tax aspects   14.3.21,
    14.3.22

Funding – *cont*
  lease financing   8.2.9, 8.5.23
  limited recourse finance   8.3, 8.5
    achieving in PFI project   8.3.2
    meaning   8.3.1
  risk allocation   8.4.4–8.4.17, *see also*
    Risk allocation
  risk analysis   8.4
  security, *see* **Security**
  sources   8.2.2–8.2.10
  stand-by facility   8.5.3, 8.5.10
  structure of   8.3, 8.5
  subordinated debt   8.2.2, 8.4.8, 8.5.8
    intercreditor agreement   8.5.20–8.5.23
  syndicated project loan   8.2.3, 8.2.4, 8.5.1
  termination rights, and, *see* **Termination**
  transferability of interest   8.4.19
  viability   8.4
  working capital facility   8.5.3

Gift, corrupt
  termination for   10.7.10, 10.7.11
  compensation   10.9.22
Goods
  alternative product, provision for   7.6.2
  purchase or hire contract, rules   3.2.1, 3.2.6, 3.2.16
  quality   7.6.2
Government Actuary's Department (GAD)   15.11.1–15.11.3
Government (central)
  accommodation project
    core activity, not contracted-out   2.2.20
    departmental estate occupancy agreement   11.3.8–11.3.12
    property structure for   11.4.7
    residual value risk transfer   2.2.28
    risk sharing   10.5.3
  investment in PFI   18.4.3, 18.4.6
  planning control   13.1.19–13.1.21, *see also* **Planning permission**
  powers   4.2.2, 4.2.8
  risks, share in   18.2.6
  tax   14.3.1
  VAT   14.4.2, 14.4.5, 14.4.7, 14.4.8
Government Circular 6/93   11.5

Government grant   8.2.10
Guarantee   2.2.19, 2.5.8, 7.6.16, 7.7.13
Guidance   1.3.11, 1.3.22, *see also* **Taskforce**

Health and safety
  Executive   7.6.37
  legislation   10.5.3
  variation affecting   10.6.4
Health authority
  statutory body, powers as   4.2.2, *see also* **Vires**
Health sector
  see also **Health authority; Hospital; NHS**
  plans to combine with educational facilities   18.4.5
High Court
  action for breach of tender process   6.2.2
    possible orders   6.2.5
  litigation in   16.1.3, 16.1.6
Highway, *see* **Road**
Highway authority
  planning application, involvement   13.1.9
Hospital
  bond issue financing   8.2.5
  design, build, finance and manage only projects   18.4.4
  law change, and
    effect on costs   10.5.3
    termination right   10.7.8
  NHS trust powers, *see* **Vires**
  non-clinical services   10.4.12
  project   1.2.15, 1.3.9, 1.3.15
    core activity, not contracted-out   2.2.20
    service fees   2.2.23, 2.2.25
    standards   1.3.24
  project agreement   10.1.5
    standard   18.4.4
  separate service provision   18.4.4
Housing association
  VAT   14.4.5, 14.4.9

Illegality, *see* **Vires**
Income
  stream   9.1.6–9.1.9
    protection   9.1.8, 9.1.9, *see also* **Direct agreement**

Income – *cont*
　tax aspects　14.3.26, 14.6.3, 14.7.3, *see also* **Taxation**
Indemnity
　redundancy costs, against　15.6.6, 15.6.7, 15.6.9, 15.6.10
　transfer of undertaking costs
　　generally　15.7.1, 15.7.6–15.7.8, 15.15.2
　　unfair dismissal etc claims, for　15.18.2
Indexation　10.4.9, 10.4.11, 10.5.1, 10.5.2
Industrial action　8.5.19, 10.3.15, 15.8.10
Industrial building or structure, *see* **Capital allowances**
Information
　tenderer, to, *see* **Tender**
　transfer of undertaking, on, *see* **Transfer of undertaking**
Information technology project
　funding　8.3.1
Insolvency (of construction company)　7.7.14
Insolvency (of project company)　2.2.29–2.2.35
　event of default, as　2.2.32, 8.5.19
　'pay when paid' clause　7.6.33
　risk　2.2.19, 2.2.29
　risk mitigation　2.2.31–2.2.35
　　methods　2.2.31, 2.2.35
　　performance bond, *see* **Bond (performance)**
　　securing use of equipment etc　2.2.34
　　termination arrangements　2.2.32, 2.2.34, 2.2.35
　transfer of undertaking, contract variation　15.9.12, *see also* **Transfer of undertakings**
Inspection　7.6.18, 7.6.28
Insurance　2.2.21, 2.3.5, 7.6.33, 8.4.14, 8.4.15
　covenant as to　8.5.17
　first call on proceeds　8.4.14
　insured parties　8.4.14
　notice of claims　8.5.16
　reinstatement of asset obligation, and　8.4.15
　relief event, for risk of　10.3.14

　uninsurable events, *see also* **Compensation: events; Force majeure**
　　Taskforce guidance　10.3.14
Intellectual property rights　7.6.33
Intercreditor agreement　8.5.20–8.5.23
　contents　8.5.21
　negotiation of　8.5.20
Interest costs
　tax aspects　14.3.21, 14.3.22
International aspects　18.5
　countries interested in PFI　18.5.1
　examples　18.5.2–18.5.6
　dispute resolution　16.1.4, 16.8.2
　exportable product, PFI as　18.5.7
Investment in Britain Fund　18.4.3
Invitation to negotiate (ITN), *see* **Tender**
Irrationality, *see* **Vires**

Joinder of parties　16.7
Joint venture　1.2.15, 1.3.5, 14.2.4
　limited recourse structure　14.2.4
　tax　14.3.27
Judicial review　4.3.13, 6.1.1, 6.4
　alternative remedy principle　6.4.8
　planning permission decision, of　13.1.13
　public law element, need for　6.4.1, 6.4.3
　public procurement decision　6.4.1–6.4.10
　　cases　6.4.2–6.4.7
　　statutory underpinning　6.4.4, 6.4.6, 6.4.9, 6.4.10
　　ultra vires decision　6.4.9
　　uncertainty over　6.4.7

Labour Government　1.2.1, 1.3.7, 1.3.36
　commitment of　1.3.36, 1.4.2, 18.1
　reappraisal by　1.3.17–1.3.19
Land
　see also **Lease; Site**
　interest in
　　grant of, and stamp duty, *see* **Stamp duty**
　　grant of, and VAT　14.4.2, 14.4.8
　　trading loss relief　14.3.26
　see also **Property issues**
　report on title　8.5.8
　risk allocation　8.4.12

Land – *cont*
  surplus   2.2.12, 11.2.2, 11.7, *see also*
    Crichel Down Rules; Surplus site/property
Landscaping
  planning application, and   13.1.9–13.1.12
Laundry, *see* **Service; Services contract**
Law, change in   10.5
  compensating event, as   10.3.9, 10.3.10
  indexation as compensation for   10.5.2
  mitigation of impact   10.5.4, 10.5.5
  risk of   8.4.11, 10.5.1 *et seq*
  Taskforce guidance   10.5.2, 10.5.4–10.5.6
  Transfer of Undertakings Regs   15.7.1
  VAT   10.5.6
Lease   9.1.6, 11.4.5 *et seq*
  see also **Property issues**
  capital allowances, and   14.3.17, 14.3.20
  contaminated land, of   13.2.3
  copy of   8.5.8
  duration   9.1.6
  full repairing and insuring, PFI structures distinguished   11.8.2
  grant back to awarding authority   11.4.7–11.4.14
    Crichel Down Rules, application   11.5.5
    sub-lease   11.4.15–11.4.24
    see also **Property issues**
  rents   14.5.1, 14.7.4
  stamp duty on grant   14.5.1, 14.5.3, 14.5.4
    lease back   14.5.5, 14.5.6
    rents   14.5.1
Lease financing   1.3.5, 8.2.9, 8.5.21, 8.5.23
Legal compliance   7.6.33, 8.5.13
  see also **Consents**
  costs, tax aspects   14.3.23
Licence   2.5.3, 8.5.17, 11.4.5, 11.4.6
  capital allowances, and   14.3.17, 14.3.19
  copy   8.5.8
  Crichel Down Rules, application   11.5.5
  grant to project company   11.4.25–11.4.27, 11.4.34, 14.3.26

  stamp duty, avoids   14.5.7
Limited recourse finance, *see* **Funding; Joint venture**
Litigation   16.1.3, 16.1.6
Loan
  project, of, *see* **Funding**
  protection of lender to local authority   4.3.10, *see also* **Third party**
  restriction on project company   8.5.18
Loan life cover ratio   8.5.8, 8.6.4
  breach of   8.5.19
Local authority   1.3.12, 1.3.24, 1.3.27
  borrowing transaction   4.3.4 *et seq*, *see also* **Third party**
  buildings project   4.3.3
  capital finance regime amendments   4.3.1–4.3.3
    credit cover   4.3.1, 4.3.3
    DBFO schemes   4.3.3
    private finance transaction   4.3.2
  delegation limits   4.2.21, 4.3.7
  disposal of land by, price   11.5, *see also* **Property issues**
  EU public procurement rules apply   3.2.2
  fiduciary duty   4.2.25
  heating and lighting system   4.3.3
  standing orders of, own compliance   4.2.26
  statutory body, powers as, *see* **Vires**
  swap transaction   4.1.2, 4.2.9, 4.3.4
  third party protection, *see* **Third party**
  VAT   14.4.5, 14.4.6
London Underground   1.3.7, 2.2.28, 18.2.2, 18.2.4
  EU rules   3.2.3, 3.2.7

Machinery, *see* **Asset; Capital allowances; Equipment**
Maintenance
  failure   7.6.30
  obligation   1.2.9, 7.2.6
  work, as 'construction work'   7.6.33
Management consultancy services   3.3.1, *see also* **Services contract**
Market testing
  comparable pension provision as condition   15.11.4
  contract lost on, redundancy payment liability   15.12.4

Market testing – *cont*
  payment   10.4.13–10.4.16, 10.5.2
  services contract, for   15.6.6, 15.6.12
  variation   10.6.9
Mediation   16.3.3
Monitoring   7.6.18, 10.4.28, 10.4.29
Mortgage, *see* **Security**
Mortgagee in possession, as   9.3.12

NHS
  see also **Hospital**
  bank margin reductions   18.3.1
  Conservative Government
    approach   18.2.4
  equal pay claims   15.7.5
  equipment project, funding   8.3.1
  injury benefits for employees
    15.7.3, 15.12.2
  public procurement rules apply
    3.2.2
  redundancy benefits for employees
    15.7.3
  trust, powers
    compulsory purchase, for   13.3.2
    VAT   14.4.5, 14.4.7, 14.4.8
    validity, abuse, etc, *see* **Vires**
National Asset Register   18.4.3
National security   3.2.22
Natural justice   4.2.26, 6.4.2, 13.1.13
Negotiated procedure, *see* **Public procurement rules (EU)**
Negotiating the project agreement
  10.1 *et seq*
  background to   10.1, 10.11
  complexity   10.1.3, 10.11.1
  constraints   10.1.2
  core issues   10.2 *et seq*, *see also* **Law, change in; Payment; Step-in; Termination; Variation**
  draft agreement   10.1.4–10.1.6
  events preventing performance, *see* **Compensation; Force majeure; Relief events**
  precedents   10.1.2, 10.1.4, 10.11.2
  standard form agreement, guidance
    10.1.7–10.1.13, 10.2.1, 10.3.2, *see also* **Taskforce**
Non-governmental public body
  EU public procurement rules apply
    3.2.2
  Policy Statement on   1.3.29

Notice
  national   3.3.20
  OJ, in, *see* **European Union**
  tender, for   5.4
Novation agreement   9.2.1, 9.3.27–9.3.31
  effect of   9.3.31
  novatee
    awarding authority's objection
      to   9.3.28–9.3.30
    outstanding defaults etc, position as
      to   9.3.31
    revision and resubmission   9.3.30
  undertaking compliance   9.3.31

Occupation, *see* **Property issues**
Offences   7.6.33
  dismissal/removal for   15.17.2
  previous convictions   15.17.1, 15.17.2
Offer, *see* **Bid**
Office accommodation   11.4.12, 11.4.18, *see also* **Government (central)**
Operating period   8.5.1, 8.5.11, 9.5.32
  see also **Service**
  contract for   7.3.3, 9.1.6
  variation during   10.6.9, 10.6.11
Operational risk   2.2.20–2.2.25
  see also **Performance (project agreement)**
  changes in   17.5.7
  factors for consideration   8.4.7
  transfer of   2.2.20, 8.4.7
Option testing   1.3.8–1.3.10
Origins   1.3, 1.6
Output specification   1.2.3, 2.2.1, 2.2.7
  construction contract to identify
    7.7.7
  design and build contract, 7.3.5, 7.4
    approach to   7.4.1, 7.4.2
    contents   7.4.3, 7.6.2
    design risk transfer, and   2.2.8, 7.4.2
  design requirements of, meeting   7.6
  Writing an Output Specification
    2.2.8, 5.6.13
Overage   12.1 *et seq*
  anti-avoidance   12.4.20
  background   12.1
  benefits, ways for authority to
    enjoy   12.5.2

Overage – *cont*
    calculation   12.4.15–12.4.19
    clawback distinguished   12.2.2–12.2.5
    disposal statement, covenants, etc   12.4.21
    disposal triggering   12.4.4–12.4.6
        'actual' and CGT rules   12.4.9
        deemed   12.4.10, 12.4.11, 12.4.14
        small   12.4.12
    evolution   12.2
    form of   12.4.1, 12.4.2
    meaning   12.1.3
    non-land interest   12.4.5, 12.4.13, 12.4.14
    planning permission
        grant triggering   12.4.10
        land sold without   12.3.2
        protection inherent in   12.3.3
    reasons for   12.3
    tax, *see* **Taxation**
    third party developer   12.4.4, 12.4.10, 12.5
        authority contractual link with   12.4.6
        contracts with   12.5.2
        disposal statement   12.4.21
    time considerations   12.3
        obligation to pay   12.2.1, 12.4.7–12.4.14
        period   12.4.7, 12.4.8
Overseas element
    see also **International aspects**
    dispute resolution   16.1.4, 16.8.2

Partnership, public/private sector   1.3.7, 18.2, 18.4.3
    development and forms of   18.2.2, 18.4.6
    Public Private Partnerships Programme Ltd   1.3.12
Payment   1.2.13, 10.4
    see also **Price**
    adjustment   10.4.8–10.4.10
        variation, basis for   10.6.9–10.6.13
    affordability   1.2.14, 10.4.37
    amount of   10.4.8–10.4.10
        availability element   2.2.22, 10.4.3, 10.4.4
        tax   14.3.26
    unavailability, *see* **Deductions**

    compensation, *see* **Compensation**
    cost, out of line with   10.4.11–10.4.19
    elements   2.2.22–2.2.25, 10.4.3–10.4.7
        availability, *see* 'availability element' *above*
        performance, *see* 'performance-related' *below*
        volume element, *see* 'volume-related' *below*
    failure by authority   10.7.7
    guidance   10.4.1
    interim or stage   7.6.33, 7.7.5
    JCT81-based contract term   7.7.5
    mechanisms for   10.4
    obligations, start of   2.2.19, 2.2.29, 7.6.27, 8.2.6
    performance-related   2.2.22, 8.4.7, 10.4.20
        over-performance   10.4.37, 10.4.38
        performance element   10.4.2, 10.4.3, 10.4.5
        under-performance, *see* **Deductions**
    purpose clause in credit agreement   8.5.3–8.5.5
    results, by, *see* **Deductions**
    risk transfer   10.4.2, 10.4.8, 10.4.9
    service provision, *see* **Service**
    step-in period, during   9.4.5
    suspension for non-payment   7.6.33
    variability   10.4.8–10.4.10
    volume-related   2.2.25, 10.4.3, 10.4.6, 10.4.7
    withholding sums, notice of   7.6.33
Pension rights   15.10–15.13
    enhanced schemes, rights after transfer   15.12.1–15.12.3
        calculation methods   15.12.3
    General Whitley Council rights   15.12.1, 15.12.2
    Government Actuary's Department role   15.11.1–15.11.3
    project company, comparable level provision   15.10.4–15.10.7, 15.11
        'broadly comparable' test   15.11.1
        GAD certificate   15.11.2, 15.11.3
        remuneration package as whole   15.11.3, 15.11.4

Pension rights – *cont*
   protection of accrued   15.11.4,
     15.12.5, 15.12.6
     'bulk transfer payment'   15.12.5
     individual transfer payment
      15.12.6
   reform proposals   15.13
     UK compliance   15.13.2
   transfer of undertaking, effect on
     15.2.4, 15.10
     'excluded rights'   15.10.1, 15.12.1,
      15.12.2
     government schemes, and good faith
      duty   15.10.4–15.10.7
     interpretation   15.10.2, 15.10.3
     rights passing to project
      company   15.10.3
Performance (employee), *see*
   Workmanship
Performance (project agreement)
   1.2.9, 2.2.7, 2.2.20
   element of payment   2.2.22, 8.4.7,
    10.4.3, 10.4.5
   events preventing, *see* **Compensation**;
    Force majeure; **Relief events**
   monitoring   2.2.18
   over-performance   10.4.37, 10.4.38
    credits for   10.4.38
   services, *see* **Service**
   standards, *see* **Standards**
   under-performance   8.4.9, 10.4.5,
    10.4.38, *see also* **Deductions**
Performance bond   2.2.31, 2.2.33,
   2.5.7, 7.7.14
   circumstances for   2.5.10
   construction company default or
    insolvency, for   7.7.14
   use of   2.2.19, 7.6.16, 7.6.17
Planning authority   13.1.1
   government client dealing with
    2.2.11
   permission, obtaining, *see* **Planning
    permission**; **Planning risk**
   planning agreement   13.1.7, 13.1.8,
    13.1.14
    Crown entering   13.1.22
   'non-material considerations'
    13.1.8
Planning permission   13.1
   acceptable for project company
    13.1.5
   appeal, non-determination   13.1.8

   application for   13.1.4
    mistake in   13.1.13
    preparation   13.1.9–13.1.13, *see
     also* 'full' *below*
   conditions   13.1.3, 13.1.4, 13.1.6
   decision on
    judicial review of   13.1.13
    political nature of   13.1.1
   detailed   13.1.4
    need for, 13.1.6, 13.1.8
   full   13.1.4, 13.1.9–13.1.13
    environmental statement
     13.1.10–13.1.12
    highway improvements, traffic
     impact studies etc   13.1.9
    visual impact study   13.1.10
   government department, position
    of   13.1.19–13.1.22
    case on   13.1.21
    immunity of Crown   13.1.19,
     13.1.20
    informal procedure for   13.1.19,
     13.1.20
    planning agreement   13.1.22
   land sold without   12.3.2
   outline   13.1.4, 13.1.6, 13.1.8
   planning agreement   13.1.7, 13.1.8,
    13.1.14
   project agreement conditional on
    13.1.14
    circumstances for unconditional
     agreement   13.1.17
    responsibility for   11.3.4, 11.3.5,
     13.1.14
   risk transfer, *see* **Planning risk**
   stages leading to grant   13.1.3
   surplus site, for   13.1.18
Planning risk   11.3.3–11.3.6, 12.2.1,
   13.1.14–13.1.17
   consent as condition   2.2.12
   funders' considerations   2.2.11–
    2.2.13, 13.1.6
   managing   13.1
   'planning gain'   13.1.15, 13.1.16
   projects to which relevant   2.2.11
   surplus sites part of consideration
    2.2.12
   transfer difficulties   2.2.11, 2.2.12
Planning supervisor   7.6.33
Plant and machinery, *see* **Asset**; **Capital
   allowances**; **Equipment**
Police authority   3.2.2

Political objectives   1.2.1, 1.4.1
Power, *see* Vires
Price   2.2.37. 10.4.11–10.4.19
  see also Cost(s); Tender; Value for money
  alteration   5.7.15, 7.6.31, 7.7.7, 10.4.17, 10.5.1
  completion to price   2.2.17, 7.6.31
  disposal of land by local authority, controls   11.5
  indexation   10.4.9, 10.4.11, 10.5.1, 10.5.2
  target price contract   7.7.9–7.7.11
  transfer of risk, of,   1.2.10, 1.2.11, 7.7.9, 8.4.8
Prison project
  contracting out, scope of   2.2.20
  default by project company   10.9.4
  increased costs   10.5.3
  number of prisoners, and payment   2.2.25
  ownership issues   2.2.27
  project type   1.2.15
  public procurement procedure   3.3.9
  specifications   2.2.8
  standardising of agreement   1.3.14, 1.3.24
Private Finance Panel   1.3.6, 1.3.13
  guidance   2.3.8, 10.1.8, 10.3.3
  winding up of   1.3.20
Private finance transaction
  definition   4.3.2
Private Finance Unit   1.3.12, 1.3.22, 1.3.31
  guidance on transfer of undertakings   15.6.6
Private sector
  asset, responsibility for   1.2.2–1.2.6, 1.2.9, 1.2.15
  risk transfer to, *see* Risk allocation
  role, outline   1.2.1–1.2.3
Procedure
  complexity   1.4.3
  impropriety in, *see* Vires
  improving   1.3.23–1.3.30
  public procurement rules, *see* Public procurement rules (EU)
Process   1.3.23–1.3.30, 18.4
Profits   2.2.38, 2.3.3, 2.3.4
  refinancing gains, *see* Refinancing
Project
  early examples   1.3.2–1.3.4, 1.3.14

  nature of, effect   1.3.15, 1.3.16, 2.2.2, 2.2.3
  priority   1.3.9, 1.3.21, 1.3.26
  sale as going concern   9.1.9
  series, one procurement   18.4.2
  'significant'
    factors for   1.3.20
    overseeing of   10.1.2
  take over of
    debt funder, by   9.2.3, 9.3.5, 9.3.12
    third party, by   9.1.9, 9.2.3
  types   1.2.15, 1.2.16
Project agreement   1.3.23–1.3.25, 2.5.2
  access provisions   7.6.18, 7.6.23
  agreeing terms, *see* Negotiating the project agreement
  amendments
    creditor agreement   8.5.21
    prohibition on   8.5.18
  assignment of rights   9.3.26, 9.4.2
  boilerplate clauses   1.3.11
  breach   8.5.19, 9.2.4, *see also* Default; Direct agreement
  commissioning provisions   7.6.23–7.6.26
    defect and re-commissioning   7.6.25
    forfeit of right   7.6.26
    'windows' for   7.6.23, 7.6.24
  compulsory purchase
    condition, as   13.3.4
    indemnity for costs   13.3.4
  consistency   1.3.25, 15.7.8
  construction contract based on, types   7.7, *see also* Construction contract
  contractors of awarding authority, provisions for   7.6.20–7.6.22
  decanting provisions   7.6.19
  design and construction issues   7.6
    alternative product, provision for   7.6.2
    approval of documents   7.6.5, 7.6.6, 7.6.9
    construction company input   7.7.6
    detailed drawings   7.6.7
    development after acceptance of tender   7.6.3–7.6.10
    development after execution of agreement   7.6.6–7.6.10

Project agreement – *cont*
  design and construction issues – *cont*
    form of provisions   7.6.1, 7.6.4, 7.6.5
    outline drawings, numbering and acknowledgement   7.6.4
    project company's liability   7.6.5, 7.6.9, 7.6.10
    rejection or revision of documents   7.6.7, 7.6.8, 7.6.10
    standard of care and performance   7.6.1, 7.6.2
    time limits   7.6.6, 7.6.8
  extension of term   2.2.16, *see also* **Completion**
  flexibility   2.2.40
  health and safety file   7.6.36
  guidance on   10.1.7–10.1.3
  intervention rights of awarding authority   9.3.25
  legal compliance obligations   7.6.33
  model   5.6.15, 10.1.4
  monitoring provisions   7.6.18
  negotiating, *see* **Negotiating the project agreement**
  parties   2.5.2
    differing objectives   2.6
    see also **Awarding authority; Consortium; Debt funder; Project company**
  planning permission, condition for   13.1.14, 13.1.17
  preservation of, *see* **Direct agreement**
  'relief events', *see* **Relief events**
  specialist contractors, provisions for   7.6.20–7.6.22
  standard form agreement, guidance   10.1.7–10.1.13
  structures for   1.3.23, 1.3.24
  termination, *see* **Default; Insolvency (of project company); Termination**
  terms   2.5.2, 7.6.33, 10.2 *et seq*, *see also* 'design and construction issues' *above*; *see also* **Negotiating the project agreement**

Project company
  agreement
    awarding authority, with, *see* **Project agreement**
    construction company, with, *see* **Construction contract**
    covenants   8.5.15–8.5.18
    default by   2.2.19, 2.2.30, 8.5.19, *see also* **Default**
  defect liability   7.3.4,, 7.6.29, 7.5.30
  delegation to   4.2.17
  developer, as   7.3.1, 7.3.3, *see also* **Design and build contract**
  direct agreement, party to   9.2.1, 9.2.2
  drawing on funds, conditions   3.5.9
  'economically advantageous' solutions to output specification   7.4.4
  extension of time   7.6.18, 7.6.21, 7.7.7
  finance for, *see* **Funding**
  guarantor for   7.6.16
  income, tax aspects   14.3.26, 14.6.3, 14.7.3, *see also* **Taxation**
  indemnity, *see* **Indemnity**
  insolvency of, *see* **Insolvency (of project company)**
  land tenure   8.4.12, 8.5.8
  payment to, *see* **Unitary payment**
  progress reports   8.5.16
  property ownership issues, *see* **Property issues**
  proposals   7.3.5, 7.5
    construction company input   7.5.1
    construction contract to identify   7.7.7
    design documents forming part of   7.6.5
    form of   7.5.2
    pre-contract award   7.5.2, *see also* **Tender**
  representations and warranties   8.5.13, 8.5.14
  restrictions on   8.5.18
  risk limitation   2.4.4, 2.4.5
  shares in, transfer restrictions   8.4.13
  special vehicle company, as   2.2.29, 2.3.6, 7.6.11, 7.6.16
  step-in rights   7.6.12
  sub-contractors   7.6.11–7.6.15
    agreeing prior to project agreement   7.6.13
    approval by awarding authority   7.6.13
    collateral agreements   7.6.12–7.6.15
    contract amendment   7.6.15

Project company – *cont*
  sub-contractors – *cont*
    debt funder vetting   7.6.11
    review of appointment of   7.6.15
  tax issues, *see* **Taxation**
  transfer of undertaking liabilities
    15.6.5–15.6.7, *see also* **Transfer of undertaking**
  undertakings   8.5.15–8.5.18, 9.3.3
Property issues   11.1 *et seq*
see also **Planning risk; Site**
  choice or identification   11.3.1, 11.3.2
  compulsory purchase   11.3.6, 11.3.13, 13.3
  Crichel Down Rules, *see* **Crichel Down Rules**
  disposal at 'best obtainable price' 11.5
    consent of Secretary of State 11.5.3
    Government Circular on   11.5.1
    whole arrangement taken together   11.5.2
  freehold scenarios   11.4.5, 11.4.6
    awarding authority has   11.4.15–11.4.24, 11.4.32–11.4.34
    outright transfer to project company   11.4.28, 11.4.29
    project company has   11.4.5–11.4.14, 11.4.30, 11.4.31
    risk mitigation for authority 11.4.11
  grant of interest, time for   11.6
  lease grant back to authority 11.4.7–11.4.14
    default by project company 11.4.8, 11.4.11, 11.4.14
    duration   11.4.7
    increase/reduction in occupied area   11.4.12
    landlord   11.4.10
    repair etc obligations   11.4.9
    reversionary interest, and protection of authority   11.4.11
    termination options   11.4.13
  lease grantback to authority, sub-lease to project company   11.4.30, 11.4.31
  lease(head) grant to project company   11.4.32, 11.4.33
    disadvantage   11.4.33
    uses   11.4.32
  lease(head) grant to project company, sub-lease back to authority 11.4.15–11.4.24
    control of authority   11.4.19, 11.4.24
    duration   11.4.16, 11.4.23
    right of authority to buy out 11.4.23
    terms   11.4.22
  licence   11.4.25–11.4.27, 11.4.34
    disadvantages   11.4.26
  mixed-use, structures for   11.5.10
  occupation after project   11.4.2
    awarding authority, by   11.4.5
    change of use, and Crown development   13.1.20
  occupation before project   11.3.7–11.3.11, 11.3.13
    awarding authority dealing 11.3.7, 11.3.12
  DEOA, *see* **Departmental estate occupancy agreement**
  ownership   11.3.6, 11.4.2, 11.4.6, 11.4.23
  role of   11.2
  structure   2.5.3, 11.4, 14.6.5, 14.6.6
    imposition timing   11.6
    issues determining   11.4.2–11.4.4
    legal restrictions on   11.5.11
    new, opportunities for   11.8
  sub-lease grant back to awarding authority   11.4.15–11.4.24
    benefits of structure   11.4.19, 11.4.20, 11.4.24
    duration   11.4.16, 11.4.23
    extent   11.4.18
    terms   11.4.21
    uses   11.4.15
  sub-lease grant to project company 11.4.30, 11.4.31
  surplus, *see* **Surplus site/property**
  third-party ownership, in   11.3.2, 11.3.3
  title, report on   8.5.8
  vacant possession   11.3.3, 11.3.4
Public
  end-user   1.2.1, 1.2.3
Public body, *see* **Awarding authority; Government (central); Health authority; Local authority; NHS: trust; Non-governmental public body**

Public procurement rules (EU)   3.1
  et seq
  aims   3.3.39
  application   3.2
  background   3.1.1–3.1.3
  breach, remedies   6.1.1, 6.2, 6.3
    complaint to European
      Commission   6.3
    damages   6.2.5, 6.2.6
    High Court orders   6.2.5
    mechanisms for   6.2.1
    notification duty   6.2.3
    right of action in High Court
      6.2.2
    time limit   6.2.3
    writ   6.2.4
  compliance duty   3.1.3
  evidence of no breach   8.5.8
  implementation in UK   3.2.1, 3.2.2
  national security exclusion   3.2.22
  negotiated procedure   3.3.1, 3.3.4–
      3.3.11 *et seq*
    advertisement duty (OJ), 3.3.12–
      3.3.20
    competitive (OJ notice)   3.3.7–
      3.3.21, 3.3.30, 5.2.2, 5.3.1
    contract notice   3.3.13–3.3.19,
      5.4.1
    national notices   3.3.20, 5.4.2
    negotiation invitation   3.3.24,
      3.3.32, 5.6.12
    non-competitive (no OJ notice)
      3.3.5–3.3.6, 5.2.2
    pre-qualification stage   3.3.24–
      3.3.28, 3.3.35, 5.5
    prior information notice (PIN)
      3.3.12, 3.3.23
    shortlist candidates   3.3.29,
      3.3.31, 3.3.36, 3.3.38, 3.3.39
    time limits   3.3.21–3.3.23
    urgency   3.3.22, 3.3.23
    wording standardisation   3.3.16–
      3.3.18
  post-award of contract   3.3.48
  procedure   3.3
    accelerated   3.3.22
    award criteria   3.3.32–3.3.35
    exclusion of candidate,
      automatic   3.3.25
    exclusion of candidate, reason to be
      given   3.3.50, 5.5.13
    four types   3.3.1
    negotiated, *see* 'negotiated
      procedure' *above*
    negotiations after selection
      3.3.45–3.3.47
    notice of award   3.3.48
    open and restricted, limitations
      3.3.3
    pre-selection stage   3.3.24–3.3.28
    records   3.3.49
    short-listing   3.3.29–3.3.31
    tender, *see* 'tender' *below*
    time for response to contract
      notice   3.3.21, 3.3.22
    two-stage negotiations process
      3.3.39–3.3.44, 5.6.5–5.6.8
  'public sector contract', meaning
      for   3.2.2
  public works concessions, *see* **Works
      contract**
  subject-matter categorisation   3.2.1,
      3.2.5–3.2.11
    guidance   3.2.9
    multi-faceted contracts   3.2.6–
      3.2.10, 3.2.16
    'services' contract, *see* **Services
      contract**
    significance of   3.2.10, 3.2.11
    'supplies' contract, *see* **Supplies
      contract**
    'works' contract, *see* **Works
      contract**
  tender   3.3.2–3.3.4 *et seq*, 5.2.1, 5.2.2
    invitation to   3.3.24, 3.3.32
    minimum number of tenderers
      3.3.30
    selection of candidates, criteria
      3.3.25–3.3.28
    standard questionnaire/database
      3.3.27, 5.5.7, 5.5.8
    submission   3.3.37
    submission, period for   3.3.23
    use of   3.3.36–3.3.38
    see also **Tender**
  unfair discrimination prohibition
      3.3.38, 3.3.44, 3.3.47, 5.3.2, 5.6.25
  value, thresholds   3.2.16–3.2.19
    contract valuation rules   3.2.18,
      3.2.19
    1998–1999 values   3.2.16
Public sector
  authority awarding contract, *see*
      Awarding authority
  contract, scope of   3.2.2

Public sector – *cont*
'outputs', prescribing   1.2.3, 2.2.1, 2.2.7
service provider, as   1.2.3
  accounting aspects   1.2.4
service purchaser, as   1.2.3, 2.2.1
purchaser and user, projects   1.2.15
vires for PFI project, *see* Vires
Public sector comparator
  disclosure of   5.6.22
  draft   5.6.21, 5.6.22
  guidance on   1.3.34
  use of   2.2.37, 5.6.21
Public sector contract   3.2.2
Public works concession, *see* Works contract
Public works contract, *see* Works contract
Publications   1.3.11, 1.3.22

Quality
  completion to   2.2.18, 2.2.19
  goods and materials, of, *see* Goods
  value for money, factor   2.2.37

Railway, light   8.2.10
  Docklands   8.2.5
  Dublin, in   18.5.6
Receiver   8.4.17, 9.1.7, 9.2.3
  debt funders' use of   9.3.4, 9.3.5, 9.3.13, 9.3.14
    fettering of right   9.3.13
    right, clause for   9.3.14
Redundancy   15.2.8, 15.2.10
  enhanced benefits for NHS employees   15.7.3, 15.12.3
  project company liability continuing after contract loss   15.12.4
  risk of, covering for   15.6.3, 15.6.6–15.6.9
  employees of existing contractor   15.6.9
Refinancing   8.6, 18.3
  cost savings in   8.6.1, 18.3.1
  profits from, authority share in   8.6.2–8.6.4, 18.3.2
  suggested limits   8.6.3
Refurbishment
  decanting   7.6.19
  service provision after, whether 'transfer of undertaking'   15.5.9

Rehabilitation of offenders   15.17
Relief event   2.2.21, 10.3.5, 10.3.13–10.3.16
  compensation event distinguished   10.3.14
  insurance   10.3.14
  liquidated damages   10.3.13
  meaning   10.3.13, 10.3.15
  notice of   8.5.16
  termination, and   10.3.16
  time occurring, different treatment   10.3.13
Remedy
  see also Compensation; Default; Termination
  breach of tender process, *see* Tender
  defect or failure, for   10.4.26, 10.4.32, *see also* Defect
  period, extension of   9.4.4, *see also* Time limit
Rent, *see* Lease
Repayment, *see* Credit agreement; Payment; Unitary payment
Representative, employee, *see* Transfer of undertaking: information duty
Reserves level   8.4.7
Residual value risk   2.2.26–2.2.28
  accounting treatment   17.5.7, 17.7.5
  amortisation   2.2.26, 2.2.27
  meaning   2.2.26
  option for awarding authority   2.2.28
  termination options, and   10.7.3, 10.9.2
  transfer of   2.2.26
Retention   7.2.3, 7.2.4, 7.7.14, 7.7.17
Revenue
  intercreditor agreement, application provisions   8.5.22
  project company receipt, and repayment formula   8.5.12
  risk   8.4.9
Review, *see* Bates Review
Review Board, Disputes   16.1.1, 16.2
Review, judicial. *See* Judicial review
Risk, *see* Insurance; Relief event; Risk allocation
Risk allocation   1.2.5–1.2.12, 2.2.5 *et seq*
  see also Completion; Design risk; Insolvency (of project company); Operational risk; Planning risk; Residual value risk

Risk allocation – *cont*
  accounting treatment, for   1.2.13,
    18.2.3, *see also* **Balance sheet treatment**
  agreement on   5.6.29
  approach to, in invitation to negotiate   5.6.15
  awarding authority's powers   8.4.10, *see also* **Vires**
  consortium view   2.3.5
  construction risk   10.4.8
  contaminated land   13.2.7–13.2.9
  control of   1.2.10
  degree of   2.2.37
  demand risk   17.5.7, 17.7.5
  funding viability, and   8.4.4, 8.4.5
  genuine, need for   1.5
  insurance to offset risk, *see* **Insurance**
  key risk types   2.2.5–2.2.35
  land conditions, tenure etc   8.4.12
  law change   8.4.11, 10.5.1, *see also* **Law, change in**
  not possible   2.2.8, 2.2.21
  objective of awarding authority   2.2.3, 2.2.4
  performance at heart of   1.2.9, 2.2.7, 8.4.7
  price   1.2.10, 1.2.11, 7.7.9, 8.4.8
  revenue   8.4.9
  sponsor   8.4.13
Road   1.3.14, 1.3.24
  see also **Design, build finance and operate (DBFO)**
  access   13.1.9
  bond issue financing   8.2.5
  bridges   1.2.15, 1.3.3
  capital allowance availability for   14.3.10, 14.3.11
  default by project company   10.9.4
  highway concession   14.3.11
  law change, effect on costs   10.5.3
  London Underground   1.3.7
    rolling stock ownership   2.2.28
  model project agreement   10.1.4
  number of vehicles using   10.4.6
  ownership   2.2.27
  specifications   2.2.8
Ryrie rules   1.3.1

Sale of project   9.1.9
Savings
  examples   1.2.7

School, maintained   3.2.2
Secretary of State (Environment, Transport and Regions)
  consent of, to land disposal   11.5.3
  delegation, *see* **Vires**
  discretion   4.2.24
Security
  awarding authority taking   2.2.31
  debt funder, for   8.3.2, 8.4.21
    consent to   9.4.2
    contractual rights, over   9.1.6–9.1.9
    protection afforded by   9.1.2
  see also **Charge; Direct agreement; Funding**
  mortgage over project company shares   9.1.5
  priority   9.1.2
Service
  availability and take-up   2.2.22, 10.4.4, 10.4.5
  benchmarking   10.4.18, 10.5.2
  continuity   2.2.40
    insolvency, on   2.2.35
  fee, discrete   10.4.5
  market test, *see* **Market testing**
  'performance failure' and accounts   17.5.7, 17.7.10–17.7.12
  performance points for   10.4.27–10.4.36
  pricing of   10.4.11–10.4.19
    risk   8.4.8, 10.4.17
  relief from provision   10.3.13
  termination   10.7.4
  third party revenues   10.4.9
  unavailability, *see* **Deductions**
  usage   10.4.6
Services contract
  see also **Contractor**
  change of provider
    redundancy issues, *see* **Transfer of undertakings**
    Transfer of Undertaking Regs not applying   15.5.9
  EU procurement rules   3.2.1, 3.2.6, 3.2.9
    categorisation   3.2.1, 3.2.6 3.2.9, 3.2.20, 3.2.21
    Community Product Classification   3.2.21
    cross-border competition element   3.2.20

Services contract – *cont*
  EU procurement rules – *cont*
    'Part A' and 'Part B' services
      3.2.20, 3.2.21, 3.3.1
    procedure   3.3
    value threshold   3.2.16
Set-off   10.9.23, 10.9.24
Sewerage   1.3.26, 3.2.3, 3.2.4
  capital allowance availability
    14.3.9–14.3.11
  services contract   3.3.1, *see also*
    Services contract
Shares
  equity finance   8.2.2
  mortgage over   9.1.5
  overage, and   12.4.5, 12.4.13, 12.4.14
  security over   8.4.21
  transfer restriction   8.4.13
Sharing experience   1.3.25, 1.3.32
Site
  access   7.6.18, 7.6.23, 8.5.17
  compulsory purchase of   11.3.6,
    11.3.13, 13.3
  deficiencies in, cost associated with
    11.3.5
  inspection   7.6.18, 7.6.28
  location   11.3.1, 11.3.2
  ownership and occupation issues, *see*
    Property issues
  planning permission, *see* **Planning risk**
  risks associated with   8.4.12, 11.3.3–
    11.3.6
    awarding authority retaining
      11.3.5, 11.3.6
  security, fee for   7.7.5
  vacant possession   11.3.3, 11.3.4
  valuable asset, as   9.1.6
Special vehicle company   2.2.29,
  2.3.6, 7.6.11, 7.6.16
Sponsor   2.3.2, 2.3.7
  equipment manufacturer   8.3.1
  equity investor, as   8.2.2
  failure by   8.5.19
  financial etc strengths   8.4.13
  liability, limits   8.3.2
  payment to   8.5.22
  refinancing, and   8.6.2
'Sponsor risk'   8.4.13
Stamp duty   12.5.5, 12.5.6, 12.5.10,
  14.5
  licence to avoid   14.5.7

private sector   14.5.3–14.5.7
calculation   14.5.4
leases   14.5.3–14.5.6
sub-sale relief   14.6.5
public sector   14.5.1, 14.5.2
exemption   14.5.2
rents, on   14.5.1
Standards   1.3.24, 7.6
see also **Quality**
employee   15.18
failure in, giving termination right
  10.7.6
goods, *see* **Goods**
service   10.4.31
workmanship   7.6.2, 7.6.5, 7.6.11
  covenant as to   8.5.17
training   15.16
Standing orders   4.2.26, 4.2.27
Statute, body created by   4.2.2
Step-in   10.10
  awarding authority rights   7.6.12,
    7.6.14, 7.6.22, 9.3.25
  cost reimbursement   10.10.5
  exercise of   10.10.2
  extreme step   10.10.3
  forms of   10.10.2
  notice   9.3.4
  temporary nature of   10.10.4
  unitary payments during period
    9.3.25
conflicting   9.3.25
debt funders' rights   8.4.17, 9.2.2,
  9.2.3, 10.9.7
  accrued liabilities/pre-existing
    defaults   9.3.19–9.3.21, 9.5.1
  circumstances for, and limits on
    9.3.32
  date   9.3.6
  end of period   9.3.17, 9.3.31
  liabilities during period   9.3.22,
    9.3.23, 9.5.1
  notice   9.3.4
  option of using   9.3.16
  payments by authority during
    period   9.4.5
  period   9.2.3, 9.3.7, 9.3.8, 9.3.31
  remedy period extension   9.4.4
  step-out right   9.3.17
  transfer of project during period
    9.3.27
  undertaking clauses, *see*
    Undertaking (step-in)

Sub-contractor
see also **Service; Services contract**
construction company, of   7.5.1
contract   2.5.9
    arm's length   2.3.4
    assignment of rights   8.3.2
    liability limitation   2.3.6
    Transfer of Undertakings Regs application   15.6.13
    see also **Project company**
direct agreement with   2.2.19, 2.2.35
failure or breach by   10.4.34
identity of   7.6.13
project company, of   7.6.11–7.6.15, see also Project company
risk passing to   2.2.24, 2.3.5, 2.4.3
Sub-lease, see **Property issues**
Subordinated lending   8.2.2, 8.4.8, 8.5.21
    subordination agreement   8.5.20–8.5.23
Substitute entity, see **Third party: taking over project**
Supplies contract
    EU procurement rules   3.2.1, 3.2.6, 3.2.16
Surplus site/property   11.7, 12.1, 14.6
see also **Overage**
capital generation from   11.2.2, 13.1.18
grant of land interest in, time for   11.7.1
NHS trust disposal, power for   4.4.3
offer to former owner, see **Crichel Down Rules**
part of consideration   2.2.12, 2.2.31
planning permission for   13.1.18
price/share in uplifts   11.7.2, 13.1.18
tax issues   14.6
    awarding authority, VAT for   14.6.2–14.6.5, 14.6.7
    project company direct taxes   14.6.2, 14.6.3, 14.6.5, 14.6.7
Syndicated loan agreement   8.2.3, 8.2.4, 18.5.2

Taking over project, see **Debt funder; Direct agreement**
Target price contract   7.7.9–7.7.11
Taskforce
    Bates Review   1.3.18, 18.4.6
    conferences   1.3.33
contract structures   1.3.23
draft direct agreement   9.5.1, 9.6
guidance   1.3.22, 1.3.34, 3.2.9, 3.3.27, 8.6.3
    change of law risk   10.5.2, 10.5.4–10.5.6
    performance monitoring   10.4.28, 10.4.29
    project agreement, on   10.1.7–10.1.13, 10.3.9, 10.3.12, 10.7.6, 10.9.13
    relief events   10.3.13–10.3.15
    'unavailability' of service   10.4.24
projects arm, duration   1.3.20, 18.4.6
questionnaire   3.3.27, 5.5.8
responsibility   1.3.21
road-testing, see **Testing**
tendering, selection   3.3.27
Taxation   14.1 et seq
awarding authority, and exemptions for   14.3.1, 14.3.2
impact on   14.3.3
capital allowances   14.3.7–14.3.20, see also **Capital allowances**
compliance costs   14.3.23
construction costs   14.3.8–14.3.20
financing costs   14.3.21, 14.3.22
government department/Crown   14.3.1
grossing up of compensation payment   10.9.25, 14.7.5
overage, issues on   12.5
    back-to-back land contract   12.5.3
    CGT aspects, see **Capital gains tax**
    direct contract with developer   12.5.8–12.5.11
    stamp duty   12.5.5, 12.5.6, 12.5.10
    unitary payment reduction   12.5.2, 12.5.12
    VAT   12.5.7, 12.5.11
payments and receipts arising from project   14.2.2–14.2.4
private sector, and   14.3.4, 14.3.5
reliefs
    availability/time for   14.3.25
    limiting factors   14.3.26
    list of direct   14.3.24
stamp duty, see **Stamp duty**
start-up costs   14.3.6, 14.3.7
surplus land, see **Surplus site/property**

Taxation – *cont*
  termination compensation
    payments 14.7
    construction period, during
      14.7.2
    grossing up 14.7.5
    operating period, during 14.7.3
    rent under leases continuing
      14.7.4
  trading expenses 14.3.24–14.3.26
  trading losses 14.3.26, 14.3.27
  VAT, *see* **VAT**
Tender 5.1 *et seq*
  acceptance, *see* 'preferred tenderer'
    below
  bid costs, evaluation etc *see* **Bid**
  breach of process, remedies 6.1 *et seq*
    implied contract breach action
      6.5.1–6.5.3
    judicial review, *see* **Judicial review**
    public procurement rules, *see* **Public procurement rules (EU)**
    tort, in 6.5.4
  competitive, transfer of undertakings
    case 15.9.9
  conflict of interest case 6.5.2
  contract
    detailed, time for introduction of
      5.6.29
    implied, arising, breach claim
      6.5.1–6.5.3
    model 5.6.15
    terms 5.6.15, 5.6.29, 5.6.30
    fairness 6.5.3, *see also* **Unfair discrimination**
  information request from tenderer
    5.6.26, 5.6.27
    provision of, issues on 15.14.1
  invitation to negotiate 3.3.32,
    5.6.12–5.6.20
    accuracy 5.6.23
    conduct of negotiations, instructions
      on 5.6.17
    confidential information 5.6.17,
      5.6.19
    detail in 5.6.18, 5.6.19
    disclaimer 5.6.17, 5.6.23
    heads of terms 5.6.15, 5.6.29
    necessary restrictions 5.6.14
    output specification 2.2.8, 5.6.13
    public sector comparator as part
      of 5.6.22
    revised version 5.6.24
    submissions, evaluation 5.6.16, 5.7.2
    invitation to tender 5.6.24
  negotiations
    commencement 5.6.28
    issues for 5.6.29
  negotiations phase 5.6
    approaches to 5.6.5
    complex project 5.6.7
    decisions for structuring 5.6.1
    feedback from tenderers 5.6.10
    ITN, *see* 'invitation to negotiate'
      above
    interim submissions 5.6.7, 5.6.9,
      5.6.10, 5.6.11
    single-stage 5.6.9
    two-stage, advantages 5.6.6–
      5.6.8, 5.6.16
  non-discrimination 5.3.2
  number of tenderers 5.5.11, 5.6.1,
    5.6.3
    Bates Review 3.3.30, 5.6.4
    maximum 3.3.30
    minimum 3.3.30, 5.6.4
    resource restrictions 5.6.29
  preferred tenderer 3.3.45, 5.7.2
    consultation with employee reps
      (TUPE Regs) 15.8.7, 15.8.13
    continuing negotiations with
      5.7.8–5.7.14
    design development with 7.6.3–
      7.6.10
    pre-qualification document 5.5.4–
      5.5.6
    contents 5.5.5, 5.5.6
  pre-qualification stage 3.3.34 *et seq*,
    5.5
    application 5.5.4
    evaluation of candidates 5.5.7–
      5.5.12, 5.6.16
    initial culling process 5.5.1, 5.5.2
    methodology for assessment
      3.3.28, 5.5.9, 5.5.10, 5.7.3
    methods of approach to 5.5.1
    no initial culling 5.5.1, 5.5.3
    questionnaire 3.3.27, 5.5.7, 5.5.8
    re-evaluation, circumstances
      5.5.14
    result of 5.5.11, 5.5.12, 5.6.1
    technical capability/economic
      standing of candidate 3.3.26,
      5.5.2, 5.5.4, 5.5.10

Taxation – *cont*
  pre-qualification stage – *cont*
    unsuccessful candidate, debriefing of   3.3.50, 5.5.13, 5.7.7
  public procurement procedure, rule details   3.3, *see also* **Public procurement rules (EU)**
  publicity notices   5.4
    contract notice   3.3.13–3.3.19, 5.4.1
    national   5.4.2
    OJ, in   5.4.1
    project outside Regs   5.4.3
  risk allocation
    agreement on   5.6.29
    intended approach   5.6.15
    timetable   5.5.5, 5.6.17
Tenderer
  aggrieved, remedies for   6.1 *et seq*, *see also* **Tender**
  bid, *see* **Bid**
  contaminated land   13.2.7, 13.2.8
  information to, *see* **Tender**
  number of, *see* **Tender**
  preferred   5.7.8–5.7.14, *see also* **Tender**
  public procurement rules, *see* **Public procurement rules (EU)**
  selection, transfer of undertaking issues   15.8.7, 15.8.13
Tenders Electronic Daily (TED)   3.2.11, 3.3.19
Termination   10.7–10.9
  advance notice of   2.4.6, 2.5.5, 9.3.2, 9.3.3
  assets, treatment on   10.8.2
  at will   10.7.2–10.7.5, 10.9.2, 10.9.3
  awarding authority
    default   10.7.7, 10.7.8, 10.9.16–10.9.18
    rights   2.5.6, 2.5.7, 10.7.2
  compensation   8.4.18, 10.9
    calculation options   10.9.2, 10.9.3
    default by awarding authority   10.9.16–10.9.18
    default by project company   10.9.4–10.9.15, *see also* **Default**
    grossing up   10.9.25
    none   10.7.3, 10.9.2, 10.9.4
    pre-agreed   10.9.3
    set-off   10.9.23, 10.9.24
  corrupt gift, *see* **Gift, corrupt**
  debt funders' rights   8.4.16–8.4.18

  effect   10.8, *see also* **Step-in**
  force majeure, and, *see* **Force majeure**
  notice, effect of   9.3.11
  payments, *see* **Compensation**
  project company, events list   10.7.6, *see also* **Insolvency (of project company)**
  redundancy costs, *see* **Redundancy**
  security enforcement, and   9.17
  service or part service, of   10.7.4
  Taskforce guidance   10.7.2
Terrorism   10.3.4, *see also* **Force majeure**
Testing (of works)   7.6.23–7.6.25
  re-testing   7.6.26
Testing (PFI)
  meaning   1.3.8
  'road testing'   1.3.10, 1.3.21, 1.3.24, 2.3.2
  universal   1.3.8, 1.3.9
    abolition   1.3.10, 1.3.17
Third party
  bonds from   7.6.16, 7.7.14
  counterparty   9.2.5–9.2.7
  direct agreements, advantages from   9.2.5–9.2.7
  guarantor   7.6.16, *see also* **Guarantee**
  local authority contract, protection   4.3.4–4.3.13
    certified contract   4.3.9–4.3.12
    compensation for contract set aside   4.3.8, 4.3.13
    discussion note   4.3.5
    judicial review, and efficacy of   4.3.13
    'provisions contract'   4.3.7
    'relevant discharge terms', enforceability   4.3.12
    safe harbour provisions   4.3.4–4.3.13
    scope   4.3.7
    statute   4.3.6 *et seq*
  services to   1.2.8
  taking over project as 'substitute entity'   9.1.9, 9.2.3, 9.3.5, 9.3.15, 9.3.16
    debt funders' control   9.3.15
    novation, *see* **Novation agreement**
    step-in period, during   9.3.27
    variation, carrying out   10.6.8

Third party revenues   10.4.19, 17.5.7
Time limit
  see also **Timetable**
  action for breach of procurement
    rules   6.2.2
  extension   2.2.16, 10.3.6, 10.3.13
    construction contract, in   7.7.3
  see also **Project company**
Timetable
  completion   2.2.15, 2.2.16
  length of time, issue of   18.4.2
  tender process   5.5.5, 5.6.17
  transaction closing, for   1.3.14,
    1.3.15, 1.3.23
Title to property, see **Property issues**
Tolls   2.2.25
Tort claim
  awarding authority, against
    duty of care to bidder   6.5.4
    misrepresentation   6.5.4
  contaminated land, for   13.2.5
Trade union
  dissatisfaction with project, disruptive
    action   15.8.10
  information to and consultation
    with   15.2.2, 15.2.9, 15.8
  involvement of   15.8.13
  official, as representative   15.2.9
  pension scheme enhanced rights
    15.12.3
  recognition   15.2.5, 15.7.1
    provision in project agreement
      15.8.11
Trading expense
  deductibility for tax   14.3.24–
    14.3.26, see also Taxation
Trading loss   14.3.26, 14.3.27
Training
  PFI projects, on   1.3.31
  workforce   15.16
    inherited on transfer   15.16.2,
      15.16.3
    obligation on project company
      15.16.1, 15.16.3
    warranty on competence   15.16.2
Transfer of interest
  debt funder, by   8.4.19
  restrictions on   2.3.8, 8.4.19
Transfer of risk, see **Risk allocation**
Transfer of undertaking   15.2–15.10
  acquired rights Directive   15.1.2,
    15.2.1
  amendments   15.3.1, 15.3.6

asset transfer   15.3.2, 15.4.3, 15.4.11,
  15.4.12
background and relevance   15.1.2,
  15.1.3
consultation   15.8.5–15.8.9
  procedure   15.8.9
continuity of service   15.2.6
contract of employment, change to
    after transfer   15.9
  agreement, after legal advice
    15.9.8
  agreement, ineffective   15.9.6
  competitive tender, to enable
    15.9.9
  contractor's options   15.9.11
  crucial issue   15.9.1
  dismissal and re-engagement on new
    terms   15.9.2–15.9.6
  dismissal preferable to   15.9.7
  protection of employee by unfair
    dismissal remedy   15.9.4,
    15.9.5
  remuneration fixed by national
    bargaining process, case on
    15.9.10
  trade union agreeing with employer,
    insolvency transfer   15.9.12
  uncertain position as to   15.9.6
  whether transfer reason for
    change   15.9.2, 15.9.3, 15.9.6
contract of employment, transfer
  of   15.2.2, 15.2.4
  objection to, effect   15.2.11
contracted-out services   15.3.3–
  15.3.6, 15.4, 15.5
  contractor agreeing to take on
    employees   15.6.4
  contractor choosing not to take on
    employee   15.5.1–15.5.6,
    15.5.9
  helicopter services to oil rigs, CA
    decision   15.4.9–15.4.11
  project company sub-contractors
    15.6.13
  school cleaners, ECJ decision
    15.4.2–15.4.8, 15.5.1
  convictions, disclosure of employees'
    previous   15.17
  costs   15.7
    equal pay claims   15.7.5
    indemnity   15.7.1, 15.7.6–15.7.8,
      see also 'redundancy' below
    list of   15.7.1

Transfer of undertaking – *cont*
  costs – *cont*
    market testing, bearing on   15.7.7,
      15.12.4
    public sector benefits, cost of
      matching   15.7.3–15.7.5,
      15.12.3
    tender pricing reflecting   15.7.2
  dismissal of employee   15.2.2,
    15.2.7, 15.7.1
    automatically unfair   15.2.8
    compensation limit, raising of
      15.2.8, 15.9.5
    constructive   15.2.11, 15.10.4
    'economic, technical or
      organisational reason'
      15.2.8, 15.9.4, 15.9.7
    liability for   15.2.8
  documentation   15.6, 15.7.3, 15.14.1
    options   15.6.1, 15.6.2
    project company liabilities
      15.6.5–15.6.7
    redundancy claim risk, *see*
      'redundancy' *below*
    requirement to take on staff
      15.6.5
  'economic entity' or 'activity'
    15.3.2, 15.5.7, 15.5.9
  excluded rights   15.10, 15.12.1,
    15.12.2
    proposal to remove exclusion
      15.13.2
    see also **Pension rights**
  information duty   15.2.2, 15.2.9,
    15.8
    confidence duty   15.14.3, 15.14.4
    early provision and accuracy,
      importance of   15.14.5,
      15.14.6
    employee representatives   15.2.9,
      15.8.2
    existing employees, on   15.6.12,
      15.7.2, 15.8.1, 15.14
    failure in   15.8.8
    indemnity for awarding
      authority   15.15.2
    'measures' in relation to transferring
      employees   15.8.3, 15.8.5,
      15.15.1
    preferred tenderer selection, and
      15.8.7, 15.8.13
    scope   15.8.3

    standing committees for   15.2.9,
      15.2.10
    time for   15.8.4, 15.8.7, 15.8.12
  pension rights   15.2.4, 15.10.1, *see*
    also **Pension rights**
  redundancy   15.2.8, 15.2.10
    change to employment terms before
      transfer   15.6.12
    enhanced benefits for NHS
      employees   15.7.3
    indemnity for costs   15.6.6,
      15.6.7, 15.6.9–15.6.11, 15.7.2
    new employees, terms for   15.6.8
    risk of claim   15.6.3, 15.6.6, 15.6.7
    third party employees   15.6.9
  reform, consultation on, *see* 'TUPE
    forum' *below*
  'relevant transfer'   15.3.1 *et seq*
    amended definition   15.3.1
    circumstances when not   15.5.9
    entity retaining identity   15.5.8
    PFI, and   15.3.4, 15.3.5
    test for   15.3.2, 15.3.3
    tightened circumstances for
      15.3.6, *see also* 'contracted-out
      services' *above*
  summary of effect on employees
    15.2.2
  TUPE forum   15.3.6, 15.9.12,
    15.14.6
  training, competence etc of inherited
    workers   15.16.2, 15.16.3
  'transferee'   15.2.3
    obligations   15.2.3, 15.2.4
  'undertaking'   15.3.1, 15.3.2
  union recognition agreement, *see* **Trade**
    union
Transfer to substitute vehicle   2.4.6
Transport   3.2.3, 3.3.1, *see also*
  Railway, light; Road; Services
  contract
  capital allowance availability
    14.3.10
Treasury
  accounts of public sector
    approval of   17.2.1
    guidance on   17.4
  see also **Balance sheet**
  Taskforce, *see* **Taskforce**
Tunnel
  see also **Channel Tunnel**
  capital allowance availability
    14.3.10

Unavailability of service, *see* **Deduction**
Undertaking (step-in)
  alternative to   9.5.1
  bond financing, and   9.5.2
  debate over   9.5, 9.6
  debt funder   9.3.24, 9.3.31
  project company   8.5.15–8.5.18, 9.3.3
Undertaking, transfer of, *see* **Transfer of undertaking**
Unfair discrimination   3.3.38, 3.3.44, 3.3.47, 5.3.2
  costs related to   15.7.1
  indemnity for claims   15.18.2
Unfair dismissal   15.18.2, *see also* **Transfer of undertakings: dismissal**
Unitary payment
  see also **Payment**
  adjustment for compensating event   10.3.12
  deduction from
    defect, for   7.6.14, 7.6.29, 9.3.25
    liability, to cover   9.5.1
    overage benefit, for   12.5.2, 12.5.12
  elements, *see* **Payment**
  events entitling re-opening   2.2.39
  indexation   10.4.9, 10.4.11, 10.5.1, 10.5.2
  market testing, effect of   10.5.2
  monitoring of level   8.4.20
  security of, debt-funders' interest in   8.4.9
  step-in period, during   9.3.25
  VAT   10.5.6
University   3.2.2
  VAT   14.4.5, 14.4.9
Utilities company   3.2.3, 3.2.4
  failure to provide service   10.3.15, 10.4.25
  privatisation, clawback arrangements   12.2.2–12.2.4

VAT   14.4
  change in   10.5.6
  exempt supply   14.4.2, 14.4.9
  government department   14.4.2, 14.4.5, 14.4.7, 14.4.8
  housing association or university   14.4.5, 14.4.9
  local authority   14.4.5, 14.4.6
  overage, and   12.5.7, 12.5.11
  public sector, issues for   14.4.4–14.4.9
  types of public body   14.4.5
  recoverability   14.4.1–14.4.3, 14.6.2–14.6.5, 14.6.7
  termination payments, and   14.7.2–14.7.4
Vacant possession   11.3.3, 11.3.4
Value for money   2.2.36–2.2.39
  awarding authority securing   2.2.36
  calculating   2.2.38, 2.2.39
  competitive tendering assists   5.2.2, 5.8
  factors for   2.2.37
  fiduciary duty of local authority   4.2.25
  reviews   8.4.20
  risk transfer, and   2.2.6, 13.2.7, *see also* **Risk allocation**
  test   1.2.12
Value thresholds, *see* **Public procurement rules (EU)**
Variation   10.6
  approval by debt funder   10.6.5
  awarding authority right   10.6.1
    restrictions on   10.6.3–10.6.5
  compensating event   10.3.9
  drop dead dates   10.6.5
  implementation   10.6.7
  negotiations for   10.6.1, 10.6.2
  physical   10.6.2, 10.6.4, 10.6.7, 10.6.8, 10.6.10
  pricing and funding of   10.6.7, 10.6.9–10.6.13
    adjustment to payment   10.6.10, 10.6.12
    objective measure   10.6.9, 10.6.13
    provisions for   10.6.11, 10.6.12
    savings   10.6.13
    standby funding   10.6.11
  project company
    responsibilities   10.6.7, 10.6.8
    rights   10.6.5, 10.6.6
  service, to   10.6.2, 10.6.8
  Taskforce guidance   10.6.3, 10.6.7, 10.6.10
Vires   4.1–4.4
  background   4.1.1
  Bates Review   1.3.29, 4.1.2
  debt funders' interest in   8.4.10
  grounds for challenge   4.2
    flowchart   4.2.1
    illegality   4.2.1

Vires – *cont*
  incidental powers   4.2.3–4.2.9
    'complete code' concept   4.2.9
    limitations   4.2.5
    'reasonably incidental', power 4.2.3
    'sufficient nexus' requirement 4.2.6–4.2.8
  irrationality   4.2.10–4.2.25, 4.4.7
    bad faith, entered in   4.2.13
    delegation limits, and   4.2.16, 4.2.21, *see also* 'Secretary of State, delegation' *below*
    discretion, fetter on   4.2.22–4.2.24
    improper purpose   4.2.14
    relevant consideration not taken into account   4.2.12
    unfairness/abuse of power   4.2.15
    value for money, and fiduciary duty   4.2.25
    Wednesbury unreasonableness, circumstances   4.2.11, 4.2.18
  local authority   4.3, 4.4.7
    capital finance regime   4.3.1–4.3.3
    delegation   4.2.21, 4.3.7
    incidental powers   4.2.4–4.2.9
    procedural impropriety   4.2.26
    standing orders   4.2.26
    statutory powers   4.2.2, 4.2.4–4.2.9
    third party protections   4.3.4–4.3.13, *see also* **Third party**
    unreasonableness   4.2.11
  NHS trust   4.4, 8.4.10
    documentation   4.4.5, 4.4.6
    early problems   4.4.4
    'externally financed development agreement'   4.4.5–4.4.7
    incidental powers   4.2.4, 4.2.8
    new facilities   4.4.2, 4.4.3
    specific power to enter PFI transaction   4.4.5–4.4.7
    standing orders   4.2.27
  statutory powers and functions 4.2.2, 4.2.4, 4.2.8, 4.4
  surplus site disposal   4.4.3
  procedural impropriety   4.2.27
    NHS trust   4.2.27
  Secretary of State, consent to land disposal   11.5.3
  Secretary of State, delegation 4.2.16–4.2.21
    Carltona principle   4.2.17, 4.2.18
    project company, to   4.2.17–4.2.20
  Secretary of State, discretion of 4.2.24
  standing order, compliance   4.2.26, 4.2.27
  statutory bodies   4.2.2–4.2.9
  ultra vires transaction, cases on 4.1.2, 6.4.9

Warranty
  collateral   2.5.12
  credit agreement, in   8.5.13
Waste, *see* **Service; Services contract**
Water project   1.3.26, 3.2.3, 3.2.4
  capital allowance availability 14.3.10
Weather   7.2.4, 7.7.8, 10.3.15
Workmanship   7.6.2, 7.6.5, 7.6 11, 15.18
  covenant as to   8.5.17
Works contract
  categorisation   3.2.1, 3.2.6, 3.2.8
  public works concessions contract 3.2.12–3.2.15
    definition   3.2.12
    examples   3.2.13
    procedure   3.2.14, 3.2.15
    valuation   3.2.18
    value threshold   3.2.16

HEIRLO

Catherine-Esther Cowie was born in St Lucia to a Tobagonian father and a St Lucian mother. She migrated with her family to Canada and then to the USA. Her poems have been published in *PN Review*, *Prairie Schooner*, *West Branch Journal*, *The Common*, *SWWIM*, *Rhino Poetry* and others. She is a Callaloo Creative Writing Workshop fellow.

HEIRLOOM
CATHERINE-ESTHER COWIE

CARCANET POETRY

First published in Great Britain in 2025 by
Carcanet
Main Library, The University of Manchester
Oxford Road, Manchester, M13 9PP
www.carcanet.co.uk

Text copyright © Catherine-Esther Cowie 2025

The right of Catherine-Esther Cowie to be identified as the author
of this work has been asserted in accordance with the
Copyright, Design and Patents Act of 1988; all rights reserved.
No part of this book may be used or reproduced in any manner for
the purpose of training artificial intelligence technologies or systems.

A CIP catalogue record for this book is
available from the British Library.

ISBN 978 1 80017 479 5

Cover image by Catherine-Esther Cowie, *Heirloom*, 2021
Book design by Andrew Latimer, Carcanet
Typesetting by LiteBook Prepress Services
Printed in Great Britain by SRP Ltd, Exeter, Devon

The publisher acknowledges financial
assistance from Arts Council England.

CONTENTS

Manman: Tifi   11

Prelude
  Origin Begs for Hymns   15
  Colour Flood   17
  In the beginning   18

Leda
  Blessed Be My Unwed Head   21
  Daughter   23
  My Englishman   25
  The War   26
  Christmas Day   27
  Body Talk   28
  Poem in which I am Nèg Mawon   29
  When the Storytellers Found Me   30
  Mimorian   32

Marie
  The Swan's Daughter   37
  Early Morning Rescue   39
  The Outside Child   40
  First and Second Abandonment   41
  Elegy   42
  Marie   45
  Easterners   47
  unElegy   48
  What I Know   49
  Reasons to Hit A Child   51

The Daughters
   On Repetition   55
   She Got that Music in Her   56
   After a Funeral: An Object Lesson   57
   Haunting   58
   An Inheritance   61
   A Bedtime Prayer   63
   Time Travel   65
   Rescue   66
   Still, I listen for news of your breaking —   68
   Trigger   69

Catherine
   Catherine   73
   Rogue Memories, AKA The Beast   76
   Mother: Frankenstein   77
   You, Again at 2 a.m.   78
   Outside My Window   79
   A Name I Will Not Call My Daughter   80
   Blès ing   81
   Survival Strategies   83
   Head Malady   87
   Aftermath   89

Notes   93
Acknowledgements   96

'Because this is how you mark a child, make her yours forever. Press your story like a blessing into her still-bruised forehead.

If I tell you all the stories, how will you know which ones are true—which you can eat, which ones will eat you?'

—Julia Bouwsma, *Work by Bloodlight*

'All cultures and all individuals without exception participate in violence… violence is what structures our collective sense of belonging and our personal identities.'

—Rene Girard, *The One by Whom Scandal Comes*

HEIRLOOM

MANMAN: TIFI

Image of my own making,
more paper and ink than flesh,
I am the god filling your breath,
a threadbare story I give arms
and legs to—
Move. Live. Speak.

PRELUDE

ORIGIN BEGS FOR HYMNS

Then I devoured their wooden faces, their
invisibility. Disappeared
the scent
        of ochre earth and savannas,
carried their people to a new sun. I

stole the letters,
        shoved A B C D E down
their throats. How they stumbled
blind,
begging for a mirror,
        a piece of glass.

And as it pleased me,
they brought forth cane and cocoa,
        and every fruiting tree.
And as it pleased me, when I said,
        dance, they danced.
And when I said strike
        your brother's cheek, they struck.

Wasn't I a servant to them too? Their
        stifled sounds pressed
into the letters I gifted, they begot
a bastard tongue,
        a burst. Shout. Long song.
Without me they are without jazz,
reggae or calypso tune. Without me
there is no speech
        of the world.
If there are flowers,
give me flowers, praise songs.
        Without me, you are not, I am

    your father's hand
against your mother's mouth,
her ear filling with dirt.
    I build a loom in her belly,
spin you, daughter—
complete with claws and fangs and fur.

COLOUR FLOOD
St Lucia, 1841

The women broke out
into split oranges and red suns—
wore reams of madras spun
into headpieces and jupes,
petticoats trimmed
with bodwi angléz,
washed with blue soap
and left out in the sun
to bleach a blinding white.
They loved the clang clang
of bangles rattling
up and down their wrists.

Sundays, they flooded the streets,
crowded through the church doors.
Too loud for God, the priest
said. The women pressed
into the pews like bodies
corralled in plantation cabins.

The sugar planters sat together,
bunched in with the Governor,
some gawked, others kept dem eye
trained on the altar—
too much colour.

IN THE BEGINNING

the man ate,
bit right through the sweetbitter of her,
and how could he not—
He swore she begged, didn't she—
like a mango in a white bowl begs for teeth.
And so he ate again and again wounding her until he pleasured.
He begot girls, too many girls, running around with ribbons
in their hair, the sound of his end in their playground songs.
He escaped to the jungle, hunted what was small—warbler and finch—
weighed their small hearts, the knitting of muscle.
His wife sent word: *the village boys are circling.*
The woman sent word: *the village boys are circling.*
He kept hunting: taking down bird after singing bird.

LEDA

BLESSED BE MY UNWED HEAD

To what angel did I concede: Let it be as you decree.
Body for the will of a man.

That I was sixteen, that he married to my sister,
did not matter, body for an apathetic god.

No spirit overshadowed, ruptured his seed,
or the throbbing vein in his sun-spotted neck.

I am consoled: At least I wasn't dragged into
the bush by some nobody.

O hail the extra-marital bed of the kitchen floor.

And nature, indifferent to circumstance,
to my will, does not break her order, her law—

       mercymercymercy—

There must be miracle.

No wise men visit. Only the matriarchs,
rotten-toothed and stinging, their gifts:

the back of a hand, fists, and a crown called Sketel.

What figure do I cast in this family portrait,
a darkening frame for this haloed child.

She has put on his power: her pale skin
blessing her bastardness clean.

To tend, to tend, to suckle and bath,
another body siphoning my life.

How the noise in my head grows and grows,
splinters into phantoms and shapes,

graceless muses for her cot-mobile.
How I terror.

DAUGHTER

Curious thing. Spit and flesh.
Huge black eyes.
You weren't ugly. That helped.
And wasn't I tender?
Gathering you to my warmth,
your lolling head, breakable body.

And of the hate I brewed and brewed
while you were tethered inside,
you bore no mark of it,
no trace of your forced conception.
You came out well-formed and wailing,
and I felt nothing.
But knew you were mine.
Mineness. A feeling. Is there such a thing?
Like owning a cat. A thing to do.
A small butt to wipe. But wasn't I tender?
Isn't that why you beg me not to leave, my tender looks.

Listen: I fed you, so that I could be fed.

Haven't I lived like a prisoner,
my survival threading through your squalling body?
But now you are weaned and walking,
a body not so flimsy, so tender.

And I am but twenty-two, full of shadows
and shadowing,
there are things my teeth edge for.

Already I have gone, out of mind
into that crooked picture on the wall, there.
What am I but that long road running
through those watercolour fields.

If you follow, I warn you,
I will be as much a weight around your neck
as you have been around mine.

MY ENGLISHMAN
St Lucia, 1942

He here for di war,
he a captain of a ship.
His skin red like a slap,
he hair fine fine.

I meet him in di rum shop,
jut my hips so-and-so,
shake up my shoulders
like dat... like dat.

He face catch a look
like eh, eh,...bon!
Soon we living up
together in di capital.

THE WAR
St Lucia, 194—

A disturbed hour, the sky loud
with the memory of assault.
But still, it's Sunday, the trees shake
like shac-shacs in the breeze,
and the sea goes on and on
with its lullaby like it has never
given cover to the enemy.

It is Sunday,
and we go on with our lovemaking.
I refuse to hush, let my pleasure rise
against the weary tones
in the thin-walled rooms like ours,
it was yesterday, only yesterday,
another body washed ashore...

Forever and forever,
death our only guarantee.
Haven't I died already,
years ago, on a kitchen floor,
under the weight of a different man,
my girlhood shot through,
I learnt the body as machine—
dead heart, dead pubis.

It is Sunday,
I teem with life like the flies
swarming the torpedoed ships
in the harbour.

CHRISTMAS DAY

I sing no hymns,
I want to get on bad.

Christmas Day,
and the neighbour ponging
his music so loud—
mento, calypso,
old tune, new.
I want to get on bad.

Christmas Day
And I am out on the porch
sorrel drink in hand,
belly full up
I eh want to hear
no carols,
no red-hot gospel sell,
I want to get on bad.

Christmas Day,
I already say my prayers,
Lord, doh strike me down
'cause I live up with my man,
we common-law and so it will be
forever and amen.

Christmas Day,
no one singing hymns,
I wining up my waist so hard.

BODY TALK

What siren belled?
What loud-mouthed sentry screamed her warnings?
It was only the sound of your enormous heart   himhimhim.
And wasn't he good to us?
Weren't you fed, sheltered, didn't I hear you pleasure?
How you glowed when you poofpoofed out with child.
A child we made on purpose, not like the first one.
Now you slow, slow and shutter, hold onto your bruises longer.
Please stop. He can smell it on you: how far, far away you want to go.
And where will you go? Back to Manman's to be cursed?
Her loud tsk, tsk, tsk, like a mosquito in your ear.
Isn't he better than the first man?
Didn't you get turned on when he called you his. And his alone.
Stop shrinking when he draws near.
Don't look at him like that.
Things will get better, are better than before.
Only stay, keep me always, always by his side.

POEM IN WHICH I AM NÈG MAWON

The door in the cow field cried, *come*.
Through the kitchen window I saw—
I left everything, my sons, my daughters.
And   *himhimhim*.

I smalled myself into the door's dark entry,
my body followed, heavy-footed
and full o' blood-scent,
of course, he pinned her face down in the mud,
dragged her back to the house.

What happened after, I don't know.
Of her suffering, do not tell me.
I only know that she gave me up.

Now, we sit together in the asylum's white-walled room,
her tongue swole and chewed through,
her fingers flick at the ants trailing out of the cracks in the walls.
I small myself again, squeeze through—

WHEN THE STORYTELLERS FOUND ME

Most nights I don't think of it,
the blood on my teeth,

my white dress, stained
with soot and wet grass,

how the mud hugged my feet
like bedroom slippers.

I hid in the bush until the storytellers found me.

They enjoy the music of split-open things,
stretched my skin into a drum.

*

The first time God pulled me
into a body, I imagined myself
a fruit,

soft and spilling.

What if I am also the seed,
hard white knot of a mango,
when aimed can wound.

*

Beat this dumb drum,
beat this troubled song:

my skin, I painted red with clay,
my hair, I laced with lavender.

Even when the man hurt me,
my body could not forget
awakening.

I returned to rip the sun
out of his window.

We pitched forward in the dark;
he had the knife,
I was the ram
undoing him with my teeth,
our desecration darkening
his fingertips.

Each time I offered my body,
he grew a vision—
a rain tree,
the sky aflame,
children,
burning.

MIMORIAN
after Carlos Drummond's 'Residuo'

Only a little of me remains, a fixture,
Madwoman locked in a downstairs room,
four-walled gag, muffler. Of my ravings,
the upstairs hear nothing, nothing.
But still a little of me will stay, the stink of me
in the sheets, on the walls, on their tongues,
wagging, wagging all night long about
my bad romances—chupid woman,
sad woman
                object lesson.

Of my illness, they talk too much,
I am spectacle, spectre, fire-lover
wandering off into the bush, the market square.
My early morning peep shows, the breaking
day, someone forgot to lock my room, again,
the music loud in my head, how I shook,
shook the neighbourhood awake with my naked breasts,
my grandchildren cried, their friends can't come over.
And of those things I remember
so little
      so little
why can't they *do* the same?

Of the things I enjoy,
they won't remember, the mourning doves
nesting in the monstrous breadfruit tree,
rum thrown back, going deep
down, deep down between my legs,
my hair brushed and slick and smoothed
into a bun, my yellow satin ribbon.

Of God, am I against, for
or indifferent, they've never asked
or cared to know. My mother,
father, their names…
already they've forgotten.
Of my love of white, they'll remember
cotton dresses bleached in a blinding sun,
my men, always, always fair.

Of me so little will remain, stripped
and pared down to a fear,
bright and blossoming in the back
of a young girl's head: ou fou ou fou
ou fou
                    ou fou.

MARIE

THE SWAN'S DAUGHTER

What heralds your birth—
the feathered air, bloodied,

your father exposed;
his wife crowns your head with a curse.

And your mother swears
she sees the sky collapsing into a flood,

or is it a star falling
      like lightning?

    But you are the wingless girl with an axe.
Felling a tree. Carving a boat.

You will not drown in anyone's visions.

What marks your way—
the darkening of a blood line,

a coming Messiah exchanged for
a he-already-done-come Messiah encircling your neck.

And what blow you strike—

Your father's land, peopled and seized
by those hands who grew the breadfruit trees,

dug the fields and made your meals.
Those hands your father blessed holy unclean.

What your birth does not halt—

His light shows, stars spinning
hips emptying
of love,

the boom and clatter of laughter,
praise songs
by those same hands.

He is handing out feathers.

Before he plucks himself clean,
you return, put on his power,
those glorious wings,

watch your shadowed kingdom rise,
spire—

EARLY MORNING RESCUE
Castries, 1951

You search the blue dawn for your mother.
She scents of smoke and burnt matches.

You steer her back to the house.

Soon, your stepfather will wake,
      demand tea and bread,

snatch her by the hair, rattle
      until you yell, *I'll make it.*

Sometimes, you want to push her
      towards the open gate,

watch as she walks right into
      the side of a speeding pick-up truck.

There would be no more sound,
      the hitting and the wailing,

and the insults when you snatch the box
      of matches from her hand.

THE OUTSIDE CHILD

I will not disappear, dead myself
in a bush somewhere.
The freak lives, sucks air.
I have a face that is not so unlike hers.
Perhaps that's what troubles,
I am the final blow. The betrayal,
so close, under her roof, in her bed.
The man she so loved, loved me,
raised me in her house, unnatural thing that I am,
a sin, offspring of a predator and a prey,
that grows and grows, has a mammalian face,
hands, feet, a voice like the blackbird's,
high-pitched and singing.

In my wildest dreams, I hug her
children, my cousins.
They are my brothers and sisters.
How they insult, *mother-killer,*
daughter of a sketel.
I blossom bright, draw nearer still,
allow their biting, bites. The sharp of their teeth,
the only intimacy:
my flesh an epiphany.
                I am, love me.

FIRST AND SECOND ABANDONMENT
St Lucia, 1978

Headless. But still, your heart beats gleefully
as you dance naked on my front porch singing,
sugar bum, sugar bum bum,
gimme the sugar bum bum.

And you won't have my interfering, slap my face
as I steer you towards the door.
My own heart trembles enormous at your sting, Manman;

yesterday, only yesterday, you let me brush your hair.
And I was five again, begging you, *stay.*
How gentle I brushed, I did not pull,
not even one, not one strand.
But you did not stay. Returned to the capital.
To your Englishman.

Even this is abandonment,
your long stays in the land of Nod.
And I am the (un)happy jailer—
to have the body and not the woman.
I beg you, *return now.*

A shock returns your head.
Head in which I am the enemy,
face of your first harm. That man.
Your body follows your lucidity—flight.

Months later, I'm called to fetch you, a body
streaking through the market, loud with song.

ELEGY
> *for Papa*

1.

Of our Sundays, I say little.
They are mine. Ours.
The pots of rice and peas,
and black mackerel we shared.
How after, we licked
the oil off each finger,
the loud clap of your voice,
c'est bon.

2.

You were too white to live like that—
In a hut. On the beach.
Cooking fish on a coal pot.
Yellowing your ragged shirts
with the suck of mango.
Your hair thin and spare.
A jumbie.
A white jumbie.
Left me alone, too often alone
for the jungle to hunt manicou and iguana.
Even when the fer-de-lance
took your left leg,
you wouldn't stay,

hobbled to and fro,
paid the village boys
to carry you here and there.
The house, the land,
you refused to care.
Lived only for the sound
of the sea in your ear.
The shine of a dead fish
in your palm.

3.

Another blue night.
My girl-ear sweats against the locked
bedroom door. The love sounds.
The scent and silence after.
I trouble the lace curtains
greying with dust.
Outside, the trees, thick and nameless
rim the plantation's edge.
I ask about my mother.

4.

Of
That.

Only the old women talk—
Men. Their ways.

The young ones rage—
Rights.

Isn't that how most of us
came to be?

Have our being:

Fair skin.
Good hair.

Not out of love
or rightness.

But hips banged open.
Forced.

Still, I was your favourite
child, wasn't I?

MARIE

After the virgin, who paid her prayers no mind.
What she wanted so? The blood-knot of a child
sliding down her inner thigh. Toilet waste.
She believed Mary would understand, she'd chosen her
condition, hadn't she?
Understood a body must be willing, pliable for miracle.

*

Because she did not drown.
But grew a fish tail. Slick and shiny.
And a taste for salt. His fine linen skin.
How else to survive a body on top of you?

*

The tale I tell myself:

I was born when the sky collapsed,
flooded our tiny village,
softening the soil into muddy rivers.
Trees fell, pitched forward down hillslopes,
blocked roadways, plunged into the dark gutters of ravines.
And the sea dared to walk on land.

*

The brightness of my skin.
Its clarity: the green mapping of veins.
I was his. Landowner.
Her favourite colour: what it promised.
She made her wish:
Marie, Marie, Marie,
build me a large house near the sea.

I built a house. Not for her.
With a view of the hills.

EASTERNERS

You a butcher man's son
I a landowner's daughter.
Some people doh like the song of us.

You a dark-skinned man.
I a fair-skinned woman.
My people doh like our gettin' on.

But I sing my victory sweet.
You a staying man,
never blacked my eye,
never cursed me out.

And when the lights laid low
you pull out a banjo,
woyoyoy oy.

Ou sé lavi mwen,
ou sé tché mwen,
ou sé lanmou mwen,
mesi, mesi bondié.

UNELEGY
for Manman's husband

An English specimen, ruddy-faced and balding,
he strung himself up like a fruit. A mango.

Or a guava.

Which did he prefer, I never cared to know.

I found him there. Dangling
from the rafters.

I had wished him gone, as in, go back
to where he came from, England. As in,

pa bat manman mwen. As in,
my name is not djanmèt or sketel.

But I must speak well of the dead.

His pleasures, simple—
cursing people out of their skins,

calypso: *don't go January girl,
don't you know even summers grow cold,*

dancing with Manman, then after,
purpling the skin around her eyes.

His displeasures—
Me, child of another,
child of another man in his house.

He loved rum.

WHAT I KNOW
> *'Men are threatening presences.'*—Lucy Ellmann

I.
    St Lucia, 1950

I hit Auntie in the face.
She tried to sell my sisters.
I hit her again. We hid.
The spoon was wooden,
broke Auntie's nose.
She said our mother wasn't coming back.
She said tourists love mixed girls,
I was too old.
I told my sisters, if Auntie finds us,
brings them to a big white ship,
remember, our mother is the sea,
                      jump.

II.
    St Lucia, 1990

I hit my daughter. Even now,
she throws the past at me,
some sports uniform I burnt
when she was thirteen.
Netball, she says, netball.
She came home after five.
What did she expect? I cuffed her ear

when she refused to undress.
Yes, the sun was only beginning to set,
yes, she barely had breasts.
But when had that ever put them off?
You stopped me from being me, she cries.
I tell her, this is what I know,
my hands staving off men.

REASONS TO HIT A CHILD

Because the sun grows in her left eye.

Because a misfired belt buckle.

Because her skin hasn't turned, and

Because the neighbours gossip that a white man
sleeps under your bed.

Because if you spare the rod, you spoil the child.

Because the porridge-sticky pan still sits on the stove.

Because her mouth is so full of your name,
Mama, Mama, Mama…

Because as a child, you snapped branches in two,
kept time to a hand slapping your mother's face.

Because rage has its own flight.

Because there is a pleasure in pinching flesh
until it flashes red.

THE DAUGHTERS

ON REPETITION

Give me Sunday afternoons   my front porch

my child right here   by my side banging

some toy into its broken parts   Hear my tongue

winged and repeating   the same blues

a woman shuttered and struck   I ruffle my daughter's hair

sing   I touch the woman   bruised cheek

touch my face   stinging   my mother said she never

touch my face   in that song   the man hit the woman

in that song   my mother said she never

SHE GOT THAT MUSIC IN HER

When the music blares,
Granny chases the morning
right onto the front porch
wearing only her underwear:
Gran Stan please everybody,
Seraphina please everybody,
when I go home....

We wrestle her inside.

When the music goes on for days,
Granny wears a lampshade
like an English lady's hat,
answers the telephone,
one, two, three, four, bye.

We tell our friends don't come over.

When the music shadows into arms, a head,
Granny hunts for her husband,
his rum and vetiver, *over there*
she fondles a shadowed corner,
gestures at the ceiling, calls to him,
get down from there.

There are no ghosts here, we cry.

Sometimes the music stops,
we loop hands,
we spin, Granny sings,
there is a brown girl
in the ring tra la la la la.

AFTER A FUNERAL: AN OBJECT LESSON

We press our fingers to their plastic shrines,
to their glass coffins,
visages captured in film.
What do we say now, how pretty,
how fat, how fair, how dark, too young,
how badly the man she slept with treated her.
Divide the spoils, the silk,
the chiffon, the 100% cotton,
squabble over her gold hoops, bangles,
a nearly empty bottle of Casmaratti.
There are lessons here, the old women murmur,
how living with a bad man killed you,
the stress raging the cells
until they collected, fisted into a lump.
I plastic-bag a purse and leather sling-backs,
O body of my sister, body I loved.
They expect me to talk about your sin,
how your friends only remember how
good you looked, copper-coloured girl
who caught all the men.
As though sin is without hands,
your hands, slender,
copper-coloured, holding mine.

HAUNTING

We frighten the children.

My hair ragged in red cloth,
I speak a language they don't understand,

their ears tuned to English, tuned
to American cartoons.

And Leda, Gwanmanman Leda runs
cracks up the walls,
through the centre of our dinner plates.

It's their own fault, you know,
they won't stay in their rooms.

How she endures, endures,
Gwanmanman Leda. Leda.

Even after I married,
after she died, she endures.
Tanbou mwen.
Jab mwen.

But the children,
the children.
They stare.
Regard me strangely, sadly.
There will be no walk to the park today.
No jump rope high.
Only their rooms.
They will stay in their rooms.

Alé, alé. I chase.
They hide behind a wall. Spy.

I must clean my house like I cleaned Leda's room.

Scrubbing. A form of memory.
A song. Trojan horse for my own blues.

Keeper of the madness.
The mad. Leda.
Mwen faché.
I was only a child,
only a child
made for play,
not the washing of soiled sheets,
of shit-stained walls,
of an old woman.

But the children,
how they stare.
Their blink-less eyes.
Pouty lips.
Why won't they go into their rooms?
Leave me to Leda.

We are a pair.
She, because of her bad head.
Mal tèt. And I,
because I was a child.
Small. Piti.
Crushable.
Like a roach.

The mad and the little,
The mad and the little,
Give them a tickle,
Then a prickle.

Leda, stop your singing.

And I must stop this fool parade.
This arm muscling towards memory—

You've made it up,
Isn't that what they said?
Mal tèt, bad head.

No one ever hit you. Mantè.
Isn't that what they said?

But Leda, Leda,
my sweet Leda.
Mad monument.
Rogue memory.

But we must think of the children.
They cry for us, *Mommy, Mommy.*

AN INHERITANCE

Grandfather, we gather around your effigy,
    sew in a slip of bone,
finger your blonde hair,
    we want your acres of green
to build a house
    white-walled with vaulted ceilings,
we will hide your hands there,
    sun-stained and soil-worn
they smell of her
sex,
    her blood, salt
and pinking shame.

    And I can hear our mothers singing,
    a man is a man is a man.

    I can see the seed of an orange
        splintering into a green shoot,
    the white husks folded into the dark soil.

    I can see the wall of a volcano collapsing,
        a flood of sea water emptying
    turtle, seal and bird into the crater.

    I can see shanty houses and concrete buildings spiralling
        upwards, the mangroves,
            swamp, manatee and turtle, gone.

We set fire, let it lick, lick, lick
        your moon-blue stare.

And still, we wear you like a crown,
                fair skin and long hair.
    On the playgrounds,
in the market square, on the street
        named after you
and under the cocoa trees,
     we chant you,
           a beginning.

A BEDTIME PRAYER

We ate the fruit Lord,
boiled and buttered we ate.
Thought nothing of it.

It was pleasing to the eye.
Filled our mouths, our bellies.

It was the fruit of a breadfruit tree.
A tree as old as the first city.

How it grew taller than the house.
Those monstrous leaves.

Its roots echoing— cracks in the walls.
Its shadow falling through the back door, the corridor,
lengthening towards the front—

Ghost of our first father,
ghost begetting ghosts,
our lives thinned into his weakness,
his terror.

But we were fed, fed, fed.

*

Lord, you have cast us off,
left us to starve,

Sent that girl.

Girl born with a veiled face,
a caul, calling.

How did she find the axe?

She wouldn't eat the fruit,
refused its sweetness,

weight of our father,
the first city.

Lord, she went down to the garden,
an axe flowering in her hand.

It was you Lord, the bouden blan
chirping in her ear.

What cruel instructions?

Didn't we do your will,
kept a remembrance—
the tree,
our father,

we were hungry, Lord.

The tree fell into the house.

TIME TRAVEL

Escape through the hair,
a coiled end, pinned
between thumb and index,
the middle finger twirling
this soundless lullaby,
drumming out your husband's
early morning banging,
fixing the roof,
fixing the car, fixing,
fixing, whiting out this morning's
discovery: a web of decay
across your daughter's
front teeth, dark markings
of your failure. You spin,
arrive at the same place:
your mother banging
through the front door,
yelling about the dirty
kitchen floor, the light
left on in the bathroom,
stomping into your bedroom,
tossing the sheets and pillows,
calling your name, you hid
in the closet. Your hand,
moving like a hummingbird
from lock to lock,
tearing the fragile ends.

RESCUE

1.

The freak, dark-haired beast
knocks at my cupboard door.
I have kept quiet,
not a sound,
even when the daddy-long-legs
mounted my nose.
She has sniffed me out,
calls, Mommy.

What terrifies, the oven, the flour
the butter pooling on the counter.
What a test of love,
my husband wants homemade bread,
It's easy, he said.
What a test of love
to understand the workings
of a clock,
a rug,
a water filter,
the proportion of yeast
to flour,
the measure of a dash,
a dab, a dabble
of salt,
a Ms. Fixer-upper,
Maker-of-things
I am not.

The bread is hard,
hard like a rock
it will break the teeth
of our guests coming for dinner.
O what terrifies,
he'll turn into Mama,
how you kah cook up to now?

2.

My daughter knocks again.
She is four, a voice so sharp, a seam-ripper.
I lead her to the sea roiling
at the back of our house,
our arms full of bread rolls, stones.
What is a daughter,
small rescue tearing
towards the shoreline,
rolls falling like a trail of droppings.
She flings the bread into the waves.
I will tie my waist with a string to hers,
                     my little buoy.

STILL, I LISTEN FOR NEWS OF YOUR BREAKING—

Your wife has left you. You are exposed—a fraud.
You are bald. Impotent.
I measure the ways I could harm. How your life
would rupture and spray. How the loud puckering
of your mouth would shrink, shrivel, silence.
Yes, I see the flap of my own sin, bright and bloody.
I wanted it too. The sticky feast. I wanted you.
But I was too Mother, receiving your confession
bare-chested and giving. Now, my intuition,
peacock-feathered, parades its knowing,
fool, fool, fool, the self-flagellating loop
troubles my waking. I remember your text
while you trembled on a Jerusalem night,
the echo of bombs bursting your drug-laden vision.
What did you see? Your limbs heavy and furred.
Your lumber towards birth. And the girl,
you mentioned a girl, her laughter
smashing against a closed window,
smearing the glass bright and bloody.
I was small like that too and bright.

TRIGGER

We smashed the plates   flower-patterned
into the back steps   again and again   a song
seaming a tear our mother left
unseen bruise   welting and wilting.

In the kitchen   a wet stack of white plates   dripped
on the countertop   our husbands said   *One thing*
I asked you   to do   one thing
like how our mother would say—

We smashed the plates   our children saw
we didn't want them to see   the breaking
of things   our hands
high-pitched and frenzied   repeating
our mother's fists against our faces.

Our husbands took off up the road   *some air.*
We searched for the children   found them
in their bedrooms   sucking on the blue ears
of their bunnies   trying to stuff
sheets down their throats.

CATHERINE

CATHERINE
St Lucia, 1848

When slavery ended,
                Catherine
mashed up her name,
became
        Catiche,
        discarding the sound
        of breeze
                rifling through the cane,
        discarding the sound
        of massa (master)
between
                her thighs.

       *

St Lucia, 1986

Because she did not have your colouring,
because of your own affliction—

        you name her after your likeness.

Then you thought of your errant climb
up the rain tree. A midnight dare:
        tied your school ribbon to a branch.
How it is still there. Blue. Tattered and flailing.
        Gave her a second name.

> *A hyphen, I walk the plank between the two names*
> *—call me Esther.*
> *The Hebrew three-root letters mean to hide, hidden.*

She is her father's daughter.
You teach her hands your quiet ways—

> A plate, an open mouth.
> The gift of white shatter:
> never having to say, *I hate you.*

    *

Chicago, 2018

These days I wear my blood-hemmed name,
write Catherine on every application,
every journal, every poem, sound of my mother,
name I once detested,
sound of an image that is not me.
Sound of my fear. Repetition.

Sunday afternoons, she sprawls
on the couch, her white legs peeking
from under her skirts. Her voice singing,
dou-dou darling stay sweet.

> *Am I then, memory or prophecy—*
> *swell of her hurt. Her sweetness.*
> *Unscrew my skull,*
> *dislodge the tape,*
> *strew her sound through the trees.*

I wear my name like my hair,
the way it screams of a different sun, of makola blue,
of the great odoum, I will not knife the French and English
out of my tongue, this heirloom, cruel and sweet.
My white ancestors roll, roll, roll—
I've been sewn into their line.

ROGUE MEMORIES, AKA THE BEAST

What shrieks cupboards until emptied,
falls down the backstairs scattering

into tiny, tiny pieces.
Has no face. Bares no teeth.

Chases the children here and there
with a flick, a lick, licks.

Only a small girl stays, puffy with hurt,
suckling the ear of her teddy bear.

Louds the clamour of thrown pots, choruses
the accompanying damn yous, through a window

hems a woman in. She is under the bed.
She won't come out, won't come out, she says.

Possesses no hands but conducts
the symphony of another's undoing

a sound. Slim, slender fingers smash
an heirloom, undo a sound,

thread a ghost into the small,
small ear of a girl.

Amasses, legion, at the thin membrane
demanding tending. A witness.

Tears through anyway, a thousand
thousand little feet running through your head.

MOTHER: FRANKENSTEIN

Raise the dead. The cross-stitched
    face. Her eye-less eye. My long
longings brighten, like tinsel, the three-fingered
hand. Ashen lip. To exist in fragments.
    To exist at all. A comfort.
A gutting. String her up then,
figurine on the cot mobile.
And I am the restless infant transfixed.
Her full skirt, a plume of white feathers,
    blots out the light.

YOU, AGAIN AT 2 AM

       Does your life so stun, I turn you into a ghost—
dress you up in a white cotton frock and yellow ribbons,
fasten your wrists and ankles to the rack,
pin your eyelids firmly back. I call you stronghold. The thing to resist.
To cut down. I call you my propensity for psychosis, muse,
reach through your body for the beast, feel for its teeth.
       Did it speak to you when you wove
a yellow ribbon through your thick black hair? *Come outside.* Then again
as you hung the clothes
out to dry. *Into the bushes.* You saw it, a cat you never had, walking through
the corner of your right eye. You tried to hush your insides, reason,
but it only badgered until you lit the match, watched the fire blacken the wood,
then lit another, and another, and another.
       I've only known the shadow of the beast—a voice going off in my
       head
eight, twelve, twenty-one times a day; do I, do I, do. And I wanted to—
       I prod and prod at your pinking shame, unveil and expose. The
       trigger
for your disease. But I am more freak than compassionate, thrill
in touching the wound. Knit titles for my unscathed forehead—
Girl of the tawdry beginnings. Girl of the troubled family history.
       Like Walcott's girl in a lemon frock hunting yellow wings,
I pin and maim. Label. To know.
       To witness, I console my anxious heart,
spin into verse the bat, bat, batting
              of your bloodied left eye.

OUTSIDE MY WINDOW

A dog. Her underbelly.
Fat hanging tits.
I think of the Dahomey Amazons.
Women who never knew a man,
never bore a child. Whose breasts
so stunned the Frenchmen. They couldn't shoot.
The Amazons severed their heads.
I have longed to suckle at their tits.
Mino. Mothers. I would cry.
Each drop possessing what—
pride. Prophecy. A way forward.
My own legend:
A woman forced.
A woman forced. Who stayed.
Because sugar cane and cocoa failed.
Because a 1930s rural town.
He, a landowner.
Because she was only a girl, sixteen.
Because, because, because
a song of shame fattens
on its own repetition,
I reach for another.
But what of Mino's song,
wild march to the battlefield,
her shame:
We are men, not women.
If I am the call: Mino. Mother.
What of her response:
I have no daughter.

A NAME I WILL NOT CALL MY DAUGHTER

When Granny Leda died
                          her nightgown was stripped off,
       her body sponged, cleaned of urine.
And after the funeral, the stories circled our house—
             Leda, who set the lace curtains on fire. Leda, shuttered
                 behind doors,
Leda, who ran well on an electric shock. Leda,
       whose hugs I refused.

                 Now, when I witness my own fraying,
                 I tongue your name, Leda. Forbidden sound.
                 Imagine your secret place, under a breadfruit tree,
                 Leda, your gold hoops
                 clanging against your jaw.
                 Leda, how you caress your broken things,
                 that man who bruised
                 then left you, his body
                 dangling from the rafters.
                 Leda, how you weep over your dreams,
                 a house on a hill with a view
                 of the sea, your children running
                 in the garden, flinging green mangoes at each other,
                 their mouths full of your name,
                 Mummy, Mummy, Mummy.

BLÈS ING

I.

a shadowed song held at bay
a forgetting

now stains aloud at the opening
of my buttons

at your hands pressing and pressing—
the work of another man

a blès ing

what blessing I sought from you
but your spit

only your spit

to shine a mouth who for so long
had not known another

II.

into the tree outside your window
I release a songbird

weighted with my grief
your fear

You shoot the bird
I release another and another

until the rot rises
freights your lungs

SURVIVAL STRATEGIES

1.

Leda, you wanted to eat, believed, *through a body now, miracles*,
spun out your lines of milk-white children,
carved out ease, so you imagined,
a pathway with your body, through his.

Girls, so many little girls you made, dark-haired and fair,
pretty-enough so that one day men would break their backs
to put them in houses with running water,
with shiny white toilet bowls,
carry them off to England.

You imagined London, the bush firmly pinned back,
paved roads, places to walk without being run over.
So much glint and bauble, and bread, and milk and tea.
One of your children would send for you,
because what is love, if not survival.

No one sent for you.

2.

I wanted to survive an ocean crossing,
fondled his skin, echo of glass and glossy steel,
song of a cowboy, a Wild Wild West,
                        a forgetting.

I played the exotic bird,
the shoal against a pale decolletage,
accepted his small violence,
his tiny, tiny horrors.

3.

I exposed my affliction,
that of an arrivant,
of a woman hunting the scent of rainfall,
the dusty roads I walked as a child.
He smelt like me. Hungry.

4.

ungod the man in my head
his hundred-year-old lease
unbelieve a string of words
through a body now miracles
unsound the body trying to sing through his
unsing oak unsing pine unsing America
return to me bazodee
return to me ezer 'z-r
return to me breadfruit leaf

unforget the small violence
the little horror
unforget the serpent swinging
high through the trees
their mocking chants 'z-r 'z-r 'z-r
unforget the sound of myself

return to the tongue the razed notes
return to the tongue its fly-ridden fruit

ungod the man in my head
unbelieve the thought
skin: shelter
unbelieve the thought
his body: ladder
believe the thought
through a body now miracles

god the limbs stiff and unmoving
god the tongue maker of light
god the tongue shriek shrike shank
god the hand singing his away, away away
remove his blessing his spit his oils
god the tongue *Dear God please*
god the tongue *don't make me first*
the first face—

5.

Consider Adam, the first alien,
first human on planeta terra,
his upright posture marked his difference,
how the animals drew near, curious,
prodding, biting, swiping, cowering,
turning away at his need to be held.

*

Before me there was no other daughter,
begotten of the first-born son of the first wife,
there was no other before me walking around with his face.
I make his face female, a variant of his chin,
his jaw, I did not soften him there.

6.

The tongue cannot renounce nor abjure the alien.
The alien is the tongue,
announcing what was first, what preceded.
The alien can only grow an additional appendage(s)
resembling the place where she is not indigenous,
as in a marked difference to what is native,
as in a marked difference to what preceded,
as in your accent mashed up,
as in the tongue will grow some of the sounds of the new environment,
as in the tongue will go native, as in the tongue remains native.

7.

Leda, look at me,
I am the colour
of your dark root
yet I live,
eat,
send for you.

HEAD MALADY

Esther,
anoint the back of your thighs
with coconut oil. Kiss
the insides of your shoulders.
Today, you are thirty-one
and have not known the inside
of a straightjacket,
of Clozapine,
of Alice's Wonderland.

Those troubling genes
lie listless, mute,
eyeless and dusting.

Retire the sentry
who stands vigil
at the thin membrane
in your head.
You are safe,
for now.

But what of the shadows
that peek at the corner of your eyes?
The sound of your name, called
when no one else is around?
Glitches.
The brain glitches
like the tremor of blue
flashing across your computer screen.

It is only your fear,
only your fear that has knotted
itself a voice.
How often do you hear it? Rarely.
How often do you obey it? Never.

Esther,
crack open a window. Scream.
Today you are thirty-one.
Past the peak. Over the hill
and tumbling, tumbling
down past the peak. Forget
what they say,
it is all in your head,
tèt wèd, tèt lèd.
Listen: the jolt of electricity you feel
when you flick the switch
on and off, on and off,
is real, real, real.
Trust the knowing of your flesh,
a body that refuses to lie.

AFTERMATH
To Great-Grandpa

O hands that wound, even you grew flowers,
the red-petaled hibiscus, the soft trumpeting
yellow bells, even you grew banana trees
and the dasheen root, and we too
are your blossoms.

I am here, I am here,
Mwen la, mwen la,
the animal of my body
chants my praise. I strip
to my underwear,
press against the cool tiles,
let the sun trample my skin,
let the light take root inside.

Tonight, I'll listen to the unlit sky
teeming with rain,
tomorrow the hills will sparkle
emerald, and one day I will tell another,
these hills live in me,
Morne Fortune and Belle Vue.

And you too threaded this place
through your bones,
abandoned the great house
for a hut on the beach, its siren songs.

We thought Grandma would tongue
your name, a curse,
she called you, *Daddy*,
spoke of the coconut heads you split,
gave her the water to drink.

Who wants to begin in violence,
we pressed our fingers to our wound,
felt its widening mouth chorus,
we are ashamed.

O hands that wound,
no one sung this song to you,
no one rimmed your neck with shame.
But sew into a girl-child
what is hidden and hurts.
O dead man, with your ears
stuffed with dirt,
I string you into verse—
a vengeance,
an attempt at teasing out the light,
to bear witness.
I call you monster.
I call you father.
How this song blues the kitchen floor,
bloodies our feet.

NOTES

'Manman: Tifi'
Manman is pronounced MUH-MUH. It means mother in Kwéyòl. Tifi is pronounced TEE-FEE. It means daughter in Kwéyòl.

'Origin Begs for Hymns'
The lines "Without me they are without jazz,/reggae or calypso tune. Without me/ there is no speech /of the world" references *Poetics of Relation* by Edouard Glissant.

'Color Flood'
This poem references Chapter 9 in *A History of St Lucia* which documents the changes in the social landscape that occurred after Emancipation: "As for the women, nothing can surpass the sumptuousness of their Dress, which generally consists of jupes or petticoats, made up of the finest chintz, with richly worked cambric chemises shown from the neck, to the waist, and madras handkerchiefs, all of the most radiant colors..."

    bodwi angléz: the lace on the ankle length skirt of the St Lucian national dress.

'In the beginning'
Borrows the line "the village boys are circling" from an interview with Toni Morrison in the documentary film, "Toni Morrison: The Pieces I Am". And the line "bringing down bird after singing bird" from Brigit Pegeen Kelly's "Garden of Flesh, Garden of Stone."

'Poem in which I am Nèg Mawon'
"Nèg Mawon" refers to St Lucian runaway slaves, who were also referred to as Brigands. They played a pivotal role in the French Revolution in St Lucia, 1794–1804.

'Mimorian'
"ou fou" means "you are crazy" in Kwéyòl.

'First and Second Abandonment'
The lines, *sugar bum, sugar bum bum,/gimme the sugar bum bum*, are borrowed from the calypso, "Sugar Bum Bum" by Lord Kitchner.

'unElegy'
The lines, *don't go January girl,/don't you know even summer grows cold*, are borrowed from the calypso, "January Girls" by Lord Kitchner.

'Grandfather'
Borrows the line "pinking shame" from Kwame Dawes, *City of Bones: A Testament*

'Haunting'
Tanbou mwen means my drum in Kwéyòl.
Jab mwen means my devil in Kwéyòl.

'Trigger'
Borrows the line "welting and wilting" from Vievee Francis' "Taking It" and borrows the line "One thing I asked you to do one thing" from Tiana Clark's "Black Champagne".

'Catherine'
This poem references Chapter 9 in *A History of St Lucia* which documents how ex-slaves changed their names after Emancipation. And borrows the phrases "makola blue" and "great odoum" from Kamau Brathwaite's "The visibility trigger".

'Blès ing'
Blès is Kwéyòl for internal wound.

'Survival Strategies'
Bazodee is Caribbean English for mental illness.
Ezer is a Hebrew word meaning 'be strong/rescue'. Used in Genesis 2:18 to refer to the woman.

ACKNOWLEDGEMENTS

Many thanks to the journals in which these poems—sometimes in earlier versions, first appeared: *SWWIM, West Branch Journal, PN Review, TriQuarterly, MAYDAY Magazine, Prairie Schooner, Cider Press Review, Bear Review, Small Axe, RHINO Poetry, Portland Review, Southern Humanities Review,*

Special thanks to my parents and my beloved sister, Kelsey. My thanks to Carrie Beyer, Joshua Boettinger, Ana Michalowsky, John Robert Lee, Celia Sorhaindo, Cindy Beebe, Pablo Otavalo, Linda Burch, Mariana Lin, Dr Tina Trigg; the staff and faculty at Pacific University including Kwame Dawes, Mahtem Shiferraw, Ellen Bass, Chris Abani and Scott Korb.

Thanks to the Barbara Deming Memorial Fund, Callaloo Creative Writing Workshop and the Glen Writing Workshop.